Studies in Animal and Human Behaviour

VOLUME II

KONRAD LORENZ

Studies in Animal and Human Behaviour

VOLUME II

Translated by Robert Martin

HARVARD UNIVERSITY PRESS
CAMBRIDGE, MASSACHUSETTS
1971

First published in collected form in Munich
by R. Piper Verlag under the title
Über Tierisches und Menschliches Verhalten
(Gesammelte Abhandlungen, Band II)
Copyright © Konrad Lorenz, 1971

First published in the USA in 1971

SBN 674–84631–1

Contents

Part and parcel in animal and human societies (1950). A methodological discussion

Psychology and phylogeny (1954)

Methods of approach to the problems of behaviour (1958)

Gestalt perception as a source of scientific knowledge (1959)

Contents

Bibliographical Note

These papers appeared originally in the following books and journals, under the titles given, in order of publication in this book.

A scientist's credo, in *Counterpoint: Libidinal Object and Subject*, ed. Herbert Gaskill, International Universities Press, New York, 1963.

Vergleichende Bewegungsstudien an Anatinen, *Journal für Ornithologie*, **79**, 1941 (special volume).

Ganzheit und Teil in der tierischen und menschlichen Gemeinschaft, *Studium Generale*, **3/9**, 1950.

Psychologie und Stammesgeschichte, in G. Heberer *Psychologie und Stammesgeschichte*, 2nd edn, Jena, 1954.

Methods of approach to the problems of behaviour, Lecture delivered before the Harvey Society, New York on Nov. 12, 1958, published in *The Harvey Lectures* 1958–59 by the Academic Press, New York and London, 1960.

Gestaltwahrnehmung als Quelle wissenschaftlicher Erkenntnis, *Zeitschrift für experimentelle und angewandte Psychologie*, **4**, 1959.

Haben Tiere ein subjektives Erleben? *Jahrbuch der Technischen Hochschule München*, 1963.

'Methods of approach' and 'A scientist's credo' were not included in *Über tierisches und menschliches Verhalten* Band II published by Piper Verlag. Included in the Piper volume, but omitted from this one, is 'Phylogenetische Anpassung und adaptive Modifikation des Verhaltens' (*Zeitschrift für Tierpsychologie*, **18/2**, 1961) since it has been published separately in English in book form as *The Evolution and Modification of Behaviour*, by Chicago University Press, and Methuen, London.

Translator's Foreword

As Konrad Lorenz has pointed out in his introduction, the composition of this second volume of his papers differs quite considerably from that of the first. This is partly due to the question of his *choice* of papers for publication; but it is also a reflection of the greater stability of ethological (behavioural) theory achieved by the time most of the present papers were published. The intensive investigations carried out by Lorenz, von Holst, Tinbergen and other major pioneers in this field had already provided an established backbone of fact and theory when most of these later papers were written. This, to some extent, explains why Lorenz thought it more rewarding at this stage to spend much time and energy replying to the vitalistic and mechanistic philosophers who were sniping at the flanks of the adolescent science of ethology. The papers in the first volume represent *pioneering* studies carried out during the early stages of development of ethology, whilst the papers in the second volume are primarily works of *consolidation*. Nonetheless, there are some important developments in the scope of ethology. Perhaps the most important is the clear demonstration of how useful behaviour patterns can be for considerations of the *evolution* of animal groups. Lorenz's paper on the distribution of behaviour patterns in the Anatinae (ducks and geese) is a classical work which underlines the close relationship between studies of animal behaviour and the theory of evolution.

To some, it might seem that Konrad Lorenz need not have devoted so much time defending ethology against attacks from armchair philosophers of the vitalist kind, since their comments generally have little appeal to anyone trained in the application of scientific method. As Theodosius Dobzhansky recently said: 'As to the mechanism/vitalism contest, it has been a dead issue in biology for about half a century.' However, such philosophical criticisms still carry tremendous weight in certain quarters, and anything that can be done to clarify the various problems (or pseudoproblems) raised by opponents of ethological theory is surely worthwhile. In particular, it is essential to give due

attention to the philosophical problems of analysis of human social
behaviour. The reader will find that such problems are dealt with in
various parts of this volume more thoroughly than is the case in any of
the recent popular books on this subject . . . though some philosophers
and anthropologists will doubtless never be satisfied with a defence of
ethological methods of analysing human behaviour, however well it
may be argued.

   Philosophical objections to ethological studies, usually linked to some
implicit or explicit vitalistic leanings, still appear from time to time.
One cannot escape the conclusion that the recent attacks launched by
Ashley Montagu, Bernard Towers and others on the ethological
approach to human behaviour fall clearly into this class. And one cannot
avoid the impression that these attackers have not really understood
what most ethologists are trying to say. For instance, in attempting to
study human behaviour with ethological methods, responsible investigators (such as Lorenz and Tinbergen) would never claim that they
intend to explain *everything* about man. The ethologist's approach is
(generally) much more modest; it is merely hoped that ethological
studies of human behaviour will make a complementary contribution to
a vast range of knowledge about human activities. The ethologist is
not (usually) aiming to *debase* man, but to identify some contributory
features of his overall make-up which can be traced to his evolutionary
links with the animal kingdom. Konrad Lorenz has tried to explain
this point of view – and it is extremely interesting to see, in a number
of the present papers, how he goes about this. The latest insult to be
hurled at ethology is that of 'reductionism'. The use of this term really
underlines a basic misunderstanding about what ethologists are trying
to do. Critics often say that analysing complex, integrated phenomena
such as human behaviour *destroys* the integrated whole and thus makes
any interpretation meaningless. The ethologist, on the other hand,
believes that it is possible (conceptually and/or experimentally) to dismantle systems, look at their parts and then re-examine the whole
system with new insights into the way it operates. Lorenz uses the
analogy of the motor car engine to underline the divergence between
the attitude of the covert or overt vitalist and that of the ethologist. In
some ways, he does not go far enough. One really has the impression
that many critics of ethology actually believe that it *soils* a 'car' (behavioural system) to open up the bonnet and take a peek inside; that
it is not merely useless, but actually *sinful* to try to work out how a
'carburettor' (behavioural component) operates. In the face of such
criticism, it is understandable that Lorenz should have spent a great
deal of time dealing with various aspects of the theory of knowledge
(epistemology) and trying to explain the ethologist's approach. In a

neighbouring field, Claude Levi-Strauss – in following through his structuralist concepts of social anthropology – has encountered criticism of exactly the same kind. At a recent meeting in London, he countered this criticism by explaining that a knowledge of the physical processes of evaporation and expansion of gases by no means destroys the aesthetic properties of the hearthside scene, with the kettle bubbling away on the fire. Understanding of processes and aesthetic appreciation of the overall phenomenon are not necessarily mutually exclusive. Many philosophers seem to think that *all* the scientist sees when looking at a kettle boiling is a cloud of hypothetical molecules buzzing around in a manner which is of purely mathematical interest. It is, of course, possible that *some* scientists see things in this way; but it is rather naughty to generalize.

Lorenz also devotes attention to attacks launched from an entirely different, diametrically opposed direction – by mechanistic behaviourists who would claim to explain all animal (and human) behaviour in terms of ever-increasing aggregations of very simple basic units, such as the conditioned reflex. These are the ultimate reductionists, and *they* have accused ethologists of incomplete dissection of behaviour. One thing which is of great importance here is the fact that, from the outset, ethological theory has been intimately linked with the theory of organic evolution. The typical behaviour of any animal species is adapted for a particular natural environment, and the behaviour can only really be understood as an overall system in terms of that environment. Now, as is well known, mechanistic behaviourists traditionally conduct their studies on a small range of animal species – nearly always domesticated, and always captive. They therefore have no means of understanding the integrated *function* (as opposed to mere *operation*) of behaviour under natural conditions. Exclusion of the concept of natural selection under given environmental conditions prevents mechanistic behaviourists from coming to terms with animal behaviour as a dynamic product of the interaction of a genetic programme with the natural environment. To take the analogy of the motor-car engine once again, the mechanistic behaviourist approach is almost equivalent to trying to find out how a motor-car engine works *by studying it under water*. This is not to say that behaviourist studies cannot produce meaningful results at some levels. One could, for example, see that one basic principle of the motor-car engine is the operation of moving parts and that nuts and bolts represent frequent basic components; but it would be impossible to understand the overall functioning of the motor-car engine in this alien environment.

Konrad Lorenz – along with other ethologists – has thus taken the middle road between ultimate reductionism and vitalistic imagery. It should be clearly evident from this second volume *why* he has done this, and *how* he defends his choice.

Overall, the selection of papers in these two volumes of Lorenz's papers gives an extremely good idea of the gradual development of his work, ranging from the first tentative steps in the field to philosophical considerations of the wider implications of the established science of ethology. In addition, there are – at every level – fascinating ideas which are given out in profusion. Some of them may have proved to be wild goose chases; but then again, Lorenz has more than adequately shown that chasing wild geese can be an extremely profitable occupation. This second volume includes a classical paper of the 'ideas' type in the discussion of the behavioural concomitants of human evolution ('Psychology and Phylogeny'). This discussion could be read with profit by anybody interested in the current wave of speculation about the origins of human behaviour.

The translation of this paper proved to be an extremely long and demanding task, and Konrad Lorenz's continued encouragement certainly eased the burden. The greatest source of satisfaction, now that this task is completed, is the knowledge that Konrad Lorenz himself is satisfied with the translation. I, myself, had the privilege of working for two years in Seewiesen with Konrad Lorenz and his colleagues, and my main motivation in trying to translate these papers with a maximum of accuracy has been the possibility of paying a tribute to all of those who provided me with friendship and assistance during my stay in Seewiesen. As Hans Selye once wrote: 'To discover does not mean to see, but to uncover sufficiently that many can see and continue to see forever.' Through his continued hospitality, Lorenz has enabled many people to see what they did not see before; by translating some of his major papers, I hope that I have enabled some people to see what they could not see before.

R. D. MARTIN

Introduction

Though the papers included in this second volume were all written at later dates than those contained in the first, they are all still 'basic' in the sense that each can easily be understood by itself without any previous scientific education, particularly without any previous reading in ethology. The reader who, perhaps, is not interested in the philosophy of science, nor in the political inferences of ethology, should not be deterred by the fact that there was an ulterior motive guiding my choice of papers for the present volume: the aim is definitely different from that of the first volume, which was chiefly meant to give some idea of the lines along which ethology, as a young science, began to evolve. The present volume is intended to convey, to the interested reader, some understanding of the philosophy as well as of the theory of knowledge on which ethological approach is based. In fact, I believe that the same epistemological attitude underlies *all* truly scientific procedure. In particular, this collection aims at explaining the strategy of research imposed upon the scientific investigator by the nature of his object whenever the latter happens to be a complex system. Though the obligatory rules of this strategy have, long ago, been adequately formulated by Otto Koehler, Ludwig von Bertalanffy, Paul Weiss, Erich von Holst and others, it still seems to be unknown to many otherwise quite admirable scientists that a system can *not* be approached by operationalist methods, at least not before a considerable number of altogether different cognitive procedures have been successfully performed.

As D. S. Lehrman has aptly expressed in his contribution to *Essays in Memory of T. C. Schneirla*, the predominant opinion of the behaviourist school of American psychology is 'that questions about the processes internal to the subject that give rise to the observed behaviour are unnecessary, misleading, non-scientific and/or irrelevant to an inclusive system of behaviour analysis'. In other words, knowledge of the *machinery* of the living system, the behaviour of which we hope to understand and, if possible, to control, is deemed unnecessary to this purpose.

All the papers included in the present volume were written at a time when I had not yet fully realized how vastly different the behaviourists' attitude is, in its fundamental theory of knowledge, from that of all branches of natural science. Nevertheless I cherish the hope that these old papers explaining the strategy of research obligatory in analysing systems might suffice to make it clear to an unbiassed reader why it is a vain hope ever to arrive at an understanding of behaviour without understanding the physiological machinery which causes it.

A little more, however, should be said, here in the introduction, about the behaviourists' way of thinking. Though indubitably copied from modern physics, the behaviourists' attempt to find a direct, lawful relationship between the experimenter's influence and its effects on the organism's behaviour, _without trying to analyse the causal chain leading from one to the other_, is strangely lacking in understanding of the nature of physics itself and of its relations to other natural sciences. All true science is 'physicalistic' in one sense. In all our daily work we act on the hypothesis that, if ever we should arrive at the ultimate and utopian goal of completely understanding Nature, including our own nature, we should have explained the universe and everything in it on the basis of a number of very general laws of physics and chemistry, and _of the complex structures in which these laws are at work_. Our endeavour is to push analysis 'downwards' (that is, in the direction of more basic and more general laws) and, as investigators of behaviour, we hope ultimately to arrive at its understanding on the basis of the physico-chemical processes which take place in synapses, or at the charged cell membranes of ganglia and the like, not forgetting, of course, the immensely complicated structural systems into which synapses, ganglia and other elements are integrated. This, of course, is exactly the way in which the physicist, or, for that matter, any engineer would go about trying to analyse any complex system whose composition is unknown to him, as, for instance, a computer built by somebody else. No physicist or engineer in his right senses would, in order to get the hang of how this contraption works and how it can be used, programmatically restrict himself to studying the probabilistic relationships between input and output. He would instead take the thing to pieces and see how it is wired.

The analogous procedure, though dictated by common sense, is very far from the mind of true behaviourists. They hold the entirely unfounded belief that it is, indeed, possible to find laws which hold true for the behaviour of all animals, irrespective of whether they happen to be amoebae, pigeons, rats or men, irrespective of whether they are healthy or ill, and irrespective of the physiological processes on which their behaviour is based. They proceed as if there were no structures to be studied. They also proceed as if there were no such thing as evolution and phylogenetic adaptedness of form and function to the ubiquitous necessity of survival.

In other words, the behaviourist school treats the organism, and whatever goes on within it, as if it were as *unknowable*, as sub-atomic processes which transcend the forms of thought and of visualization with which we are endowed *a priori*. If, in this hazy borderland of that which is accessible to human knowledge, physicists resort to the exclusive application of operationalistic and probabilistic methods, they do so *only because they have to*, because our common sense and our everyday forms of thought (like causality and substantiality) as well as the corresponding forms of visualization (like space and time) cease to be applicable to that which is to be explained.

Let us suppose, by contrast, that physicists or technicians were misguided enough to apply behaviourist methods. Suppose that a team of extra-terrestrial physicists or technicians had arrived from Mars, and were, for some really unearthly reason, determined to apply nothing but operationalist and probabilistic methods to the study of (for instance) the behaviour of railway locomotives, completely neglecting – in approved behaviourist fashion – to ask what makes locomotives run. The student of steam locomotives would then quickly find himself in disagreement with the investigator of electric engines when the latter asserted that the cutting of high tension wires had a negative effect on the behaviour of trains. If ever these two, through their misguided method, should find the same lawful relationship between their randomly chosen experimental influences and their effects on the behaviour of locomotives, it would be in the cases in which the mechanisms experimentally influenced in steam and electric locomotives happened to be identical or strictly analogous. The bending of rails, for instance, would have the same effect on both kinds of engines.

Correspondingly, the behaviourist attempt to cut blindly across all species differences can demonstrate common lawfulness prevailing between the experimental influence and the resultant changes in behaviour only in those cases in which the behavioural mechanism affected by the experiment is either identical or strictly analogous in each of the investigated species.

Indubitably the physiological mechanism which achieves reinforcement has been independently evolved in at least three phyla of animals, in Vertebrates, Cephalopods and Arthropods, and possibly, among the latter, again three separate times – in Arachnomorphs, Insects and Crustacea. The 'invention' of evolving a receptor apparatus ascertaining success or failure, and of feeding back, to the mechanisms of precedent behaviour, the reports of 'this was right, do it again', or alternatively of 'this was wrong, avoid this in the future', had, as a prerequisite, a rather complicated organization of receptor and effector mechanisms which simply do not exist in animals devoid of a central nervous system. It is, therefore, quite futile to expect, in an amoeba or a coelenterate, the capability of learning through reinforcement. Understandably, behaviourist research concentrates on animals which do possess the physiological mechanisms forming the prerequisite of conditioning by reward. If this is the case, as D. L. Lehrman pointed out, 'the same techniques, the same formulations of problems can very readily be applied, with the same quantitative methods and sometimes with the same instruments, to the studies of rats, of pigeons, of monkeys, of psychotic human beings and of normal human beings'. However, the remarkable uniformity of the behaviour of all these creatures in the operant conditioning situation depends largely upon the fact that, as Lehrman aptly puts it, 'the technique and the philosophy which it expresses, carefully avoid a good deal of what makes a guinea pig a guinea pig, and a pigeon a pigeon – to say nothing of what makes a person a person'.

Of course, this sort of comparison is a process which is altogether different from the one implied by the word 'comparative' when used as an attribute to morphology, anatomy or ethology. In these cases, the connotation of the word is that of a very special methodological procedure which, from a study of the similarities and dissimilarities of species, deduces their phylogenetic relationship and reconstructs their genealogical tree. The importance of this type of investigation is by no means purely historical. Quite on the contrary, we owe most of our insights into the causation of evolution to comparative studies: it was purely on their basis that Charles Darwin developed his theory of natural selection. If the cat has crooked, sharp claws, well-fitted for catching mice, this is a so-called *adaptation*, brought about, as we have sound reasons to assume, by natural selection which *bred* cats with that useful form of claws. If we say that the cat has such claws 'to catch mice with', we are not professing a teleological philosophy, but just stating, in an abridged way, the above-mentioned knowledge. This is the *teleonomic* aspect of the form and function of organic systems. (The term was coined by Colin Pittendrigh, who wanted to divorce teleonomic considerations from teleological ones as far as astronomy is removed from astrology.)

As has been explained, the programmatic restrictions of behaviouristic research preclude participation of any consideration of structure, or of causal chains of events. This, in turn, blocks the way to any phylogenetic approach, which can only be achieved on the basis of a thorough knowledge of structure. Avoidance of the evolutionist viewpoint makes it impossible to consider adaptation, and, consequently, the *loss* of adaptation, that is the pathological miscarrying of phylogenetically adapted structures and their functions. In other words, the behaviourists' programme excludes practically all the questions which biological science is asking, one is tempted to say all problems which are really interesting to us as live creatures and human beings.

Rejection of the teleonomic aspect of behaviour constitutes an inconsistency in behaviourist thought. It is an admitted, and even emphatically proclaimed, aim of their research to manage social relations by 'shaping' human behaviour . . . by 'controlling', during education, the contingencies of reinforcement. I do not see how this kind of shaping and controlling can mean anything else than an attempt at *adapting* behaviour, nor do I see how one can hope to adapt something of which one knows neither the structure, nor the survival function, but only the changes wrought by arbitrary experimental influences. The extensions of behaviourist assumptions and techniques into the realm of pathology make particularly clear the consequences of total rejection of physiology. In the paper on inductive and teleological psychology included in the first volume, I tried to make it clear that any hope of finding the means to repair a system which has got out of order rests on insight into the causality of its 'normal' functioning, that is to say of the kind of function which provides survival value, the selection pressure of which brought about evolution of that function. There is no simpler way of defining the 'normal' and the 'pathological', and even so the borderline between the two seems disturbingly vague when we consider its immense practical, medicinal importance. Without that borderline (i.e. without the concepts of adaptation and its disturbance, of survival value and its loss), health and illness are indistinguishable from each other. At the same time, a health-preserving factor in an animal's environment cannot be distinguished from a reinforcing one, as can be demonstrated by many erroneous interpretations of deprivation experiments, in which the effects of ill-health, for instance atrophy of the retinae in an animal reared in darkness, were mistaken for the consequences of lack of conditioning.

The dogmatic restrictions of the behaviourists' research programme are psychologically amazing; it is extremely hard to understand their motives for renouncing not only quite normal, everyday functions of human cognition, but practically all sources of knowledge which, to 'nous autres', make life worth living. I have two tentative explanations of why this renunciation is so fashionable nowadays. One is that quantum or 'acausal' physics is regarded as the one and only 'exact' natural science – which it is not – and that it must therefore, at all costs, be imitated in every detail – which it cannot. The second explanation is, I am afraid, political: the fundamental negation of all that makes a person is necessarily welcome to all those who wish to *manipulate* great masses of people. The belief that a man is exclusively the product of the conditioning which he received during his childhood and adolescence encourages the attempt of 'social engineering' which Lenin proposed and which Aldous Huxley has so horrifically described in his satirical book *Brave New World* and in its sequel *Brave New World Revisited*. It is unlucky for the happiness of present-day humanity that the doctrine of the unlimited conditionability of man is untrue: One cannot *teach* a man how to be happy under the neurosis-producing circumstances which the great manipulators on all sides of all curtains are trying to force upon us. It is lucky, however, for our humanity – for everything that *does* make a man a man – that this is not so, though it will take some real men to take a stand against the deleterious influence of an ideology which, even at present, has become a world religion. Even the scientist himself, as a propagator of the behaviourist's doctrine, is threatened by this danger: As D. L. Lehrman has recently pointed out, 'it is not only the subject which is denatured by behaviourist psychology; the experimenter himself is not permitted to be entirely human'. An epistemological lobotomy which prevents an intelligent man from using the normal cognitive functions nature gave him, does indeed constitute an act of dehumanization.

Were it not for the fact that behaviouristic philosophy, by gaining political ascendancy, constitutes a real threat to the very essence of human freedom, it would be redundant to expound the philosophy of natural science. As matters stand, however, it does seem necessary to explain, in some detail, what we, the natural scientists, are trying to do, and also *how* we are going about it. Enlarging on the methodology of research seems all the more necessary, as the methods of many younger students of behaviour have undoubtedly been dangerously influenced by behaviouristic fashion. Most of them are tarred with the behaviourist brush of exclusive or predominant operationalism, some slightly, some heavily and some beyond redemption. Even among those who regard themselves as ethologists there are men who regard the experiment as the only legitimate source of scientific knowledge, and operationalistic procedure as the only way to gain it. J. P. Hailman's review of the first volume of my collected papers may serve as an example of this attitude. He 'laments the vagueness' of many of my concepts and 'the apparent lack of interest in operationally formulating and rigorously testing initial hypotheses'. He says 'Nothing summarizes Lorenz's epistemology so well as his own phrase "inductively determined facts".' In another place, arguing against 'Lorenz's conception of scientific method', he says that my joint paper with Niko Tinbergen on the egg-retrieving response of the greylag goose 'is the only one in the collection that would be likely to be called scientific by modern criteria', and this only because Tinbergen's excellent experiments form the essential part of this paper. I myself am indeed a very poor experimenter; but I hope to have shown in most of the papers included in this 'second volume that *induction*, the fundamental cognitive process of all science, which consists in the abstraction of a general law out of the observation of many special cases in which it prevails, is *not* absolutely dependent on the experiment: the hypothesis which allows prediction can just as well be verified or falsified by further observation of single cases which are not intentionally contrived by an experimenter. The important point is that one cannot 'test initial hypotheses' concerning complex systemic functions in any other way than this, nor can one, at an early stage of analysis, formulate any but provisional and vague concepts. To pretend that one has, at that stage of investigation, any sharply definable concepts, would be sheer fabrication. If some people, like J. P. Hailman, believe that 'Lorenz fails to convince one that he understands the cycle from observation through induction and prediction back to subsequent observation', I can only humbly hope that this second volume might convince at least some people that indeed I have! I also hope that I succeed in making it clear that operational formulation and rigorous experimental test, though desirable, are not indispensable to making a scientific legitimate assertion. Isaac Newton, for one, was in no position to test, by rigorous operational tests, the inductively determined facts which he abstracted from the observation of astral bodies (experiments on gravitational forces are extremely difficult to perform in laboratories); but I do lament a generation of scientists who deny his results the honorific attribute of being 'scientific by modern criteria'.

Considering these ulterior aims of this collection of old papers, I thought it best to make an exception from the otherwise chronological arrangement, by putting first a paper which I called 'A Scientist's Credo'. In fact, it is a paper which I have never written: some years ago, my late friend John Benjamin, psychiatrist at the University of Colorado, asked me to speak to the medical freshmen of that year about the philosophical fundamentals of natural science. I did, and he had my speech recorded on tape. In order to preserve the directness of the spoken word, he prevented me from doing any editing, and in deference to his wish I have not changed anything in what this great scientist thought worthy of taking down from that tape.

The next paper, dealing with a comparative study of the innate motor patterns of ducks, is put in as a paradigm illustrating what the term 'comparative' means in biology, as opposed to its connotation in behaviouristic 'comparative' psychology. Both the publishers and myself at first had some doubts about including it in this collection, and

if I finally insisted on doing so, it was because I regarded it as necessary
to show to readers not familiar with the study of phylogeny what a toil-
some, patient work truly comparative science is, what a hard-won
accomplishment the craftsmanship of its experts is, and that the reliability of its results can actually be computed by a consideration of
probabilities. The reader who is not interested in phylogeny may skip
this paper, but then it is probable that he would be better off to skip
the whole book.

The third paper, 'Part and Parcel in Animal and Human Society,'
was originally written in opposition to the tendency of certain social
psychologists to generalize principles of gestalt psychology, particularly
the ascendancy of the 'whole' over the 'parts', and to treat all living
systems as if they were the results of gestalt perception. Although this
error is virtually the exact opposite of the above-discussed fallacy of
behaviourist thought, it results in the same disastrous conclusion that
causal analysis is unnecessary. Both the behaviourists on one hand, who,
in imitation of quantum physics, replace causality by probabilistic computation, and 'holists', on the other hand, who believe in a miraculous
'whole-producing' factor neither accessible to nor requiring a causal
explanation, both unanimously hold the opinion that it is unnecessary
and even unscientific to disentangle the host of causal interactions which
take place between the parts, or 'sub-systems' of an organic entity,
which are dependent on the structure and function of these parts, and
which, in their totality, determine and *cause* the functional properties –
in other words the behaviour of the whole. In this paper I have tried to
explain the strategy of approach which is obligatory in the endeavour
to analyse any living system. The verb 'analyse' means making the
function of an entity understandable on the basis of already-known,
general laws, *and of the special structure* of the system in which these
laws prevail. The paper can give quite a good general idea of how far
the ethological analysis of 'behaving' systems had progressed 20 years
ago, and also of the rôle which comparative, phylogenetic considerations played in this progress.

The fourth paper deals with the application of phylogenetic-com-
parative methods in the field of psychology and behavioural study. As
it touches on problems also discussed in other papers, certain redun-
dancies could not be avoided. As in several other cases, the slowness
with which I have developed certain ideas has the undesirable effect
(already mentioned in the introduction to the first volume) that things
that ought to have been said in the summary of an earlier paper are only
explained in a later one; or, conversely, that in an early paper certain
phenomena which really are essential to its understanding are only just
touched upon, while their more thorough explanation follows several

years later. Thus the methodology of comparision, which is not sufficiently discussed in the paper on the motor pattern of ducks, where
such a discussion should be (p. 14/15), is more clearly summarized in
the fourth paper (p. 197 etc.). The latter contains, on the other hand, some
short and rather inadequate remarks on the function of Gestalt perception as a source of scientific knowledge, while this important subject is
dealt with more thoroughly in the next paper, published four years later.
Another overlap, between this paper and the next-but-one, concerns
the discussion of the historical circumstances which retarded the application of phylogenetical methods to the study of behaviour; these are
much more clearly discussed in the sixth paper (which I read as a
Harvey Lecture at the Rockefeller Institute, New York, 1959).

The subject of the fifth paper included in the present collection deals
with so-called *Gestalt* perception. For several reasons, this treatise is
very close to my heart. For one thing, it contains a theory of cognition
on which, as I have the temerity to believe, most natural scientists,
consciously or unconsciously, are founding their work, and which was
called hypothetical realism by Donald Campbell, to whom I owe a great
debt of gratitude for editing not only the translation but actually the
original, improving on it very noticeably. For another, this paper
analyses a very wonderful, but by no means miraculous, form of neuro-
sensory organization, and by this procedure may make it more acceptable to some scientists – or so I hope. It is one of the tragi-comical
paradoxes of perverted scientific fashion that it is necessary to *legitimize*
a procedure in the eyes of men who unavoidably use it in their daily
work. Perception is the first step in any process of gaining knowledge
of outer reality, and even the most 'hard-nosed' behaviourist *looks* at
the graphs excreted by his Skinner-boxes, though he would (in order
to de-humanize the 'scientific' procedure one step further) really love
to publish them without doing so. However, even research workers who
are otherwise epistemologically sound have some inhibitions against
confessing (even to themselves) their dependence on their own, healthy
sense organs. It is the sense organs, to which the physiological mechanisms belong, which, by complicated and non-conscious computations,
abstract perceptions out of the chaos of innumerable sensory data.
Much is known about these mechanisms. A long time ago, Wilhelm
Ostwald had exactly the right idea of their function; Erich von Holst,
Wolfgang Metzger and others have analysed them with the greatest
possible success, but modern theory of knowledge does not seem to have
drawn, from their results, some highly relevant inferences which, in
my opinion, are inescapable. The man who is otherwise my authority
in the field, Karl Popper, never mentions the cognitive functions of
Gestalt perception, nor do I quite understand his rejection of *inductive*

processes as means of cognition. All constancy functions, and also true Gestalt perception, perform the objectivating function of extracting, from hosts of sensory data, the lawfulness prevailing in them. In order to achieve the separation of the essential from the accidental, they need an enormous sensory input, which must be the greater, the lesser the content of essential and the greater that of the accidental. As Grey Walter said, it is redundancy of information that compensates noisiness of channel. Perception is the function of a computer which, on an unconscious level of our neuro-sensory system, achieves knowledge by an inductive procedure. On the conscious level of cognition, we never start out from the immeasurably lower level of unselected and unprocessed sensory data, but rather from the sophisticated reports made to us by our perception, particularly by our Gestalt perception. These reports do in fact already contain hypotheses, and quite well-founded ones at that. Of myself, for one, it is simply not true that my first step in approaching any phenomenon I have observed consists in creating a rather random hypothesis and subsequently trying to find fault with it. Knowing about the functions of my perception as I do, I feel inclined to suspect that the sequence of events is, at least partly, the reverse of this. I strongly suspect that, at the time when a set of phenomena seriously begins to fascinate me, my Gestalt perception *has already* achieved its crucial function and 'suspected' an interesting lawfulness in that particular bunch of sensory data. If I then spend more and more time in observation of these particular phenomena, it is already a consequence of a hypothesis which my perception has formed, though I may still be quite unconscious of it. The increased observation accelerates the input of sensory data until, when sufficient redundancy is achieved, the consciously perceived lawfulness detaches itself from the background of accidentals, an event which is accompanied by a very characteristic experience of relief expressed, as Karl Bühler described many years ago, in the sigh: 'Aha!' After this 'Aha-experience' I proceed to cast about for further observations in which the suspected lawfulness plays a rôle. In doing so, I tend to increase the redundancy of information, and therewith, the probability of being right. It would, however, be a falsehood to say that I am hopefully searching for evidence disproving the hypothesis suggested to me by my perception. I must never, of course, forget that there really is no such thing as verification, and that I can only increase the probability of being right by collecting more and more cases in which my hypothesis was not falsified, and by assiduously searching for circumstances under which there is maximum improbability that any other than my chosen hypothesis could furnish a satisfactory explanation. But, however conscientiously I pursue this work, it would be dishonest to deny that I am rather fervently hoping that my hypothesis will stand all these strenuous tests.

If it were not for the non-conscious neuro-sensory functions just discussed – in other words, if our conscious effort at cognition really had to start at the level of miscellaneous, unprocessed sensory data – we really should have to approach them with nothing but a consciously built-up hypothesis, as yet unsupported by any factual evidence. Inductive procedure would, I think, really be impossible and it would indeed be the best strategy of research to do one's best to disprove a hypothesis which, in this case, would be highly unlikely to contain any appreciable amount of truth. Gestalt perception, on the other hand, when based on a sufficient wealth of unbiassed observation, has a way of being *right*, and if one is familiar with its occasional trick of being altogether wrong and knows when to discount its assertions, it is an invaluable and quite indispensable guide.

The next paper, the sixth, attempts a short survey of the history of behavioural science. In 1949, at a symposium of the Society of Experimental Biology in London, I read a paper in which I analysed the shortcomings of different schools of behavioural study, of behaviourists, purposivists and of Jakob von Uexküll's 'Umweltlehre'. That paper has a disagreeable 'mother knows-best' flavour and certainly does not do justice to the merits of the scientists criticized in it. The paper presented here actually has the same subject, yet it is, in a manner of speaking, doing penance for the seeming aggressiveness of the one just mentioned by laying stress not on the errors, but rather on the lasting merits of different schools. This 'inversion of sign', far from impairing the factual content, is more conducive to a just appreciation of the historical process by which thesis and antithesis bring about a dampened oscillation of scientific opinion which, in the end, becomes stabilized at a point which represents a much nearer approach to truth than any of the opposing doctrines had achieved. This holds true, for instance, for the different views concerning instinctive and learned behaviour held by behaviourists and purposivists. It does not hold true, however, for the fundamental philosophy of behaviourism, that is to say of its attempt to circumvent the necessity of *causal* and *structural* analysis. At the time when I wrote that paper, I was not yet conscious of this fundamental and devastating fallacy. Although the reader will find that I do indeed keep harping on analysis of structure and causal interactions, he will soon realize that I still considered explanatory monopolism and atomism to be the only errors for which to reproach behaviourists.

The seventh and last paper tackles a problem which, in my experience, regularly crops up late at night, at the end of epistemological discussions when the protagonists have become very tired: the good old, and reliably insoluble, body-mind problem. Far from attempting the impossible, I have endeavoured merely to describe functional properties of nervous processes which are correlated with subjective experience. In fact, these correlations contribute some interesting paradoxes that make the body-mind problem appear even more of a great enigma, which is impossible to solve with the cognitive functions evolution has provided us with. This seemed a tolerably good final note on which to conclude a collection of epistemological papers.

Of these, two (the first and the sixth) were originally written in English by myself* as, I am afraid, will be painfully evident to the reader, particularly with *A Scientist's Credo*. The paper on Gestalt perception was translated by Charlotte Ghurye and edited by Donald D. Campbell who, as I have already mentioned, decidedly improved on the original. For the rest of the papers I have to thank my friend Bob Martin for an immense amount of meticulous, conscientious and often really inspired work invested in his translation. One reviewer of the first volume, Arthur Bourne, has said, 'Even in translation these papers are beautifully written.' I can assure the English reader that in the German original they really are not, so the word 'even' should be deleted and tribute paid to Dr Martin.

* As was this introduction.

A scientist's credo

We are living in a time in which it has become fashionable to assess the exactitude, and with it the value, of any scientific result by the extent to which quantitative methods have taken part in producing it. Now this is one of the dangerous half-truths which fashion is prone to accept unquestioningly. This concerns the relationship of exactitude and value. The exactitude of any scientific result is in direct proportion to the amount of quantification that is possible, and quantification has of course the last word in all verification of discoveries, but it is an entirely erroneous assumption that you can attain any scientific result by quantification alone. If you feel that you *only* want to quantify, then please become mathematicians, but for heaven's sake do not try to become doctors. The prejudice under discussion has been expressed in hundreds of very clever-sounding aphorisms! Every science is just science to the degree to which it contains mathematics. It sounds beautiful! It is entirely false. The very dangerous consequence of the overassessing of the cognitive functions of quantification is that it devalues all other cognitive functions, and therewith the other branches of science in which these other cognitive functions, for instance, observation pure and simple, play a large rôle. All descriptive natural sciences like anatomy, taxonomy are just nothing, and the paragon of science is physics, and everybody thinks so, except the physicists themselves, because, believe it or not, atomic physicists are quite intelligent people.

The term naturalistic has – in the sense in which at least some behaviouristic psychologists use it – assumed a definitely derogatory implication. All that I do is considered 'just naturalistic' and case histories are 'just anecdotal' unless you have thousands of case histories on the basis of which to make quantitative statistical studies. I am *not* saying that these studies will not become necessary, later on, but in the present state of medicine you still have to observe, to keep your eyes open.

My friend, Wolfgang Metzger, Professor of Psychology in Münster, once said scathingly of some philosophers that they are incurably prevented by epistemological considerations from using their sense organs as sources of scientific recognition. '*Es gibt Leute die durch erkenntnis-theoretische Erwägungen am Gebrauch ihrer Sinne unheilbar behindert sind.*' And this may be said with equal justification of some natural scientists who study highly complex organisms and sincerely believe that the use of the sense organs is only legitimate and scientific when it comes to reading instruments. If you observe the object directly, then it is naturalistic and not doctored. Please do not believe that I am exaggerating. All this, I am very sad to say, really is so. However, the 'patron saint' of our society and one of the greatest scientists of the present times, Max Planck, was of an entirely different opinion, and in 1942 he wrote a sweet little paper which is quite generally intelligible, you need not be an atomic physicist to read it, under the title of 'Die exakten Naturwissenschaften', published in *Die Naturwissenschaften*, in which he explained that the way in which the physicists arrive at their picture of the world is in no way different from that in which a baby arrives at its own though simpler picture of the world. What do we do when confronted with an entirely new set of facts? We scan, we take into account the chaotic multiplicity of stimuli, and then we begin to see sets of stimuli belonging together, configurations of stimuli, objects.

This already contains the beginning of systematization. We recognize syndromes regularly occurring together and we say then to one syndrome 'wow, wow' and to another syndrome 'mama, mama', and then gradually we see that other 'wow, wow' and 'mama, mama' exist, and so the purely describing and naming functions gradually merge into systematization, and this systematization provides us with the sudden recognition of lawfulness, of laws of nature. Regularities are generally improbable. The probability is that of complete disorder. So, regularities ask for an explanation, we ask *why* it is so and little Adam, after having said 'wow, wow' for a while, goes about and asks his indefatigable 'why, why, why', which is exactly what the scientist does. Windelband in his classical disquisition on the development of natural sciences speaks of three phases through which every natural science has to go; the descriptive, the systematic, and the nomothetic.

First, description, then systematization, and lastly the quest for lawfulnesses; these phases, as Max Planck points out, follow each other in the same way when the baby develops its picture of the world and when the scientist does so in a quantitatively more detailed way. So you see in understanding something, in giving the explanation of something, you need your sense organs and that of the senses which is the most important – common sense. In the middle range of science, common sense is very important.

Let me exemplify what I have just said. Let us suppose you find some phenomena in your environment in which a lawfulness prevails and you ask why it exists. Remember, lawfulness always needs an explanation. For instance, you see a clock hanging on the wall and observing it you discover lawfulness, the very important one to twelve law of the clock. I ask you if this is a law of nature or not? The answer is yes, it is law of nature, though a very special one. And now we want to explain this law of nature. Our attempt to 'understand' is equivalent to the procedure of reducing the special law which you see to more general, more widely applicable laws of nature and the structure in which it prevails. Whenever I say 'and the structure' please read capital letters. The complete knowledge of this structure in which these more general laws prevail is quite indispensable. Of course in order to explain our 'one-to-twelve law' of the clock, or my watch, you have to know about the laws of levers, and of the pendulum, you have to know the properties of the metals out of which the clock is made. But, however deeply you go into these basic laws and basic properties of matter involved in the working of the clock, nothing will ever excuse you or make you exempt from counting the cogs in the cogwheels in which you will find represented, in some way, the mechanical system controlling the two hands, the one-to-twelve relationships observed in their movement. In other words, nothing will ever exempt you from the absolute duty to study structure.

The nature of the real explanation – understanding a special lawfulness of nature on the basis of more general lawfulnesses and the special structure in which these wider lawfulnesses prevail, thus producing a very special one such as the 'one-to-twelve' law of the clock – puts certain obligations on the scientist taking part in this great collective undertaking of humanity to explain nature. These obligations are quite as easy to understand as the 'one-to-twelve' law in the clock. What you must know in order to explain something is the structure of the matter which you are investigating and the laws of nature which are the *next* more general ones to the lawfulness you are observing and trying to explain to yourself. And the accent is on the *next* more general laws. When Sutton and Boveri were attempting to explain the laws of Mendelian segregation, on the basis of the division of chromosomes in the maturation on the one hand and division in miosis and fertilization on the other – and indeed succeeded in doing so – all they needed to know was the gross structure of the chromosomes and the way they split up in miosis and in mitosis. All that we know today about the biophysics and the biochemistry of the chromosomes would have been of no use to them. Of course the explanation of why the chromosomes split and how they reproduce needs the man still further downstairs, in other words, Professor Puck. So you see every scientist is under a strict obligation to know what goes on directly downstairs. He need not know a thing about what goes on 'upstairs'. Let us take another example. The organic chemist need not know anything about the physiology of metabolism, but he will be sunk if he does not know anything about inorganic chemistry. The consoling thing about this is that every man may restrict his knowledge to his own layer, but he may not restrict it to parts of this layer. I am now talking particularly of biology and the biological sciences. Your outlook must be a broad outlook, while it may be thin (if I may put it in this metaphor); what is illegitimate is the jumping of layers. If you try to explain the Mendelian laws directly by the biochemistry of chromosomes without first studying the grosser mechanical processes of miosis and mitosis, in other words, when you jump from the Boveri level to a much lower level of biochemistry, you undertake the ambitious and impossible task to do yourself all the analyses going all the way down and to do the work of all the men on all the layers that are between, and this is on principle impossible.

The whole of natural science is like a system of Chinese boxes, slightly more complicated, because one box may have several boxes in which it is sitting. But on the whole every box sits in a wider and more general box, until everybody sits in the great box of atomic physics. There is a German saying: '*Vergleiche hinken*', 'Metaphors limp', and if ever a metaphor limped, this one is limping on all four feet. For one thing it is only valid in the middle ranges of science, in the ranges in which naïve or bestial realism (that is, the philosophical attitude which takes things as we perceive them for direct and ultimate reality) does no damage to understanding. In these middle ranges it is still legitimate to assume that physics or, at the slightly earlier stage of our knowledge, classical mechanics, are the all-embracing basis of all our explanatory and analytic attempts. If we speak of a 'mechanist' or a 'mechanistic' explanation of behaviour and so on, we still use the terms as if classical mechanics were the ultimate rock bottom of all explanation, although we long ago know that it is not true at all and the physicists themselves have long since lost their ultimate trust in classical mechanics. We know that classical mechanics themselves need a further explanation, that it is not at all a matter of course that you cannot stick two objects into each other, that causality is not that nice and really reliable category of thought, as it has been shown to be non-applicable to the smallest elements of matter and energy.

To the biologist who regards the human brain and all its functions as something which has grown to be as it is through evolution, it is not at all surprising that our thought categories and our forms of ideation behave in the ultimate and the most difficult ranges of knowledge quite like man-made theories. One of the greatest revolutions in modern thought occurred when Max Planck treated the categories of causality exactly as any scientist would treat a man-made hypothesis, at the point at which this hypothesis failed to explain essential fact, in putting it aside and substituting other methods of approach, namely, by statistical quantification. The limited applicability of our thought categories becomes apparent at the two ends of natural science: downwards in the analysis of the atom and upwards in the analysis of ourselves where the body-mind problem puts, at the present state of our mental development, an insurmountable barrier to further progress. In studying the atom, scientists have found it necessary to take into consideration the limitation of our thought categories, of our world-depicting apparatus, much as a man working with a microscope has to know the limitations of his instrument in order not to ascribe properties to the object which are really only projected onto it by properties inherent in the instrument. You know that when in a microscope the first diffraction spectrum of a grating no longer falls into the aperture of the objective, you do not see the structure. You do not see the grating, but surprisingly and rather inexplicably you see a smooth, brown object. If you take a look at a diatom which gives you a nice grating, you can show perfectly that when the numerical aperture of the objective is insufficient you do not see the grating any more but the diatom becomes brown. That is a very good metaphor illustrating the manner in which the atomic physicists had to treat their 'microscopes' in order not to mistake properties of the 'microscope' for the properties of the object.

You all know that certain phenomena can be looked at from the viewpoint of two categories. Some properties of radiation can only be explained on the assumption that they are corpuscular, and others can only be explained on the basis of the assumption that they are waves. What is the answer to this seemingly irreconcilable contradiction? In nonsubjective reality there is no corpuscularity and there is no wave as we conceive of it but a 'thing in itself' which to grasp fully we have no satisfactory means of conceptualization.

The philosopher here foregoes a source of knowledge by dogmatically declaring our categories of thought as well as our forms of ideation as something absolute, something given *a priori*. The biologist knows that, like any other structure or function of living organisms, they have evolved phylogenetically and only fulfil the requirements of our life. He regards them as evolutionally developed working hypotheses; that is to say, he examines them at work and assesses their value by the explanations they are able to furnish. In examining phenomena which they fail to explain, he discards them as he would discard any man-made hypothesis. We cannot know more about the reality that surrounds us without furthering our knowledge of the apparatus by whose function we become aware of it, nor can we do the latter without expanding our insight into the reality. Loren Eiseley, in a book I recently read, expresses this state of affairs very beautifully by saying: 'The value of knowledge is not only in what is known, it is more a change wrought by it in the knower'; and P. W. Bridgman, in a commentary to a paper by Niels Bohr, puts the same thought more succinctly: 'The process of knowledge and the object of knowledge cannot legitimately be separated.' So you see, the system of Chinese boxes is not just a pyramid, but surprisingly it turns out to be a circle because the widest box 'physics' definitely sits in the box of the theory of knowledge, and the theory of knowledge in turn sits in the physiology of the brain. So the most specialized branch of biology, which treats the most specialized and narrowest laws of nature, is really the supporting column on which physics rests. If I drew a diagram of this mutual independence of sciences, it would appear so Jungian that all the psychoanalysts would run away.

Now let us talk a little bit about the knower, about the one who knows. The theory of knowledge as it is pursued by most philosophers, professional philosophers, is what I call 'leicology'. *Leicology* is the *ology* of a *Leica* or photographic camera pursued without consideration of the fact that the Leica has been developed by Leitz-Wetzlar, out of simpler ancestors, under the selection pressure of making better and better pictures.

Even if you forget, for the moment, function and development, and therewith the rôle of interaction between our world-depicting camera and our environment, and concentrate on the inner lawfulnesses of the camera itself, you will still find a lot of things worth knowing. Among other things, you will find all the laws of logic and mathematics, but I think you will miss much and fall very short of any real understanding of the Leica if you forget that it is made to photograph with. And very much the same is true in epistemology. In these matters the physicists and the ethologists all but fall on each other's necks, so perfect is their agreement, while neo-Kantian philosophers agree that both sorts of scientists have not even grasped the basic principles of epistemology. One of the two parties is wrong. Whether the considerations I am expounding here to you are 'epistemology', in the philosophical sense or not, they are necessary for the strategy of human research. We have to know the apparatus with which we are trying to make a picture of outer reality.

Now at school we learn a lot about some aspects of this apparatus. We learn a lot about logic and mathematics and we do not learn anything about a basic and much simpler cognitive function, which to know thoroughly is also very important to the observer, and that is the lawfulness of perception. Perception is something very, very wonderful, though not at all miraculous. Our cognition of the outer world would be impossible without Gestalt perception and all the lower perceptive functions which are its prerequisites like those of space orientation, of size constancy, the very complicated computers built into our brain which prevents us from thinking that a thing grows larger when it comes nearer, the functions of colour constancy which enables us to see this paper as white whether I hold it here under the yellow light or here in the more bluish daylight and so forth. All these functions are performed by highly complicated computing mechanisms which obey all the laws of logic. They obey all the laws which our rational computations have to obey. They are 'ratio-morphous' as the late psychologist E. Brunswik expressed it.

One of the most important functions of perception is form constancy. If you realize what complicated computations are implied in my seeing this pipe as a constantly formed object while I turn it before my eyes, you are amazed. Only think what amount of stereometry and interpretation goes into the function which enables me to interpret all the changes of the retinal image which occur while I turn this pipe before my eyes correctly as movements of the pipe and not as changes of its form. If this pipe, while I turn it, would suddenly really retract its tail and waggle it, I would probably drop it with a yell of fright and would certainly not for a moment interpret the movement of the pipe as a perspective foreshortening.

The important function common to all these constancy phenomena is that of abstracting properties which are essential, constant and inherent to the object, from the background of the accidental data of perception. They extract a constant out of a background of accidental data which are strictly analogous to what is called 'noise' in information theory. The apparatus excluding accidental data as noise and extracting constant syndromes from a background is among the most indispensable instruments of human knowledge, and it is the more indispensable the more complicated the system is which you try to investigate. In a way it lies at the basis of all taxonomy and of all systematization. It is an early phase in the development of science, according to Windelband, in which description, systematization, nomothesis follow each other in this order. In all three, Gestalt perception plays a large role. In recognizing things as syndromes all these functions are already comprised. The little boy, Adam, would not even say 'wow, wow' if he did not find something constantly recurring in mother's retriever, uncle's mastiff, and aunt's pug. This is the truly abstracting function of Gestalt perception which is strictly analogous to rational abstraction. The same principle is contained in all three steps of scientific cognition, and it is quite indispensable. In a way, Gestalt perception is similar to what cybernetists building perceiving computers have called 'hunch generator',

Let me give you a few examples of Gestalt perception. My daughter Agnes when she was five years old diagnosed, in a large bird collection in a zoo, all the birds belonging to the family of *Rallidae*, railbirds. Though her judgement was biased and her basis of induction very small, as she knew only the coot and the green-legged *gallinule*, she recognized the Gestalt of the railbird. There are rails which are long-legged and look rather like waders, and there are others which are quite short-legged and live on dry land and look very much like gallinaceous birds, but she was never mistaken in classifying all these birds.

Gestalt perception collects data, exploits them in a way analogous to, if not actually identical with, that of true induction. Like the latter, Gestalt perception needs very many data as a basis and the more data it has, the more reliable its 'conclusions' are. Inductive natural science is the building of a very flat pyramid which needs data to the square of the height attained. What has been termed a clinical eye, or a green thumb, or intuitive knowledge and so on, is nothing but the function of Gestalt perception. Some scientists pretend it is nonexistent, as an old wives' tale, and repress, in the Freudian sense, the recognition of their own perceptions. They use it nevertheless because no man would ever find anything if that reliable hunting dog, Gestalt perception, would not point its nose at the interesting object, the one which promises results.

As we have to use the functions of perception we ought to know its strength as well as its extreme weaknesses so as to be able to exploit the first and to avoid the pitfalls of the latter. The strength of Gestalt perception is that it endows us with the faculty to discover the unexpected – which is exactly what no other cognitive function is able to do. You look at a patch of grass on which many protectively coloured grasshoppers are sitting, you look for quite a while and you see nothing, and another few minutes and you still see nothing until, quite suddenly, the contours of one animal seem to jump out from the background – even if the grass-hopper did not jump. When you are vaguely looking for something which you never saw, for bacteria in the microscope's visual field and many other situations, you have to look for a long time. No real discovery in this world was ever made in any other way; our Gestalt computer is our discovery generator.

The second very great strength of Gestalt perception is of course that it can take into consideration many more individual data than you would ever be able to keep in mind simultaneously by rational thinking. Gestalt perception has the beautiful ability of accumulating data over a long period of time. You can look at a thing, and you sort of feel there might be something interesting. The first thing that Gestalt perception does, is to claim your attention. Like a good hunting dog, it starts to pull at the leash in the direction of an object, and it achieves that by making the object subjectively attractive and interesting. Then you can look at it and it sort of catches you, you have to look at the object for the necessary stretch of time without as yet knowing in the least what is happening until suddenly a little bell rings and you know *why* it was interesting. This long summation of stimulus data gathered like inductive material in long periods of time makes it easily understandable why some great men of science stayed with one object for practically all their lives. Karl von Frisch studied bees for three quarters of a century with the most amazing discoveries cropping every ten years.

The third great strength of Gestalt perception is that its function is a pleasure, that it is not 'work'. You just sit and look, absolutely lazy, and in a way it is a drawback that diligent men just do not have time enough to be good Gestalt perceivers. So whether you put that with the advantages or disadvantages of Gestalt perception is left to you.

This brings us to the drawbacks or the dangers of Gestalt perception. As I said, Gestalt perception is made to be a hunch producer. Its function is to take up the slightest hints and work them into a hypothesis. The microphone is most sensitive just before the molecular movements make it sing (feedback); as the microphone is tuned finer and finer, it begins to reverberate in itself and that is the limit of sensitivity to which the microphone can be tuned. Something analogous happens with Gestalt perception. It is so finely tuned that it will be set off by a ridiculously small stimulation, perceiving the most tenuous indications of a lawfulness and finally even suspecting the existence of a lawfulness where there is none. In other words, if you stimulate it too much, it will offer you pseudo lawfulnesses which are not existent in the sensory data at all.

Alex Bavelas, information and communication theorist, once made a rather cruel but highly revealing experiment. He presented to his subjects randomized data and told them to press a key when they thought they saw a lawfulness. If their discovery was right, a light would flash. Now in this really hellish apparatus everything was randomized. The data were randomized, the flashing of the reward of the reinforcing signal was randomized, everything was randomized, yet only about 5 or 10 per cent of the subjects said this is random, the majority believed they had found lawfulnesses. They all got very, very furious when told about the deception. One really hardy man wrote to Bavelas months after the experiment that his *randomizer had been wrong*! He had been calculating and recalculating the data all the time and finally had succeeded in convincing himself that there had been an unsuspected and unintentional lawfulness after all and that his Gestalt perception had been right.

Such false reports are closely akin to hallucination, which is one danger; the other immense danger is that it camouflages as a revelation. In German, perception is called *Wahrnehmung* which already implies that you take as truth what perception tells you. A stereoscopic picture tells you that a certain object is far away though you know that the two slides are really before your eyes. The report given to you by Gestalt perception has all the earmarks of absolute truth – and do not ever believe it, it is *not* absolute truth. It is just as fallible as any optical illusion of perception and, like such an illusion, it is inaccessible to rational corrections. That is why good Gestalt perceivers often will fight incorrigibly, and with the fervour of a fighter for a religious conviction, for one of the convictions induced in them just by Gestalt perception.

As medical men you must key yourselves to the utmost finesse of sensitivity to Gestalt perception. At the same time you must always be ready to hash up completely its results if your quantitative verification fails to agree with it. That is one of the most difficult duties of the scientific man.

Now let us talk a little bit about the incentives of knowledge in the knower. There are in human science two main motivations for the striving for truth; as you are medical students, both ought to be present simultaneously. One is plain and simple curiosity. Curiosity is not at all specifically human. Curiosity is something characteristic of many young animals as well as of the human infant. Why it remains a characteristic of man up to his old age is a story in itself. The other incentive for wanting to know is wanting to help. And if you are medical men, this ought to be one of your incentives. As I am now delivering something which is more or less of a sermon, I ought to warn you that the existence of these two independent incentives can throw you into very difficult and conflictual situations in which wanting to know and wanting to help may require different things from you. Often it is not so easy to just concentrate on the human incentive of wanting to help, because if you knew, you might be able to help more people. This quandary has been wonderfully described in American literature by Sinclair Lewis in his novel *Arrowsmith*. That is a very beautiful and highly moral story.

Before I close this lecture, let me say just a few things about your object of knowledge, about man in health and sickness. One of the things you must keep realizing is that any living being, and most of all Man, is a system. In investigating systems some methodological rules, governing our strategy of research, must be observed. In striving for an understanding of the inner workings of nature, we are necessarily mechanists, or to be more exact, physicalists, as we believe that the universe is a unit and that all its phenomena can, at least on principle, be explained in the manner already discussed. That means that we do not subscribe to naïve or bestial realism but keep aware of the fact that we ourselves are the measure of everything we experience. We do not regard the fact that organisms are wholes (or systems) as a miracle, but we do keep aware that their system character prevents us from using some very simple methods of approach. We find that it is impossible to pursue one single chain of causality, as physics and chemistry can legitimately do, because, in an organism, everything is causally interacting with everything else; there are, so to speak, no single and straight causal chains, but an all but inextricable network of causal relationships in which, to make matters worse, the effect usually exerts an influence backwards on its cause. In analysing the working of such a system you are confronted with the same difficulties which you encounter in trying to explain what you know about the system to a pupil. Suppose you try to explain the simple and man-made system of a gasoline engine to a complete ignoramus, you will find that you have to choose, arbitrarily, a point at which to begin. Most people will begin with the structure and function of the crankshaft, because it is easy to represent by histrionics, then explain how the piston goes up and down, sucking the 'mixture' out of the 'carburettor', using all these terms although your audience as yet cannot possibly know what these things are. So you just hope that he will form, from all of this, a sort of mental diagram in which he keeps a few reserved spaces free to be filled in by conceptions later to be formed. On principle the listener to such a description cannot understand the workings of one of the parts described before he has understood all of them. In other words, it is a law that you can understand the subsystems of a system only simultaneously or not at all. This simultaneous understanding is a task which quantification alone cannot fulfil, nor can at that point experiments, nor the conceptualization of the cutest operational concepts. That is where you just have to sit wide-eyed and humbly take in as many details as you can.

In a science like medicine you cannot do without Gestalt perception and the naming of syndromes, naming them provisionally a long, long time before you know what they causally are. This is strategy forced on you by the nature of your object. With a simpler object this is not so binding. If you analyse that clock, you may get along without studying the structure of the clock. You may see the one-to-twelve law and then, if you are clever enough, you may just suck your fingers and invent the clock. You see, atomism, the fault of trying to get along without knowing structure deriving the special one-to-twelve law from the atomic physics in one jump, is just bad research strategy. Atomistic procedure, though very bad strategy, is not on principle impossible, because knowing the laws of the levers and the laws of the pendulum and the properties of iron and steel, you could possibly invent a clock. This is exactly what cybernetists have actually done. It is something of a shame to biologists that their real appreciation of homeostasis, of self-regulating cycles, came from another branch of science, from cybernetists who were real atomists but clever enough to invent homeostatic cycles. Only afterwards biologists say, 'Oh, but look it is just the same as thermal regulation of homeothermic animals.' So this is possible. But you poor men and ladies are confronted with a most complicated object, with something very much like yourself. Furthermore, you are confronted with a system going wrong, with a system out of order, and there, even with a human-made machine, an attempt to invent would not be successful.

If you have a highly complicated computer which has gone wrong and you call the cybernetical technician of another institute to repair it, he would not try to invent it, he would say: 'Now give me your plans, your chart explanation,' and he would go into the structure of the thing before trying to repair it. That is your task too.

Apart from atomism there is another dangerous fault against which you must guard and that is explanatory monism, which is quite different from atomism, though among psychologists both usually coincide in one and the same person. While atomism is the error of looking into the functions of the car without studying the structures, trying to invent it, explanatory monism contains a much more fundamental fallacy. Suppose you are a Martian arriving in a flying saucer. You find a car; you get down to analyse it and dismantle it. The first thing you get is a hubcap and the screw of the radiator. Now what you do is to pocket these two things, go home to the laboratory, put the two things together and try to resynthesize the car out of these two elements. In psychology the two elements are the reflex and the conditioned reflex. No, I have a better example. You unscrew a bolt and a nut and go home with these and try to resynthesize. Bolts and nuts are certainly highly important things whose function is to keep the car together, but you will not get any explanation of the car. You will not get any resynthesis of the car on the basis of these two explanatory principles, though they may be, as they actually are, what holds the car together. So this metaphor of the reflex and the conditioned reflex is no exaggeration of the fundamental impossibility of explanatory monism.

Now the Martian arriving in his flying saucer and finding this car will have very little success in his causal analysis before he has found something else; the function of this car. In other words, he would have to find out that this locomotor organ is 'homo sapiensally' made. What for, is a question often branded as finalistic, teleological, or mystical. In the mouth or in the pen of the biologists, the statement that the cat has pointed, crooked claws 'to catch mice' does not mean anything more than that catching mice is the function which caused the claws to evolve in just that manner. The evolutionist is the last man to be a finalist. He could not be. The finding of a finality in the sense just defined, the finding of a function shows only the existence of a problem but does not give you its solution. If I drive my car across country to deliver a very illuminating, beautiful lecture somewhere – this high aim may buck me up tremendously. I may sit there meditating on the beautiful way in which this car is constructed and so on and so forth. And then the motor may suddenly cough a few times and peter out. At this moment I will become painfully aware that the finality, the goal of my drive does not make my car run. And I had better forget all about the goal for a minute and concentrate on the causality of the disturbance; probably there is water in the jet or I am not the good diagnostician I flatter myself to be. You see my point? Without knowledge of the function, without knowing the aim, you will be seriously handicapped in causal analysis because one very important evolutionary factor remains unknown to you. On the other hand, the recognition of an aim does not exempt you from the duty of finding out the causality of it. There are no whole-producing factors, and meditation on the beautiful system of the construction of man does not help a man in the least in whose appendix vermicularis a cherry stone got stuck. But the youngest pupil in the surgical clinic who knows the cause of the man's illness can help him. He need not be a very bright fellow. He just needs to know the technique of taking out an appendix. I think that this example shows you very clearly the relationship between aims, between values, on one side and the cause of investigation on the other. Causal investigation would be meaningless if man did not strive for high aims. The aim of your profession is to help suffering people, to help humanity. Causal investigation without aims is meaningless; but the pursuit of aims without causal insight is powerless. So, far from being opposite aspects and incompatible with each other, the causal and the final questions only make sense when we apply both of them together.

Well, that is the sermon I wanted to deliver to you on this occasion. Thank you very much.

Comparative Studies of the motor patterns of Anatinae (1941)

I Introduction and aims

In zoological systematics, more than in any other branch of biological research, the success of the investigator is dependent upon a 'feel' for the subject matter. This property can be acquired, but it cannot be taught. In the introduction to his contribution (*Die Vögel*) to Bronn's *Klassen und Ordnungen des Tierreiches*, Gadow set out a neat theoretical experiment in the form of a 'thirty character classification'. He selected thirty generally applied characters of undoubted taxonomic importance and proceeded to compile a tabular classification of groups of birds based purely on the presence or absence of each character. The classification which emerged – although exhibiting extensive agreement in respect to some groups – in some sections showed amazingly crude departures from the 'obvious' and generally employed classification corresponding to the genuine relationships between the birds involved. Primarily, this is to be explained on the basis that so-called 'systematic intuition' is dependent upon subconscious evaluation of a *much larger number of characters*. These characters, which are extremely elusive on the conscious plane, are woven into the overall impression which an animal group makes upon the investigator. Such unanalysed complex qualities incorporate individual characters of the finest degree, which cannot be extracted from the overall impression even though they have a qualitative influence on the latter. This fact, which is self-evident to perceptual and Gestalt psychologists,[2] must be considered if one wishes to analyse 'systematic intuition' and to determine the reasons for one's own judgements regarding the degree of taxonomic affinity of different animal species.

The inadequacy of a classificatory system based on a limited number of specific, pre-determined characters is not only based on the fact that the *number* selected is too small. Far greater difficulties are presented by the fact that within the different subdivisions of a fairly wide systematic unit a given character *will by no means carry the same weight throughout*.

14

The rate of differentiation, the variability of a given character can differ even between two closely related species. The assumption that a specific character (e.g. the absence of the fifth pinion or the form of the furcula) exhibits the same taxonomic relevance in all of the Orders and Families of the entire Class Aves is wrong from the outset. The weight which must be attributed to a given character as an indicator of the degree of phylogenetic relationship must be determined in each individual case on the basis of its behaviour relative to the other characters of the group investigated. The statement that a given character is 'conservative' or 'variable' can only apply to a restricted selection of closely related species. This applies not only to fine systematic characters of restricted distribution but also, in many cases, to generally distributed characters. Even the characters of ontogeny (e.g. the juvenile plumage of many bird groups), which are usually very conservative, can be affected by caenogenetic changes within a narrowly defined taxonomic unit to such a degree that it would lead to great confusion if one were to attribute to these characters in the unit concerned the same taxonomic value as that applying to the same characters in general. For example, one can imagine the results if the details of the juvenile markings – which are so extremely conservative and taxonomically important for the Anatidae – were to be given the same importance in the classification of the rails, in which caenogenetic differentiation processes serving a releasing function overlay the basic features. Thus, the *number* of characters known to the investigator of phylogenetic relationships is not only operative through the determination of certain group-specific 'complex qualities'. Over and above this, the *relative taxonomic weight of an individual character* can be determined with greater exactitude as the number of characters known to the investigator (consciously or subconsciously) increases. All of this leads to 'systematic intuition' without necessitating analysis of this property by the possessor. However, the outcome of this property only becomes scientific when this analysis has been successfully conducted.

Even from this brief summary of the basis of conscious or intuitive estimation of phylogenetic relationships, it is possible to conclude that the most reliable assessment is produced not by investigators acquainted with *one* organ in all of its various manifestations within a large systematic unit (a goal often set by comparative anatomists), but by those who can survey a *small* systematic unit in consideration of a *maximum* number of characters. The opportunity for drawing reliable taxonomic conclusions increases in geometric (and not arithmetic) progression with the number of recognized characters, since each additional character investigated in all members of the group involved leads to greater accuracy of our estimation of the previously investigated characters. It is at once clear why zoologists who are acquainted (as zoo attendants or as amateur naturalists) with a large number of living representatives of a given group of animals manage to achieve outstanding 'systematic intuition' and critical illumination of phylogenetic relationships. Heinroth's Anatid studies and the Equid studies performed by Antonius provide two good examples. A zoo attendant who is acquainted with the anatomy, and possibly palaeontology, of a large number of representatives of an animal group is obviously provided with a significant advantage over any pure museum systematist through knowledge of *the characters of species-specific innate behaviour*. This undeniable fact is of significance and value not only for the systematist, but also – most particularly – for the psychologist. It has been emphasized for some time (since Wundt) that the theoretical approach of comparative phylogeny is just as indispensable in psychology and ethology for the understanding of the existing human and animal structures as it is in morphology. Even in the psychological field, living organisms are phylogenetically derived entities whose specific origin and form can only be interpreted in the light of their phylogentic history. Thus, comparative psychology (unfortunately little more than a programme as it now stands) is presented with the pressing primary task of performing purely descriptive behavioural research on a suitable group of animals, in order to incorporate the characters thus recognized, together with the maximum number of assessible morphological characters, into a fine classification of the group. Above all, correspondence with the related morphological characters would permit solid defence of the application of the phylogenetic *homology concept* to species-specific behaviour patterns, such that the pre-conditions for *comparative* psychology in the narrowest sense would be provided. Only such fine systematic studies of an exactly investigated group of animals is able to provide us with information about the manner in which phylogenetic alterations of instinctive motor patterns, taxes, innate schemata, and – later on – of all psychological mechanisms, occur. The basic importance of such information – which is entirely lacking at present – need not be emphasized here. The pathway along which research must proceed lies clearly before us, though it is extremely tedious and hazardous. This present paper represents a far from complete attempt to provide a fine systematic study of a single group, including behavioural characters, as a contribution to the described task.

II Technical information

The task of establishing initially purely descriptive behavioural catalogues (ethograms) of a large number of animal species makes great demands upon the observational capacity of the investigator. In order to reach even an approximation to satisfactory catalogues, the investigator must live with the animals day after day, year after year. This alone would seem to exclude the possibility of acquiring the necessary information from field studies. Even after keeping the species studied for a period of years, conscientiously recording every observation in a diary, individual items of information which would be extremely important for comparison are still missing when the work is concluded. This paper unfortunately shows this only too well. The animal group investigated must therefore be one which can be maintained well in captivity. In addition, the group must contain a large number of comparable species and genera exhibiting the maximum possible range of degrees of relationship. The individual species themselves should exhibit a large complement of species-specific behaviour patterns, which exhibit interspecific resemblances and are yet distinct enough to present a test case for the application of the homology concept. All of these requirements are fulfilled in an ideal manner by two groups of animals, both of which I have employed as objects for the research purposes discussed here: the *Anatinae* among birds and the *Cichlidae* among fish. This paper is concerned with the former. The Anatinae have been subjected to particularly exact investigation by Heinroth, Delacour, von Boetticher and others. In addition, they present a special advantage in comparative phylogenetic studies in that *interspecific hybrids* can be obtained with particular ease. In very many cases, these hybrids are actually fertile so that they can be employed for investigation of the inheritance of species-specific behaviour patterns. This represents a fertile area for synthesising phylogeny and genetics. In many cases, hybrids can lead to phylogenetic conclusions regarding species-specific behaviour patterns because of a special peculiarity whereby they exhibit, morphologically and behaviourally, a condition which is distinct from that of the two parental species (rather than intermediate) and is in fact *more primitive.* The hybrids have a further significance in that the degree of fertility can be employed as a measure of the degree of relationship between the parental species, as Poll has shown.

I have been able to investigate the following species within the Family Anatinae and the two adjacent Families Cairininae and Casarcinae: ANATINI: mallard, *Anas platyrhynchos* L.; Meller's duck, *Anas melleri* Scl.; Japanese spot-billed duck, *Anas zonorhyncha zonorhyncha* Swinhoe; Indian spot-billed duck, *Anas z. poecilorhyncha* Forster; pintail, *Dafila acuta* L.; South-American pintail, *Dafila spinicauda* Viellot; Bahama pintail, *Poecilonetta bahamensis* L.; Red-billed pintail, *Poecilonetta erythrorhyncha* Gm.; common teal, *Nettion crecca* L.; South-American teal, *Nettion flavirostre* Viellot; gadwall, *Chaulelasmus strepera*; wigeon, *Mareca penelope*; South-American wigeon, *Mareca sibilatrix* Poepp.; garganey, *Querquedula querquedula* L.; shoveller, *Spatula clypeata* L. – CAIRININI: Muscovy duck, *Cairina moschata* L.; American wood-duck, *Lampronessa sponsa* L.; mandarin duck, *Aix galericulata* L. – TADORNINI: shelduck, *Tadorna tadorna* L.; ruddy shelduck, *Casarca ferruginea*, Pallas; Egyptian goose, *Alopochen aegyptiacus* L. The hybrids will be discussed elsewhere.

III General discussion of motor display patterns

I. THE TAXONOMIC RELEVANCE OF MOTOR DISPLAY PATTERNS

In 1898, Whitman clearly emphasized that instinctive behaviour patterns require the same time intervals for phylogenetic development as morphological structures, and later Heinroth published his Anatid studies (1910) and his paper on the systematic distribution of certain motor patterns among vertebrates (1930). Since then, the applicability of innate, species-specific behaviour patterns as taxonomic criteria has gradually become a basic feature of zoological systematics (Stresemann on *Aves* in Kükenthal's *Handbuch*). Several years ago, I myself drew attention to the fact that certain instinctive behaviour patterns are quite particularly suited for taxonomic considerations and thus naturally suited for the analysis of the phylogenetic origin of innate motor patterns. Such instinctive behaviour patterns are those whose adaptive function is the *transmission of stimuli which evoke a specific response from conspecifics*, i.e. patterns referred to as 'releasers' (Lorenz 1935). Motor patterns of this kind are particularly common among birds, since responses to perception of movements play a very important part in their behaviour. In other groups of animals, the major rôle is played by chemical, acoustic or tactile releasers, which are by no means as favourable for comparative and experimental investigation by man – also an optically oriented animal. But quite apart from technical reasons of perceptibility, the optically operative motor display patterns of birds are particularly fertile objects for research (as is also the case with teleost fish). In the first place, there is a great abundance of characteristic and conspicuous individual characters, which provide a good foundation for inter-specific and inter-group comparisons. This abundance of characters is closely associated with the signal function involved, since animal releasers – just like human signals – must be *unmistakable* if they are to fully perform their functions. I have discussed this subject in detail in a special paper (Lorenz 1935), in which I demonstrated that the main characteristic of an unambiguous, easily perceived signal is a combination of maximum *simplicity* with maximum general *improbability*. Understandably, both of these properties render the releaser a particularly suitable object for the phylogenetic comparison of characters. The ease with which the releaser can be described itself contributes to this.

Over and above this, however, there is a second factor which makes releasers particularly useful in phylogenetic considerations: Because the special form of a releaser is not directly derivable from its function (in contrast to mechanically operative motor patterns) and is not influenced by the latter, the *possibility of convergence* can be fairly confidently excluded when there is correspondence between the elicitatory ceremonies of two related species.[3] The fact that tail-wagging in the dog represents a friendly greeting, whilst it is a sign of unfriendly tension in a cat, has nothing to do with a releaser function. The significance of the pattern depends upon an 'understanding' between production of the innate display pattern by one conspecific and corresponding innate recognition of the same by another. As far as the form of the motor pattern is concerned, the significance of the pattern could just as well be reversed in the dog and the cat. A philologist finding the same word expressing the same concept in two different human populations can virtually disregard the almost infinitesimally small probability that this is a pure product of chance and can justifiably assume that the word has a unitary historical root. In the same way, the comparative psychologist can in many cases assume that phylogenetic homology is doubtless present when the releasing ceremonies of two related species (usually incorporating a large number of characters) correspond. All of these factors have led to a situation where we know far more about the phylogenetic origin of elicitatory instinctive behaviour patterns than about the evolution of other innate patterns. Very many (if not all) patterns of this kind can be derived with great probability in two completely different ways from other, more primitive and mechanically operative instinctive behaviour patterns, although we of course do not know how the latter evolved. Nevertheless, in view of the poverty of our knowledge about the phylogeny of behaviour patterns at the present time, even this restricted demonstrable fragment of a phylogenetic process is extremely welcome.

2. THE SYMBOLIC MOTOR PATTERN

It is a characteristic feature of centrally co-ordinated, autonomous automatisms (whose operational effects are referred to as instinctive motor patterns) that even the lowest intensity levels of the excitation which they produce lead to the performance of observable movements. In this way, there emerge varying intensities of *indications* of motor patterns which only perform their adaptive function at much higher intensities of response. Weak indications, which can be observed at the lowest levels of response-specific excitation, are essentially non-functional in the adaptive sense. But an experienced observer can estimate the quality of the excitation which is developing within the organism and can judge the direction in which any resultant behaviour patterns may be expected. These incipient behaviour patterns have therefore been referred to as *intention movements*. Many instinctive behaviour patterns (e.g. the take-off flight of a duck or goose) only emerge with full and sudden intensity in response to strong *external* stimulation, whereas gradual accumulation of the *internal* drive regularly produces series of intention movements of successively increasing intensity preceding the actual adaptive, full-intensity eruption of the motor pattern concerned. This introduces the possibility that the animal species concerned may develop an 'understanding' for the intention movements of conspecifics, as a result of the evolution of innate schemata (Lorenz 1935),[4] which correspond to the stimuli produced by specific intention movements, in the same way as a radio receiver corresponds to the transmitter. In most cases, these innate schemata initially operate such that the conspecific responds with the same instinctive behaviour pattern as that evident in the stimulus-transmitting animal. Thus, the specific excitatory quality related to the motor pattern is transmitted from one individual to all of its neighbours as a result of the performance of intention movements and the activation of corresponding innate schemata in conspecifics. I have provided many examples of this form of motivational transfer in my paper *Der Kumpan in der Umwelt des Vogels* (*1935*), showing that this effect is almost always involved in cases where one finds behavioural conformity (often erroneously referred to as 'imitation'). As a result of this process, which is naturally of great adaptive significance for social animals, intention movements which were previously non-functional acquire an important function and *become subject to the factors determining further differentiation, just like any functional organ.* Consequently, elicitatory intention movements – in accordance with their 'signal' function – are regularly specialized from their original form such that they exert an *enhanced visual effect*. They come to exhibit 'exaggerated performance', as for example the nodding movements of guiding female mallard, the take-off patterns of Casarcinae and Anserinae, the nest-relief swimming pattern of Cichlid fish, etc. Exaggeration in performance often proceeds so far that the original root of the motor pattern – an intention movement of a purely mechanical, adaptively functioning motor pattern with no signalling effect – is scarcely recognizable and can only be divined through phylogenetic comparison covering related species in which the intention movement is less specialized. The take-off pattern of the Egyptian goose and the juvenile-guiding pattern of *Nannacara* (etc.) are doubtless derived from the intention movements of flying off and swimming away, respectively, but nobody who is unaware of the homologous motor patterns of related species would recognize their origin. Ceremonies of this type, which are derived from intention movements and are frequently unrecognizably 'formalized' (ritualized), are referred to as *symbolic motor patterns*.[5]

3. DISPLACEMENT ACTIVITIES

Apart from elicitatory symbolic motor patterns derived from intention movements, there are others with a fundamentally distinct origin, referred to by N. Tinbergen as *displacement activities*. At high levels of general arousal,[6] it can occur that instinctive motor patterns which are adaptively speaking quite inappropriate to the biological situation concerned are 'erroneously' elicited. This seem to occurs particularly in situations where performance of the normal, adequate motor pattern is for some reason prevented. The specific excitation then 'sparks over' into another pathway, producing a motor pattern which is both unexpected and inappropriate. Even human beings exhibit many examples of this process. The best-known case is embarrassed scratching of the head, and there are also the various well-known automatic movements performed by lecturers in the heat of their delivery. Tinbergen and Kortlandt, who independently provided the first descriptions of this process, have cited many examples, mainly from the behaviour of teleost fish and birds. In the ornithological literature, displacement activities are usually referred to as *sham-reactions*, e.g. sham-preening, sham-pecking, etc. Just as intention movements evoked by '*autochthonous*' response-specific energy can develop to represent bizarre symbols of themselves through optically operative exaggeration of characteristic motor phases, motor patterns activated by 'sparking over' can undergo formalization in the course of phylogenetic specialization to such an extent that comparison of many related species is necessary in order to determine their origin.

Most of the motor patterns of courtship to be described for the drakes of dabbling species can be interpreted as symbolic motor patterns or displacement activities. In view of the phylogenetic relationships determined, and their agreement with those assumed following comparison of other characters, this interpretation is probably highly reliable. Displacement activities are far more common than symbolic motor patterns; most of them are derived from the motor patterns of preening and body-shaking. It is also true of other animals that automatisms which, as displacement activities, are innervated by 'allochthonous' excitation (Kortlandt) are predominantly represented by the every-day automatisms of self-grooming (head-scratching in man, sham-preening in pigeons, cranes, etc.), feeding (sham-pecking in the threat behaviour of the domestic cock) and so on. For more detailed information on symbolic motor patterns and displacement activities, the reader is referred to my paper *Der Kumpan in der Umwelt des Vogels* and to Tinbergen's paper *Die Übersprungbewegung*.

IV   The mallard, *Anas platyrhynchos* L.

I. GENERAL COMMENTS

Quite apart from being the earliest and best-known object of behavioural studies, the mallard in many ways occupies a central position in the Anatini. It may be regarded as a pronounced 'primitive' character of this species that the drake – in addition to possessing the courtship whistle – 'still' has a relatively loud voice, which appears in the form of the monosyllabic, drawn out summoning call ('raehb') and the disyllabic contact call/conversation call('raebraeb'), and which is employed in the same way as the corresponding calls of the duck – alike in both rhythm and significance. In all other Anatinae, in the 3 species of Cairinini considered here, and in the Casarcine *Tadorna*, the actual voice of the male – as produced in the syrinx – is considerably reduced and replaced by a whistling call produced by a special organ, the bony drum of the trachea.

2. NON-EPIGAMIC MOTOR DISPLAY PATTERNS AND CALLS

In the mallard, the monosyllabic summoning call of both sexes arises ontogenetically in a smooth transition from the similarly monosyllabic 'lost piping' (present in homologous form in all Anatid ducklings so far investigated) and involves exactly corresponding head posture and plumage array (Figs. 1 and 2). In the same way, the contact call of all the Anatid ducklings which I have observed (i.e. including 'Anserinae) is originally disyllabic. In the genus *Anser*, this (doubtless original) condition persists only for a few hours. Thereafter, the disyllabic, generalized Anatid call develops to give the characteristic multisyllabic contact call of the genera *Anser, Eulabea, Branta*, etc. In both sexes of the mallard, the monosyllabic summoning call appears to be uttered with the same tonal qualities (at least, to the human ear) as an *alarm call*. The appearance of a strange dog elicits the drawn out 'raehb' from all drakes. In such a case, the call may be particularly long and drawn out, but I am nevertheless unable to tell from the call alone whether a drake is signalling alarm or calling his consort. In the duck in particular, repeated production of the monosyllabic summoning call indicates the intention *to move to a different place*, and the call is uttered with particular frequency before take-off. A restlessly roaming duck searching for a nest-site utters the call more softly, but with greater persistence, and the same applies when a female intends to lead her flock of ducklings on a long excursion. This form of the summoning call, referred to as the *departure call* is found in very many Anatinae and also in *Aix* and *Lampronessa*, in which the actual summoning call is no longer present in its original form or is replaced by a specialized vocalization. The 'departure call' is *lacking* in males.

The disyllabic contact call, in which the accent is placed on the second syllable, is uttered with particular intensity when mallard are reunited

Fig. 1. *'Lost piping' in a duckling of a dabbling species*

Fig. 2. *Monosyllabic summoning call of the mallard drake,* Anas platyrhynchos L.: *drawn out 'raehb'*

after a lengthy separation, or when *reassurance* is emerging after the birds have been cowed into a long period of silent crouching by a frightening stimulus. This occurs even among ducklings in a sibling flock, but it is most marked between, partners of a pair. In both cases, the drake, predominantly, augments the speed and volume of his disyllabic 'raebraeb' call, while the female begins to 'incite' at high levels of response intensity. A palaver of this kind exhibited by a pair or a flock of ducklings is strongly reminiscent of the so-called 'triumph-calling' of Casarcines and Anserines, and it probably represents a phylogenetic precursor of the latter.[7] At high levels of response intensity, roughly corresponding to the point where the duck switches to 'incitement', a specific head posture is exhibited, with the beak raised – particularly in the drake (Fig. 3). At still higher levels – though this is very rare – a

particular motor pattern known as '*down-up*' appears. (This will be
discussed later under courtship patterns.) Without doubt, there is a
connection with phylogenetic relationships in that more highly specialized
Anatines (*Chaulelasmus, Mareca penelope* and *M. sibilatrix*) possessing a
genuine 'triumph ceremony' exhibit particular differentiation of 'chin-
raising' and the 'down-up'. (This will be discussed in detail when these
species are considered.)

Fig. 3. *The 'raeb-raeb' palaver of a mallard pair, with 'chin-raising'. Note the
feather posture of the head and compare with Figs. 43, 44 and 45*

When this 'raeb-raeb' palaver of the mallard drake (with all its
resemblances to the triumph ceremony) reaches exceptionally high
levels of arousal, exceeding even the point of appearance of the down-up
movement, the drake's 'raebraeb' (and sometimes even the disyllabic
call of the female) exhibits traces of a peculiar accent which has undergone further differentiation in the gadwall. This accent depends upon
regular emphasis of the second syllable of the middle call in three
successive disyllabic calls, emphasizing this syllable against the preceding and following syllables: 'raebraeeb raebRAEEB raebraeeb'.

3. EPIGAMIC MOTOR DISPLAY PATTERNS AND CALLS OF THE FEMALE

In the same way that the females of closely-related Anatine species
differ less from one another than the males in morphological characters,
there is less interspecific variation in the behavioural repertoires of the
females. Thus, a detailed description of the female mallard will serve
for all of the other Anatines except *Mareca*.

(a) Incitement behaviour

The commonest female courtship pattern is so-called 'incitement', which occurs in a basically similar, and doubtless homologous, form in all Anatines, in *Tadorna* and *Casarca* and in *Aix*, *Lampronessa* and *Amazonetta* among Cairinini. The female turns towards her consort – or prospective consort – swims along behind him and simultaneously threatens another conspecific male over her shoulder. In the Egyptian goose these two orienting responses (general orientation of the longitudinal body axis to the existing or prospective consort, and threat towards a 'symbolic enemy') are completely independent of one another and exhibit a plastic relationship. The angle between the body axis and the direction of the threat movement of the head is determined solely by the spatial relationships of the female, the male and the threatened enemy. For example, it can happen that the enemy is located behind the male, as seen from the female's position, such that the female Eygptian goose – closely following her consort – threatens directly forwards towards the symbolic enemy. Usually, however, the inciting female is oriented with her tail towards the 'enemy', for the simple reason that she typically begins by making a slight spurt towards the latter, does not dare to translate this into actual attack and must therefore swim from the 'enemy' to the male in order to perform incitement. This process automatically provides the characteristic angle between the head and the body axis. 'Already' in *Casarca ferruginea*, however, one can frequently observe a similar incitement movement of the head directed backwards over the shoulder *without* dependence on the spatial relationship between female, male and 'enemy'. In inciting Anatines, in which incitement has been 'formalized' to a pure ceremony and in which the original significance of the instinctive behaviour pattern (provocation of the male to attack a real opponent) is completely obscured by the secondary significance of a 'declaration of love', *the movement of the head over the shoulder represents a pure, taxis-free instinctive motor pattern,* and the ducks are quite unable to perform the pattern in anything other than the definitive established manner. For example, a female mallard will incite over her shoulder even if the 'enemy' is not located in the resultant direction of the threat movement! The direction of the threat movement can only be varied within a small arc! I must emphasize that I am quite opposed to any lamarckian explanation of this remarkable evolutionary series of the incitement movement; though I am convinced that this is a genuine 'phylogenetic series', since the form of incitement found in Casarcines (and to some extent in Anserines) doubtless represents the original form of the motor pattern. Without knowledge of these patterns, the 'ceremonies' of the Anatines – which exhibit a pronounced change in significance – cannot be understood at all. I am nevertheless against the assumption that an instinctive motor pattern could evolve from an orienting response through the acquisition of a 'habit' and the hereditary transmission of acquired characters[8]. On the other hand, we know of many examples of the origin of completely rigid, centrally co-ordinated motor patterns from originally oriented movements, as for example the so-called zig-zag dance (Leiner) of the male stickleback.

The female mallard utters a specific vocalization during incitement – a peculiar 'nagging' sound, *queggegéggeggeggeggegg*, which is usually emphasized on the third syllable, thus producing a strangely 'querulous' accent. This vocalization is not to be confused with that which the duck utters when pursued by a strange drake. During incitement, the upper mandible is bent some way ventrally on the extremely mobile head articulation (Fig. 4), whilst the head and back feathers are flattened. These two features produce a peculiar 'sheepish' facial expression, and the downward flexion of the mandible assures that the chin profile closely fits the curvature of the back as the head moves along it.

Fig. 4. *Incitement in the mallard. Note the angle between the forehead and beak and compare with Fig. 5. The drake shows hind-head display and chin-raising* (*cf. Fig. 14*)

(b) *The rejection display*

The 'rejection call' of a duck followed by a strange drake, uttered particularly by females which are already incubating, bears a superficial resemblance to the incitement call; but it consists of a fragmented series of single *geck* sounds produced with the abruptness of a cough, rather than of a continuous series of *quegg* notes. With this call, the upper mandible is rotated maximally upwards on the so-called 'frontonasal joint', the feathers on the head and back are markedly ruffled, and the head is drawn back onto the nape (Fig. 5). The same body and plumage posture, associated with a very similar call, is exhibited by female Casarcinae when disturbed on the nest and by brooding *Cairina* females when a drake attempts to mount. Since in the mallard and in the other species mentioned quite mild disturbances are particularly responded to with the same motor pattern and vocalization by females leading their ducklings, it is reasonable to assume that this represents the primary significance of this display. In the mallard, the special, more specific, function of rejecting a strange drake – occurring even in non-incubating, but firmly paired ducks – would then be a secondary specialization. Because of the 'raping' response of the drake (see later), these motor display patterns and vocalizations, which would originally have occurred only in absolutely non-receptive brooding females, have found a new range of application in the mallard, pintail and probably the teal. Whenever a clucking vocalization is heard from a female mallard followed by two drakes in flight, it is virtually always the described 'rejection call' which is involved. I have only once in my life heard a female mallard inciting on the wing.

Fig. 5. *The rejection display of the mallard female*

(c) The decrescendo call

All female Anatines, including the genus *Mareca*, exhibit a quite peculiar vocalization which doubtless represents a homologous instinctive motor pattern in all forms, despite the fact that it has 14 syllables in *Nettion* and is unisyllabic in *Mareca*. In the mallard, this call usually has 6 syllables – *quaegaegaegaegaegaeg* – with the strongest emphasis on the second syllable and with gradual decline in the following syllables. This call is uttered particularly by *unpaired* ducks, and it is usually uttered by firmly paired females only when their mate has flown off. The major elicitatory factor is the *sight of a conspecific on the wing*. With pronounced threshold lowering, unpaired ducks will exhibit this response towards any flying duck and sometimes even to other flying birds.

(d) Nod-swimming

This instinctive motor pattern of the female mallard, referred to by Heinroth as '*coquettish swimming*', corresponds to the many highly differentiated motor patterns of the social courtship of the drake, termed 'social play' by Heinroth. We shall see later on that the drake can similarly exhibit the motor pattern of nod-swimming, but in the male it is coupled to other motor patterns, whereas it is independent in the female. The female usually exhibits this motor pattern only when several drakes have formed a group and indicate their courtship motivation through ruffling of the head feathers and shaking themselves. Then, the female abruptly dashes between the drakes, with the body markedly flattened and her head bobbing up and down pronouncedly. She swims in short arcs, each time swimming around as many drakes as possible. During the nodding movements, the head is held so close to the water surface that the duck's chin skims the water (Fig. 6). Nod-swimming markedly elicits the subsequent courtship patterns of the drakes.

Fig. 6. *Nod-swimming in the mallard female*

The phylogenetic origin of the nod-swimming pattern is a complete mystery, since we have not so far observed any precursors of the ceremony. Apart from occurring in the mallard, this motor pattern is found only in the closest relatives within the genus *Anas* (as it used to be) and in the chestnut-breasted teal (*Virago castanea*) and the grey teal (*Virago gibberifrons* E. Virchow).

(e) The mating prelude

This consists of jerking head movements which bear great resemblance to the intention movement of take-off, but occur in the *opposite* manner. Instead of moving the head slowly downwards and then abruptly upwards, the duck performs the reverse. This motor display pattern has obviously evolved from an intention movement towards flattening the body. Whereas in the take-off movement the head is pushed abruptly upwards with the beak held horizontally and then lowered more slowly into its original position, it is the downward movement which is abruptly accelerated in the mating prelude. This motor display pattern is probably derived from an intention movement towards flattening the body, as occurs in mating itself. This assumption is supported by the following chance observation: I once saw a mallard drake standing on the upper edge of a very steep bank and performing what I took to be the 'pumping movement' of the mating prelude. No female was to be seen, however. The next instant, the drake took off and flew down the bank to land at the lower end. The movement which I had interpreted as a mating prelude was in fact the – usually extremely rare – intention

movement for flying downwards! Thus, a downward intention movement (i.e. towards flattening) is doubtless the origin of the pumping
mating prelude of most Anatinae. In the mallard and in all other
Anatines (with the possible exception of *Mareca*), the motor patterns of
the mating prelude are similar in form in both sexes.

Fig. 7. *'Pumping' as the mating prelude in the mallard. The two partners
exhibit the extremes of the vertical head movement*

The movements of the female usually predominate in intensity, and this
usually provides the impetus for the prelude ceremony and for copulation
itself. This motor pattern is briefly termed 'pumping' (Fig. 7).

4. THE EPIGAMIC DISPLAY PATTERNS AND VOCALIZATIONS OF THE DRAKE

(a) The general form of courtship

As is well known, the males assemble for social courtship play in most
species of Anatinae, in *Aix galericulata* among the Cairininae and in a
number of species of Fuligulinae. In this, the females only participate
as spectators – apart from performing a small number of releasing
patterns which incite the drakes to courtship (p. 27 et seq.). On the
other hand, females of all Anatine species exhibiting such 'social play'
(Heinroth) play an extremely active part in the choice of partner, something which will be dealt with specifically in discussing the mandarin
duck. Along with the mandarin drakes, the mallard drakes are probably
least affected by the presence or absence of a female in performing
social play. As with male Black Grouse, Caper caillie, turkey and peacock, their courtship does not represent courting of a particular female
but a general display which occurs in more-or-less the same way, whether
a female is present or not. Within the Anatinae, we shall find all imaginable intermediates between such 'impersonal' mass courtship and the
individual courtship of a particular female. In social courtship, the drake
together perform a number of highly differentiated motor patterns which

varies from species to species. These patterns are usually accompanied by calls which are produced by the *bony drum* in the drake's syrinx. The vocally accompanied patterns, which – as we shall see later on – have arisen from extremely varied instinctive behaviour patterns via symbolic patterns and displacement activities, have one thing in common: with very few exceptions, they lead to tension of the trachea, which is obviously necessary for production of the courtship call. The actual courtship motor patterns, accompanied by calls, are always preceded by a number of instinctive behaviour patterns which possibly serve for self-stimulation of the drake.[9] The distribution of these patterns within the group indicates that they are phylogenetically older than the actual courtship patterns.

(b) Display drinking

The first such 'introductory' motor pattern to be described is one which possibly does not have an exclusively epigamic character. Whenever two ducks meet on the surface of a pond, either one will avoid the other or both will *drink*. At first, one might consider such drinking to be a chance effect. Heinroth often relates in a very illustrative manner how long it took until he himself realized in observing this motor pattern that drinking following an encounter is no chance phenomenon but possesses a specific social function and operates as a *pacific gesture*. Heinroth explains the evolution of this significance of display drinking as derivation from a symbolic pattern, to the extent that two birds which eat or drink in close proximity have no bad intentions towards one another. Thus, display drinking was originally a motor display pattern of purely social significance, and for this reason it is far from restricted to interactions between the partners of a pair, even if it occurs with great frequency between such partners. At a higher level of differentiation, the pattern is in some species coupled with the motor pattern of sham-preening behind the wing. In the gadwall and the mandarin duck (a member of the Cairininae) this coupling is quite rigid. (See under mandarin duck.) In the mallard, such coupling is just discernible; the drakes exhibit mock-preening with particular frequency immediately after exhibiting display drinking towards the female, but the two patterns are then repeated several times without any fixed sequence. At this point, it should be mentioned that rigid coupling between display drinking and sham-preening in the gadwall and the mandarin duck has occurred in reverse order.

Display drinking is very widely distributed in the Family. In the Anatinae, there is no species which lacks it (see table). As a male courtship pattern, it also occurs coupled with other epigamic behaviour patterns in the Cairininae *Aix* and *Lampronessa* as well as the two

Fuliguline forms *Netta* and *Metopiana*, which are similarly closely related to the Anatinae.

(c) Sham-preening

When a drake has exhibited display drinking towards a female he is courting, he will frequently reach back with the bill behind one slightly raised wing (Fig. 8), just as if he intends to preen at that spot. Instead, there is a brief, coarse movement of the nail of the bill across the base of the pinion quills, producing a fairly loud rrr-sound which can be heard up to several metres away.

Fig. 8. *Mock-preening of the mallard drake. The contact of the bill with the pinion quills produces a loud noise (cf. Figs. 28 and 49)*

The movement is so rapid that I still do not venture to decide whether the beak is passed over the secondaries or over the primaries. The intensity of the sound indicates the latter, but it must be remembered that the wigeon, garganey, teal, wood duck and mandarin drakes quite definitely perform sham-preening on the inside of the secondaries. The last two each perform this on *one* particular, specially differentiated feather with a specific colour (see under wood duck and mandarin). It is an interesting methodological point for the psychology of observing animals that sham-preening of the mallard drake was first discovered by us in 1939, after we had spent so many years in purposeful observation of these birds. The event which opened my eyes to this frequently observed procedure was my first observation of the homologous motor pattern of the garganey drake, which is performed in a somewhat different manner. The colours of the auxiliary wing plumage – obviously developed specifically for this motor pattern – make it impossible to overlook the behaviour. I at first vaguely realized that I had seen this ceremony 'somewhere' before, and then specific observations carried out to locate this source produced the surprising result that all of the duck species which I have kept exhibit this motor pattern (see table). Nowadays, I find it quite incredible that the extremely characteristic sound produced did not draw my attention to the motor pattern earlier on.

Mallard drakes begin sham-preening, which almost always follows display drinking (but not the other way around!), not only in encounters with females but also in encounters with drakes – possibly at even greater intensity – when motivation for social courtship is beginning to emerge. In this context, the motor pattern can be regarded as the first introductory element to what Heinroth called 'social play'.

From a phylogenetic standpoint, sham-preening is doubtless to be interpreted as a displacement activity. There is scarcely any behaviour pattern which can assume such varied functions as displacement preening within the Class Aves. Apart from its extremely common application as a courtship pattern, it can be employed as threat (e.g. in the crane) or as a prelude to mating (as in the goosander and the rock dove). In the last case, however, there are justifiable doubts as to whether the preening ceremony has evolved from a genuine displacement activity and not from an autochthonous behaviour pattern, i.e. as a symbolic motor pattern. This could have occurred in roughly the same way as assumed by Heinroth for display drinking (q.v.).

(d) Introductory body-shaking

When several drakes have gathered together in the manner described above, the augmentation of their specific courtship motivation is at

Fig. 9. *The introductory posture of mallard drakes assembled for 'social play'* (*Heinroth*). *Head feathers ruffled; back feathers flattened (cf. Fig. 19 and Fig. 48)*

first expressed by means of a particular body and plumage posture. The head is drawn right in between the shoulders, so that the white neck-ring completely disappears; the down feathers are lightly ruffled, so that the bird swims high on the water in a 'demonstrative' manner, and the back feathers are markedly flattened to produce a 'contrived' contrast to the normal resting position. The head feathers are erected to the extreme so that the green sheen disappears for almost any angle of observation and is replaced by a deep velvety black (Fig. 9). This posture differs from that assumed by a mallard immediately before normal body-shaking only in that it is maintained for longer periods – often several minutes. In normal body-shaking, the retraction of the head and the ruffling of the head feathers last only for a number of seconds, increasing in intensity. The experienced observer can exactly determine from this increase the point at which body-shaking will occur, in a manner completely analogous to determining the instant of sneezing by a neighbour from the degree of distortion of his face. In the social play of the mallard, by contrast, the expected shaking appears much later, and even when it does occur it does not bring about relaxation, or liberation from the preparatory posture. Instead, the first shaking action – in which the head is hesitantly thrust upwards

Fig. 10. *Schema of the movement in introductory body-shaking*

(Fig. 10) in a strangely inhibited and yet nervously rapid manner – is followed by a second and a third after only a few seconds.[10] The intensity of the movement increases very gradually from one movement to the next until the shaking movement seems to pull the drake high out of the water as if in convulsion. When this intensity level has been reached, the movement is regularly followed not by another shaking action but by one of the three courtship motor patterns to be described next (grunt-whistle, down-up, head-up-tail-up). All of the drakes then perform courtship. Thereafter, the entire assembly is relaxed for some time and either ceases to exhibit courtship, or commences (after a short pause) to exhibit a new bout of low-intensity introductory shaking, and so on. The introductory shaking movement definitely represents a *displacement activity*. It is found in all Anatinae with the exception of *Spatula*.

(e) *The grunt-whistle*

As with the normal shaking movement, the beak is at first lowered, so that the shaking movement commences low down and is performed upwards (Fig. 11a). However, this lowering action is so pronounced that the bill-tip scoops the water-surface in the first transverse movements, throwing up a shower of droplets in a wide arc. This fact has not been recorded by any previous investigators of drake courtship, and we only noticed it ourselves on observing that the 'scattered black dots due to faulty emulsion' persistently re-appeared specifically in photographs of the grunt-whistle.

Fig. 11a & b. *Mallard: 2 motor phases of the grunt-whistle. Note the arc of upward-flying water droplets*

In contrast to the normal shaking movement, the rearing of the body precedes that of the head to such an extent that the body is already fairly erect in the water when the head is still quite low with the bill close to the water surface. This peculiar re-curved position (Fig. 11b) obviously performs a mechanical function in the tensing of the trachea. At the instant where the movement is at its peak, a loud sharp whistle is produced. This is followed by a deep grunt as the head is straightened again and the body sinks back to the water surface. The grunting sound gives the impression of the escape of a pocket of air compressed during the whistle.

The distribution of the grunt-whistle within the Order Anatinae is peculiar (see table) to the extent that not all Anatinae exhibit this motor pattern or a homologue of it, while both the Cairininae *Aix* and *Lampronessa* and the Casarcine *Tadorna tadorna* exhibit definite homologues, even if these are differentiated in another direction. Apart from the species of the genus *Anas* (in its narrower sense), which exhibit virtually no differences from the motor pattern of the mallard, the grunt-whistle is exhibited in almost identical form in the pintail (*Dafila acuta*), the

South American pintail (*Dafila spinicauda*), the European and South American teal (*Nettion crecca* and *N. flavirostre*). Probably, all of the other species of these genera which I have not observed have this pattern as well. The grunt-whistle is also present in the chestnut-breasted teal (*Virago castanea*) and (in somewhat modified form) in the gadwall (*Chaulelasmus strepera*); but it is lacking in the Bahama duck (*Poecilonetta bahamensis*),[11] the African red-billed duck (*Poecilonetta erythrorhyncha*), garganey species and the shoveller.

In view of the intermediate form between the grunt-whistle and body-shaking found in the wood duck and the mandarin (see later) and the incipient shaking movement evident at the beginning of the grunt-whistle in the mallard itself, there can be no doubt that the grunt-whistle has evolved through gestural exaggeration of 'incipient' body-shaking originally occurring as a displacement activity. In the mallard, other Anatines and the wood duck there are – in addition to normal body-shaking – 2 ritualized forms of this motor pattern present as display activities, and in the mandarin there are actually no less than four clearly demarcated derived courtship motor patterns which are distinct from the original shaking action. In *Tadorna*, on the other hand, a quite peculiar contrasting form of behaviour is found: The male *Tadorna* exhibits demonstrative shaking very similar to the corresponding motor pattern of the mandarin drake, in which the head is initially lowered as if indicating a subsequent grunt-whistle, and is then shot upwards with a shaking motion accompanied by a trilling whistle, but without involving rearing of the body. In contrast to all other Anatid males performing homologous motor patterns, however, the sheldrake exhibits this motor pattern as the only form of shaking. In other words, the original, normal, mechanically functional body-shaking movement has been absorbed into this display pattern. For example, if a sheldrake is seized and then released, there is no subsequent reflex performance of body-shaking, as would emerge with all other drakes. Instead, the described demonstrative gesture always appears. One would think that this movement has a much lesser ordering effect on the feathers than the original pattern 'constructed' expressly for this purpose. I should like to draw a comparison between the phylogenetic process underlying this change of a mechanically operative instinctive motor pattern into an elicitatory ceremony for courtship and (for example) the differentiation of morphological structures which can be seen in the wing of a nightjar[12] and an Argus pheasant. Without doubt, these two extremely different courtship organs originally developed on the basis of a specific form of use of the wing in courtship which was already present before their formation. Whereas in the 'goatsucker' a second, specific 'courtship wing' has been developed on the normal wing, leaving the original flight organ intact and functional, in the Argus pheasant the wing has been 'absorbed' into the courtship organ to such an extent that its original mechanical function has been quite considerably impaired by the secondary function of elicitation. In exactly the same way, the original motor pattern of body-shaking has remained in existence alongside the courtship motor pattern arising from the courtship organ in *Anas* and *Aix*, whereas the former has been absorbed in the latter in the sexually motivated *Tadorna* male.

(f) *Head-up-tail-up*

In addition to the grunt-whistle, the mallard drake exhibits two further, equally important courtship motor patterns – the 'head-up-tail-up' and the 'down-up'. Which of the 3 patterns follows the introductory body-shaking seems to be a matter of chance.

Fig. 12. *Head-up-tail-up in the mallard drake; the same movement seen from different sides. Note the prominence of all particularly colourful and morphologically differentiated parts of the plumage (cf. Figs. 20, 25, 35 and 41)*

Heinroth writes that it is usually *one* drake which performs the grunt-whistle, while the other drakes involved in the social play respond with head-up-tail-up or down-up. This is indeed frequently the case, but it is definitely not an absolute rule. All other possible combinations can occur.[13] Head-up-tail-up is possibly the most conspicuous of the courtship patterns of the mallard drake; it is definitely the most complex. The drake first jerks his head backwards and upwards with the chin drawn in, accompanying this with a loud whistle. At the same time the rump is bent upwards with the rump feathers extremely ruffled. The result is that the bird has a peculiarly shortened and raised profile. The elbows are also raised, so that the protruding curled feather of the rump remains visible (Fig. 12). This phase lasts about one-twentieth of a second, and the body then sinks back into the normal posture. The head remains reared for a moment, and the beak is directed towards a particular female among those present at the social play of the drakes. With mated drakes, the beak is always directed towards the consort (Fig. 13).

Fig. 13. *Turning of the head towards the female appearing immediately after the head-up-tail-up. Note the posture of the head feathers*

A moment later, the drake moves off rapidly across the water surface, performing 'nod-swimming' (see p. 27 et seq.) with a flattened body posture and usually circling around the courted female (Fig. 14). Towards the end of the performance of nod-swimming, when the drake gradually returns to the normal swimming posture, the head is raised and the back of the head is turned towards the duck previously presented with the male's beak (Fig. 15). During the head-up-tail-up and 'burping' the head plumage already assumes a remarkable 'coiffure': The lateral head feathers are flattened, while the median feathers are ruffled so that the head forms a flattened elevated disc. Seen from the side, the head has a marked sheen – providing a conspicuous contrast to the matt black ball formed by the head during introductory body-shaking. During nod-swimming, this 'coiffure' is again altered in such a way that the entire head plumage is flattened, apart from a small group of rigidly erected feathers evident on the nape (Fig. 14). This feather arrangement can

Fig. 14. *Nod-swimming of the mallard drake, as coupled with head-up-tail-up and hind-head display*

only be understood from the following phase – the display of the back of the head: in this, the courted duck is presented with the sight of a conspicuous pattern composed of a small black area entirely framed in green.

It is appropriate at this point to consider the comparative morphology of these feather postures, taking the word 'morphology' to cover the study of both the form of the movement *and* the organic form. The feather postures, which are purely *functional* in the mallard drake, have quite definitely come to represent an invariable form in the pintail, teal, wood duck and mandarin drakes. All of these four species – and probably a large number of others – exhibit homologues not only of the mallard drake's motor patterns but also of the corresponding feather postures. However, these species also possess colour and shape characters which delineate as *persistent* morphological characters the same profiles which are produced by different feather postures in the mallard drake. The disc-shaped 'coiffure' which the mallard drake exhibits at the moment of 'burping' presents a sharp edge exactly corresponding to the course of the fine white line which separates the green eye-patch

Fig. 15. *Hind-head display of the mallard drake without chin-raising; Usually coupled with nod-swimming. Note the posture of the hindmost head feathers and the highlights (cf. Fig. 23)*

from the matt colour of the top of the head in the European teal. In the Carolina wood duck, a corresponding white line is accompanied by extension of the feathers, which produces a spatial development of the edge indicated merely by the white line in the teal. The hoods of *Lampronessa* and *Aix* 'serve' primarily as 'disc-coiffures'. In the mandarin drake, the same line is underlined even more sharply by the border of the white temples set against the colourful crown feathers. In this species, extension of the feathers has gone so far that the spatially prominent edge is even present when the feathers are in repose. In the pintail drake, the 'disc-coiffure' is less conspicuous than in the mallard drake, but the hind-head display and the accompanying erection of the nape feathers is particularly well developed (see also Fig. 23). The black velvety patch which appears on the nape of the mallard drake in this posture has developed to a persistent morphological character in *Dafila acuta*. The corresponding feathers are not only deep black, with a white line framing them to the left and right (as is well known) – they are also longer than the surrounding plumage, so that the feather posture of hind-head display produces a spatially protruding feather cushion. There can be no doubt that with all of these body and feather movements *the motor pattern is older than the organs differentiated to magnify their optical effect*. The broad systematic distribution of the motor patterns, the much narrower range of the individual feather forms and colours, and the obvious relationship of the latter to the common basic motor patterns (obviously an extremely ancient attribute of the Family) allow no other conclusion. A further indication is that the characteristic bodily movements are performed in a fashion completely homologous to that seen in the mallard even in the males of the other *Anas* species not equipped with a 'Prachtkleid' (nuptial plumage). The feather postures are also demonstrable in these species, but their extent is conspicuously less than in duck species with glossy or even extended head feathers.

The head-up-tail-up pattern is much less common within the Family than is the grunt-whistle (see table). Apart from the true *Anas* species, it occurs only in the pintail and European teal drakes. It is also found in the Bahama drake, as the only courtship motor pattern. Interestingly, the head-up-tail-up is lacking in *Dafila spinicauda*. In *Nettion flavirostre*, only parts of the motor pattern are present – 'burping' with subsequent head-turning towards the female. At the moment, it is not possible to speculate about the origin of the head-up-tail-up. As with the grunt-whistle, the marked flexure of the vertebral column is obviously related in some way to the tensing of the trachea in the production of the whistle. However, it is not yet possible to decide whether the motor pattern itself is derived from some originally mechanically operative instinctive behaviour pattern, via either a symbolic pattern or a displacement activity.

(g) The down-up pattern

Instead of the grunt-whistle or head-up-tail-up, the drake can perform a third motor pattern in which the bill is rapidly dipped into the water and the head is then almost immediately reared up without raising the breast from its deep position in the water (Fig. 16). At the moment where the head is at its highest point and the breast at its lowest, the whistle is uttered. Once again this occurs when the tension of the trachea is greatest. As the bill is swept out of the water, the rapid movement frequently produces a fountain of water, which may well have a visual effect on the duck, in view of the short response time typical of birds. Immediately after this extremely brief movement, the drake (still with the chin raised) very quickly utters the *raebraeb*. With the down-up pattern, more than with any other courtship motor pattern, one has the impression that the drakes must influence one another in some way. With a frequency far beyond that expected by chance, most or even all of the drakes in a courtship group will perform this particular motor pattern. The subsequent *raebraeb* palaver usually concludes the courtship sequence.

Fig. 16. *The down-up pattern of the mallard drake, showing a drake at the lowest point* (left) *and another* (right) *at the highest point immediately afterwards. Note the column of water drawn up from the water-surface, showing the extreme rapidity of the movement*

The down-up pattern is the only motor pattern occurring in courtship which can exceptionally occur *outside* of courtship. This always happens in a particular situation – following a *raebraeb* palaver (see p. 23) of maximal intensity, which occurs especially after alarm or a fight between two drakes.

The distribution of the down-up pattern among the close relatives of the mallard exhibits (so to speak) the reverse direction to that shown by the head-up-tail-up. Apart from occurring in *Anas* species (in the narrowest sense) it is only found in definitely homologous form in the gadwall and the various widgeon species. A probably homologous differentiated form is also found in *Virago castanea*. The pattern is lacking in all pintails and teal species, which otherwise exhibit great similarity to the mallard in their courtship motor patterns.[14] A possibly homologous motor pattern is the extreme lifting of the head which represents the most important courtship pattern of the rosy-billed pochard drake (*Metopiana peposaca*).

The origin of the down-up movement can be stated with some certainty. It probably represents a ritualized exaggeration of the display drinking found in almost all Anatidae. If the motor pattern of *chin-raising* (as performed by the mallard drake after the down-up movement and generally following pronounced *raebraeb* palaver) is interpreted as a low intensity form of the down-up, the motor pattern in fact exhibits a somewhat wider distribution within the Family and simultaneously shows a more distinct relationship to display drinking. In particular, display drinking is frequently followed by chin-raising and hind-head display in the male Carolina wood duck.

(h) 'Gasping'

Sometimes, at the very moment when other members of the courtship group produce the whistle, individual drakes will utter a peculiar hoarse note without performing a particularly conspicuous movement. This can best be imitated by hoarsely saying the three syllables *chacha-cha*, alternatively breathing out, in and out again. This call is particularly heard from weak, or otherwise relatively unresponsive, drakes. In addition, I have heard this uttered in the same way, though with a corresponding transposition of pitch, by a female Khaki Campbell duck and by a female hybrid between *Virago castanea* and *Poecilonetta bahamensis*, which displayed interest in the social courtship of the mallard drakes. The origin and significance of this call are unknown, and the further distribution has not been established.

(i) Fighting between drakes

Fighting mallard drakes draw in their necks and grasp one another by the crop feathers, each pushing towards and trying to displace the other. As a result of this remarkable form of combat, one can observe round bare patches in the crop feathers quite early in the Spring. The drakes only begin to strike at each other with the wing shoulders at very high levels of intensity of fight motivation. It is then observed that the peculiar retraction of the head, with the neck shortened, is adapted from the out-set to the subsequent performance of this second motor pattern. Other Anatidae which strike with the wing shoulders in fight also hold the opponent against their breast with the neck retracted, exactly at the point where the shoulder strikes.

(k) Post-copulatory play

This is characterized by a specific motor pattern in the mallard drake. Immediately after treading, whilst still holding on, the drake suddenly pulls the head and neck far back towards his rump, without extending the head upwards. Frequently, the nape feathers of the female are still grasped in the drake's beak, so that her head is drawn back too (Fig. 17). Then, as if this backward movement were merely necessary as prepa-ration for a gestural exaggeration of head-nodding, the drake darts off and nod-swims in a circle around the female, just as with the head-up-tail-up (see p. 36). The motor pattern of upward and backward pulling of the head, which will be termed 'bridling', sometimes occurs as a component of the motor pattern of head-up-tail-up. This occurs in such a way that 'bridling' and subsequent nod-swimming follows head-raising and bill-turning to the female in the same way as when following treading.

The same post-copulatory play is found in all *Anas* species, in *Nettion flavirostre* (I do not know whether it occurs in *N. crecca*) and in *Virago castanea*. In the latter two species, 'bridling' can also occur as a completely independent motor pattern in social play (table). In *Nettion flavirostre*, there is no subsequent nod-swimming; in *Virago castanea*

Fig. 17. *'Bridling' of the mallard drake following copulation. The same movement occurs after the head-up-tail-up (Fig. 12) with head-turning towards the female (Fig. 15) and preceding the subsequent nod-swimming (p. 37)*

the pattern is either isolated in the same way or (see later) occurs as a component in a single, fixed chain of motor patterns, which begins with the grunt-whistle and concludes with nod-swimming and hind-head display.

V The spot-billed duck, *Anas poecilorhyncha* Forster and *Anas poecilorhyncha* Swinhoe

For these two species, all that can be reported is that they agree entirely with the mallard in all motor patterns and vocalizations. The only difference which I was able to observe concerned the feather posture of the head in the motor patterns described on p. 38. The characteristic 'coiffures' are actually present, but they are markedly less extreme than those of the mallard. The mallard, the spot-billed duck and Meller's duck regard each other as 'the same' to the extent that the drakes will fight together like conspecifics and that these species will produce interspecific pairs just as easily as conspecific pairs. In the 'rape' response alone, there is a remarkable elective response to conspecifics: spot-billed ducks and Meller's ducks are very seldom pursued by mallard drakes, and conversely the drakes of these species never exhibit the inclination to 'rape' female mallard. All the same, actual pairing occurs just as easily between as within these species.

VI Meller's duck, *Anas melleri* Sclater

Whereas the spot-billed drake is quite distinct from the female in plumage and beak colour (though there is no actual male display plumage) the male and female of Meller's duck are almost identical. The male's plumage exhibits the typical, longitudinal shaft spotting of the *Anas* female plumage, with no trace of the tendency to transverse banding indicated in both the spot-billed drake and the black drake (*Anas rubripes*) and reminiscent of the summer plumage of the mallard drake. Behaviourally, the Meller's drake differs from the mallard and spot-billed drakes in its extraordinary predisposition for fighting and the accompanying strong tendency to exhibit chin-raising and *raebraeb*-palaver. The drakes defend their consorts against strange drakes more intensively than the male mallard, and they exhibit much more fighting when courting females. Interestingly, female Meller's duck seem to respond particularly readily to drakes of other species. In particular, one large hybrid between mallard and Muscovy duck was continually favoured with the love – and thus the most intensive pressure of incitement behaviour – of a whole series of Meller females. This lack of species specificity is doubtless correlated with the lack of a characteristic male nuptial plumage. The Meller's drakes, on the other hand, make up for their lack of display plumage with their extraordinary fighting spirit. In a contest between a mallard drake and a Meller's drake, it is always the the latter who carries off the bride. Even the Meller's drake whose 'legal' consort had fallen in love with the mallard-Muscovy hybrid eventually managed to prevail over his rival through the stubbornness of his attacks, despite the fact that the hybrid was twice his weight and far from cowardly. This marked fighting spirit, and particularly the tendency towards wildly defending the consort, indicated that there might be some form of male brood-care. The complete lack of sexual dimorphism would fit with this supposition. However, this expectation has so far not been fulfilled: in the few cases (3) in which I allowed Meller's duck to lead their offspring at liberty, in order to examine this question, the drake in each case paid just as little attention to his ducklings as would a mallard drake.

Both the male and female epigamic and non-sexual motor display patterns and vocalizations differ so little from those of the mallard that it is sufficient to mention the differences exhibited. The incitement call of the duck has a high, thin ring and can be immediately and reliably distinguished from that of the mallard or spot-billed duck (which has an identical ring in both). The decrescendo call is also somewhat coarser and thinner. One could say that both calls sound as if they were uttered by a smaller duck. With the drake, the greatest difference from the drakes of the spot-billed duck and mallard occurs in the social contact call and palaver, where the *raebraeb* is replaced by a trisyllabic *raebraebraeb*, which may even become quadrisyllabic at high levels of arousal. This struck me optically at first – and not acoustically – because the lower mandible of Meller's drakes moved with remarkable rapidity during the palaver. In the social play of the Meller's drakes, one can observe all of the motor patterns noted for the mallard drake; *but in addition, the drake performs nod-swimming, which is only performed as a discrete motor pattern by the female in the social courtship of spot-billed duck and mallard.* This nod-swimming of the Meller's drake also corresponds to that of the *Anas* female in the manner in which it is exhibited. In contrast to the nod-swimming incorporated into the head-up-tail-up of the mallard drake, which only emerges after a long introduction incorporating many other motor patterns, that of Meller's drake is (so-to-speak) used as an introduction and invitation to courtship, just as in the female. There is no introductory shaking, display drinking or sham preening. It is possibly no chance effect that the only really female-coloured dabbling drake should also possess this female courtship pattern.[15]

VII   The pintail, *Dafila acuta* L.

1. GENERAL OBSERVATIONS

The general structure of the courtship groups of the pintail, and therefore the significance of the individual motor patterns under comparison, differs from that of the duck species so far discussed in that the drakes do not begin their courtship play independently of the presence of the females and do not dispense with the presence of these (so-to-speak) 'invited' onlookers. Instead, the drakes decidedly perform courtship in front of the females and virtually force their courtship motor patterns upon them – something which mallard drakes never do. A mallard drake never swims towards a female, or even *after* her, in order to perform courtship motor patterns before her eyes; but the pintail drake does just this. This does not absolutely exclude formation of a small company of drakes and initial performance of courtship in the absence of a female, but as soon as a female appears on the scene, the drakes begin to crowd around her. Having reached the female, however, they 'have to' perform introductory beak-shaking a couple of times before the grunt-whistle or head-up-tail-up can emerge. When observing this procedure, one always has the impression that the pintail drakes actually 'want' to perform courtship on the spot after a long 'ceremonial' introduction, just like mallard drakes, but that the restlessness of the watching female forces them to repeatedly change the scene of courtship display.

I am not quite sure that under natural conditions the female pintails do not exhibit more interest for the drakes' courtship than was the case on my lake. This possibility is backed up by the fact that the mallard females bred much more successfully than the female pintails. Nevertheless, it should be emphasized that mallard drakes will not interrupt their social play, let alone move to a place nearer the female, if the females display lack of interest.

2. NON-EPIGAMIC MOTOR DISPLAY PATTERNS AND VOCALIZATIONS

The social contact call and the summoning call of the young ducklings, together with the corresponding body postures, are the same as in the mallard. Even before acquiring the ability to fly, at the time that the voice breaks, the drake loses the disyllabic social contact call. His voice changes to give a thin, peculiar compressed sound – a fine, nasal *gaaaay* – reminiscent of certain song-bird calls. This is produced in a drawn-out monosyllabic form, even when its significance corresponds to that of the disyllabic *raebraeb* of the mallard drake, e.g. when tame drakes are driven along. Under such conditions, the mallard drake angrily utters the fastest form of the *raebraeb* and the females of both species produce the disyllabic *quegegg, quegegg*. As in the mallard drake, a drawn-out monosyllabic social contact call combines the function of both summoning and alarm calls. The motor display patterns of motivation for take-off and moving-off in the pintail are completely comparable to those of the mallard, except that the voice is considerably deeper and coarser and extremely rich in rolling r-sounds.

3. THE EPIGAMIC MOTOR DISPLAY PATTERNS AND CALLS OF THE FEMALE

(a) Incitement

The incitement behaviour of the pintail female does not differ from that of the mallard, either in conditions of performance or in significance. However, although the motor patterns of the two species are definitely homologous (female hybrids of different parentage exhibit all conceivable transitional stages), the form of the movement and the call in the pintail differ considerably from those of *Anas*. When inciting, the pintail female markedly raises the anterior end of the body, so that she is more-or-less reared up when on land (Fig. 18), and the head is moved backwards in much closer contact with the body. The original movement of the beak towards the adversary, which is still clearly recognizable in the female mallard, is scarcely noticeable and the entire motor pattern is considerably farther removed from the primitive form (as found in Casarcinae) than in the mallard. The lowering of the bill around the head-articulation is much less marked than in the mallard. In the pintail vocalization, individual *quegg*-sounds can scarcely be distinguished. These sounds are uttered in much more rapid sequence than in *Anas* and (in accord with the vocal pitch of the pintail) they flow into a virtually continuous *arrrrrrrrrr*. However, the peculiar 'querulent', scolding rise and fall of the call can still be heard, just as in *Anas*.

Fig. 18. *Incitement behaviour of the female pintail. Note the raised forequarters. 'Burping' of the pintail drake. With the extreme type of performance illustrated, a whistle regularly follows*

(b) *The rejection display*

This is more intensive and more easily elicited in the pintail female than in the mallard female. Even when driving tame individuals along, a slight degree of roughness can elicit raising of the upper mandibles and ruffling of the head feathers in the females. The 'cackling' has a similar ring to that of *Anas* females, but it is coarser and deeper. During brooding pauses, female pintails will indulge in veritably 'hysterical' outbreaks of rejection display, even without the approach of a drake. This is often the first sign indicating to the keeper that there is an incubated clutch on hand. The drakes, which otherwise behave like *Anas* species with respect to 'raping' chases, appear to leave such brooding females completely undisturbed.

(c) *The decrescendo call*

This is heard more rarely than with the mallard, appearing most frequently in fading twilight when take-off motivation is greatest in intensity. The call consists of an extremely loud and deep disyllabic *quahrrquack*.

It is not quite clear whether this is derived from two slow or a large number of extremely rapid *quegg*-calls. The lowering of the amplitude and pitch in each syllable exactly corresponds to that heard with *Anas*.

(d) *The mating prelude*

This resembles that of the mallard, but it seems to me that – in contrast to the mallard – the pintail female does not act as the initiating partner towards the drake. However, this may be a result of reduction of the reproductive motivation of my female pintails under the conditions of captivity, which usually affects females more than males.

4. THE EPIGAMIC MOTOR DISPLAY PATTERNS AND VOCALIZATIONS OF THE DRAKE

(a) *Sham-preening*

Just as with the mallard drake, sham-preening can occur with or without display drinking. Since pintails (both *acuta* and *spinicauda*) exhibit sexual differences in the speculum, with the male exhibiting a much more colourful pattern, the function of the speculum as a take-off signal emphasized by Heinroth seems to have been superseded by an epigamic rôle in these species. In the pintail species, just as in the mallard, the female almost always flies in advance of the male, although she does not carry colourful markings on the wing like those of the male. It is certainly no chance phenomenon that sham-preening of the wing plays the greatest part in the very species in which sexual dimorphism of the wings is at its greatest, as in *Aix*, *Lampronessa*, *Chaulelasmus* and *Mareca*.

(b) *Display drinking*

This is in every respect identical in performance to that of the mallard.

(c) *Introductory body-shaking*

In the body posture and head-shaking which precede the actual courtship motor patterns, the pintail drakes give an impression of particular length and elegance. The drawn-in, greatly ruffled head provides a peculiar and attractive contrast to the stretched body and the almost horizontally oriented tail-spike (Fig. 19). Body-shaking tends to occur less frequently and less persistently than in the mallard drake, but this is balanced by the introduction of a specific motor pattern between this introductory display and the more highly differentiated courtship patterns.

(d) 'Burping'

While the head feathers take on the 'disc-coiffure' described for the mallard drake on p. 38, the head is pushed far upwards with the beak held horizontally or even inclined somewhat downwards. The motor pattern is not performed with abrupt rapidity like the down-up movement of the mallard drake, but slowly and steadily. At the same time, the

Fig. 19. *The introductory posture of the social play of the pintail drake (cf. Fig. 9)*

monosyllabic social contact call is uttered with a rising pitch of questioning quality. The next moment, the head moves downward again, whilst a second social contact call – this time with falling pitch – is uttered. The head and vocal trajectory can be equally represented with the symbol $g\,e\,e\,e\,e\,e\,{}^{eg}e\,e\,e\,e\,e$, whilst the term 'burping' provides a good – if scarcely poetic – representation. In contrast to the combined courtship motor patterns and whistles of the mallard drake, the 'burping' of the pintail drake is not bound by an 'all-or-none law'. The appearance varies according to intensity, exhibiting variation in both the range of the head movement and the scale of pitch covered. In addition, the accumulated response-specific energy is far from depleted by a single performance of burping to the extent seen with utterance of the grunt-whistle. Instead, especially at low intensity levels, it operates quite definitely as a self-stimulatory pattern like introductory body-shaking. At higher levels of response intensity, 'burping' is extended by a soft, whispering, flute-like whistle sounding like *pfeuh*. This occurs exactly at the culminating point of the head and vocal elevation, as is the case with all bony drum vocalizations of drakes of dabbling species, thus occurring at the time when the trachea is subjected to maximum tension. During the whistle, the utterance of the social contact call is not interrupted, and the entire tone-picture can be represented by:

pfeuh

$g\,e\,e\,e\,e\,e\,e\,e\,{}^{eg}\,e\,e\,e\,e\,e\,e\,e$

Without doubt, the increase in pitch of the *geeee* is also mechanically induced by the extension of the head and the consequent tensing of the trachea, since one can predict very exactly from both the head movement and the rise in pitch whether a whistle will occur and at what point, or whether the movement will decline again without reaching the threshold of the whistle-call (Fig. 20).

Fig. 20. '*Burping*' *of the pintail drake, less extreme than in Fig. 18. In such cases, there is no whistle – only the social contact call (cf. Figs. 24, 39, 46 and 50)*

The only motor pattern of the mallard drake which is possibly directly homologous with 'burping' is the peculiar rearing of the head accompanied by head-turning towards the female and utterance of a drawn-out *raeaeb*, described on p. 36 as the second component of the head-up-tail-up. In the gadwall drake there is a motor pattern incorporating extension of the head and soft utterance of the summoning call (almost voiceless in this species). This pattern is much more similar to that of the pintail drake, but at the same time it is definitely homologous with the pattern seen in *Anas* species. Apart from *Dafila spinicauda*, in which the pattern is performed in exactly the same way as in *D. acuta*, a definitely homologous form of burping is found in *Virago castanea*, *Nettion crecca* and *N. flavirostre*. The pattern is performed without a whistle but with a very similar social contact call by *Poecilonetta bahamensis* and *P. erythrorhyncha*, and the burping pattern of the latter represents a clear transition to that of the garganey group and – further removed – to that of the shovellers. But even *Aix* and *Lampronessa* exhibit corresponding head-movements, although the calls are entirely different. As regards its origin, I regard the burping pattern as a gestural exaggeration of head-raising accompanying utterance of the summoning call. This is supported firstly by the questionably intermediate form of head-raising which is incorporated in the head-up-tail-up of *Anas*, and secondly by the fact that an utterly unmistakable burping pattern is also coupled with the head-up-tail-up of the pintail drake (q.v.). Thirdly, the 'burping' pattern of the pintail, teal and garganey drakes functionally represents the summoning call, and can thus be performed *independently of courtship* without introductory body-shaking. This provides a complete analogy to the drawn-out *raeaeb* of the mallard drake, in that it occurs in the same characteristic stimulus situations. Thus, the burping pattern can be seen and heard when a drake has lost contact with his consort, when a female flies over him, when a female utters the decrescendo call some way off, and – above all – with the function of an alarm call, just like the *raeaeb* of the mallard drake.[16] The 'burping' patterns of *Aix* and *Lampronessa* are indeed also homologous to the *raeaeb*, but they have presumably evolved from the summoning call independently of the 'burping' pattern of the *Dafila-Virago*-teal group.

(e) *The grunt-whistle*

In the pintail, this pattern is exactly the same as that of the mallard. As in the latter, the beak skims the water surface and the whistle occurs at the point of greatest tension in the trachea. On the other hand, the grunting sound characteristic for the *Anas* species is lacking and the whistle itself is less sharp and has more of an *uu* sound (Fig. 21).

Fig. 21. *The grunt-whistle of the pintail drake (cf. Figs. 11b and 38)*

(f) *The head-up-tail-up*

This motor pattern differs somewhat in appearance in the pintail drake from the form in *Anas*. In particular, the elbows are held flat against the back and the rump feathers are not ruffled. For the remainder, the head, back and tail movements – including coupling with head-raising and beak-turning towards the female (Fig. 22) – are exactly the same as in the mallard drake. *Dafila acuta* completely lacks the subsequent bridling and nod-swimming. Among all the Anatinae, the closest similarity to the head-up-tail-up of the pintail is found in that of the Bahama duck. *Dafila spinicauda* lacks the head-up-tail-up.

(g) *The hind-head display*

This orienting response definitely plays a particular rôle as a courtship pattern in *Dafila acuta*, since its effect is of course magnified by special differentiation of the plumage, i.e. the black plush cushion on the back of the drake's head already mentioned on p. 38. This motor pattern differs fundamentally from that of the mallard drake – which is only partially homologous – in that it is not coupled with chin-raising. Chin-raising and the down-up (which possibly represents no more than a gestural exaggeration of the former) are lacking in *Dafila acuta*, as is the disyllabic contact call which accompanies these patterns in the mallard drake. In all biological situations in which the mallard drake utters the *raebraeb* call, the courting pintail drake 'employs' the burping pattern

and the $g\,e^{\,e^{\,e^{\,e^{\,eg}\,e^{\,e}}}}\,e\,e$ call (with or without the whistle) in exactly the same way as this call takes the place of the drawn-out *raeaeb* as a summoning and alarm call. Thus, *Dafila* exhibits only one response in place of two different responses found in *Anas*. Both from a comparative point of view and from the ontogenetic development, it seems to me that this situation is definitely a secondary effect (see p. 23 and p. 46).

Fig. 22. *Head-up-tail-up of the pintail drake* (right) *with subsequent head-turning towards the female* (cf. Figs. 12 and 13)

Thus, the pintail drake continuously exhibits courtship – even when quite alone with the female – through 'burping' rather than through chin-raising, and the orienting response of turning the extremely colourful back of the head towards the female, which is elicited in this situation, usually occurs in the initiating position for 'burping' or (more frequently) immediately after the latter pattern has expired. Orientation of the bill towards the female, as has been mentioned, occurs only in burping coupled with the head-up-tail-up. In the initial position with the head drawn in, which exactly corresponds to the posture introducing social courtship, the plumage of the head is uniformly and completely ruffled. It is then possible to see very clearly how the cushion on the back of the head also projects spatially (Fig. 23).

The pintail drake lacks any further epigamic motor patterns and calls, unless one is to include a peculiar threat posture which represents a ritualized form of the attack posture of the mallard drake. Immediately before two fighting mallard drakes launch their bills at each other's breast feathers, they swim towards one another with the bills lowered almost to the water surface. This posture is adopted as a threat posture by the pintail and the Bahama drake even when an actual attack with feather-grasping does not result. In contrast to the mallard drake, these drakes will also adopt this posture when walking or swimming rapidly towards a strange female with the intention of 'raping' her.

Fig. 23. *Hind-head display of the pintail drake, always without chin-raising. Note the differentiation of the rear head feathers, particularly operative in this motor pattern (cf. Figs. 14 and 42)*

(h) Fighting between drakes

Reciprocal frontal pushing between drakes which have grasped one another by the breast feathers has a very similar appearance to that of mallard drakes, but the pintail drakes exhibit a much greater aversion to rough, physical treatment of their plumage by an opponent. They are therefore more inclined than *Anas* drakes to release their grasp and to beat with the wing 'shoulder', and in contrast to the latter they may exhibit wing-beating without prior grasping of the opponent with the beak. The fighting behaviour of Bahama drakes is even more specialized in the same direction.

(i) Post-copulatory play

Dafila acuta does *not* possess a special motor pattern restricted to this situation. After completion of copulation, the drake swims around the female, while she begins to bathe, and exhibits repeated 'burping' (with or without the whistle).

VIII The Chilean pintail, *Dafila spinicauda*

I. GENERAL OBSERVATIONS

Despite all its similarities, this small pintail – which lacks the male nuptial plumage – is much more distinct from the endemic pintail than *Anas* species without a male display plumage differ from the mallard. This small duck is peculiarly temperamental, even impulsive, not only in performance of its individual motor patterns but also in its general behaviour. I was unable to observe any behavioural signs of close relationship to the Chilean teal (*Nettion flavirostre*), which is very similar in coloration.

2. NON-EPIGAMIC MOTOR DISPLAY PATTERNS AND VOCALIZATIONS

These correspond exactly to those of *Dafila acuta* except that the male *Dafila spinicauda* tends to omit the *geeeeegeeeee* in the summoning call and to utter the whistle alone. The common pintail drake only exhibits this at high levels of arousal.

3. THE EPIGAMIC MOTOR DISPLAY PATTERNS AND VOCALIZATIONS OF THE FEMALE

These also correspond to those of the pintail; in particular, the extremely frequent, continuously grating incitement call seems to me to have an identical ring in both species. On the other hand, the decrescendo call is polysyllabic and is far more similar to that of the mallard than the call of *acuta*. It sounds extremely similar to that of *Poecilonetta bahamensis*.

I am not able to give any information on the rejection display, since this species did not breed in my care.

4. THE EPIGAMIC MOTOR DISPLAY PATTERNS AND VOCALIZATIONS OF THE DRAKE

(a) The general form of courtship

The drakes exhibit courtship almost throughout the year, assembling in small groups which differ from those of the mallard and the European pintail in that the birds do not stay still for a moment. Instead, they exhibit continuously hurried and restless movements within the group. This same behaviour is also exhibited by the females, once again in contrast to the species previously discussed.

(b) Display drinking and sham-preening

I have only occasionally seen these two patterns. The described rapidity and restlessness of social play itself determines that neither display pattern can play a large rôle.

(c) Introductory body-shaking

For the same reason, this motor pattern is also extremely limited and it is only performed a few times in a brief period prior to appearance of the actual courtship motor patterns.

Fig. 24. *'Burping' in the Chilean pintail*, Dafila spinicauda. *Note the 'disc coiffure' of the head feathers (cf. Figs. 2, 15, 20, 34, 46 and 50)*

(d) The 'burping' pattern

In the rapid-moving mêlée, the drakes exhibit 'burping' at very short intervals. The higher the intensity of response, the more rapid is the sequence and the stronger is the suppression of the social contact call *geeeeegeeeee* in favour of the whistle. Whenever my three drakes were strongly motivated, anybody familiar only with the courtship of the mallard would have estimated that there was a tenfold assembly of drakes, if trying to judge the number according to the frequency of the whistles (Fig. 24).

(e) *The grunt-whistle*

This pattern is also performed in rapid succession, occurring in an irregular sequence with the more frequent 'burping' patterns. Although both individual motor patterns are absolutely similar to those of *Dafila acuta*, the overall impression of social play in *Dafila spinicauda* is completely different.

(f) *The head-up-tail-up*

This pattern is completely lacking,[17] as is the hind-head display which is coupled to it in *Dafila acuta*. This important difference is connected with the special differentiation of the head plumage in *Dafila spinicauda*. The feathers on the temples and the crown of the head are greatly extended, and in the 'disc-coiffure' described on p. 38, which is coupled with 'burping', they form a virtual crest. This, together with the 'snub-nose' and its underlining bill markings, lends a particular and (despite its simplicity) attractive appearance to the little drake.

(g) *Post-copulatory play and fighting pattern*

Both post-copulatory play and the mode of fighting correspond exactly to the condition in *Dafila acuta*, except that *D. spinicauda* is even more inclined to beating with the shoulder of the wing. But this latter is quite generally a peculiarity of *small* ducks. This may be correlated with the sensitivity of the plumage. Smaller birds in general tend to fight less 'at close quarters' than larger species which are sufficiently closely related to permit a worthwhile comparison.

IX   The Bahama duck, *Poecilonetta bahamensis* L.

1. GENERAL OBSERVATIONS

This duck provides a contrast to the species just discussed, to the extent that the drake is not equipped with the female type of plumage; instead, the female is equipped with a 'Prachtkleid' (nuptial plumage) and exhibits both the colourful rust-red plumage coloration and the white cheeks with blue-red bill found in the drake. As a result of its particular ceremonial quality and site-fidelity, the social courtship of the drakes similarly presents a contrast to the mercurial quality of *D. spinicauda*, although this duck otherwise exhibits many similarities to the Bahama (presumably mainly because it is in many ways a small pintail). Finally, the Bahama duck seems to be the more specialized of the two in some respects, for example in the development of the head-up-tail-up as the only (and 'exaggerated') courtship motor pattern and in that the drake lacks the whistle completely (probably as a secondary feature).

2. THE NON-EPIGAMIC MOTOR DISPLAY PATTERNS AND VOCALIZATIONS

These are less distinct between the two sexes than in the two *Dafila* species, to the extent that the drake 'still' has a soft *g'e g'e* which can only be heard in the immediate neighbourhood. Although the grace-note is scarcely more than a trace of a second syllable, this call doubtless corresponds to the disyllabic social contact call of the ducklings and of both mallard sexes. In general, the motor display patterns and vocalizations of the female are the same as in the females of the *Dafila* species. It is, however, interesting that the preponderance of *rrrr*-sounds in the female voice has been even further developed. Just as in the *Dafila* species, where the succeeding *quegg* calls of the inciting female have developed to give a continuous, rolling *arrrrr*, the same process has proceeded in the Bahama duck to affect the monosyllabic departure call as well. Whereas the latter still consists of separate *quegg* sounds, in *Poecilonetta bahamensis* it has also come to represent a soft, but quite continuous, rolling sound.

3. THE EPIGAMIC MOTOR DISPLAY PATTERNS AND VOCALIZATIONS OF THE FEMALE

(a) Incitement behaviour

The voice of the female Bahama is higher than that of the two pintail species, but (as already stated) it tends still more towards rolling *rr*-sounds. Incitement itself is quite similar to that of pintails, but the call is possibly even more continuously rolled.

(b) The rejection display

This display is just the same as in pintails and is very easily elicited, as in *Dafila acuta*. I am well acquainted with it although *Poecilonetta bahamensis* has never yet bred in my care and the actual physiological prerequisites for the response were thus never obtained. The upward rotation of the upper mandible is extremely conspicuous because of the latter's bright coloration, as is the ruffling of the back feathers as a result of the elongated and pointed 'drake-like' form.

(c) The decrescendo call

The decrescendo call corresponds roughly to that of *Dafila spinicauda* in the number of syllables, but it is very coarse (in correspondence with the characteristic voice of this species) and still more peculiar and con-spicuous than that of *Dafila acuta* (p. 46–47).

(d) Gasping

The female *Poecilonetta bahamensis* exhibits great interest in the social courtship of the drakes. The display call of 'gasping' (p. 41), which is only exceptionally performed by female mallard, and is therefore only hesitantly listed in the normal response inventory, represents one of the regular courtship calls of the female Bahama duck. It is typically uttered at the moment when the drakes perform their almost voiceless courtship motor pattern. It has a sharper, more vocal ring than in the mallard and domestic duck, but its rhythm is almost identical – a trisyllabic, sharp gasping *cheh' chehcheh*. This 'participation' of the females in the drakes' social play is strongly reminiscent of the garganeys. This might be re-garded as a chance effect if it were not for the fact that the African red-billed duck (the female of which I have unfortunately not investigated) exhibits such a clear-cut link between Bahama ducks and true garganeys. In view of this fact, the gasping of the Bahama duck gains a particular taxonomic significance.

(e) Nod-swimming

This is completely lacking.

(f) The mating prelude

This corresponds exactly to that of the ducks so far discussed.

4. THE EPIGAMIC MOTOR DISPLAY PATTERNS AND VOCALIZATIONS OF THE DRAKE

(a) Sham-preening and display drinking

Both of these patterns are present, but little differentiated. It would be difficult to convince a sceptic that the two motor patterns are not in-cidentally performed, autochthonous products of the relevant instincts.

(b) Introductory body-shaking

Just as in the mallard drake, the Bahama drake requires a relatively long period of self-stimulation through introductory body-shaking in order to whip itself up to the performance of its only highly differentiated courtship motor pattern. Body-shaking is only performed after cere-monial close aggregation and immobilization of the drakes. If the courted female swims away from the drakes, so that they are forced to change the site of their 'social play', they are compelled to go through the rigmarole of beginning to body-shake afresh before they can perform their dainty head-up-tail-up. This necessary rigmarole provides a sharp contrast to the pintail drakes, particularly *Dafila spinicauda*. Introductory body-shaking often pulls the drake high up out of the water, just as in the mallard drake. With such vigorous body-shaking, the initiated observer of other Anatinae quite automatically expects performance of the grunt-whistle. which of course has an external appearance quite close to that of body-shaking at this intensity level. The observer tends to think that the small drake *must* perform the grunt-whistle in the next instant. Instead, however, this highly intensive form of body-shaking is always followed by the head-up-tail-up. 'Burping' is only possible as a sequel to less intensive introductory body-shaking.

(c) 'Burping'

The form of this pattern is identical to that of *Dafila* species. The call is still finer and even more like a song-bird vocalization than in the latter, and it is perhaps better represented as *hiiihiii* rather than *geeeegeeee*. The whistle is lacking, even at high intensities. As with the pintail drake – perhaps even more marked – the 'burping' pattern of the Bahama drake is used for individual courtship of a specific female, often alternating with hind-head display.

(d) The head-up-tail-up[18]

Following the described high intensity body-shaking, the drake abruptly swings up the tail and extends it so far forward over the retracted head (which is pressed against the shoulders) that a virtually horizontal position is reached. The elbows, back feathers and rump plumage are kept tightly flattened, but the former must be displaced some way laterally in order to make way for the tail. Both wings are always

Fig. 25. *The head-up-tail-up of the Bahama drake,* Poecilonetta bahamensis L. *The only courtship motor pattern of the species – but greatly differentiated. The extreme posture is maintained for several seconds by paddling. The light-coloured under tail-coverts are very conspicuous*

swung to the same side so that the tail is never brought between the two (Fig 25). The light, rust-coloured under tail-coverts produce a very conspicuous impression in this movement; they are quite markedly ruffled. At the peak of the motor pattern, the drake *holds the position* for about ¾ second by paddling backwards and holding the tail bent forwards. After settling back into the normal position, 'burping' (usually followed by very exact turning of the bill towards the female) is performed in a similar manner to *Dafila acuta*. In the course of this, exaggerated head-up-tail-up, the Bahama drake (in contrast to mallard, pintail and Chestnut teal drakes) *does not utter a whistle*. Instead, he utters a vocal, very soft *ee-heeb, ee-heeb, ee-heeb*. This has a rhythm very reminiscent of that of 'gasping' in the mallard drake and the female *Poecilonetta bahamensis*.

Fig. 26. *Hind-head display of the Bahama drake (cf. Figs. 14 and 23)*

(e) The hind-head display

This display is quite the same as in *Dafila acuta* (p. 52 et seq.). When seen from behind, the white cheeks are particularly evident. The cheeks are not so exposed in swimming with the head drawn in when there has been no preceding courtship, and this leads me to believe that this area of the head plumage is ruffled more than the rest (Fig. 26).

(f) Fighting between the drakes

The fighting behaviour of the drakes is initiated with the flattened posture, with the head drawn in and ruffled, as is characteristic of *Dafila acuta*. This motor display pattern, derived from an intention movement towards grasping of the opponent, is far removed from its phylogenetic origin to the extent that in the Bahama drake there is no actual subsequent grasping of the opponent with the bill. Instead, the bill is merely opened wide in threat, thus displaying the equally conspicuous red-blue coloration of the gape. The drake dashes past his opponent and displays this posture whilst swimming rapidly. Both partners dash past one another, each dealing out a 'broadside' of wing-shoulder beats at full pelt, producing a sound like the rattle of miniature machine-guns. This form of fighting behaviour is exactly comparable to that of *Lampronessa*. In *Aix*, interestingly enough, this behaviour has been toned down to a courtship ceremony, which is no longer utilized for the conquest – or even the intimidation – of an opponent. In *Poecilonetta bahamensis*, however, it is entirely functional mechanically, and the small drakes, dashing around like torpedo boats, often succeed in chasing off even much larger opponents.

(g) Post-copulatory play

I have so far observed only two matings in *Poecilonetta bahamensis*. In both cases, post-copulatory play resembled that of *Dafila acuta*, except that 'burping' was possibly less intensive than in the latter.

X   The African red-billed duck, *Poecilonetta erythrorhyncha* Viellot

I. GENERAL OBSERVATIONS

I have unfortunately only been able to observe one drake of this species, but it was an individual which I kept for many years in excellent physical condition. The red-billed duck is by no means as closely related to the Bahama duck as one is inclined to think after external examination of the plumage. The markings of the white cheeks with their characteristic graduated shading towards the lower side of the head, together with the dark head-cap, are reminiscent of *Querquedula versicolor*. As I was able to establish with Heinroth's magnificent collection, the bony drum represents an exact intermediate between that of *Poecilonetta bahamensis* and that of the true garganeys.[19]

2. THE NON-EPIGAMIC MOTOR DISPLAY PATTERNS AND VOCALIZATIONS

Apart from the courtship call, the drake appears to be relatively silent. There is indeed a social contact call in the drake, but this is so soft that it can scarcely be heard in the open with an individual which is not very tame. I cannot say whether it is mono- or disyllabic. As with the pintail group, 'burping' acts as a summoning call.

3. THE EPIGAMIC MOTOR DISPLAY PATTERNS AND VOCALIZATIONS OF THE DRAKE

(a) *Display drinking and sham-preening*

I have unfortunately been unable to observe either of these patterns. Undoubtedly, neither is particularly conspicuous, like the specialized patterns of the garganeys for example.

(b) *Introductory body-shaking*

Introductory body-shaking is clearly marked, but it is not as ritualized as in *Poecilonetta bahamensis*. It is usually immediately followed by 'burping'.

(c) *The 'burping' pattern*

'Burping' is the only motor pattern of 'social play' performed by my drake. Since he exhibits intensive courtship in the company of the Bahama drakes, however, I do not believe that this is an effect of behavioural loss in captivity. The motor pattern is quite the same as in *Dafila* and *Poecilonetta bahamensis*, and the call which is uttered with the movement is also very similar to that of these species. At the same time, however, a peculiar separation of the individual vibrations is extremely reminiscent of the wood-rattle call of the garganey drake. In contrast to mallard and Bahama duck, and once again in common with the garganey, the call is not uttered with the entire up-and-down movement of the head but only with one component of the movement. Whereas the garganey drake 'brings down the call from the top', the red-billed drake pushes up his head with a grating call and brings it down again in silence. As with both the Bahama drake and the garganey drake, the red-billed drake lacks the whistle.

XI The garganey teal, *Querquedula querquedula*

1. GENERAL OBSERVATIONS

Without a trace of doubt, the garganey differs far more from the other ducks discussed than these do from one another. In the other hand, *Querquedula versicolor*, whose behaviour I have unfortunately not yet observed, is evidently a garganey as regards the bony drum and a number of other characters, and yet exhibits distinct relationships with the African red-billed duck and the Bahama duck in its head markings, bill coloration and other characters. This links *Q. querquedula* to these species (and thus to the mallard group). Yet, in addition, this garganey exhibits an equally distinct phylogenetic relationship to the shoveller group through *Q. cyanoptera* and *Spatula platalea*. As we shall see, this is evident to some extent in the response repertoire of *Querquedula querquedula*.

2. THE NON-EPIGAMIC MOTOR DISPLAY PATTERNS AND VOCALIZATIONS

The drake exhibits a short, monosyllabic *gegg* . . . . *gegg* . . . . *gegg* as a social contact call. This is uttered in exactly the same behavioural situations as the *raebraeb* of the mallard, that is particularly when angered – for example when two drakes are separated by cage-wire and are unable to grasp one another by the feathers. The summoning and social contact call of the female are far more similar to those of the female mallard than the calls of the species previously discussed, which have an aberrant rasping quality. The female vocalizes very rarely. The departure and take-off motivational states are advertised just as in the female mallard, but the tendency towards vertical 'pumping' of the head in any situation of pronounced general arousal is greater. In this, *Querquedula* is very reminiscent of the shovellers.

3. THE EPIGAMIC MOTOR DISPLAY PATTERNS AND VOCALIZATIONS OF THE FEMALE

(a) *Incitement behaviour*

Incitement by the female differs both from that of members of the mallard and pintail group and from that of the chestnut-breasted and common teal in that it lacks the characteristic series of individual notes with rising pitch giving the impression of anger. Instead, each incitement movement is accompanied by monosyllabic, truncated *gaeeg*-call. In addition, the incitement call – in fact every vocalization – is coupled with a *pumping movement,* as if the female has the intention of taking off. *In both points, the garganey resembles the shoveller.* However, the female does represent an intermediate between the latter species and the other female dabbling ducks to the extent that she performs, between the pumping movements, a typical incitement movement over the shoulder, which is even combined with a distinct extension of the head towards the 'adversary'. The shoveller 'no longer' does this.

(b) *The decrescendo call*

This call is very rare; for some time, I believed it to be lacking in this species. It is disyllabic, or at most trisyllabic, and the final syllables have a swallowed sound. The rise and fall takes place so rapidly that a peculiar roaring emphasis is produced, and this is also reminiscent of the shoveller.

(c) The backward stretch

Remarkably, the female garganey exhibits the most striking courtship motor pattern of the drake, in which the head is stretched backwards onto the back with the crown downwards, and is then brought back to the normal position through a large arc. The female accompanies this movement with a *quaeh-gegg* vocalization emphasized on the first syllable. This call is uttered by the female when she participates with particular intensity in the social play of the drakes, i.e. when motivated in a manner roughly comparable to the Bahama female uttering the *chaeh-chaeh-chaeh*. Like nod-swimming of female mallard and chestnut-breasted teal, this motor display pattern is evidently an 'aretic' one, i.e. a character taken over from the male sex.

(d) The mating prelude

I have never seen the mating prelude, but judging from the generally great tendency of the female garganey to exhibit the pumping movement the prelude probably corresponds to that of the species so far described.

Fig. 27. *The initiating posture for 'social play' in the garganey teal,* Querque-dula querquedula L. *Note the protrusion of the tensed trachea in the neck*

(e) Post-copulatory play

I have never seen post-copulatory play. Reliable observations on this behaviour would be greatly appreciated!

4. THE EPIGAMIC MOTOR DISPLAY PATTERNS AND VOCALIZATIONS OF THE DRAKE

(a) Introductory body-shaking, display drinking and sham-preening

These three patterns play a remarkable rôle in the garganey. Display drinking is found not only as an independent introduction to social courtship, but also as a rigidly incorporated component of specific courtship patterns. Conversely, sham-preening is a major component of the introduction to courtship and occurs repeatedly in some courtship sequences almost as frequently as introductory body-shaking. In contrast to the majority of the other dabbling duck species, garganey drakes perform sham-preening on the *outside* of the wing, which renders the light blue wing coverts very conspicuous (Fig. 28; see also p. 31, 86).

Fig. 28. *Sham-preening in the garganey drake. Note that the outside of the wing is preened, thus conspicuously displaying the light blue wing coverts (cf. Figs. 8 and 9)*

The drakes swim around in a mêlée even during the introduction to courtship (Fig. 27), and the continuous performance of body-shaking and preening gives the impression of feverish 'nervousness'.

(b) Wing-flapping

Among all of the duck species I have observed, the garganey is the only one in which Heinroth's 'Sichflügeln' (wing-flapping) has developed to give a courtship motor pattern. During the restless swimming mêlée described above, increasing arousal in the body-shaking, preening drakes leads with mounting frequency to individual drakes rearing up in the water and flapping briefly and exaggeratedly with the wings. This wing-flapping has doubtless developed as 'displacement preening behaviour' (to use Tinbergen's terminology), to provide a releasing ceremony derived from the original instinctive motor pattern in a manner analogous to sham-preening and introductory body-shaking. Even before performance of the two courtship motor patterns to be described next, the drake's throat exhibits protrusion of the trachea. (The neck is drawn in as in a mallard drake performing introduction to social courtship.) The tracheal protrusion resembles that in *Dafila*, though this is seen only at the actual instant of utterance of the courtship call (Fig. 27).

(c) The 'burping' pattern

All of the motor patterns so far described belong to the category of 'introduction' rather than to the actual courtship, to the extent that they do not abreact the specific arousal state but evidently serve for self-stimulation, as has been explained with the introductory body-shaking of the mallard drake in contrast to the 'actual' courtship motor patterns. The first 'consummatory' courtship pattern which is observed in the social courtship of the garganey consists of the following: One drake, keeping the beak virtually horizontal, swings the head upwards and backwards and then lowers it again with equal speed and abruptness. The observer acquainted with the *Anas* species and the chestnut-breasted teal is forcibly reminded of the first phase of nod-swimming following 'bridling' (Fig. 29). Nevertheless, the motor pattern of the garganey drake would appear to be unrelated to the latter. In contrast to 'burping' in the African red-billed drake (p. 61), lifting of the head occurs in silence. Instead, the rapid retraction of the head to the normal position is accompanied by a short *rerrrp*, whose major characteristic is the extreme difficulty of localization. One may hear a drake which appears to be several yards away and yet the next instant see that he is close by. The quality of the call is deceptively reminiscent of that of the 'Ratsche' (a South German colloquial term for a wooden rattle used in the place of bells during Easter week to produce a loud noise by jerking a wooden splint over the teeth of a hard wooden cog). Thus it is that the garganey is referred to by the inhabitants around the Neusielder See exclusively, and very aptly, as the 'Ratsche-duck'. When one is aware of the motor pattern and the call of the red-billed duck, in which 'burping' is already slightly backwards in direction, there is no room for doubt that the 'burping' pattern of the garganey is homologous to that of *Dafila* and *Poecilonetta*. By contrast, there is some doubt about the origin of the motor pattern to be described next.

Fig. 29. *'Burping' of the garganey drake. Note the tracheal bulge in the drake's neck and compare with Figs. 20, 24, 34, 39, 46 and 50*

(*d*) *The backward head-stretch*

In this conspicuous motor pattern, the head is stretched far back onto the dorsal feathers, so that the forehead comes to lie on the tail-root (*Bucephala clangula*), given by P. Bernhardt (*Joural für Ornithologie* 1940, p. 490).

The head is then brought back into the normal position in a vigorous arc, accompanied by a loud 'Ratsche-call'. In the course of this, the tensed trachea springs forward like the string of a bow to the front of the neck, producing a pronounced skin-fold. This pattern is absolutely coupled with subsequent display drinking. At higher intensities of courtship, this motor pattern is performed with greater frequency than the 'burping' pattern just described, but at lower intensities it is less frequent. Thus, there is a relationship between the two patterns which is not evident between the completely 'optionally' performed motor patterns of the mallard drake. Although there are no revealing intermediates between 'burping' and the backward head-stretch of the garganey drake, I am nevertheless inclined to believe that the latter pattern is derived from 'exaggerated burping'. This assumption is supported by the similarity of the introduction and the identical coupling to display drinking found in both. I was not able to discover anything about the distribution of the pattern, particularly as regards the American garganeys *Querquedula discors* and *Q. cyanoptera*.

Fig. 30. *The backward head-stretch of the garganey drake*

The similarity to *Bucephala* is quite definitely a convergent effect based on the common necessity to attain a particularly pronounced tension of the bony drum.

(e) *The lateral head display*

The garganey also exhibits a specific orienting response, by means of which the markings of the sides of the head are presented in an optimal posture to the gaze of the female. However, in contrast to all other dabbling drakes known to exhibit such movements of the head, it is neither the bill nor the back of the head, but the *side of the head* which is presented. As with other drakes, this spatial relationship of the head is maintained for several seconds through a marked 'nystagmic' follow-up orienting movement. With a group of rapidly swimming drakes performing courtship in a group around a female, several males may exhibit abrupt nystagmic movements of the head. Of course, in this particular movement, the head feathers are so arranged that the white eye-brow stripe is maximally displayed.

(*f*) *Fighting between drakes*

The fighting behaviour of the drakes is not particularly distinctive. It has already been mentioned that the drakes utter monosyllabic bony drum calls like *gegg gegg gegg* when angered.

(*g*) *Post-copulatory play*

I have unfortunately never seen post-copulatory play in this species.

XII The shoveller, *Spatula clypeata* L.

I. GENERAL OBSERVATIONS

Quite certainly, the shoveller represents an extreme type allied to the garganeys. This is obvious not only in the behaviour but also in certain coloration characters common to the two groups. The reader is reminded of the characteristic, and almost identical, marking patterns of *Querquedula cyanoptera* and *Spatula platalea*, both natives of South America. According to all previous information, shoveller drakes do not appear to exhibit social courtship like the drakes of other dabbling species. However, scarcely a zoological garden or private enthusiast has kept an adequate number of healthy shoveller drakes together at the same time, and in view of the extremely differentiated 'Prachtkleid' (nuptial plumage) of the species I believe that the shoveller in fact exhibits a form of courtship which has so far escaped observation.

2. THE NON-EPIGAMIC MOTOR DISPLAY PATTERNS AND VOCALIZATIONS

In contrast to all of the other Anatids which I have studied, shoveller ducklings have two distinctly different forms of the distress-call ('lost piping'). The somewhat hasty *toot toot toot . . .* etc. uttered at low intensities abruptly changes to a drawn-out *tooht tooht tooht . . .* etc. at higher levels. The social contact call and summoning call of the female are generally similar to those of the mallard, but the drake exhibits only one call – a hoarse *chutt* – which is uttered in slow or rapid succession and has to fill the rôle of both the long *raeaeb* and the disyllabic *raeb-raeb* of the mallard drake. The shoveller exhibits one trait which is peculiar among all of the dabbling species (indeed, all of the Anatidae) which I have studied, in that *display drinking* is lacking. In its place, the shoveller performs the displacement activity of *gabbling*, which is quite as prominent as the corresponding special differentiation of the bill and which is functionally completely analogous to display drinking in all other Anatids. During this *display gabbling*, the drake very rapidly utters the *chutt . . . chutt . . . . . chutt . . .* sequence.

Any kind of arousal induces shovellers to perform the pumping head-movements which other Anatidae perform only during the mating prelude. Even ducklings and sub-adults exhibit this behaviour, and small ducklings exhibit a peculiar response which Heinroth has already described: They swim around in tight circles, closely following one another and gabbling whilst sifting the water. Each swims in the wake of the other, gabbling into the water and evidently catching small organisms churned up in front.

3. THE EPIGAMIC MOTOR DISPLAY PATTERNS AND VOCALIZATIONS OF THE FEMALE

(a) Incitement behaviour

Incitement by the female, as far as the associated movement of the head and neck is concerned, corresponds in detail to the 'pumping' of all true dabbling ducks exhibited as a prelude to mating. In its rhythm and timbre, and also in significance, the vocalization clearly represents an incitement call. However, the threatening movement of the head towards the adversary (which is still present in the garganey and alternates with pumping) is lacking in this species.

(b) The decrescendo call

This call is even more differentiated in the direction suggested in the garganey. The monosyllabic, abruptly rising and falling screech has an almost frightening quality. It sounds like the death cry of a duck which has been trampled or grasped by a predator.

(c) The mating prelude

This is worthy of special discussion here, since the motor pattern of 'pumping', which in other species exclusively serves the function of a mating prelude, has expanded so far in the shoveller that it has become a general arousal display with a wide range of performance. As has already been mentioned, this pattern has completely suppressed the original lateral movement of the head in incitement.

4. THE EPIGAMIC MOTOR DISPLAY PATTERNS AND VOCALIZATIONS OF THE DRAKE

As mentioned previously, I do not believe that social courtship of the drakes is completely lacking in *Spatula*. The bright colour-markings of the drake indicate, in my opinion, the presence of such courtship much more clearly than the lack of relevant observations indicates the contrary. In informed circles, the difficulty of keeping shovellers is usually overestimated. A female which had been reared from the egg faultlessly raised offspring in my care and – after surviving the dangers of the 1939–40 winter and the transport to Königsberg – subsequently remained in the best of health.

(a) *The hind-head display*

The only other courtship motor pattern of the shoveller drake which I have so far observed (i.e. additional to the already described 'display gabbling' performed in front of the female at every opportunity) is a conspicuous hind-head display. This involves a plumage posture exactly comparable to the 'coiffure' exhibited by the mallard drake, along with the corresponding motor pattern.

(b) *Fighting between drakes*

Since my old shoveller drake disappeared before the adult coloration of his son had developed, I do not know anything about the ritualized fighting behaviour of the drakes. In occasional moments of friction, the females typically grasp one another by the breast feathers just as in the mallard, but I have never observed wing-beating.

XIII The chestnut-breasted teal, *Virago castanea* Eyton

I. GENERAL OBSERVATIONS

This species introduces us to a new group of ducks, which is just as obviously related to the mallard as the series of Anatines so far discussed, but differs in a completely different evolutionary direction. The reader is reminded of my initial comments about the methodology of reconstructing phylogenetic relationships. Whereas the duck species so far discussed can be approximately arranged on a line leading from the mallard to the shoveller, the species now to be described form a small group in which such an arrangement is far from evident. The species belonging to this group which I have so far studied are: the chestnut-breasted teal, the grey teal (*Virago gibberifrons*), the European teal (*Nettion crecca*) and the South American teal (*Nettion flavirostre*). All of these ducks could be classified under the term 'teal' to the extent that, in addition to a quite characteristic black-and-green coloration of the speculum, they all exhibit a courtship whistle with a peculiar grace-note. This is a unique characteristic of these ducks and gave rise to their German name 'Krickente'.

The chestnut-breasted teal exhibits a marked relationship to the genus *Anas* in several features, as does *Virago gibberifrons*. The latter exhibits the same relationship to the chestnut-breasted teal as do *Anas* species without a 'Prachtkleid' to the mallard, which they resemble in all other respects.

2. THE NON-EPIGAMIC MOTOR DISPLAY PATTERNS AND VOCALIZATIONS

In the female, these patterns are quite similar to those of the mallard, but the predominance of continuous grating sounds is somewhat reminiscent of the pintail. Apart from the courtship whistle, the drake is almost silent; but he nevertheless uses his soft, hoarse 'voice' frequently. I am not able to state whether the drake has a monosyllabic summoning call and a disyllabic social contact call. On the other hand, I am quite sure that the 'Krick'-whistle (see later) – which is present both in *Virago* and in the two *Nettion* species I have studied – simultaneously represents the summoning call and alarm call of the drake,

just as with the *raeaeb* of the mallard drake and the $g\,e^{\,e\,e\,eg}\,e\,e_{\,e}$ of the pintail drake. I have unfortunately not yet been able to observe the ducklings.

3. THE EPIGAMIC MOTOR DISPLAY PATTERNS AND VOCALIZATIONS OF THE FEMALE

(a) Incitement behaviour

Because of the continuously rising grating note, the incitement call sounds somewhat like that of female pintail or Bahama duck, but the particularly pronounced, angrily rising emphasis is quite distinctive. The call sounds almost like the squealing of a small pig.

(b) The decrescendo call

This call consists of a large number of syllables uttered in rapid sequence, with the stress on the first syllable.

(c) Nod-swimming

The female chestnut-breasted teal is the only dabbling duck I have studied which shares with the *Anas* species (in the narrowest sense) a pronounced nod-swimming pattern. In comparison with that of the female mallard, the motor pattern is definitely more highly differentiated. The nodding movements are more conspicuous (i.e. far more 'gesturally exaggerated') and they are preceded by an incipient 'bridling' movement

(p. 41k), as found only in the drakes of *Anas* species. Finally, the female chestnut-breasted teal exhibits clear-cut turning of the *back of her head* towards the drake at the end of nod-swimming – something which female mallard never do. This gives the impression that the further differentiation of bridling and nod-swimming, which represents the most conspicuous character of the courtship of chestnut-breasted teal drakes, had somehow 'spread' to the female.

(*d*) The mating prelude

This is quite like that of the mallard.

4. THE EPIGAMIC MOTOR DISPLAY PATTERNS AND VOCALIZATIONS OF THE DRAKE

(*a*) The general form of courtship

In its general form, courtship would seem to be closest to that of *Anas* species among all the dabbling ducks. The assembly of the drakes, the relatively limited attention paid to any females present (which are only involved through head-turning – p. 36), the 'ceremonial' resting state prior to performance of the courtship motor patterns, and introductory body-shaking, are all quite reminiscent of *Anas*. In addition, *Virago* is the *only* species among all the Anatinae (see table) which exhibits all the courtship motor patterns described for the mallard, together with one motor pattern which the mallard lacks.

(*b*) The 'Krick'-whistle

Following introductory body-shaking, the drake does not raise his head very high – at least not to such an extreme as in 'burping'. From the rest position the drake then performs a slight, nodding and sneezing movement in which the lower mandible is abruptly swung downwards and a whistle is uttered. The whistle has a preceding grace-note and can be represented as *p-tseeh*. In combination with the head-movement, this call gives the marked impression of a sneeze. In the 'burping' pattern of the pintail, one has the impression that the rearing of the head is itself the mechanical cause eliciting the whistle. At higher intensities of the movement, and thus with correspondingly higher raising of the head, the whistle occurs in the middle of the movement, always when a quite specific degree of stretching is reached – as if a mechanical releasing mechanism in the syrinx were set off by the tensing of the trachea, rather like a trigger. With the 'Krick'-whistle of *Virago castanea*, on the other hand, the 'letting off' of the whistle is visibly determined by a muscular operation independent of head-raising and largely based on the musculature of the lower mandible. The whistle is uttered with the head held still and the neck stretched upwards.

The distribution of the 'Krick'-whistle among the species of the Family appears to be exactly the same as that of the peculiar speculum on the secondaries, which is sharply bisected in black and golden green. I have heard the whistle of *Virago* and *Nettion*. The similarity which this call in *Virago* exhibits to the burping pattern, and particularly the fact that it unites the functions of summoning and warning – just like true 'burping' in *Dafila* and *Poecilonetta* drakes and the drawn-out *raeaeaeb* of the mallard – leads me to believe that it represents a further stage of differentiation of 'burping'. In the same way, 'burping' itself is probably derived from the ordinary alert head-raising which accompanies all summoning and warning behaviour in every Anatid. This is further supported by the fact that the 'Krick'-whistle as a summoning or warning component has become more independent than any other call of the original function of all drake whistles as elements of social courtship. *Virago* and *Nettion* drakes utter the 'Krick'-whistle in the absence of courtship motivation at every opportunity, with much the same frequency and variety of meaning as the *raeaeb* uttered by the mallard drake.

(c) 'Burping'

This is extremely similar to the pintail pattern, and it occurs as an independent motor pattern just as in the latter, rather than as in the mallard drake, where it is coupled with the head-up-tail-up (p. 36). No social contact call is to be heard, but I assume from the movement of the bill that the muscular co-ordination of the breathing apparatus is still similar to that involved in the *geeeegeeee* of *Dafila* drakes. However, no more than an inaudible whisper is produced in the place of the social contact call. The whistle, which is *always* uttered with the 'burping' pattern of *Virago* and *Nettion* drakes, and not just at higher response intensities as in *Dafila*, is short and monosyllabic. It has a sharp *ee* ring rather than the fluting *oo* of *Dafila*.

(d) The grunt-whistle

The grunt-whistle is in every detail the same as in *Anas*, except that the grunting sound is lacking.

(e) The head-up-tail-up

This pattern differs from that of *Anas* in so far as obligate coupling to the subsequent motor patterns of 'burping', 'bridling' and nod-swimming *is absent*. The motor outline of the first phase, i.e. the actual performance of the head-up-tail-up, is fairly close to that of *Anas* except that the elbows are raised somewhat less and the rump is reared a little more than in the latter genus.

(f) Bridling

Bridling occurs as a completely isolated courtship motor pattern. The movement is obviously more pronounced and extensive than in mallard drakes; the head is pulled back almost to the root of the tail, but without being lifted or pulled away from the upper contour of the back. This gives the impression that the back of the drake's head is gliding along a rail on the dorsal feathers (Fig. 31). In performing this pattern, the drake utters a monosyllabic, shrill whistle like the mallard.

The distribution of isolated performance of the bridling whistle is exactly the same as that of the 'Krick'-whistle and the black-green speculum. The possible origin of this behaviour from an introductory intention movement of nod-swimming has already been discussed with the mallard.

Fig. 31. *Bridling in the chestnut-breasted teal drake*, Virago castanea Eyton (*cf. Figs. 17 and 40*)

(g) Chin-raising

With extreme frequency, several drakes will follow performance of the grunt-whistle, head-up-tail-up or bridling by one drake in the middle of social courtship by raising their heads markedly, with the chin raised. They maintain the peak of the motor pattern for several seconds, which involves paddling with the feet in order to keep the position (Fig. 32), just as with the Bahama drake in performance of the exaggerated, longitudinally extended head-up-tail-up. The motor pattern is strikingly reminiscent of chin-raising in the mallard drake, as it is performed following the down-up (p. 39 et seq.), and both the occurrence of the pattern and the involvement of several drakes in simultaneous performance present a pronounced resemblance to the mallard. This chin-raising pattern is doubtless derived from the down-up, and thus indirectly from a display drinking movement. The loss of the dipping of the bill to the water surface (present in the original pattern) presents just as little argument against this homology as the exaggeration of the subsequent raised posture of the chin. With the gadwall, we shall encounter a quite definite homologue of the mallard's down-up-pattern in which the introductory downward movement of the bill has similarly been lost.

Fig. 32. *Chin-raising of the chestnut-breasted teal drake, exhibiting pronounced gestural exaggeration. The posture is maintained for several seconds by paddling (cf. Figs. 3, 16, 42, 44, 45, and 47)*

(h) Nod-swimming

As with the mallard drake, nod-swimming is only performed coupled with another, preceding courtship motor pattern in the male chestnut-breasted teal. However, this coupling represents one of the most interesting features of the instinctive motor patterns of dabbling duck courtship, both from the phylogenetic point of view and from a behavioural standpoint. As already explained, in the mallard drake bridling and nod-swimming only occur after the head-up-tail-up (p. 36) or after mating and are thus coupled in obligatory fashion to these two extremely different instinctive motor patterns. Neither bridling nor nod-swimming occur alone in the mallard drake, whereas in the male chestnut-breasted teal the much more highly differentiated bridling pattern has become an independent courtship motor pattern. At the highest intensity level of courtship of the chestnut-breasted teal drake, quite evidently above an exactly predetermined threshold value of response-specific energy, the grunt-whistle, head-up-tail-up, 'burping', head-turning, bridling, nod-swimming and hind-head display are combined *to form a single, complex and absolutely rigidly coupled motor sequence.* Thus, in *Virago* there is either coupling of *all* described motor patterns, or each occurs in its own right – with the sole exception of nod-swimming and hind-head display, which only occur as coupled patterns. The physiological peculiarity of this phenomenon is that coupling between grunt-whistle and head-up-tail-up, between the head-up-tail-up and bridling and between bridling and nod-swimming in all cases emerges or disappears at exactly the same threshold value. Fragments of the behavioural sequence are *never* observed; one sees either individual components or the entire sequence.

Fig. 33. *Schema of the movement in nod-swimming of the chestnut-breasted teal drake (cf. Figs. 6 and 14)*

Nod-swimming itself, like the bridling pattern, exhibits much greater gestural exaggeration than in the mallard. The origin of bridling from the first backward head movement of nodding is made extremely obvious in the chestnut-breasted teal by the fact that not just in the first impulse to swimming but also in every subsequent nodding movement the head is retracted so far onto the back that the visual impression of bridling is produced (Fig. 33). The motor act and the head plumage posture of hind-head display are completely identical to those in the mallard drake, and the pattern is rendered particularly conspicuous by the fine copper-green head coloration of the male chestnut-breasted teal.

(*i*) *Fighting between drakes*
The fighting behaviour of the drakes appears to correspond to that of male mallard and plucked areas arise in analogous fashion on the breast.

(*k*) *Post-copulatory play*
This corresponds to that of the mallard, except that nod-swimming is exaggerated in the manner characteristic of the species.

XIV   The common teal, *Nettion crecca* L.

I. GENERAL OBSERVATIONS

The European teal distinguishes itself unfavourably from virtually all other Anatinae, remarkably including its close North American relative

Nettion carolinense, in that it is one of the most stubbornly shy birds that I know when trapped in the wild. Whether they were set free on the lake or kept in the smallest enclosure, these ducks would not even reach a minimum degree of tameness in my care. Thus, despite the most laborious and careful observation from afar, I know less today about the behaviour of this species than about that of any other duck which I have kept.

As regards colour, the common teal is related to the mallard and the chestnut-breasted teal. It shares with both the distinct separation of the glossy green head markings from the neck, and the black-green speculum resembles that of the chestnut-breasted teal.

The speculum of *Nettion flavirostre* is even more similar to that of *Virago*. The European teal shares with its Chilean relative (*Nettion flavirostre*) a peculiar head patterning in the duckling.

2. THE NON-EPIGAMIC MOTOR DISPLAY PATTERNS AND VOCALIZATIONS

Whereas the female in every way gives the impression of being a miniature replica of a mallard, the drake is quite distinct from the mallard drake to the extent that he is completely voiceless. The only call he possesses is the 'Krick'-whistle, which is doubtless homologous to that of the chestnut-breasted drake and similarly combines the function of summoning and alarming. Although the 'Krick'-whistle is also employed in the actual social courtship of the drakes, its frequent utterance completely obscures its function as a courtship call, and it has in every respect come to be a representative of the display calls which belong in the range of non-whistled vocalizations in the mallard. Common teal drakes will utter the whistle in situations where no other dabbling drake would, for example when greatly frightened by a human being approaching their cage.

3. THE EPIGAMIC MOTOR DISPLAY PATTERNS AND VOCALIZATIONS OF THE FEMALE

I have never seen performance of nod-swimming by my few, shy female common teal; but I do not venture to maintain that the species lacks this pattern, though I can quite definitely state that it is lacking in *Nettion flavirostre*. In all other motor patterns and vocalizations, the female European teal is quite like the female mallard, except that her voice has a much higher pitch in correspondence with the body size.

4. THE EPIGAMIC MOTOR DISPLAY PATTERNS AND VOCALIZATIONS OF THE DRAKE

(a) The general form of courtship

The complexity and 'ceremony' of the courtship is at least as great as in the mallard. The drakes have to spend a long time assembling, adjusting their position, shaking their bills, etc., before the first whistle is uttered. In this, however, they actively seek the presence of a female, in contrast to the mallard and in agreement with pintails, Bahama duck and garganeys. In some cases, they will interrupt courtship to swim after a female and then begin courtship all over again, with body-shaking and aggregation, when she has been reached. In other respects, the courtship of common teal drakes looks just like a rapid run-through of a film of mallard drake courtship; all motor patterns and whistles, along with the modified form of display drinking, display shaking, etc., are performed so rapidly and hurriedly that the observer scarcely has time to breathe. With the large group of drakes which I had, the whistling was almost continuous. Courtship subsequently wanes very rapidly, so that one only properly observes and records a fraction of the motor patterns.

(b) Display drinking and introductory body-shaking

Display drinking and body-shaking are just like the mallard drake patterns, but they are of shorter duration since the rise and fall of any arousal effect occurs more rapidly than in *Anas*, in accordance with the small body-size of the species. I have never yet observed sham-preening.

(c) The 'Krick'-whistle

As already mentioned, the 'Krick'-whistle is common outside the context of courtship. It is clearly disyllabic, and the 'Krickente' (common teal) would be more exactly termed the 'Koodick'-Ente. The lower mandible is snapped downwards to coincide with the *d* between the *oo* and the *i* just as abruptly as in *Virago castanea* and *gibberifrons*, and the bony drum mechanism is obviously the same in all these species. The head is *not raised at all* in the utterance of the call, and this presumably is of importance for the associated frequency and ease of utterance.

(d) The grunt-whistle

The motor pattern of the grunt-whistle is exactly the same as in the species already discussed. The call has a soft, fluting quality and there is no grunt.

(e) The head-up-tail-up

As I had already assumed from the marking pattern of the sides of the tail, the head-up-tail-up plays a large part in the common teal courtship.

The yellow triangles of the under tail-coverts, which are sharply demarcated from the black ground colour, are spread very rapidly and are beautifully displayed (Fig. 34). The head-up-tail-up can occur with

Fig. 34. *The head-up-tail-up of the common teal. Note the optical efficacity of the yellow triangles on the sides of the tail (cf. Figs. 12, 22, 25 and 41)*

two different forms of coupling. The more frequent in my observations was characterized by the lack of a subsequent 'burping' movement, its place being taken by *chin-raising* without any raising of the head or stretching of the neck. Alternatively, just as in the mallard drake, the head-up-tail-up is followed by *'burping'*, which is always accompanied by very intensive turning of the head towards the female (Fig. 35). My observations so far indicate that this alternative coupling occurs at higher levels of response intensity.

Fig. 35. *'Burping' in the common teal drake*, Nettion crecca L. (*cf. Figs. 20, 24 39, 46 and 50*)

The head is raised only slightly in 'burping', and a *'Krick'-whistle* is uttered when the peak is reached. The fact that this whistle occurs in exactly the same coupling as the normal 'burp-whistle' of the pintail and the chestnut-breasted teal very much indicates that it is genetically derived from the latter. As with the mallard drake, burping never occurs as an isolated motor pattern, but only in combination with the head-up-tail-up. When the head is raised, the plumage of the surface of the head and neck previously opposed to the back is kept flattened in an 'embarrassed' contour, whilst the hind margin, which previously formed a smooth transition to the back plumage with the head drawn in, is now exposed, giving a sharp, projecting tufted contour on the back of the head. It is in fact 'there for that purpose', and in *Nettion flavirostre* – in which morphological differentiation of the 'tuft' has gone much farther – it has the same function.

(f) Bridling

Bridling occurs only as a completely isolated, independent courtship motor pattern. The head is drawn back perhaps still farther than in *Virago*. Wormald, in his description of the courtship of the common teal and the mallard, has confused this strong bridling action with the head-up-tail-up, since he says of the head-up-tail-up of the mallard drake that the same motor pattern is even more pronounced in the common teal: 'He makes his head and his tail meet over his back.' Wormald is doubtless referring to the bridling pattern, which – as is obvious from all that has been said – is not at all homologous with the head-up-tail-up. The associated whistle is monosyllabic.

(g) Chin-raising

Chin-raising is always performed very slowly, usually outside of actual courtship play. Just as in the chestnut-breasted teal drake, the posture is maintained for some time, with the head drawn back on the neck, exactly as with the chin-raising in the pintail species. The function of the motor pattern is the same as in the mallard. It is seen repeatedly performed by a drake 'courteously' paying attention to a female.[20]

(h) Hind-head display

In contrast to the mallard, chestnut-breasted teal and wood duck, the hind-head display of the common teal does not occur with the described head posture, with the chin high and the feathers markedly flattened. Instead, as I had already suspected from the marking pattern and feather structure of the back of the head, this display is performed with the head drawn in, the nape pressed out and the head and nape plumage ruffled.

(i) Fighting between drakes and post-copulatory play

Both of these behavioural features have so far escaped observation.

XV The South American teal, *Nettion flavirostre* Viellot

I. GENERAL OBSERVATIONS

This species is without doubt extremely closely related to *Nettion crecca*, but at the same time it is further specialized than the latter in a quite characteristic manner. The completely identical coloration of the two sexes, which is possibly related to the brood-care by the drake already demonstrated by Grey, would in itself be a character of lesser taxonomic importance (e.g. consider the corresponding variability between the so closely related *Anas* species) than the instinctive motor patterns of male brood-care themselves. It is noteworthy that there is an amazing effect of convergence with the similar performance of brood-care by the male sex of the true geese (Anserinae), in that an originally offensive motor pattern representing threat has come to act as a gesture of greeting and family cohesion. One feature which is quite unique among the Anatinae is the fact that this motor pattern is already performed by one-day-old ducklings, just like the neck extension of young Anserinae. One peculiarity which has been emphasized by many taxonomists is the great similarity evident in the bill and plumage coloration between *Nettion flavirostre* and *Dafila spinicauda*. On this basis, von Boetticher established the sub-genus *Dafilonettium* for the South American teal and presented this form as a virtual transitional stage between the teals and the pintails. I am completely opposed to this view. Despite all of its peculiarities, *Nettion flavirostre* is a true teal as far as the body posture, motor display patterns and duckling plumage is concerned, and it is doubtless much more closely related to the chestnut-breasted teal than to *Dafila spinicauda*. Take, for instance, the coloration of the speculum (p. 31 et seq.), the bridling whistle (p. 79) and the 'Krick'-whistle (p. 77 et seq.). The similarity in bill coloration to *D. spinicauda* is doubtless based on homologous mutations, which can produce absolutely similar marking patterns even in the absence of close relationship, as for example with the so-called 'mottling' on the wings of extremely different wild pigeon and dove species and races of the domestic pigeon. *Anas undulata* also has virtually the same bill markings, although this species is quite definitely not closely related to *Nettion flavirostre* or *Dafila spinicauda*. In addition, the plumage of these two species corresponds only in the coloration and not at all in the fine details of the markings, which are typically teal-like in the first species and typically pintail-like in the latter.

2. THE NON-EPIGAMIC MOTOR DISPLAY PATTERNS AND
    VOCALIZATIONS

The social contact calls and summoning calls of both sexes are generally comparable to those of *Nettion crecca*. Apart from the latter, this represents the only species I know in which the drake is able to whistle without a special movement of the head and neck. In contrast to the common teal drake, the usual summoning and alarm call is monosyllabic and is uttered even more easily and frequently than in the mallard, sometimes almost completely with the rhythm and significance of the latter's social contact calling. It can be said that in the drake of *Nettion flavirostre* the replacement of the actual social contact call by the courtship whistle has proceeded the farthest.

Figs. 36 and 37. *The first and second phases of the greeting gesture of the South American teal drake,* Nettion flavirostre

In addition, any form of arousal brings the drake to perform a very peculiar, indeed unique, greeting ceremony – particularly when he re-locates his mate after a short separation. This ceremony has nothing to do with the actual courtship ('social play') and is never performed in association with the latter. The drake extends his head, exactly like a *threatening* dabbling duck (including the ordinary domestic duck), and holds the bill horizontally close to the ground. Whilst performing this movement, he utters a rapid, polysyllabic twittering call, approximately *rootweetweetweetweetwee*. Before the head is extended, it is first inclined sharply downwards (Fig. 36), thus displaying a protruding tuft on the neck. The next instant, the goose-like extension of the neck completely obliterates the tuft (Fig. 37). The drake is particularly prone to perform this motor display pattern in response to incitement by the female. I once arranged for a miniature hen to brood three eggs laid, but then abandoned, by my female *flavirostre* and subsequently took the three healthy ducklings into my charge. To my utter amazement, all three responded to my imitation of the duck guiding call with the described ceremony in its complete form, and uttered the twittering call with very little difference from that of an adult drake. The ducklings greeted in this way both towards me and towards each other after each separation, and the motor pattern was also elicited by other arousing phenomena. The mode of employment and the corresponding stimulus situation were amazingly comparable to the overall situation eliciting neck-extension in the greylag goose. In this comparison of these two evidently analogous motor display patterns of *Anser* and *Nettion*, the question of homology is of interest. Both are derived from a *homologous* root, that is from the threatening extension of the neck common to virtually all Anatinae with very few exceptions (*Chloëphaga!*). However, the fact that this 'outward-

directed threat' has in both given rise to a 'gesture of amicability towards family members' through the agency of the close family co-
hesiveness determined by male brood-care, represents – in view of the
many Anatid species lacking this phenomenon and separating *Nettion*
and *Anser* – a convergent effect, a stimulating special case for defining
the concepts of analogy and homology! Since all three of my *flavirostre*
ducklings developed into drakes, I unfortunately do not know whether
female ducklings also possess this motor pattern and later lose it, or
whether the sexual dimorphism in the motor display repertoire is completely developed from the first day of life. Either way, this is an
extremely interesting phenomenon!

3. THE EPIGAMIC MOTOR DISPLAY PATTERNS AND VOCALIZATIONS OF THE FEMALE

(a) *Incitement behaviour*

This is similar to that of the European teal, but there is a distinct
similarity to the characteristic cadence of the chestnut-breasted teal.
As in the mallard, the head movement is markedly downwards and
backwards. The raised posture of *Dafila* (including *D. spinicauda*) is
completely lacking, as is the very characteristic rasping *rrrr* of the
pintails.

(b) *The decrescendo call*

The decrescendo call holds the record among all dabbling ducks for the
number of syllables. The second note is the loudest, as for example in
the mallard and common teal. I have counted up to 21 syllables, each
gradually falling in amplitude and pitch and giving the impression that
the female is gradually *moving away* from the observer as the call
progresses.

(c) *The mating prelude*

This is similar to that of the mallard; nod-swimming is lacking.

4. THE EPIGAMIC MOTOR DISPLAY PATTERNS AND VOCALIZATIONS OF THE DRAKE

(a) *The general form of courtship*

The introduction is at least as ceremonial as that of the mallard. Eruption
of the courtship motor patterns in the midst of swimming, without
renewed aggregation and body-shaking – as occurs in pintails and
garganeys swimming after a female – is virtually inconceivable. My four

drakes paid less attention to the presence of a female than common teal drakes, but nevertheless more so than mallard or mandarin drakes. The slow, regular sequence of the individual courtship motor patterns is just as little reminiscent of the European teal drake as the restless, mingled swimming courtship of the drakes of *Dafila spinicauda*. On the other hand, there is a resemblance to the common teal in that each individual courtship pattern is usually repeated frequently so that one often observes literally only one and the same motor pattern throughout a courtship sequence.

(b) Introductory body-shaking

This corresponds to that of other species. I have never observed sham-preening.

Fig. 38. *The grunt-whistle of the South American teal drake. Note the tuft on the back of the head (cf. Figs. 11b and 21)*

(c) The grunt-whistle

The grunt-whistle resembles that of most other dabbling drakes; the grunting call is lacking. The tuft on the back of the head is erected during the downward movement of the head (Fig. 38).

(d) The 'burping' pattern

Since the head-up-tail-up is lacking, 'burping' occurs as a completely independent motor pattern without coupling to other patterns. However, it is reminiscent of the 'burping' coupled with the 'head-up-tail-up' in the mallard, pintail and common teal drakes, to the extent that it is always accompanied by turning of the head towards the female. During this head-turning movement, the head plumage forms an almost astoundingly high and slim disc. The dark tuft on the back of the head projects free like a horizontal thorn, and the two together give an extremely conspicuous image. There can be scarcely any doubt that the function of the extended head plumage, which almost forms a crest, is vested in the optical efficacity of this particular motor pattern (Fig. 39).

There is a structural peculiarity in that the feathers of the temples and sides of the head are much more extended than those of the crown so that in the 'disc-coiffure' a flat lens-shape with a sharp contour in the upper mid-line is produced. This contrasts to the corresponding 'coiffure' of mallard, common teal, wood duck and mandarin drakes, in which the upper region of the head is demarcated from the sides with a sharp, and visually underlined, border.

Fig. 39. *'Burping' with head-turning in the South American teal drake. Note the 'disc-coiffure' and compare with Figs. 13, 22 and 24. There is no preceding head-up-tail-up in this case*

The whistle accompanying 'burping' is almost always like that of the common teal, a disyllabic *koodick*.

(e) Bridling

This is the most conspicuous, and probably most frequent, courtship motor pattern of *Nettion flavirostre*. In vigour and range of movement, it exceeds the homologous motor patterns of all other dabbling drakes. The head not only passes back along the dorsal feathers almost to the tail root, it even moves *laterally* away and downwards from the middle of the back, while the drake is reared up above the water in front (Fig. 40).

Fig. 40. *The bridling pattern of the South American teal drake. Compare the extreme gestural exaggeration of the motor pattern with that in Figs. 16 and 31*

(f) Fighting between drakes and post-copulatory play

I have no knowledge of fighting between drakes and post-copulatory display, and there may possibly be other courtship motor patterns of the drake which I have so far missed.

XVI   The gadwall, *Chaulelasmus streptera* L.

1. GENERAL OBSERVATIONS

However close the gadwall may be to the mallard in many ways, this species nevertheless represents a departure in a specialized direction leading a long way away from all other dabbling ducks and bringing the gadwall close to the wigeons, which in their habits and motor display inventory are just as far removed from all other dabbling ducks as in their coloration and duckling plumage. In addition, it is known that wigeons always produce infertile hybrids with *Anas* species, whereas the gadwall stands between both groups to the extent that it will produce fertile hybrids with both. Finally, there is a relationship to the teals, since the Asiatic falcated teal (*Anas falcata*) represents in its plumage markings a remarkable link between *Nettion* and *Chaulelasmus*.

2. THE NON-EPIGAMIC MOTOR DISPLAY PATTERNS AND VOCALIZATIONS

The female and the duckling exhibit all the vocalizations and motor display patterns of the mallard, but in addition they exhibit an extremely characteristic motor pattern which is only fully developed in the *male* mallard, whereas the female only indicates the pattern weakly and the ducklings completely lack it – this is the *chin-raising* pattern. In any arousing situation, particularly when gadwalls are driven into a corner, when they crowd around the keeper begging for food or when separated individuals are reunited, even quite small ducklings perform the movements and the same rhythm with the disyllabic social contact call which we have encountered in the *raebraeb*-palaver of the mallard drake (p. 23 et seq.). When performed in this manner by a flock of ducklings, the ceremony resembles more the *triumph ceremony* than the mallard palaver. When the mother takes part in the ceremony (as she doubtless normally does), this analogy must emerge even more clearly than it did with my artificially-reared orphans. The corresponding motor pattern of the wigeons, which is without doubt homologous, has quite definitely assumed the function of a triumph ceremony. The disyllabic social contact calls are lacking in the drake, but he nevertheless utters a soft whispered summoning call, which is certainly homologous to the drawn-out *raeaeb* of the mallard drake.

3. THE EPIGAMIC MOTOR DISPLAY PATTERNS AND
   VOCALIZATIONS OF THE FEMALE

(a) Incitement behaviour

The incitement behaviour of the female is quite remarkable. The actual incitement movement over the shoulder is regularly alternated with a *chin-raising* movement. The drake reliably responds to incitement with exactly simultaneous performance of *chin-raising*, as will be described in more detail later (Fig. 42). The cadence of the vocalization is that of genuine dabbling duck incitement, but the rhythm of the *raebraeb*-palaver known from chin-raising mallard drakes (p. 23) is at the same time evident. In order to follow Heinroth's example and express the rhythm with an easily remembered sentence, we rendered this in South German dialect as: 'Sö, gehn s'weg da, Sö!' (approximately: 'you, go away, you!'). This at the same time expresses the significance of the ceremony, which usually occurs when two pairs aggravate one another in the wigeon manner and attempt to drive one another away. As with wood duck, mandarin, *Amazonetta* and some Casarcinae, the inciting female now and again taps the drake's breast with her bill.

(b) The decrescendo call

This is extremely rare in the female gadwall. It is higher pitched and has fewer syllables than that of the mallard.

(c) The mating prelude

I have never observed this with the two very shy adult pairs which I kept.

4. THE EPIGAMIC MOTOR DISPLAY PATTERNS AND
   VOCALIZATIONS OF THE DRAKE

(a) The general form of courtship

The general form of courtship in gadwalls and wigeons differs fundamentally from that of all other dabbling ducks (with the possible exception of the shoveller) in that a definite social courtship involving aggregation of several drakes is absent. Somewhat as in the wood duck, the motor patterns and vocalizations of courtship are predominantly recognized when two pairs are aggravating one another or when two or more drakes are competing for a female. The gadwall lacks any positive taxes between the drakes as found in the dabbling ducks and the mandarin duck (*Aix galericulata*). Although social courtship of the drakes is lacking, the male gadwall exhibits motor patterns which are certainly homologous with those of the social courtship of other dabbling drakes. The instinctive motor pattern in fact frequently proves to be more conservative in phylogeny than its orienting taxes. Even the introduction to courtship is similar to that in other drakes. A male gadwall swimming after his female 'employs' body-shaking and sham-preening for self-stimulation in a manner very similar to that of these other drakes.

(b) Introductory body-shaking

Exactly as with other Anatinae, introductory body-shaking precedes actual courtship.

(c) Sham-preening and display drinking

These two patterns play a special part with the gadwall drake. Both are fused to a solidly coupled ceremony. Whereas display drinking and sham-preening follow one another in an irregular sequence in the mallard drake (p. 31 et seq.), so that it is almost impossible to provide direct proof that these motor patterns have a signal function if faced with a convinced sceptic, the ceremony of the gadwall drake clearly demonstrates its signalling rôle: Sham-preening is always immediately followed by display drinking. The phylogenetic amplification of the introductory motor patterns through rigid mutual coupling is all the more interesting because we know of a case where this has occurred in the opposite direction: In the mandarin drake, display drinking always precedes sham-preening. As with the mandarin drake, the gadwall drake has undergone, in parallel with further differentiation of sham-preening, specialization of the plumage areas particularly presented in performance of the pattern. The conspicuously coloured feathers on the speculum and on the large wing coverts are located on the very area which is particularly presented and moved by the sham-preening bill.

(d) The 'burping' pattern

'Burping' is clearly further differentiated, and to some extent more pin-tail-like, than in the mallard drake. Even without the head-up-tail-up, occurring in complete isolation, it is one of the most frequent courtship motor patterns of the gadwall drake. The call, the production of which is evidently dependent upon head-raising and the consequent tensing of the trachea, is a very peculiar, squashed nasal sound falling roughly between *oe* and *ae*. It is very questionable whether the unusual *oe*-calls of the gadwall drake are comparable to the social contact call, *raeb*, of the mallard drake. In its sonantic character (I have never heard a whistle uttered in accompaniment), the 'burping' pattern of the gadwall drake is much more reminiscent of the drawn-out *raeaeb* of the mallard drake, which functions as the latter's summoning and alarm call, than of the corresponding vocalizations of the pintail drake, which are frequently coupled with a whistle (p. 48). Strangely enough, the gadwall drake has in addition to the grunting *oe* the soft, whispered summoning call mentioned on p. 85, which I regard as certainly homologous to that of the mallard on motor grounds.

(e) The grunt-whistle

Even the gadwall exhibits this motor pattern. In this species, the pattern is peculiarly incomplete, abruptly truncated. The rearing of the body does not proceed anywhere near as far as in other dabbling drakes, the re-assumption of the normal posture occurs in a strangely hasty fashion and the posture with the head held downwards is maintained only very briefly. The head is immediately swung up again and pressed fairly vigorously onto the nape. During the downward inclination of the head,

Fig. 41. *The head-up-tail-up of the gadwall drake,* Chaulelasmus strepera L. *Note the particularly prominent plumage areas appearing in the movement and compare with those in Figs. 12, 22, 25 and 34*

a penetrating grunting note – *oeh* – is uttered, and this is followed in smooth transition by a fine, sharp whistle. The entire utterance thus sounds like *oeoeoeiii*. Thus, the sequence of calling of the grunt and the whistle is exactly the converse of that in the mallard drake.

(f) The head-up-tail-up

The head-up-tail-up (Fig. 41) of the gadwall drake is remarkably coupled with the down-up pattern, which does not occur as an isolated courtship motor pattern in this species. The raising of the rump is by no means as extensive as in the mallard drake, but on the other hand the subsequent 'burping' is very pronounced and is coupled with a quite marked turning of the head towards the female. The movement of the rump, despite its restricted extent, is rendered very conspicuous by ruffling of the very long and dense pitch-black upper and under tail-coverts. The head-up-tail-up is sometimes followed by a little empha-sized forward swimming movement, which lacks any indication of nodding head-movements but is terminated – exactly like nod-swimming of the mallard drake – by extremely pronounced hind-head display. Much more often, however – in fact almost regularly – the down-up movement follows immediately after the head-up-tail-up and 'burping'.

(g) *The down-up*

The down-up occurs *only* coupled, as explained. The term is ill-fitted for the motor pattern of the gadwall drake, since the introductory downward movement is scarcely indicated whilst the subsequent chin-raising movement is very pronounced.

Fig. 42. *Reciprocal chin-raising in a gadwall pair. The arrow indicates the direction of the lateral neck movements incorporated between successive chin-raising movements (cf. Figs. 3, 44 and 45)*

(h) *Chin-raising*

Because of its significance as a ceremony analogous to the triumph ceremony of the Anserinae and Casarcinae, as has already been mentioned in discussing the motor patterns of the female, chin-raising plays a quite particular rôle in the gadwall. The *loong shortloongshort loong* rhythm already evident in the *raebraeb*-palaver of the mallard is found in *both* sexes of the gadwall, occurring both in incitement by the female (p. 86) and in the motor pattern of the drake now to be described. In response to incitement by the female, the drake raises his bill (without previously lowering it) far above the horizontal, at the same time lowering hs head somewhat deeper into the water by inclining the neck vertebrae. As a rule, this chin-raising movement is repeated three times in accordance with the rhythm described. With the first and last raising movements, the drake utters his grunting call, while the middle movement is accompanied by a shrill whistle. The entire strophe thus sounds like *oeh, oe-eeh-oe, oeh*. As mentioned before, the female performs her alternating chin-raising movement synchronously with this movement of the male (Fig. 42), usually such that the incitement movement (i.e. the 'weg' in the sentence 'Sö, gehn s'weg da, Sö') coincides with the whistle of the drake. The incredibly rigid correlation of the calls of the two partners is reminiscent of the homologous triumph-call ceremonies of wigeon species, which are also accompanied by chin-raising. The use of this behaviour in reciprocal annoyance between pairs, the relative moderation in fighting and the brief after-effect of a 'victory' are the same in both gadwalls and wigeons. At low intensity, the vocalization of the drake shrinks to two syllables – a grunt with a subsequent whistle – and this can be heard with great frequency.

Fig. 43. *Hind-head display of the gadwall drake. The dark patch on the back of the head is produced only through posturing of the feathers and not through dark pigmentation (cf. Figs. 15, 23 and 26)*

(i) The hind-head display

This also plays a large part in courtship by the gadwall drake. In this display, the head plumage assumes a very extreme and conspicuous posture: the forehead plumage is ruffled to give a broad round expansion and thus gives a dark visual effect; the plumage of the crown forms a high ridge along the mid-line of the skull, which spreads out to give a broad, maximally ruffled (and therefore almost black) area on the back of the head. With the head drawn in (that is, in the introductory position), this area is opposed to the back. Before performance of the hind-head display, the head is raised just far enough for the area to become visible, and thereupon it is turned towards the female. The black cushion on the back of the gadwall drake's head stands out so clearly from the colour of the rest of the head that anybody who was only acquainted with the drake with this feather posture would ascribe to him dark pigmentation of the back of the head as in the pintail drake.

(k) Fighting between drakes

Fighting between drakes occurs just as in the mallard. I have never seen mating or post-copulatory play.

XVII   The wigeon, *Mareca penelope* L., and the Chiloë wigeon, *Mareca sibilatrix* Poeppig

I. GENERAL OBSERVATIONS

These two species are dealt with only in appendix form, since I do not know them well enough. Because of the lack of social courtship and the presence of highly specialized pair-bonding (almost reminiscent of the Anserinae in *Mareca sibilatrix*), both are quite distinct from the other dabbling ducks. The almost uniform coloration of the female plumage in *Mareca penelope* – which lacks the otherwise common longitudinal spotting of the flight feathers – the dark chestnut-brown eclipse plumage of the drake, and finally the exclusive female display plumage and duckling plumage of *Mareca sibilatrix* (the former with green head feathers and the latter with an almost uniform head coloration without longitudinal stripes) represent important taxonomic characters markedly separating the two species from the other Anatinae.

2. THE NON-EPIGAMIC MOTOR DISPLAY PATTERNS AND VOCALIZATIONS

In both sexes the social contact and summoning calls are reduced in a peculiar manner. The female *Mareca penelope* really has only one call, a grating *rerrr* which corresponds to a deeper *arrr* in the South American female. The drakes of both species have completely lost all social contact calls and are dependent upon their highly specialized courtship whistle for all motivational displays. In the drake of the European species, this is a monosyllabic call something like *veeer*, whilst it is disyllabic in the *sibilatrix* drake and sounds something like *veebuerr*. Both employ the whistle as a summoning and alarm call; it is just as easily elicited by a cat creeping past as by a female flying across the lake.

3. THE EPIGAMIC MOTOR DISPLAY PATTERNS AND VOCALIZATIONS OF BOTH SEXES

In both species, these are concentrated into a ceremony which consists of fused chin-raising and incitement, and which is quite definitely homologous to that of the gadwall. Interestingly, *Mareca sibilatrix* still exhibits a rudiment of the introduction to courtship, something which I never observed with *sibilatrix*. The drake swims towards the female whilst uttering a disyllabic whistling call, which can be represented by the English name *wigeon* given to this species. The drake shakes his head briefly in introduction and then follows this with extensive sham-preening, which is sometimes responded to by the female with performance of the same motor pattern.

Fig. 44. *Reciprocal chin-raising by a wigeon pair*, Mareca penelope L. *The small arrow indicates the direction and range of the trembling, vertical incitement movement of the female (cf. Figs. 3, 32, 42 and 45). Note the differentiation of the plumage on the drake's forehead*

Usually, however, the female responds by beginning her peculiar, trembling and jerky chin-raising movement. The drake then reacts by performing an exactly synchronous chin-raising pattern, with the root of the neck lowered markedly into the water. In contrast to the repeated, trembling performance of the female, however, the male exhibits the pattern only once and in combination with a loud whistle (Figs. 44 & 45). The grating call of the female, which is accompanied by the repeated chin-raising movement indicating a large number of upward movements, sounds like a fairly continuous *errr*, and its emphasis indicates that it is probably a form of *incitement* sharply distinct from that of other dabbling ducks. The stimulus situation corresponds to that of incitement.

Fig. 45. *Reciprocal chin-raising in a pair of the Chiloë wigeon*, Mareca sibi-latrix. *Both partners perform the same motor pattern. In its significance, this motor pattern is strongly reminiscent of the triumph ceremony of geese*

In *Mareca sibilatrix*, the trembling, repeated performance of the head movement is not evident in the female. Both sexes exhibit one single chin-raising movement, which is preceded by an incipient downward movement of the bill. The voice of the female has a deeper ring, more like *arr*, and the whistle of the drake is a disyllabic *veebuerr*. In both species, the movements and vocalizations of the two partners are so rigidly co-ordinated that the entire, peculiar vocal sequence sounds quite simple. In fact, Naumann attributed the two calls, whistling and grating, to both sexes of the wigeon. The ceremony quite plainly exhibits the character of a genuine triumph ceremony; its function is identical to that of the triumph ceremony in Anserinae and Casarcinae. For this reason, I have a slight suspicion that the European wigeon also exhibits at least certain indications of male brood-care.

XVIII   *Mareca sibilatrix* x *Anas platyrhynchos*

1. GENERAL OBSERVATIONS

Although I do not wish to include in this analysis the many duck hybrids which I have already observed and whose behavioural inventory I have been able to compile with some accuracy, I cannot omit a short discussion of the above hybrids. These were obtained from the Zoological Garden of Berlin, where a free-flying female mallard had been paired off with a *sibilatrix* drake for some years. The hybrids were morphologically fairly exact intermediates between the parental species. The colour pattern of the drake exhibited far less of the mallard pattern than the hybrids in Poll's (1910) illustration; in particular, there was less green on the head, distributed just as in the Chiloë wigeon. The two hybrids were mated with one another, laying and brooding infertile eggs every year. They were free-flying for some years until the female flew off for good in the 1939–40 winter. The drake, which had survived this harsh period, was frightened by the trapping of the other ducks prior to my transfer to Königsberg and flew away too.

2. THE NON-EPIGAMIC MOTOR DISPLAY PATTERNS AND VOCALIZATIONS

The hybrids were entirely mallard-like in this respect; the drake exhibited the monosyllabic and disyllabic calls of the mallard drake, though the voice was softer and hoarser.

3. THE EPIGAMIC MOTOR DISPLAY PATTERNS AND VOCALIZATIONS OF THE FEMALE

(a) *Incitement behaviour*

Incitement cannot be described more briefly than with the statement that it does not resemble the behaviour of either parent species – it is the same as in the gadwall, down to the last detail. The tendency to respond to any sexual arousal with an outbreak of chin-raising, inherited from *Mareca sibilatrix*, was combined with the drive towards performance of the incitement movement backwards over the shoulder, which the duck inherited from the maternal side. This occurred such that an incitement jab over the shoulder always separated two chin-raising movements. Since the drake exhibited chin-raising in exact synchrony with the female, a ceremony was produced which did not differ greatly from that of the gadwall.

(b) The decrescendo call

The decrescendo call was coarser and more truncated than in a female mallard. Nod-swimming was lacking.

(c) The mating prelude

This corresponded to that of the female mallard. Sometimes, however, both birds performed distinct *intention diving movements* prior to treading, instead of the prelude, just as at the beginning of play-diving preceding the midday bathe. Unfortunately, I do not know whether diving occurs as a mating prelude in *Mareca*. Heinroth has described corresponding behaviour for *Tadorna*.

4. THE EPIGAMIC MOTOR DISPLAY PATTERNS AND VOCALIZATIONS OF THE DRAKE

(a) The general form of courtship

The general form of courtship exhibited a peculiar bifurcation. On the one hand, the drake courted the female in the wigeon manner; but on the other hand he joined in the social courtship of the mallard drakes without taking the slightest notice of the female. Leiner described a similar bifurcation of taxes for hybrids between the substrate-nesting three-spined stickleback and the nine-spined form, which builds its nest in water plants.

(b) Introductory body-shaking, display drinking and sham-preening

Introductory body-shaking, display drinking and sham-preening were roughly comparable to the mallard drake patterns, but sham-preening was emphasized in the typical wigeon manner.

(c) The grunt-whistle

The courtship motor patterns of the hybrid male were represented by the grunt-whistle and an extremely common, heavily emphasized down-up movement followed by intensive chin-raising. The head-up-tail-up was lacking.[21]

(d) Post-copulatory play

Post-copulatory play was characterized by the absence of nod-swimming. The drake exhibited an incipient rearing movement after treading and then – without nodding – swam around the female in a very leisurely manner, bringing her to a halt and orienting the back of his head exactly towards her.

(e) Reciprocal chin-raising

Reciprocal chin-raising, which resembles the triumph ceremony, corresponded exactly to that of the gadwall drake.

XIX The Carolina wood-duck, *Lampronessa sponsa* L.

I. GENERAL OBSERVATIONS

This brings us to a group which is classified with the true dabbling ducks by some authorities and with the Cairininae by others. The truth of the matter is that this very independent sub-family, which consists of only two general – *Lampronessa* and *Aix*, is roughly intermediate between the two. They share with the Cairininae certain characters of the duckling plumage, certain morphological characters resulting from arboreal life and hole-nesting (e.g. the very long femur and thus the apparent anterior position of the legs), and the long, broad tail. In addition, they share an undoubtedly extremely primitive motor character. Along with the wood-duck and the mandarin, the true Cairininae are the only Anatinae which perform orienting head-movements before take-off, surveying the surrounding space through parallactic image displacement. In addition, the genera *Aix*, *Lampronessa* and *Cairina* have a common feature in that the nystagmic head-nodding, which occurs when the bird is on the alert when walking, does not accompany every step (as with virtually all other birds), but occurs in a very characteristic manner with every second pace. Thus, the head is always pushed forward simultaneously with one leg, almost giving the impression that the bird is limping. Without a doubt, the genus *Cairina* is extremely rich in primitive characters, as has already been indicated by Heinroth, Delacour and von Boetticher. The black-and-white plumage markings and the bald facial mask are reminiscent of *Abseranas*, while the almost reptile-like 'rape' of the female and the lack of pair-bonding presumably represent further primitive characters. However, although *Aix* and *Lampronessa* are doubtless highly specialized forms quite closely related to the true dabbling ducks, I feel driven to classify them quite definitely with the Cairininae – in agreement with Delacour and von Boetticher. Despite the conspicuous relationship of this group to species with numerous primitive characters, there are also several highly differentiated characters present. This is analogous to the Herpestoids among the Carnivora, which include types (e.g. *Mungos* and *Cross-archus*) exhibiting characters of a virtually insectivore degree of primitiveness and yet at the same time include some forms whose specialized character provides an almost smooth transition to the generally more specialized Felidae (e.g. the civet-cat, *Viverra*, the palm civet, *Para-doxurus*, and the fosa, *Cryptoprocta ferox*).

The motor display patterns were exhaustively described by Heinroth in 1910, and they are merely summarized here in order to provide a ready comparison.

2. THE NON-EPIGAMIC MOTOR DISPLAY PATTERNS AND VOCALIZATIONS

Except in very small ducklings, the disyllabic social contact call of the Anatinae is lacking. In the distress call, the monosyllabic piping note does not occur at regular intervals as in Anatines, but (particularly at high intensity) usually in groups of two, though the notes are never so close together that a disyllabic quality is produced. The intention movements for take-off, which are characteristic of the entire group, have already been discussed. The 'departure call' of the female, which is uttered particularly during the search for a nest, is a soft, rapid *tetetetet*. The corresponding call of the drake, in agreement with his vocal pitch, is a fine *yibyibyibyib*. The drake utters as a social contact call a short *yeeeb* emphasized on the second syllable. This is heard particularly when the male is behaving 'courteously' towards the female. The drake's summoning call is a drawn-out *ye-eehb*, whilst that of the female is a coarser *koo-eck*. Whereas the calls so far listed represent functional analogues of the presumably homologous vocalizations of many Anatini, the alarm call of the female is a peculiar, short *hoo ick*. As with Anatini the alarm call of the drake corresponds to the summoning call. However, whereas the alarm call of Anatini cannot be distinguished from the summoning call, the alarm call of the Carolina drake can be fairly distinctly recognized by its truncated quality.

3. THE EPIGAMIC MOTOR DISPLAY PATTERNS AND VOCALIZATIONS OF THE FEMALE

(a) *Incitement behaviour*

Incitement is performed across the shoulder in the manner typical of dabbling ducks, but the female characteristically exhibits between the individual incitement movements jerks of her beak towards the drake –

particularly towards his breast. Mandarin ducks exhibit this in the same way, whereas the female Brazilian teal, *Amazonetta brasiliensis*, remarkably turns her bill towards the drake between the individual incitement jabs. This gives exactly the same impression as the head-turning of some dabbling drakes (p. 37 et seq. and p. 51 et seq.). Between the incitement movements, female wood-duck frequently perform aiming head-movements, which represent general arousal gestures as in *Cairina*.

(b) The 'coquette'-call

The 'coquette'-call (Heinroth) is a relatively soft call which is difficult to represent on paper. It has a sound something like *hooey* and is functionally roughly equivalent to nod-swimming of female mallard and chestnut-breasted teal (i.e. provokes the male to perform courtship).

(c) The flight-call

The flight-call a peculiar loud *oo-eeh*, corresponds to a drawn-out and gradually waning summoning call. It has a strange owl-like quality; nobody not familiar with the call would recognize it as a duck vocalization. It is heard particularly towards sunset and when other wood-duck fly over the bird concerned. Since ducks sometimes utter this call when alone, it may also have the subsidiary function of a decrescendo call, with which it has no genetic ties. The primary significance of the call is doubtless the display of flight intention, and this is not evident with the decrescendo call of the Anatinae.

(d) The mating prelude

In contrast to the mating prelude of all Anatini, that of the wood-duck female consists of completely silent flattening of the body and forward extension of the neck. A female will exhibit this posture while swimming after her (frequently sexually disinterested) mate and will maintain it for several minutes. For his part, the drake displays copulatory intention by repeated display drinking and aiming head-movements. Sometimes, this is mixed with sham-preening. Almost the same mating prelude is exhibited by the *mergansers*, which Delacour regards as definitely closely related to the wood-duck/mandarin group.

4. THE EPIGAMIC MOTOR DISPLAY PATTERNS AND VOCALIZATIONS OF THE DRAKE

(a) The general form of courtship

More than the males of any species of Anatini with which I am acquainted, the wood-drake courts a specific female. Whereas the courtship of garganey and wigeon drakes – with the threatening and irritation of other pairs – is strongly reminiscent of courtship in Anserinae and Casarcinae, the courtship of *Lampronessa* is almost like that of some gallinaceous birds in which the male repeatedly spreads his conspicuously differentiated feathers. The drakes completely lack any sign of mutual interaction in courtship. This is all the more striking and interesting to the extent that this minimal social courtship of *Lampronessa* contrasts with the maximal social courtship exhibited by the closely related genus *Aix*. It is noticeable that the wood-drake exhibits many *different*, though usually little specialized, motor patterns. This may be a primitive condition.

(b) Introductory body-shaking

This occurs only rarely, emerging when the drake meets the courted female in a certain rest-posture. The pattern is then performed from an initial body posture corresponding closely to the introductory posture of Anatini. It is combined exceedingly frequently with *display drinking*.

(c) Sham-preening

Particularly at high response intensities, display drinking is regularly followed by sham-preening. As with *Aix*, it never occurs without prior display drinking, though *Lampronessa* can also exhibit display drinking at lower response intensities which – in contrast to *Aix* – is not followed by sham-preening. During sham-preening, the wood-drake reaches far back behind the wing. Despite the rapidity of the movement, I have the marked impression that a *specific* feather (the 'brass feather' of Heinroth) is touched from beneath the wing and thus moved. With the extremely short response time of birds, they exhibit a whole range of optically operative releasers whose display time is only too brief for human observation. One only needs to think of the 'water-play' of the mallard drake described on pp. 34 & 40, which was first revealed through the short exposure times of the camera.

(d) 'Burping'

This is relatively rare in the wood-drake. It is doubtless homologous with that of the Anatini and of the mandarin drake. The call which is uttered in accompaniment, a whistling, sneezing *pfeet*, has a sound quite different from the drawn-out *pfrrrooeeb* of the mandarin. The movement of the head crest, which is particularly conspicuous when this motor pattern is performed, is exactly the same in both species. The outline of the 'disc-coiffure' already mentioned on p. 38 is displayed just as sharply as the partly white feathers of the back of the head, which are extended to give a long veil and account for the German name for the species (lit. 'bride-duck') – see Fig. 46.

Fig. 46. *'Burping' of the Carolina drake,* Lampronessa sponsa L. *The 'disc-coiffure' has a particular optical effect as a result of the white lines fringing the forehead and elongation of feathers (cf. Figs. 20, 24, 35, 39 and 50)*

(e) The down-up movement

This motor pattern is presumably only homologous with that of the Anatinae to the extent that it has also definitely been derived from display drinking through gestural exaggeration. The bill is first briefly lowered and then swept up almost to the vertical as a short whistling call is uttered. A labile coupling of this motor pattern with chin-raising shows that both presumably have the same origin.

(f) Chin-raising

Just as with the 'courteous' mallard drake, chin-raising is combined with *hind-head display* (Fig. 47). As with the mallard, the plumage of the back of the head is flattened so that the surface turned towards the female shines rather than exhibiting a conspicuous matt black quality, as with pintail and garganey drakes and with the second head-turning pattern of the mallard drake (p. 38). In this case, however, the plumage posturing of the Carolina drake has a further characteristic in that the crest is not only flattened against the nape, but simultaneously *laterally* spread so that the shiny green-and-white surface turned towards the female is considerably broadened (Fig. 47). This hind-head display is one of the most frequent courtship patterns of the drake, who exhibits almost uninterrupted courtly behaviour towards his female. A second specialization of the feathers is also brought into play. A drake swimming in front of the female, continuously uttering the short *yeeeb . . . . yeeeb . . . . yeeeb* and exhibiting hind-head display, also twists the raised tail such that the dark purple-violet markings of the side – with the dangling, orange-red sickle-shaped plumes – are displayed to the female just like the spread surface of the head crest (Fig. 47).

Fig. 47. *Hind-head display with chin-raising and tail-slanting of the Carolina drake. The white-ridged surface of the 'bridal veil', together with the violet side of the tail root with its decorative orange-yellow plumes, are so oriented towards the courted female that they are vertically presented in her field of view*

Thus, with the Carolina drake every individual detail of the richly differentiated plumage is (so to speak) optically operative in a specific ceremony, acting as a 'visual adaptation' (Süffert) or 'releaser' (Lorenz). When simultaneously displaying the back of the head and the tail, the drake – since he cannot orient his tail perpendicular to his body – swims with a pronounced slant 'shoulder on' in front of the female. He is always oriented such that the purple surface is presented in an exact vertical position to the female's gaze. The male changes frequently from left to right, and each time the tail is swung from one side to the other in a very conspicuous fashion.

(g) *Whistle-shaking*

I have deliberately refrained from calling this motor pattern a grunt-whistle, since I believe that they are only homologous to the extent that both are derivatives of introductory body-shaking. On the other hand, it is just this motor pattern of the Carolina drake (which is actually far closer to the original form of body-shaking than the grunt-whistle of the Anatinae) which represents for me the most convincing proof for the correctness of the proposed phylogenetic derivation of the grunt-whistle. With the Carolina wood-duck, even with a quite autochthonous, mechanically operative body-shaking movement, the 'upswing' is always accompanied by lowering of the head down to the breast. Thus, the subsequent rearing motion is itself very reminiscent of the grunt-whistle pattern of the Anatini, and also of the 'demonstrative shaking' of the male *Tadorna tadorna* (p. 34). The 'whistle-shaking' of the Carolina drake, compared to the 'true' body-shaking of the species, exhibits very little, but nonetheless recognizable, gestural exaggeration. However, in combination with the linkage to introductory body-shaking, the fact that the drake *utters a sharp whistle at exactly the right position* provides thoroughly convincing support for the assumption that the grunt-whistle of the Anatini is derived from a similar form of body-shaking. Whistle-shaking is relatively rare in the Carolina drake.

(h) Male incitement behaviour

The male Carolina, as the only male among the Anatinae which I know, exhibits a symbolic threat movement which closely resembles the incitement movement of the female. Particularly when incited by the female – and obviously as a response to this – the Carolina drake jerks his head laterally in threat towards an 'adversary' and utters a soft *deeh* with each jerk.

(i) Fighting between drakes

The bill is not used as an offensive weapon in fights between drakes. The drakes dart alongside one another with great rapidity on the water surface and strike at one another with the wing shoulder without ever grasping with the beak. The stretched darting movement has secondarily come to represent a ritualized form of demonstrative behaviour in *Lampronessa*. The drakes often swim towards a courted female in the same way, particularly when returning to her after pursuing another drake. Even older females tend to exhibit this motor pattern towards the drake, in which case both birds dash alongside one another with a hefty bow-wave, just like fighting drakes, only to pass on to hind-head display and amicability an instant later.

(k) Post-copulatory play

Post-copulatory play is not characterized by specific motor patterns. Whilst the female has already begun to bathe, the drake exhibits particularly intensive 'courtly' motor patterns.

XX The mandarin duck, *Aix galericulata* L.

I. GENERAL OBSERVATIONS

Without a doubt this species is very closely related to the Carolina wood-duck, though not quite as closely as one tends to suppose at first. Nevertheless, in my opinion the separation of the two genera *Aix* and

Lampronessa is out of all proportion to the collection of such different ducks as the mallard and the pintails within the genus *Anas*.

2. THE NON-EPIGAMIC MOTOR DISPLAY PATTERNS AND VOCALIZATIONS

These generally correspond to those of the Carolina duck. The summoning call of the drake is not separated from 'burping' as with the Carolina drake, however; both calls are represented by a very nasal *pfrrrooeeb* uttered with the crest spread to the extreme (Fig. 50). The departure and nest-search call of the female is very similar to that of the Carolina female. In contrast to the Carolina drake, the mandarin drake does not – as far as I know – exhibit a corresponding vocalization.

3. THE EPIGAMIC MOTOR DISPLAY PATTERNS AND VOCALIZATIONS OF THE FEMALE

(a) *Incitement behaviour*
This is entirely similar to that of the Carolina duck.

(b) *The 'coquette'-call*
This is louder and sharper than in the Carolina; a sharp *kett*.

(c) *The flight-call*
This represents a gap in my observations; I can find it neither in my memory nor in my diary entries.

(d) *The mating prelude*
This is the same as in the Carolina duck.

4. THE EPIGAMIC MOTOR DISPLAY PATTERNS AND VOCALIZATIONS OF THE DRAKE

(a) *The general form of courtship*
In the performance of his courtship motor patterns, the mandarin drake pays less attention to the presence of the female than any other Anatid species I know. Even more than with mallard drakes, social courtship is a matter for the males. Almost as with non-pairing gallinaceous birds, the males display purely passively without the slightest dependence on the presence of a female. In association with this, the social courtship of *Aix* lacks even the orienting responses with which other drakes – even mallard drakes – relate themselves to any females present (i.e. head-turning and hind-head display). Only with sham-preening does the drake orient himself towards the female, but in fact this motor pattern is less frequent in social courtship. In the actual performance of social

courtship, the mandarin drakes exhibit just as little direct courtship of a particular female as peacocks, male turkeys, black grouse or ruffs. In addition, it is doubtless no chance effect that the very species in which the active rôle of partner choice is so exclusively an attribute of the female should at the same time exhibit greatest differentiation of the male 'Prachtkleid' (display plumage).

Fig. 48. *The initial posture of the mandarin drake*, Aix galericulata L., *in social courtship* (*cf. Figs. 9 and 19*)

(b) Introductory body-shaking

This plays a very minor part. On the other hand, the posture from which this pattern is performed, by all Anatinae which exhibit it, is driven to an extreme in the mandarin drake. The head is more strongly retracted and the head plumage more strongly ruffled than in all Anatini (Fig. 48).

(c) Display drinking and sham-preening

Display drinking and sham-preening have come to form *one* obligate, coupled motor sequence in *Aix*, though the sequence is the converse of that described for the gadwall drake (p. 87). Exaggerated display drinking is followed by sham-preening (Fig. 49, a–c) which is more extensively ritualized and emphasized by more extensive morphological differentiation than in any other duck species: The mandarin drake touches the large innermost rust-red tertiary from the midline, holding the latter up like a sail whenever aroused to perform courtship. Very often, the drake performs the display drinking/sham-preening pattern when standing alongside the female on the bank. Then, both partners drink at exactly the same time and the drake subsequently touches his ornamental feather, always on the side turned towards the female. During display drinking, the crest on the back of the head (Fig. 49a) is moved such that the movement is greatly emphasized.

(d) 'Burping'

This is extremely conspicuous, as a result of the size of the ruffled crest and beard feathers (Fig. 50). The enormous feather-ball which is thus projected gives an impression of great weight.

Fig. 49, a, b and c. *Display drinking of the mandarin drake, as coupled with sham-preening. Note the raising of the dark-green crest on the back of the head, through which gestural exaggeration of the motor pattern is produced. Compare the feather posture with Fig. 50*

Fig. 50. *'Burping' of the mandarin drake (cf. Figs. 20, 24, 39 and 46)*

The drake utters in accompaniment a nasal *pfrrrueeehb*. Simultaneously, the feathers of the neck – which is pressed outwards in order to increase the tension of the bony drum – are raised in such a way that the movement has an exaggerated appearance. It seems as if the bird might put its neck out of joint.

(e) Demonstrative body-shaking

The mandarin drake has no actual grunt-whistle, but he exhibits no less than three motor patterns derived by gestural exaggeration of body-shaking. The first is strongly reminiscent of the demonstrative shaking of the male *Tadorna*. The head is first lowered and then swept up very high whilst a whirring call is uttered. This call can best be represented

as:

$$fwwwwwwwwwwwwww$$
$$vrrrrrrrrrrrrrrrrrrrr$$

(The *r* and the *w* should be pronounced simultaneously and sonantically.) With this head movement, too, the crest is markedly ruffled.

(*f*) The double grunt-whistle

The double grunt-whistle is a motor sequence restricted to the mandarin drake and derived from two further motor patterns originating from displacement body-shaking. Following usual introductory body-shaking, or even without this on occasions, the drake shakes himself, dipping his bill into the water about 5 cm from his breast, spraying water and following this by swinging the bill upwards. This motor pattern actually differs from normal intensive body-shaking, as seen in the females of *Aix* and *Lampronessa*, only in that it is so exaggerated that the bill is dipped into the water in a manner reminiscent of the grunt-whistle of Anatini. This is never the case with autochthonous body-shaking. In addition, the drake utters a call in association with the movement. I recorded this as *gnk-tsit* in my diary, and this expresses its similarity to a half-suppressed sneeze. In immediate and obligate coupling with this motor pattern, the drake then performs a second pattern which is further differentiated from body-shaking. The bill is lowered vertically with a sharp inclination of the head, so that it is dipped into the water just in front of the drake's breast. Thus, the tendency towards lowering of the head observed even with the normal body-shake of *Aix* and *Lampronessa* (p. 98) is even more subject to gestural exaggeration in this movement than in the preceding pattern. Accompanying a very brief shaking movement – I suspect that only a single right–left movement is involved, as with the true grunt-whistle of mallard and pintail drakes – the markedly projecting neck is thrust upwards, and once again a brief, sneezing whistle can be heard. The body is not reared. It can be said that the first of these two coupled shaking ceremonies is scarcely differentiated from normal introductory displacement shaking, whilst the second, more specialized movement has (so to speak) stopped at a point half-way towards the grunt-whistle. Thus, both provide obvious intermediates between displacement shaking little different from autochthonous body-shaking and the grunt-whistle of the Anatini, which is scarcely to be recognized as such. This renders the derivation of the latter from a body-shaking motion virtually certain.

(g) *Fighting between drakes*

The fighting behaviour of the drakes provides a particularly interesting chapter in the ethology of *Aix*. The drakes, like many male birds with extreme social courtship and extreme developments of the 'Prachtkleid' (display plumage), no longer exhibit serious fights among themselves. Side-by-side darting, which is so characteristic of the fighting behaviour of the Carolina wood-duck, and which even in this species tends towards symbolic display and ritualization, is only present as a *pure symbolic pattern* in *Aix*, though as such it plays a large part in social courtship. Heinroth quite rightly compares the behaviour pattern of the wildly darting drakes in this ceremony with that of a flock of whirligigs (*Gyrinus*).

(h) *Post-copulatory play*

This consists merely of non-specific gestures of arousal, such as 'burping', demonstrative body-shaking and aiming movements of the head.

XXI Summary

If one wishes to carry out individual systematic study of a group, it is necessary to free oneself once and for all from the impression that a linear arrangement of the forms involved could ever reflect the genuine phylogenetic relationships prevailing between them. This of course applies to the 'approximate series' outlined for the ducks discussed so far. All animals alive today represent living branch-tips of the 'phylogenetic tree' and can thus *ipso facto* not be descendants of one another. Therefore, a comparison of their characters produces an arrangement which, taking the metaphor of the phylogenetic tree, permits spatial representation of relationships like those existing between the individual branch-tips of a rounded box-tree or yew-tree. All of the tips are located in *one* surface – a temporal cross-section of the expansively growing stock. Just as we can only estimate the probable grouping of the individual tips on common branches and the height of union and separation on the stock when looking through the thick, opaque leafy shroud of the tree, even the best systematic arrangement can only permit us probable estimations of the genuine phylogenetic relationships of a group of animals.

I should now like to attempt to give a graphic representation, in the form of a tabular schema, of the products of 'systematic intuition', which has been defined as simultaneous *survey* of a maximum number of characters. This itself provides the correct estimation of the taxonomic relevance of individual characters (p. 15).

In this connection, it is first necessary to conduct some fundamental consideration. Similarity in a series of forms need by no means correspond to a series of evolutionary *levels*, however clearly the series may be indicated by the distribution of characters. One can imagine that a given stock might have given rise to a number of forms which are all of the same age and all equally differentiated away from the basic

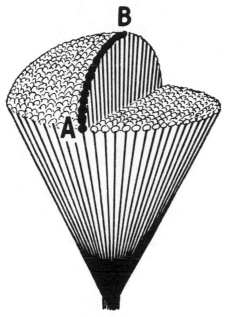

Fig. 51. *Schema of a series of similarities in recent animal species, where adjacent individuals are not linked by close phylogenetic relationship. Following loss of a proportion of the descendent lines, the remaining forms located on the line A–B can give the false impression of a phylogenetic series*

stock. This is symbolized in Fig. 51 as a kind of shaving brush. It can further be imagined that, as schematically shown in Fig. 52, a proportion of the hairs of the brush may have fallen out such that the remaining hairs are arranged in an approximate fan. The tips then represent a ladder which apparently speaks convincingly for the derivation of the forms involved 'from one another', particularly if the degree of differentiation at one edge of the fan is less than that at the other. Without doubt, it has already occurred very often that the terminal points of such 'phylogenetic fans' have been confused with phylogenetic series. Unfortunately, this has often pressed welcome weapons into the hands of opponents of the theory of evolution. On the other hand, we should not swing to the opposite extreme of this precipitate construction

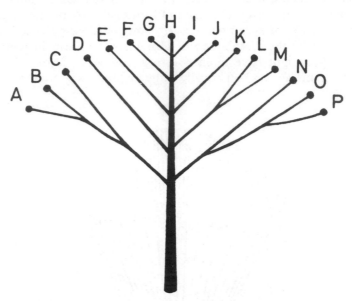

Fig. 52. *Schema of a similarity series of recent animal species based upon genuine phylogenetic relationship. Any two neighbouring forms in the series A–B owe their similarities to the common evolutionary pathway which they shared*

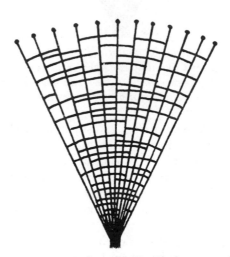

Fig. 53. *Schema of the expected character distribution among bush-like divergent and unbranching descendent lines. The cross-links represent common characters. Since similarities and differences can only be explained through greater or lesser divergence, the distributions of most characters overlap*

of 'phylogenetic' series and generalize the opinion that all similarity series among recent organisms can be explained through the principle of a fan-like arrangement of descendent lines. Without a trace of doubt, there are many cases where there has not only been monophyletic evolution of entire large animal stocks, with division into many individual forms occurring only at a later time, but also where the further evolution of the individual forms – at least in respect to individual characters – has proceeded at such different rates that similarity series rather like those illustrated in Fig. 53 have arisen. However, even when considering these genuinely phylogenetically graduated similarities *it must not be forgotten for an instant that the term 'primitive' can only be applied to one or more characters of a recent animal species and not to the entire animal.* Even *Sphenodon* or *Ornithorhynchus* are not 'primitive animals'. The fact that some, or even very many, characters of such a species are certainly primitive in phylogenetic terms by no means permits us to assume that all other characters are primitive too. Arrest in the evolution of one character tells us *nothing* about the further evolution of other characters.

The 'intuition' of a professional systematist mentioned at the beginning is generally quite adequate for distinction between similarity series based upon common origin of the type just described and those which originate from the previously discussed phenomenon of a fan-shaped arrangement of descendent lines. However, in order to obtain an objectively tenable criterion for this distinction, I suggest the following probabilistic consideration: If one assumes that all representatives of an animal group (as symbolized in Fig. 51) are derived from one source divergently and without any close mutual relationships, it would be expected that the similarities between the characters decisive for the arrangement of the individual descendent lines would be fairly evenly distributed throughout the entire 'shaving brush'. If, for the sake of simpler graphic representation, we take a longitudinal section through the brush (i.e. a number of fan-like diverging descendent lines), the similarities linking each form to its systematic neighbour would necessarily be homogeneously distributed through the whole fan of lines. Above all, there would be links to both sides (i.e. on all sides in the spatial brush schema) equally binding species to species. If common characters are represented as cross-links and the more general, older and widely distributed common characters are placed towards the origin, whilst the others are placed more towards the periphery following a lesser distribution, greater specialization and thus more recent origin, we obtain in the ideal case of radiating, divergent speciation the arrangement represented in Fig. 53.

If it is now assumed that not every species in the group of forms investigated has proceeded along an individual evolutionary pathway from the origin, but that sub-units of the group have diverged from a common origin only at a later date, then it is to be expected that one or other character would be common to forms belonging to the sub-group concerned and exclusive to them. These characters would be products of the evolution of the common phylogenetic sub-stock in isolation from neighbouring forms. If two such sub-stocks separate from one another

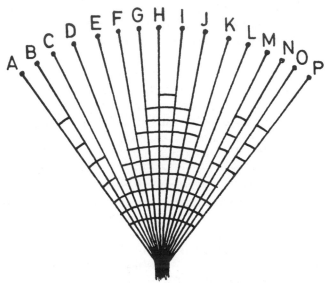

Fig. 54. *Schema of the expected character distribution with tree-like divergence of descendent lines. Since the connecting characters result from common evolutionary pathways, they are (excluding convergence) distributed according to common origin and do not overlap*

at a relatively early stage, we would expect that they would only be linked by very old characters common to larger group categories. Overlapping in the distribution of characters, as seen in Fig. 53, would not be expected for obvious reasons, as long as the possibility of convergence is excluded. Fig. 54 represents a character distribution of this type.

We shall now attempt to graphically represent the group of the Anatinae in the manner described without any prior assumptions and employing as many systematically applicable characters as possible. This will provide us with a judgement as to how far the representatives of the group can be classified into genuine phylogenetic groups and how far speciation has followed the type of straight-line divergent, brush-like evolution represented in Fig. 51. Since the brush of descendent lines can only be represented spatially, several plane projections would have to be made. Anybody who attaches great weight to illustrative techniques can draw up such projections and stick them together to give the requisite spatial pattern. I must admit that I myself used a bundle of stiff wires for arranging the species, united into sub-groups with thin wires representing 'common characters'. In order to summarize the character comparison conducted in this paper to give a single table, I am compelled to indicate specifically species which do *not* exhibit common characters indicated by crosslines. This is done with a heavy black dot. With species for which there is reason to believe that the lack of a character is not primitive but due to secondary loss, this is indicated by a cross at the point of intersection of the character cross-link and the descendent line. As can clearly be seen from the table, grouping into common stocks becomes more probable as we move down towards the origin, whereas with very many more recent characters obvious overlapping of character distribution occurs as in the schema of Fig. 53 (e.g. examine the distribution of the grunt-whistle, head-up-tail-up and hind-head display).

The few *morphological* characters distributed in the table are intended to show how similar their distribution is in many cases to that of the *innate behaviour patterns*. After filling in the gaps which are, above all, evident in the *list of species investigated*, I plan to set out a much larger table established on the same principle, including all possible morphological and behavioural characters as well as the fertility of the hybrids. However, before anything else the publication of this table must be preceded by publication of the comparative studies which Heinroth has carried out on the bony tracheal drums of the drakes, which are extremely rich in comparable characters. Even this provisional, incomplete table shows clearly the applicability of the phylogenetic homology concept to characters of innate behaviour. This fact, the demonstration of which was a major aim of my investigation, is of the greatest significance for *comparative psychology*.

Table: see overleaf

Table

The *vertical* lines represent species; the horizontal lines characters common among them. A *cross* indicates the absence of a character in a species crossed at the point concerned by a character cross-line. A *circle* indicates special emphasis and differentiation of the character. A *question-mark* indicates the author's uncertainty.

SPECIES LIST

1. *Cairina moschata*, Muscovy duck
2. *Lampronessa sponsa*, Carolina wood-duck
3. *Aix galericulata*, mandarin duck
4. *Mareca sibilatrix*, Chiloë wigeon
5. *Mareca penelope*, wigeon
6. *Chaulelasmus streptera*, gadwall
7. *Nettion crecca*, teal
8. *Nettion flavirostre*, South American teal
9. *Virago castanea*, chestnut-breasted teal
10. *Anas* as genus including mallard, spot-billed duck, Meller's duck, etc.
11. *Dafila spinicauda*, South American pintail
12. *Dafila acuta*, pintail
13. *Poecilonetta bahamensis*, Bahama duck
14. *Poecilonetta* (?) *erythrorhyncha*, red-billed duck
15. *Querquedula querquedula*, garganey
16. *Spatula clypeata*, shoveller
17. *Tadorna tadorna*, shelduck
18. *Casarca ferruginea*, Ruddy shelduck
19. *Anser* as genus
20. *Branta* as genus

CHARACTERS

Mlp	monosyllabic 'lost-piping'
Dd	display drinking
Bdr	bony drum on the drake's trachea
Adpl	Anatine duckling plumage
Wsp	wing speculum
Sbl	Sieve bill with horny lamellae
Ddsc	disyllabic duckling social contact call
I	incitement by the female
Bs	body-shaking as a courtship or demonstrative gesture
Ahm	aiming head-movements as a mating prelude
Sp	sham-preening of the drake, performed behind the wings
Scd	Social courtship of the drakes
B	'burping'
Lhm	lateral head movement of the inciting female
Spf	specific feather specializations serving sham-preening
Ibs	introductory body-shaking
P	pumping as prelude to mating
Dc	decrescendo call of the female
Br	Bridling
Cr	chin-raising
Hhd	hind-head display of the drake
Gw	grunt-whistle
Dum	down-up movement
Hutu	head-up-tail-up
Ssp	speculum same in both sexes
Wm	black-and-white and red-brown wing markings of Casarcinae

Bgsp	black-gold-green teal speculum
Trc	chin-raising reminiscent of the triumph ceremony
Ibr	isolated bridling not coupled to head-up-tail-up
Kr	'Krick'-whistle
Kd	'Koo-dick' of the true teals
Pc	post-copulatory play with bridling and nod-swimming
Ns	nod-swimming by the female
Gg	*Geeeeegeeeee*-call of the true pintail drakes
Px	Pintail-like extension of the median tail-feathers
Rc	R-calls of the female in incitement and as social contact call
Iar	incitement with anterior of body raised
Gt	graduated tail
Bm	bill markings with spot and light-coloured sides
Dlw	drake lacks whistle
Lsf	lancet-shaped shoulder feathers
Bws	blue wing secondaries
Pi	pumping as incitement
Dw	drake whistle
Bwd	black-and-white duckling plumage
Psc	polysyllabic gosling social contact call of Anserinae
Udp	uniform duckling plumage
Nmp	neck-dipping as mating prelude

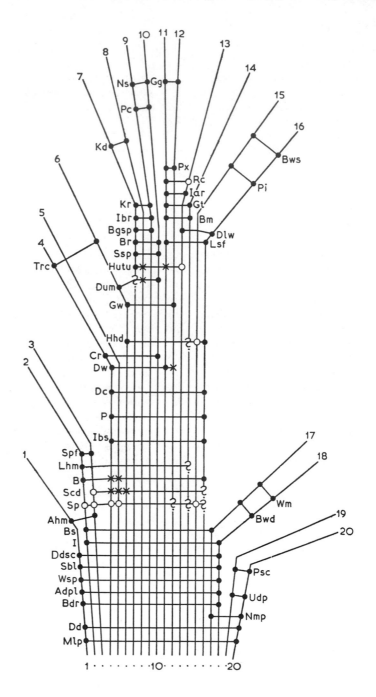

Part and parcel in animal and human societies (1950)

A methodological discussion

I Introduction

The causal interrelationships existing between the structures of the individual and those of the super-individual society, between the component and the governing system, are exposed to a peculiarly one-sided treatment by a great many modern sociologists and ethnological psychologists. Whereas the old atomic analytical approach aimed at deriving the nature of total entities exclusively from the sum of their elements, in complete ignorance of the characteristics of organic systemic entities, the pendulum of scientific 'public opinion' has nowadays swung to the opposite extreme. Now there is an almost exclusive search for the influence exerted by the society, by virtue of its specific structure, upon the personality structure of the individual growing within the social framework. There is scarcely ever an enquiry after the presence of individually invariable species-specific structures in human behaviour as determinants of certain species-typical characteristics common to *all* human societies. The focus of analysis is almost always the structural *differences* between different types of human society, and scarcely ever the structural *similarities* arising from invariable individual response patterns.

This exclusive treatment of the causal chains extending from the society to the individual, this complete neglect of causal effects in the opposite direction, represents a breach of specific methodological rules which one is obliged to follow in the analysis of any organic entity. It represents a misinterpretation of the nature of organic systemic entities, no less damaging and no less discouraging for research than the complementary bias of the atomists.

As far as I can see, complete neglect of the influence exerted by the structure of the individual within an organic system upon the structure of the super-individual society has two main origins. Paradoxically, the first reason for this offending breach of the obligate methodology applying to the analysis of any organic entity is based upon *erroneous generali-*

115

zation of certain principles of Gestalt psychology. The second reason is the neglect of the presence of innate species-specific action and response patterns in human beings. I propose to separate the methodological arguments of this essay according to these two points of view. In conclusion, I shall briefly consider certain dangers to mankind, the antidote for which requires exact knowledge of the innate action and response patterns of man.

II   Erroneous generalization of principles of Gestalt psychology

1.   EVERY GESTALT IS AN ENTITY – BUT NOT EVERY ORGANIC ENTITY IS A GESTALT

It is a major achievement in the history of psychology that it was psychologists who first formulated in an exact fashion certain constitutive properties of organic systemic entities and clearly established the methods for their analysis. Gestalt perception is indeed a virtually classic case of an organic entity. In addition, it was the attempted analysis of this phenomenon which demonstrated to research workers the unreliability of the then prevailing atomistic analytical approach. The methods of reflection and application which were developed for the analysis of the Gestalt within the framework of classical Gestalt psychology proved to be effectively applicable to other organic systemic entities as well. However, this led one to forget that the Gestalt is exclusively a perceptive phenomenon and as such represents no more than a *special case* of an organic entity and is *definitely not* equivalent to *the* entity in general. Very many Gestalt psychologists, even Wolfgang Köhler himself, are inclined to straightforward equation of the concepts of the entity and the Gestalt – take, for example, Köhler's concept of the 'physical Gestalt'. But whereas Köhler limits himself to the demonstration of Gestalt criteria where they are *really* present in other types of system, other authors only too often postulate quite dogmatically that any organic entity must *ipso facto* possess *all* the typical characteristics of a perceptual Gestalt.[22]

The most pointed formulation of the erroneous extension of Gestalt psychological principles to biological and sociological phenomena is given by H. Werner. I cite him here as a typical representative of a school of thought which is still common among sociologists and ethnological psychologists:

> The attempts to define the intrinsic basic concept of ethnological psychology, that of the structure of governing units, through its component elements (i.e. through synthesis) demonstrates more

clearly than ever before the utter unreliability of this theoretical approach. In every case, it can be shown that the total entity can be constructed in a completely different manner (i.e. that the so-called component elements can be changed) without altering the overall character. Thus, it is not an inherent property of dots that a circle can be made from them, nor is it a property of aggregation of the dots through synthesis. Given components can give rise to widely different figures in the same way that entirely different elements (e.g. crosses rather than dots) can produce the same figure.

These statements are illustrated by an oval composed of round dots, a circle composed of the same dots, and a second circle composed of crosses!

Similarly, it is not a property of individual human 'dots' that they should produce an overall unit of a particular form. Synthesis of individuals never produces a super-individual total entity. Total entities cannot be derived from their elements through mixture or synthesis of any kind. This necessarily gives rise to a transformation of the basis for theoretical analysis, as is reflected for example by a modern trend in ethnological psychology. If a total entity cannot be derived from its component elements, it follows that the total entity can only be explained through itself.

It is always extremely surprising, for a biologist long accustomed to broad application of the method of analysis, when intelligent Gestalt psychologists and sociologists do *not* see that this theoretical approach is no less unreliable and no less obscuring for the study of organic systemic entities than that for which Werner so pointedly reproaches mechanistic atomists. Whilst the latter overlook causal influence of the whole upon its components, the former neglect effects exerted upon the systemic entity by its components. It is completely forgotten that in the external, organic world each 'sub-entity' (to use the far from aesthetic terminology of Gestalt psychologists) *also possesses its own structures.*[23] In the psychology of Gestalt perception, this neglect of the properties adhering to the 'element' matters little, since they in actual fact have only a slight influence upon the character of the entity – the Gestalt. However, the situation corresponding to the extreme case of the Gestalt is certainly *not* represented in every organic systemic entity. The fact that in Gestalt perception the total entity of a melody can be composed of high or low notes from a violin, a xylophone or an organ without altering its immutable Gestalt character, by no means demonstrates that an organic systemic entity can be constructed from 'any given' elements. It is equally impossible to construct an arch from quadratic bricks or to build a rectangular wall with stones hewn to form an arch, and in the same way it is impossible to incorporate jackdaws into the total entity of a bee swarm or bees into that of a jackdaw colony.

I am much more ready to agree to some extent with Werner when he writes: 'A human being, as a member of a governing unit, possesses qualities which he achieves by virtue of his allocation to this total entity and which can only be understood through the nature of this entity,' than when he talks of 'human dots' which can supposedly aggregate to produce any given form of total entity. But even this statement must *not* be extended to imply that the individual acquires *all* of these 'qualities which can only be understood through the nature of this entity' only as a direct result of his individual life within the society. There are very many qualities of an individual which can indeed only be 'understood' through the structure of the total entity, but which the individual possesses as innate, inherited features and not as traditionally transmitted acquisitions. The individual possesses such qualities by virtue of his membership of a given *species* and not as a result of chance membership of a particular society. It is obvious that the form of a stone hewn for inclusion in an arch can only be understood from the plan of the archway. In fact, the arch can be 'understood' in a *teleological* sense without prior understanding of the form of the stones and without realization of the manner in which their form influences that of the total entity.

However, inductive natural scientists are concerned not only with teleological but also with *causal* understanding. Man owes his *power* over material objects to causal understanding! One can revel in teleological considerations of the wonderful entirety of organic systems, and one can actually achieve a certain degree of intuitive 'understanding' of them. But this type of understanding does not provide one with the means for combating even the smallest disruption threatening the function of a given systemic entity. Nobody would deny that the social structure of mankind today represents a fundamentally disrupted functional entity, and nobody *can* deny that elimination of the disruption requires *causal* understanding of both the entity and its disturbances. To return to the above simile: One can recognize the purpose of the arch without realizing the form of the stones, but one cannot *repair* it without such realization! In inductive research, finalistic and causal understanding must always go hand-in-hand. Active pursuit of a given goal is fundamentally impossible without causal understanding. On the other hand, causal analysis would not fulfil its function if human analysts were not to pursue such goals. Thus, causal analysis does not represent a form of 'materialism' blind to values in the moralistic sense, but rather a great service to the ultimate finality of organic processes.

When successfully applied, it provides us with the possibility to intercept and rectify where human values are threatened and where purely teleological observers of total entities can only lay their hands in their laps and helplessly mourn the collapsing 'entity'.[24]

Any *unidirectional* attempt at scientific understanding of a genuinely *reciprocal* causal relationship, as is usually present between components and total entity of an organic system, involves a methodological mistake which is principally analogous with that for which we criticize the 'atomistic' mechanists! It is extremely paradoxical that just this breach of the rules of inductive research should be committed by members of a school which is always producing the term 'entity.'[24]

What has been said would be thoroughly justified even in a case where the organic systems are 'entities' in the ideal sense, i.e. when they include no components which are incorporated in the plastic machinery of reciprocal causal relationships as virtually fixed inclusions or skeletal elements, affecting the form and performance of the total entity but themselves unaffected (or affected to a negligible degree) by the entity. But since, as we shall soon see, such 'entity-independent elements' play a vital rôle in the construction of *any* organism and *any* society of organisms, the theoretical approach of the mechanists (both Behaviourists and reflexologists) is actually *less* misleading, and in a certain sense more appropriate to an understanding of entities, than that of the cited observers of total entities. One-way causal relationships extending from the component to the whole *do* sometimes exist, and atomists commit no methodological error as long as their investigations are confined to such causal chains. *There is, however, no such thing as a one-way causal chain extending from the systemic entity to its components.* Postulation of such effects is a fiction which, for specific reasons which cannot be fully discussed here, is not greatly damaging in the psychology of Gestalt perception, but which can become a serious obstacle to the investigation of objective organic systems.

For several reasons, it is necessary here to consider the concept associated with the term 'entity' in inductive biological research. Firstly, this is necessary for a better understanding of what must straightaway be said about the rôle played by the entity-independent component in the mechanism of an organic system. Secondly, the nature of the entity dictates both the methods which must be employed in its causal analysis and the criticism which must be directed, from a methodological standpoint, at the great mechanistic schools. We shall return to this criticism in the third chapter and in the second section of this paper, which is concerned with neglect of innate, species-specific behaviour patterns.

2. THE NATURE OF ORGANIC SYSTEMATIC ENTITIES AND THEIR ANALYSIS ON A BROAD FRONT

If the entity is defined as a system in which every part is related to all others through reciprocal causal influence, as a 'regulative system of universal amboceptor causal relationship' (O. Koehler), this concept is freed from any metaphysical – in particular, vitalistic – formulation. Even the most convinced mechanist and 'atomist' must admit that the structural mechanisms of many organic entities represent systems of this kind, and must accept the correctness of certain methodological prescriptions governing analytical research which are determined by the nature of such entities. In a system in which there is a universal reciprocal relationship between all components (e.g. the system of internal secretory glands of man), it is fundamentally impossible to *isolate* experimentally – or even theoretically – an individual component and to consider it separately. Both the isolated components and the residue of the entity robbed of this component are converted by this (experimental or theoretical) operation to something entirely different from that which they represented in their previous relationship. The rôle played by each individual part in the mechanism of the whole can only be understood *simultaneously* with those played by all other components involved in the given entity. To quote an extremely rough-and-ready example: If we attempt to understand the function of a combustion motor, we must necessarily begin with the consideration of a component. But we will only fully understand the function of a given component such as the carburettor when we have realized how the pistons suck away the gas mixture from this element. Our understanding of the suction action of the piston requires that we should know how it is moved by the fly-wheel, the crank-shaft and connecting rod during the three passive strokes; how the cam-shaft and the valves function, etc. Finally, we will only understand that the fly-wheel possesses kinetic energy which moves the piston during the suction stroke when we have also grasped the nature and function of the carburettor among all the other members of the system. *The components of an entity can only be understood simultaneously*.

This peculiarity of systemic entities gives rise to certain conditions governing the *method* of analysis – a method which was clearly established some time ago by a number of Gestalt psychologists who were not entangled in a vitalistic/teleological conception of the entity, for example Matthaei and Metzger. Analysis must necessarily begin with a consideration of the overall mechanism of *all* components, thus providing a survey of the number and nature of the incorporated parts. Penetration into individual details must then be achieved from as many different directions as possible. The knowledge of each individual detail must be pursued at the same tempo as that of all other details until the overall mechanism of the entity presents itself in a comprehensive and comprehensible form. Matthaei aptly compares this process, which can be characterized as analysis on a broad front, with the approach of a painter, who first makes a general rough sketch of the subject and then develops all of the component parts at the same pace. The painting is thus, at all stages of its development, a depiction of the total entity of the subject, despite the fact that this development represents continual extension into ever finer details. Analysis on a broad front is obligate in all cases where the investigated object possesses the character of an entity. This underlies our criticism of the method employed by the great mechanistic schools of psychology and behavioural research. All commit the methodological error of voluntarily separating components or component functions from the most integrated of all organic systems – the central nervous systems of higher animals and man – and investigating them in complete isolation from the total entity. Even worse, they attempt to re-synthesize the entity, using as the 'element' an individual component process which they have managed to separate and analyse as a chance result of favourable technical conditions.

3. THE RELATIVELY ENTITY-INDEPENDENT COMPONENT

By no means all organic systems are covered by the definition of an entity as a system of *universal* amboceptor causal relationships! Simple examples from embryology such as the 'mosaic embryo' of ascidians, where two halves of the developing animal separated at the two-cell stage each literally give rise to a half-ascidian, prove convincingly and incontrovertibly how little one is justified in generalizing the relationships between entity and component evident in Gestalt psychology and regarding these as automatically applicable to the properties of all organic systems. There is surely not one single living organism which, as an entity, represents a unified system similar to that of the sector of the central nervous system of higher vertebrates and man which integrates sensory data to produce Gestalt perception! There are in the structural mechanism of every living organism innumerable components which, in a literal, anatomical sense, represent 'parts' or 'structural elements', to the extent that they occur as relatively fixed, immutable inclusions in the amboceptor causal reticulum of the overall system. Even in cases where such components in themselves possess the character of typical organic systemic entities, they can be treated as genuine 'elements' of the organic system in analysis. This is because they are

involved in a *one-way*, and not reciprocal amboceptor, causal relationship with the overall entity. In other words, these elements – at least in
the fully-formed organism – are not considerably affected either in form
or function by the entity, whilst they themselves have a decisive influence in the form and function of the entity. Such elements, which
exhibit a predominantly one-way causal relationship with the total
entity, will be termed *relatively entity-independent components*. It is
necessary to incorporate the word 'relatively' in the definition of these
components of an entity, because there are all conceivable transitional
stages between such components, which are absolutely independent of
the entity with which they have a one-way causal relationship, and
others which exhibit a normal amboceptor reciprocal relationship with
the entity. Examples for the extreme case of a really *absolute* entity-
independent component are difficult to find. Even the famous ascidian
half-embryo is not, exactly speaking, completely entity-independent,
since the ultimate half-ascidian which emerges is covered with epidermis
along the plane of separation, which would be absent in the complete
ascidian. Presumably, the only absolutely entity-independent components are *dead* parts of organic systems, and even these only become
so when fully formed. Cuticular formations, such as the completely fixed
external skeleton of fully-formed insects, and inorganic inclusions, such
as the spines of sponges and other organisms, can be taken as examples.
Even a solid skeletal element such as a human bone is far from being
absolutely entity-independent. For example, a human being can suffer
from softening of the bones. Nevertheless, the causal chains which pass
from the entity of the organism to such a bone are so limited in number
that they can be confidently neglected in the investigation of the function
of the skeleton and the effects of its structures on the muscular functions
and locomotor performance of the overall system. In the same way, we
would not be committing a noteworthy methodological error in investigating a short ligament reflex if we should initially neglect the fact that
the higher sectors of the central nervous system do actually exert a
minor effect upon elicitation of the reflex. (For example, elicitation of
the reflex is considerably facilitated by functional suspension of the
pyramidal system.)

It is for this very reason that the discovery of a relatively entity-
independent component, in the immeasurably complex causal reticulum
of the organic system, offers such a welcome opportunity for the operation of causal analysis – *such components can be isolated without introducing
a considerable methodological error*. For the same reason, rigid structure
also presents the first archimedian fixed point for analysis in research
and instruction. For example, every anatomy book begins with a description of the skeleton. Thus, in the investigation of animal and human

behaviour, causal analysis legitimately set out from functions associated with invariable structures of the central nervous system. Investigation of the reflex process became the crystallization centre of the entire development of physiology of the nervous system. The discovery of the conditioned response gave the impulse to the origin of the entire Pavlovian reflexologist school. Finally, the discovery of the endogenous-automatic motor pattern, which is far more entity-independent than the reflex – let alone the conditioned reflex, sparked off the development of our own research field, that of the study of comparative behaviour.

The analytical possibilities which are presented by the discovery of a relatively entity-independent component must nevertheless not obscure the fact that the method of isolated investigation is only permissible for entity-independent components *and must be rigidly restricted to the limited component area of the process concerned.* Any such component behaves to some extent like an inorganic inclusion in the amboceptor causal reticulum of the organic system. (The most completely independent components are, after all, literal inorganic inclusions!) The researcher must at all times be prepared to *return to* the otherwise obligatory holistic method of analysis on a broad front, as soon as he extends beyond the boundaries of the fixed included element and is once more concerned with a network of reciprocal causal relationships.

Our criticism of the great mechanistic schools, of Behaviourism and of the Pavlovian reflexologist school is founded on this very requirement. Both have discovered a relatively entity-independent element of behaviour – in essence the same in both cases: the conditioned response – and have achieved great and lasting research successes on the basis of this discovery. But both have, in the course of these successes, sacrificed their readiness to return to the tedious and demanding method of analysis on a broad front. They hung on to the isolating 'atomic' method long after they had extended beyond the limits of applicability of the laws they had discovered. Consequently, in a scientifically utterly unacceptable manner, they have dogmatically raised the discovered element to the exclusive explanatory principle of the entity of behaviour. In the second part of this paper, we shall be concerned with the way in which this particular explanatory monism of the great mechanistic schools – particularly Behaviourism – has prevented or delayed the discovery of certain *innate* action and response norms of animals and man. This blindness, as we shall see, is even today operative against recognition of the presence of innate, species-specific behaviour patterns in sociology, which is influenced by Behaviourism.

Different organic systems exhibit different degrees of incorporation of entity-independent components. A distinction analogous to that made by Spemann between 'mosaic embryos' and 'regulative embryos' in embryological development can be made quite generally and from many different points of view between different organic systems. To take two extreme examples from behavioural theory: When a sea-urchin is attacked by a starfish – its principal enemy – it will simultaneously flee and protect itself with its poisonous pincers. These entirely apt and adaptive behaviour patterns of the entire animal are based on a mosaic co-operation of its individual organs – ambulacral feet, spines and pedicellariae. There is no integrating activity of the central nervous system to co-ordinate the individual performances of the organs to form an entity. Instead, each individual organ is an individually operating 'reflex person', as J. von Uexküll puts it. Each ambulacral foot and each spine independently possesses the property of heading away from the stimulus source of the chemical stimulus of the starfish mucus, and, in addition, the property of subordination to and 'participation' in the locomotor direction dictated by movement of the entire animal. On the other hand, every pedicellaria bearing poisonous pincers orients itself towards the stimulus with pincers open. These response patterns are exhibited in exactly the same way by the isolated organ and the adaptive overall response is truly a mosaic. It can be synthesized in the real sense from its 'elements', for example, by joining isolated pieces of a spine- and pedicellaria-bearing sea-urchin with a piece of string. In his succinct manner, von Uexküll has summarized this state of affairs with the statement: 'When a dog runs, it moves its legs; when a sea-urchin runs, it is moved by its legs.' Although it is also possible – and therefore necessary – to extract certain relatively entity-independent components (in the form of endogenous automatisms – see later) from the running of a dog and to analyse these quite legitimately in isolation, there is no doubt that the dog's central nervous system is an extremely highly integrated system with at least approximately universal amboceptor causal relationships. The attempt to synthesize the dog's running from individual reflexes and automatisms of its legs to give a purposive overall activity is doomed from the outset. The central nervous system, which integrates overall activities of higher animals and man into units, comes *relatively* close to the ideal definition of an entity as a system of universal amboceptor causal relationships. Apart from this, it is doubtless very similar in structure and performance to the system which integrates sensory data to Gestalt perceptions and which exhibits the most universal amboceptor causal relationships among all known systems of the universe. For this reason, it is permissible and productive to carry out a *careful* comparison and transference of known principles valid in Gestalt psychology to the performance of closely related and similarly structured central nervous organ systems.

On the other hand, it is obviously complete nonsense to expect to find a systemic character related to that of the perceptual Gestalt in cases where there is no real integrating apparatus which operates, as with Gestalt perception, to provide an abundance of amboceptor causal relationships. Thus, when Alverdes takes part against von Uexküll's conception of the 'reflex republic' of the sea-urchin, stating that this denies 'the fiction of systemic character', the misunderstanding is based on the opinion that systemic character is a fiction. This is far from true where an entity is truly present, representing a quite real phenomenon. But the question of the extent to which systemic character is present is not one to be solved by metaphysical speculation and dogmatic mis-use of a motto, but one to be decided through patient inductive investigation of each individual case.

It is a basic necessity for the entire application of causal analysis of any organic system that one should correctly decide how much it is composed from a network of reciprocal causal relationships and how much from relatively entity-independent components. The result of the attempted analysis is quite simply *wrong* when reciprocal causal relationships are treated as one-way phenomena, and *vice versa*. Extraction and isolation of relatively entity-independent components is just as *obligatory* as is the method of analysis of a broad front for studying an amboceptor causal reticulum. This fact must be established at the outset.

Over-estimation of the primacy of the entity over its components and under-estimation of the relatively entity-independent component has developed from a mistaken generalization of Gestalt psychology principles and is widespread in the entire field of psychology. In addition to this, there is – particularly in sociology – a neglect of certain very special entity-independent components of animal and human behaviour, and in my opinion this plays an extremely inhibiting rôle. This has quite different causes, which we shall now consider.

III Neglect of innate species-specific behaviour patterns
THE EFFECTS OF THE MECHANIST-VITALIST CONTROVERSY

1. The overestimation of effects exerted by the entity upon the component, discussed in the first section of this paper, is derived from false generalization of Gestalt psychological tenets. The *underestimation* and *neglect* of certain fixed innate action and response norms of animals and man, which is now to be discussed, is the result of a somewhat more complex and extremely interesting situation in the philosophical sphere. This we shall examine more closely.

It has actually been recognized ever since the Middle Ages that there exist innate, and innately species-preserving, behaviour patterns. The scholastics themselves were concerned with such patterns and left behind them, as a dubious heritage, the current term 'instincts'. Even in our colloquial language, the expression 'instinct' has established itself, in actual fact retaining the scholastic concept of a *supernatural factor* which itself is neither accessible to, nor requiring, a causal explanation. On the other hand, this term is employed as a pseudo-explanation for any behaviour pattern which is evidently fitted for preservation of the species, and yet whose species-preserving function cannot be explained on the basis of a mental accomplishment of the type common in our own experience. Thus, 'instinct' has been from the very beginning one of those treacherous words which fit in just nicely where concepts are lacking! Or, to state this more exactly, the nature of the scholastic concept of instinct is such that it represents a supernatural pseudo-explanation for natural processes. This peculiarity of the instinct concept, which is so obstructive in comparative behavioural research, had the undesirable consequence that the innate species-specific action and response patterns which it was supposed to explain were thrust at a very early stage into the focus of a dispute between two schools of natural philosophy – vitalism and mechanism.

As has already been explained, the major errors of the great mechanist schools stem from clearly identifiable methodological errors, which are based upon their blindness to the nature of an organic entity as a system of virtually universal reciprocal causal relationships. However, the fact that both Behaviourism and the Pavlovian reflexologist school have produced such amazing misinterpretations and pseudo-explanations with respect to these innate species-specific behaviour patterns, is to be explained from a second source: the antagonism towards the teaching of the vitalists, who were particularly vociferous on this point. In their statements about innate behaviour patterns, the two opposing schools of thought were forced into quite untenable extreme positions, which neither of them would have adopted if unaware of the views of the opposing side! Whereas the vitalists made the holistic Gestalt of organic process a supernatural factor in the face of which any attempt at causal analysis would be sacrilege, the mechanists almost consciously blinded themselves to the nature of entities and produced an extreme, methodologically erroneous atomism, whose most harmful effect was the gestation of the explanatory monisms discussed above. Whereas the vitalists made a wonder out of the purposive nature of animal behaviour, by explaining this as the immediate attribute of a supernatural, entelechial factor, the mechanists avoided considering purposivity – even the important, indisputable fact of species-preserving purpose. With some behaviouristic authors, this has particularly given rise to a situation where *pathological* behaviour patterns are confused in an extremely misleading manner with physiological, natural lyadaptive patterns.[25] If the supernatural factor of the vitalists – whether it be called vital force, holistic or directive factor, entelechy, instinct, or whatever – in the final analysis amounted to *soul*, then the mechanists were concerned with 'psychology without soul'. They pursued this even in cases where, with clear-cut separation between objective and subjective aspects, self-analysis can produce extremely valuable conclusions about specific behaviour patterns, and where rejection of introspection consequently represents the worst of all crimes against the spirit of inductive natural science – namely the rejection of knowledge!

But by far the worst influence of this 'extremifying' mutual relationship between vitalists and mechanists was exerted in the field which especially concerns us here – the investigation of innate species-specific behaviour patterns. These presented no problems at all for the vitalists: As with other properties of living organisms which are characterized by a particular, harmonic holistic nature and conspicuous finality – such as heredity, embryogeny and restitution – innate species-specific behaviour patterns represented for the vitalists an ideal case of an immediate product of supernatural life force, neither requiring nor accessible to natural explanation. Johannes Müller, who – with the typical dualistic nature of an idealistically oriented natural scientist – simultaneously became the father of causal analysis in physiology and of vitalism, quite clearly regarded 'the instincts' as an object of the latter field rather than the former! At one point – in a publication which is unfortunately only known to me through quotations – he speaks of examples of the immediate influence of the 'vital force'. He first explains how an embryo which is still lacking a central nervous system can nevertheless develop as an entity, how organs for later use by the imago are formed in an appropriate manner in the butterfly pupa, how the spinal cord is shortened in correspondence with reduction of the tail in the metamorphosis of the tadpole to a frog, etc. And then, in the same vein, he adds that it is a similar, unconscious, organizing, entity-producing force which is operative in the instincts of insects! Since this veteran master of physiological research (whose investigation of the reflex was to represent one of the most important foundations of the later, causal-analytical study of central nervous processes) classed the 'instincts' with causally inexplicable 'wonders', why should not later vitalists, with their much lesser causal-analytical talent and their far lesser dependence upon causality, abdicate from the search for a natural explanation. Even as late as 1940, Bierens de Haan wrote, 'We observe instinct, but we do not explain it!'

For the mechanists of the opposing side, innate species-specific behavioural systems represented – because of their undeniable species-preserving function and their relatively holistic nature – an object which offered little chance of success to their atomistic approach and therefore little stimulus for research. Since the vitalists made so much fuss about the 'instincts', it was virtually a matter for scorn among mechanists even to speak about them. The few reflexologists who permitted themselves statements about innate behaviour patterns limited themselves to the opportune explanation that they consisted of chains of unconditioned reflexes. The behaviourists, on the other hand – with Watson at their head – simply denied the existence of extensive innate motor patterns. The complete untenability of these views could never come to light because no reflexologist and no behaviourist ever came face-to-face with the performance of an extended, highly differentiated chain of species-specific innate behaviour patterns. The research method of both large mechanistic schools, as is well known, was restricted to experiments in which a *change* is made in the environmental conditions affecting the organism and the *response* of the animal to this change is recorded. The presupposition that the reflex and the conditioned reflex are the only major 'elements' of all animal and human behaviour determined a quite specific, scarcely varying experimental set-up. Because of this, the investigated central nervous system to a certain extent had no opportunity at all to exhibit the fact that it can also perform processes other than the response to the operation of external stimuli. As a result of exclusive application of this methodology, the opinion that the operation of the central nervous system was restricted to the registration and answering of external stimuli *had to* become stronger.

Since none of the mechanists ever looked to see what animals do *when left to themselves*, it was impossible for any one of them to notice that they will in fact do quite a lot spontaneously (i.e. without the operation of external stimuli). In this way, the entire phenomenon of spontaneity of certain behaviour patterns – which was so extremely important in the recognition of the physiological peculiarity of the so-called *instinctive motor pattern* (see later) – remained hidden from the very research workers who wanted to learn something about the physiology, the causal relationships, of animal and human behaviour. On the one side, the vitalistic-teleological behavioural investigators did in fact *see* quite well the spontaneity of certain behaviour patterns, but took this very effect as a particular immediate effect of a supernatural factor, whose causal analysis and explanation was anathema. They did not – as was justified – employ the demonstrable spontaneity of certain motor patterns as an argument against the reflex-chain hypotheses of the reflexologists. Instead, without any justification at all, they took this as an argument against the assumption of *any* physiological-causal explicability of behaviour. If this truly tragic, almost tragicomic, dilemma in which vitalists and mechanists have involved themselves is contemporized, one is reminded of a quotation from Goethe's *Faust*. 'What one does not know is just what one needs, and what one does know is of no use.' Those who could have drawn reasonable physiological conclusions from the fact of spontaneity were quite simply unable to see them, and those who saw them were irreparably prevented by idealistic prejudices from drawing the proper inferences!

For all of these reasons, it was not only the existence of spontaneous, automatic-rhythmic stimulus-production in the central nervous system which remained undiscovered, but also the wide and fruitful field offered to inductive natural science by innate, species-specific behaviour patterns. These lay completely untouched as a no-man's-land between the front lines of two dogmatically exaggerated and opposing schools of thought. It is no wonder that this therefore became a 'playground for infertile philosophical speculation', as Max Hartmann put it!

2. THE LATE INTRODUCTION OF COMPARATIVE PHYLOGENETIC METHOD INTO BEHAVIOURAL RESEARCH

The late discovery of innate, species-specific action and response patterns – the demonstration of whose fundamental significance represents a major aim of this article – does have other reasons, however. There was not only a lack of researchers combining open recognition of the spontaneity of certain behaviour patterns with a healthy desire for their causal explanation. Above all, the first and indispensable prerequisite for permitting behavioural research to become a genuine inductive branch of natural science was missing: no more and no less than the idiographically and systematically assembled, hypothesis-free *basis for induction*! In the first place, there was a lack of investigators well acquainted with the intellectual and applied methods of inductive natural science, and in particular with those methods suited to study of entities on a broad front, who could accomplish the Herculean task left untouched by the vitalists and mechanists. There were no research workers prepared to carry out the very modest and yet very important, the very infantile and yet scientific task of conducting (without presupposition) observation of animal behaviour, quite simply 'to see just what there is'! Neither a reflexologist nor a behaviourist, nor yet a human psychologist, and still less one of the vitalistic instinct theoreticians, would have set himself the extremely painstaking and demanding task of becoming acquainted with the *entirety* of the observable behaviour of just one single animal species. It would have been unthinkable to make an inventory of the action and response norms typical of a species and to investigate the relationship of these to the natural environment. Alongside the truly penetrating experiments of the mechanists and the apparently penetrating speculation of the vitalists, this task appeared to be quite unimportant and scarcely 'scientific'. That is how the first task of all inductive natural science – straightforward idiography – all too easily appears on superficial examination.

H. S. Jennings was the first who regarded it as a worthy task for a researcher to observe and describe in all its details the behaviour of animals left to themselves. He was also one of the first to recognize quite clearly that the behaviour patterns of an animal species do not exhibit unlimited variation; the species simply 'possess' a restricted number of action and response norms in the same way that it possesses morphological structures with a particular form. By working towards the concept of the *system of actions* as the entirety of behaviour patterns possessed by a specific animal species, Jennings introduced a holistically appropriate method of study involving the investigation of the behaviour of a species as that which it really is – namely as an organic systemic entity.

Jennings was thus the proponent of genuinely unprejudiced and exact idiography of animal behaviour. It was C. O. Whitman and O. Heinroth who systematically collated action systems of related animal species and thus became pioneers of *comparative behavioural research* in the phylogenetic sense. In very many branches of biological research, the discovery of a *suitable object* has given rise to an independent research field because the properties of this object dictated a specific *method*, which itself determined the direction in which further research would be conducted. The classic example of this process is provided by the modern study of genetics. This originated from the discovery of the extremely simple borderline case where the parents of a hybrid differ from one another in only one single hereditary character. Right up to the present day, further developments in genetics are governed by the method dictated by the nature of the suitable object – hybridization.[26]

In comparative behavioural research, the position is only different to the extent that the method characteristic of this branch of research was there *first* and that this then led to the discovery of the 'suitable object', which determined the path of future research. This object, which made possible the pursuit of causal analysis in a quite specific direction, could in fact only be noticed and appreciated through the application of the comparative phylogenetic method. It is here that one must also seek the reason why the phenomenon which became the crystallization centre of an entire research field was only discovered so *late*. The existence of specific innate *motor co-ordination patterns*, occurring in the same manner in all individuals of a species and characteristic of species, genera, orders, even of classes and yet higher systematic categories, was fundamentally only open to discovery by researchers who described and ordered the action systems of phylogenetically related animal species side-by-side, using the same methodology as that employed with morphological structures in phylogenetically comparative systematics.

3. THE PHYSIOLOGICAL PECULIARITY OF ENDOGENOUS-AUTOMATIC MOTOR PATTERNS

The discovery and investigation of these innate, species-specific motor patterns provides a classic example of the necessary organic process in the development of genuine inductive natural science whereby a preliminary, unprejudiced and descriptive 'idiographic' stage leads on to a 'systematic' stage of ordering according to similarities and differences between characters, and this in turn leads to a causally explanatory and principle-seeking 'nomothetic' stage. This also provides convincing proof of the indispensable necessity for the broadest possible knowledge of concrete individual facts, collected through *unprejudiced* observation and termed the *'inductive basis'* of a natural science.[27]

The first great discovery, which can more-or-less be described as the birth of comparative behavioural research, was doubtless the identification of a genuine phylogenetic *homology* between innate, species-specific motor patterns of related animal species. C. O. Whitman and O. Heinroth were both highly trained and extremely knowledgeable comparative morphologists, and by way of a lucky – but far from chance – coincidence they also possessed the extremely broad mass knowledge of behaviour patterns of a group of related animals which is the prerequisite for phylogenetic comparison. Thus it was that they first made – independently of one another – the simple, but extremely fruitful, discovery that there are motor patterns of constant form which are performed in exactly the same manner by every healthy individual of a species. These represent characteristic features not only for the individual species, but (just like many 'conservative' morphological characters) also for even the broadest groups of related forms. In other words, they discovered motor patterns whose distribution and occurrence in the animal kingdom intimately resembles that of *organs*. One can thus safely assume that the developmental history of these patterns during speciation has followed the same lines as that of organs and organ characteristics. Therefore, their phylogenetic age can be determined with the same methodological means as that of morphological characters, and it follows that the concept of phyletic homology can be applied to the former in just the same way as to the latter. Both researchers demonstrated this fact by employing suitable characters of such motor patterns as taxonomic characters in the reconstruction of phylogenetic relationships within a given group of related animals. The end-product was then compared with conclusions obtained from the fine systematic evaluation of morphological characters. The unqualified agreement between the results convincingly demonstrated the correctness of their initial belief, which had been summarized by Whitman in 1898: 'Instincts and organs are to be studied from the common viewpoint of phyletic descent'.

The newly discovered facts demonstrated equally convincingly the utter untenability of the ideas which had been previously developed with respect to the nature of so-called 'instinctive' behaviour, both on the vitalistic-teleological side and on the mechanistic side. In the view of the vitalists, 'the instinct' was a 'directive factor' fundamentally immune to causal explanation, and the behaviour determined by instinct was necessarily characterized by the typical, plastic variability of all *purposive* behaviour. Thus, it was actually quite logical when representatives of 'purposive psychology' quite simply equated the species-preserving function of species-specific innate behaviour patterns with a purpose towards which the animal subject strives. On the mechanistic side, by contrast, there were – as already mentioned – *two* schools of thought. That of the behaviourists stated that complex, innate behaviour patterns are just as much figments of the imagination as innate 'goals' and that the species-preserving appropriate form of so-called instinctive behaviour is only *apparently innate* – in reality it is only acquired in the individual lifetime of every organism through trial and error (Watson). The Pavlovian reflexologist school admitted the existence of highly differentiated and lengthy innate motor sequences, but explained them as chain assemblies of unconditioned reflexes. Quite early on, the correct objection was raised by *purposive psychologists*, above all McDougall, that the *spontaneity* of many 'instinctive' behaviour patterns and their obvious great independence of external stimuli cannot be explained through the reflex principle.

Neither Whitman nor Heinroth have ever uttered even a supposition about the physiological nature of species-specific innate motor co-ordination patterns. Whitman still referred to them quite simply as 'instincts', whilst Heinroth avoided this term and spoke of 'innate, species-specific drive-governed patterns' (*angeborene, arteigene Triebhandlung*). And, of course, neither author at that time conceptually differentiated such patterns from innate behaviour patterns of another kind, which really do have a reflex nature (e.g. particularly orienting responses or taxes). But, in presenting an unprejudiced and hypothesis-free description and systematic order of the motor patterns concerned, both authors, as a result of their finely developed systematic intuition, involuntarily achieved an extremely remarkable feat. It was in fact later discovered that virtually all the motor patterns which they employed as taxonomic characters were of a kind which are based upon pure endogenous automatisms and are scarcely bound up with reflex processes. Above all, this applies to the courtship motor patterns of various birds, which were repeatedly taken into particular account by the two research workers. This collation of innate, species-specific motor patterns, at first a purely systematic affair, had the inevitable result that they obviously exhibited a number of common peculiarities which almost cried out for a physiological explanation.

The main fact which struck home was an unexpected correlation between spontaneity and individual invariability of species-specific motor patterns. According to the vitalistic-teleological view, a spontaneous, goal-directed behaviour pattern aimed at a specific 'drive goal' must *ipso facto* have a constant biological end-result and yet exhibit variability in the motor co-ordinations involved. According to the reflex-chain theory, on the other hand, a chain of reflexly co-ordinated individual movements determined in a rigidly innate fashion throughout its entire length cannot exhibit spontaneity. But in reality it was *just these* behaviour patterns with an overall innate, species-specific character which exhibited a particular, extremely peculiar tendency towards spontaneous eruption independent of external stimuli. The innate releasing mechanism, which in most cases acts as a 'response lock' ensuring selective response of innate, species-specific behaviour patterns in specific environmental situations, does indeed prove to be reliably reactive, but the motor pattern itself exhibits extremely peculiar behaviour which cannot at all be explained through the reflex principle. The longer the period in which the given motor pattern is not elicited, the greater the drop in the threshold level for the eliciting stimuli. Finally, in the extreme case, the pattern will erupt explosively, in the absence of demonstrable external stimuli, as a so-called *vacuum activity*. Naturally, in such a case the species-preserving 'purpose' of the pattern is in no way fulfilled.

Closer examination of the phenomena of threshold-lowering, vacuum activities, and above all response-specific habituation with raising of the stimulus threshold, led to the concept of accumulation of response-specific excitation continually produced by the organism and used up in performance of the motor pattern. This hypothesis, developed at first purely as a conceptual model, proved to be extensively accurate in the light of results stemming from an entirely different quarter – nervous physiology. Nowadays, we know from the investigations of E. von Holst, P. Weiss and others that innate, species-specific motor patterns are not based on conditioned and unconditioned reflexes, like so many other behaviour patterns of animals and man. *They are based instead upon a different elementary function of the central nervous system*, namely upon a spontaneous, automatic-rhythmic *production* of stimuli – something which was previously only known from the stimulus-production centres of the heart. Both the production and the co-ordination of the transmitted motor impulses are, as von Holst convincingly demonstrated, quite independent of centripetal nervous pathways. This is therefore not a reflex phenomenon.

The demonstration of the part played by a previously unknown basic function of the nervous system in the overall behaviour of higher animals, and doubtless of man as well, represents the most important result of comparative behavioural research to date. On the one hand, this presents us with a satisfying, causalistic physiological explanation for the spontaneity of so many animal and human behaviour patterns, which was repeatedly employed by vitalists as an argument not only against the reflex-chain theory of the mechanists, but also against the general assumption of possible causalistic physiological explanation of behaviour. As a result, vitalism is driven from a position which has always been fiercely – and previously successfully – defended. On the other hand, the demonstration of endogenous, automatic-rhythmic stimulus-production destroys once-and-for-all the atomistic explanatory monism of the mechanist schools, which regarded the unconditioned and conditioned reflex as the only explanatory principles for all animal and human behaviour. The significance of the physiological autonomy of endogenous automatisms for human sociology, which represents one of the major topics of this paper, will be dealt with later on. But in order to give some idea of this significance, suffice it to say in advance that, for example, the phenomenon referred to as the aggressive drive in depth psychology represents with almost overwhelming probability the effect of endogenous production of action-specific excitation.[28]

Through their great phylogenetic conservatism, their independence of external stimuli and above all the irrepressability of their stimulus-production and the resulting drive, endogenous automatisms are extremely self-sufficient systems which are only very slightly and indirectly open to causal influence by the organic entity in which they are incorporated. They represent an extreme case of the phenomenon described in the first part of this paper as relatively entity-independent components. Since they without doubt play a quite considerable part in human behaviour, and quite particularly – as will be shown – in the realm of social behaviour, complete neglect of their existence in sociology and ethnological psychology leads to major erroneous conclusions. Since the physiological peculiarity of endogenous-automatic behaviour patterns, and their significance for the overall behaviour of higher animals and man, has only been recognized with any clarity for a number of decades, and since these results were achieved entirely by zoologists and not by human psychologists or sociologists, knowledge of them has not yet penetrated into the circles of these latter researchers. It is only in child psychology that individual research workers are beginning to concern themselves systematically with the investigation of the endogenous automatisms of man (A. Peiper).

4. INNATE RELEASING MECHANISMS

This discussion of individually invariable, innate and species-specific action and response norms, which in their capacity as relatively entity-independent components of animal and human behaviour demand special methodological consideration in sociology, would be incomplete without treatment of a further process which plays a rôle in the social behaviour of the higher animals and man almost as important as that played by endogenous-automatic stimulus-production processes. This process is the so-called *innate releasing mechanism* or *innate releasing schema*. The study of endogenous-automatic motor patterns and their releasing mechanisms was – as will be shortly described in detail – only possible in its natural context. The discovery of endogenous production of a response-specific form of excitation, which accumulates during periods of no response and is used up by the performance of the motor pattern, resulted – as already mentioned – predominantly from a quantifying study of the behaviour of *threshold values* of eliciting stimuli during rest and performance, during accumulation and expenditure of response-specific energy. However, lowering of the threshold value can only be identified as such when a regular relationship between stimulus strength and response intensity has been successfully determined in an exact manner. As far as the response of *intact* organisms to stimuli is concerned, this had so far never been achieved in a satisfying manner in any branch of psychology or behavioural research. The first became possible through the simultaneous and functionally correlated investigation of two processes which are causally-physiologically entirely different from one another – the performance of the endogenous-automatic motor pattern itself and the process of its elicitation through specific innate mechanisms. This is a typical example of analysis conducted on a broad front.

What we can *see* as criterion for the efficacy of an external stimulus, and all that we can quantitatively record, is always the *intensity* of the elicited response.[29] Indeed, for specific reasons too complex to be discussed here, the intensity can be determined with great exactitude for some endogenous-automatic motor patterns, but it is in every case determined by *two* factors – the quantitative efficacy of the external stimulus situation and by the momentary condition of the internal motivation of the organism for performance of the motor pattern concerned. Thus, a single experiment never produces more than an equation with two unknowns. However, if one determines the inner response motivation of the animal with a second experiment, one immediately obtains a constant correlation between the stimuli and their effects. The simplest way of doing this is to present the stimulus, whose efficacity is to be measured, together with the optimal elicitatory stimulus situation, more or less 'to see how much is still there'. Just this method of double quantitative investigation demonstrated, as its most important result, the continual accumulation of specific response motivation already mentioned. At the same time, however, it also enabled us to form some idea of the nature and 'function' of releasing mechanisms.

Without doubt, these innate releasing mechanisms are – in a broad sense – the same as the *unconditioned reflexes* of I. P. Pavlov. However, the main problem of their function is by no means solved by this observation. It is not the nature of the reflex process which is paramount; it is the question of the origin of *selectivity* of the mechanism, which only permits emergence of an appropriate, species-preserving response through operation of a 'key' involving specific, characteristic stimulus combinations. Thus, the problem is not located in the physiology of the reflex itself, but to a certain extent *prior* to this – in the afferent branch. The innate releasing mechanism bears a relationship to the unconditioned reflex very similar to that between perception of a complex quality (with resultant conditioning) and the conditioned response. Innate releasing mechanisms and Gestalt perception are very probably functions of the same central nervous organ system, which processes sensory data to give perception, even though these functions doubtless take place on quite different levels and – as we shall soon see – can exhibit quite considerable physiological differences.

The function of innate releasing mechanisms permits the organism to respond in an appropriate manner, without previous experience of any kind, to the occurrence of specific, biologically relevant stimulus situations. Thus, in the observation of such behaviour, it is a natural assumption that the animal innately possesses 'knowledge' of specific response-eliciting objects (e.g. prey, sexual partner, predator, etc.), in the same way that it can recognize through acquisition response-eliciting conditioning situations. Experiments show that there is no foundation for the immediate assumption that an organism of a given species innately possesses a 'species-specific memory picture', as postulated by C. G. Jung in his theory of the 'archetype'. An enormous amount of observational and experimental material which has accumulated in recent years (Tinbergen, Seitz, Baerends, Kuenen, Ter Pelkwijk, Krätzig, Goethe, Noble, Kitzler, Peters and many others) shows quite convincingly that the innate releasing mechanism – in contrast to a conditioned Gestalt responding to a complex quality – does not respond to the overall total or even a large proportion of the stimuli accompanying a certain relevant situation. Instead, the mechanism selects relatively few of the great number of stimuli and permits these to act as a 'key to the response' (the *sign stimuli* of Tinbergen). These few stimuli are always so constituted that they adequately *characterize* the situation concerned, despite their simplicity and restricted number, such that elicitation of the response at a biologically inappropriate place cannot occur with sufficient frequency to adversely affect preservation of the species. It is just because of this function of simplified character-ization of an object or situation that the releasing mechanisms con-cerned have been termed *innate releasing schemata*. The term *schema* is misleading, to the extent that it easily gives the false impression that the organism innately possesses an overall (even though very simple) *picture* of an object or situation, whereas in reality the releasing mechan-ism never gives rise to more than *one* quite specific response. It is misleading to talk of a releasing schema of 'the sexual partner', of 'the prey', of 'the offspring', and so on, since each of the different responses elicited by one of these objects possesses its own releasing mechanism.

Even these releasing mechanisms, which each elicit just one response, have very little in common with the response to a releasing conditioned Gestalt. If dummy experiments are employed to analyse the simple combination of characters which the object of a given response must possess in order to produce the maximal elicitatory effect, one is repeatedly amazed by the paucity of resemblance to our eyes between the resulting 'optimal' dummy and the natural object of the response. For example, when a female stickleback responds quantitatively and qualitatively in exactly the same way towards a red plasticine sphere, moved in zig-zag fashion, as to a male courting with the 'zig-zag dance' (Leiner), or when a robin fights with a bundle of rust-red feathers of a few centimetres surface area just as with a real rival, the remarkable fact about such responses is that *an organism which is demonstrably capable of Gestalt perception* is not able to distinguish between a crude dummy and the natural object!

The reasonable assumption that the function of innate releasing mechanisms is greatly different from that of the response to acquired Gestalt perception is confirmed when the already simple character combinations of an optimal dummy are further dissected in 'dis-assembling' dummy experiments. This leads to recognition of the remarkable fact that *each individual character* from the total which must be possessed by an optimally eliciting dummy produces *in its own right* a qualitatively identical releasing effect, even though this is quantita-tively smaller. By means of the above-mentioned method of double quantification of stimulus strength and response motivation, it can be exactly demonstrated that the quantitative efficacity of every dummy – including an optimal one – equals the *sum* of the individual efficacities of the constituent characters. This phenomenon, which was first clearly

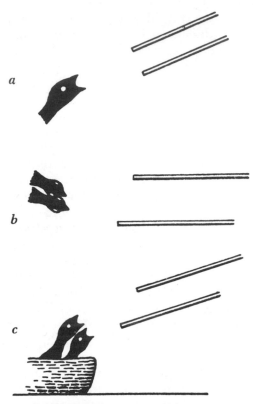

Figs. 1a and b. *The schema orienting the gaping responses of young blackbirds. With two rods at the same distance, gaping is directed at the higher (a: side view), while with two rods at the same height, gaping is towards the nearer (b: overhead view). In c, height is offset against nearness: height wins*

demonstrated by A. Seitz, is termed the *stimulus summation phenomenon* or *rule*. Tinbergen has translated this term into English as 'the Law of Heterogeneous Summation'.[30]

With innate releasing mechanisms incorporating a relatively large number of characters, one can determine extremely well the quantitative efficacity of an individual character through comparison of the efficacity of many possible character combinations. The efficacity of each character remains completely constant in all conceivable combinations and can be expressed as a percentage of the efficacity of the optimal dummy, i.e. of the sum of *all* releasing characters. By means of dummy experiments, W. Schmid has investigated the releasing efficacity of the human display pattern of laughing, and has found that in this case too – in opposition

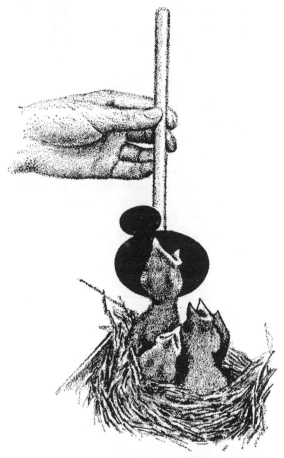

Fig. 2. *Any discontinuity in contour acts as 'head'. With a projecting triangle, it is always the upper corner which attracts gaping*

to all expectations from Gestalt psychology – the efficacity of each dummy is dependent upon the summation effect of a relatively small number of individual characters. This fact, alongside many others to be dealt with later, represents a strong argument for the assumption that the responses of a human being to specific display patterns of his conspecifics are determined to an appreciable extent by innate releasing mechanisms.

However distinct the function of a relatively complex innate releasing mechanism may be from an acquired conditioned Gestalt, the efficacity of a quite specific class of characters evoking an innate response nevertheless exhibits certain important reminders of Gestalt phenomena. When disassembling dummy experiments are carried out to separate the individual characters, one occasionally encounters very simple character combinations which *cannot be further separated* and only retain their efficacity as long as these characters are presented with a certain *relationship* to one another. The red throat coloration of the male stickleback must be on the underside, and the eyes of the mother *Haplochromis* must be horizontal and symmetrically arranged on the head in order to exhibit a specific elicitatory effect. The releasing mechanism which steers the gaping responses of young thrushes to the head of the adult bird is activated by the characters 'nearer', 'higher' and 'smaller', which differentiate the head of the adult bird – or a dummy – from the body. Among themselves, and in their interaction with other characters of the same releasing mechanism, these characters do follow the laws of stimulus summation, but in each individual character there is a *relationship* between two (as far as we know, it is always two) components which cannot be disassembled and which is the operative factor in the releasing effect.

Despite the simplicity of this relationship (itself acting as a character) in all investigated cases, it doubtless signifies a very instructive parallel to the simplest borderline case of Gestalt perception, particularly since – as Tinbergen has shown – certain parametric relationships exhibit the typical transposition effect of genuine Gestalts. Relationship characters play a particularly large part in human innate releasing mechanisms activated by display patterns of conspecifics.

5 . THE RELEASER

The almost simultaneous discovery of two so sharply defined and so extensively entity-independent physiological processes as the endogenous-automatic motor pattern and the innate releasing mechanism opened an enormous wealth of new possibilities to the progress of causal analysis, and a rapidly growing number of investigators turned in this direction. It is not possible to attempt to give in this article an extensive account of the advances and refinements which have recently marked our conception of the nature and function of the endogenous-automatic motor pattern crudely outlined above. The reader is referred to the surveys of N. Tinbergen, whose school has produced the greatest number of advances, and to Thorpe's review article (N. Tinbergen: 'An objectivistic study of the innate behaviour of animals', *Biblioth. Biotheoret*, **1**, 39–98, 1942; *Inleiding tot de diersociologie*, Gorinchem, 1947 and 'Social releasers and the experimental method required for their study', *The Wilson Bulletin*, **60** (1), 6–51. W. H. Thorpe: 'The modern concept of instinctive behaviour', *Bull. of Animal Behaviour*, **7**, 1948). What immediately concerns us in the discussion to follow, however, is the rôle played by endogenous-automatic motor patterns and innate releasing mechanisms as extensively entity-independent components in the *social* behaviour of different organisms.

Wherever an endogenous-automatic motor pattern or an orienting response (or, as usually occurs, a behavioural system based on both elements) has a *conspecific* as its object, it is not only the differentiation of the releasing mechanism developed for the object, but also the *object* itself which is governed by the factors determining the evolution of species. In addition to the receptors, *the characters operating as releasing stimuli* can undergo differentiation with respect to their 'signal' function. The stimulus-receiving apparatus and the stimulus-transmission apparatus are parts of the same organic system, and both are further differentiated, in connection with their common function of 'communication' between conspecifics, in a simultaneous and parallel process. The stimulus-transmission mechanisms which originate in this fashion are briefly termed *releasers*. A releaser is thus defined as an agent differentiated in the service of the transmission of specific stimuli, which evoke a selective response from the conspecific through a receptor correlate which has been differentiated in parallel. Genuine releasers can be found in all sensory fields – optical, acoustical and olfactory. They consist of morphological structures or innate motor patterns – in most cases *both* together, i.e. motor patterns which give particular emphasis to the stimulus-transmitting structures.

The releasers which have been best studied and are most important to human beings, who are primarily optically oriented, are visual releasers. They are also more interesting because the innate releasing mechanisms which respond to them are by far the most highly differentiated among those so far known. Nowhere is the function of the innate releasing mechanism as 'lock of the response' and that of the releaser as the appropriate 'key' so clearly analysable. It has occurred with great frequency that, in investigations concerned with the innate releasing mechanism as such, the suitable object chosen has been one which responds as a receptor correlate to a visual releaser.

When a locksmith makes a lock so that operation of a skeleton key is excluded as far as possible, he constructs the key such that it combines structural simplicity with maximum general improbability of form. For the same functional reasons, the same tendency towards maximal improbability is evident in every innate releasing mechanism (earlier referred to as the 'lock of the response'). In general, however – i.e. in every case where the releasing mechanism is the correlate of an external object or an external environmental situation – differentiation of the receptor is confined within quite narrow limits defined by the number and nature of the stimuli associated with the object or situation. To put it bluntly: A pike cannot equip a bream with a signal flag which will

Fig. 3. *Spreading of the opercular skin of* Cichlasoma meecki, *'calculated' for frontal presentation*

electively release his own snapping response. But in cases where the responding organism and the stimulus-transmitting object are members of the same species, this possibility is present. Systems composed of stimulus-transmitting organs and/or motor patterns and the responding releasing mechanisms can therefore achieve an extremely high level of general improbability for performance of their signal function. For this reason, a highly differentiated releaser can very often be immediately recognized as such by an expert. Whenever a particularly conspicuous component (i.e. improbably coloured body regions or an equivalent structure of feathers, fins, expanding organs, etc.) is found on a bird or a teleost fish, one can assume with virtual certainty that the character concerned performs an optical signal function of some kind. Of course, the same applies to certain motor patterns. Structure and movement are so intimately correlated in stimulus transmission that one can frequently predict from the structure alone the motor pattern of a novel animal species. Tinbergen and I began at the same time to study a Cichlid fish, *Cichlasoma meecki*. In two letters which happened to cross, we each predicted to the other that this species would exhibit a specific form of threat behaviour, purely on the basis of the form and coloration of the gill operculum. Just as correctly, I later predicted the form of courtship of *Apistogramma agassizi* on the basis of the form and coloration of the male's tail-fin.

The prominent quality of all of these releasers is a combination of maximal *simplicity* with maximal *general improbability*. As it happens, this is also true of all signals invented by man. This fact is easily understandable following what has been said about the relative simplicity and character limitation of innate releasing mechanisms, i.e. as a result of the functional limitation of the receiving apparatus which reacts to the signal. At the same time, the constitutive simplicity and conciseness of the releaser presents strong proof of just this functional limitation of the innate releasing mechanism: If the innate schema were able to respond selectively to complex qualities, in the same way as an acquired perceptual Gestalt (eliciting conditioned responses), *there would be no need for releasers*! The fact that these *do* exist and that they possess just the properties and functions briefly outlined here can today be regarded as an established certainty. The minor storm of discussion which the publication of my hypotheses in 1935 evoked, particularly in the English and American literature, luckily led to a large number of experimental investigations. Literally all of the major tenets regarding releasers which I set out in that paper, and which at that time were based upon an inductive basis exclusively drawn from a large range of chance observations, have since found precise experimental support. The most complete list of the decisive factual evidence which accumulated in the period 1937–50 is to be found in E. A. Armstrong's *Bird Display and Behaviour* (Lindsay Drummond, London 1947), which is by no means restricted to a discussion of birds; the best review is Tinbergen's *Social Releasers and the Experimental Method required for their Study*.

The *ease of description* of all releasers, based on their conciseness and simplicity, understandably renders them particularly suitable as objects of comparative research. The motor patterns through which Whitman and Heinroth discovered the phenomenon of genuine phyletic homology were mainly courtship patterns – i.e. releasers! However, the particular suitability of releasers for phylogenetic research and their applicability in deciding questions of fine systematics is derived from a different source: one can exclude the phenomenon of *convergent adaptation*, which is otherwise so extremely obstructive to phylogenetic considerations. With differentiation of structure or behaviour for interaction with environmental factors outside the realm of the species, one can never exclude with complete confidence the possibility that the same form has emerged in two animal species as a convergent consequence of similar function. On the other hand, where an intraspecific system of signal-transmitting and signal-receiving differentiation has emerged, the form of the signals is almost exclusively a historical product of 'convention' between the stimulus-transmitter and the stimulus-receiver, and there is only a loose relationship with the external environment. This applies to the social behavioural systems of higher animals involving releasers and innate schemata in fundamentally the same way as to the communication system of human speech, which functions on a quite different plane. The fact that tail-wagging exhibits friendly excitement in a dog and antagonism in the cat, and that this is in each case appropriately 'understood' through the innate mechanisms of conspecifics, is based exclusively upon the historical course of the differentiation process affecting the stimulus-transmitting motor pattern and the stimulus-receiving mechanism. As far as form and function of the releaser are concerned, the transmitted 'message' could quite as easily be the converse. Indeed, as long as one is not familiar with the special intraspecific 'convention', it is no more possible to recognize straight off the significance of such a motor pattern than to understand a word from a foreign language without knowledge of the historically determined conventions. As with a human language, it is virtually impossible in the evolution of releaser systems that the historical progress of the convention should twice follow the same path and thus independently produce two completely identical 'signals'. When a philologist explains the similarity of the words Mutter, *mater*, μητήρ and матъ in German, Latin, Greek and Russian, by assuming that there was a common indo-european 'ancestral form', the correctness of this assumption can be established by a probability calculation. When, in comparative behavioural research, a similarity extending into minor details is discovered – e.g. between the threat patterns of fish so different as pike, cyprinodonts, perches and gobies – one can reliably reach the same type of conclusion. *Similarity or even simple resemblance between motor display patterns bearing the same significance always indicates phyletic homology.* With reluctance, I shall forgo a discussion of the extremely stimulating and amazingly detailed analogies between releasers and the symbols of speech, such as the processes of change in meaning, restriction and extension in meaning, to which individual 'symbols' are subjected in the course of their historical development.[31]

From what has been said, it should already be evident why the comparative study of releasing motor patterns in particular frequently makes possible statements about phylogenetic relationships with a certainty which can scarcely ever be permitted in comparative morphology. It is equally understandable that we know much more about the origin and phylogeny of some innate species-specific motor patterns which function as releasers than about the origin and development of any other endogenous-automatic motor patterns. From the extremely varied processes which lead to the emergence and differentiation of releasing motor patterns, we shall consider just one, because most of the display patterns of man have arisen in just this way. It is characteristic of all endogenous-automatic motor patterns that even at the lowest levels of response-specific arousal weak *indications* of the pattern concerned will emerge. These motor patterns are, so-to-speak, governed by the reverse of the all-or-none law, i.e. there are all conceivable intermediates between the weakest indication and performance of the motor pattern at full intensity, such that it fulfils its species-preserving function. Since an observer acquainted with the intensity scale of a motor pattern can recognize from the effects of the slightest degree of arousal, from minimal indications of motor patterns, the nature of the action-specific arousal which is beginning to accumulate in the organism, and is thus to some extent able to judge the 'intentions' of the animal, Heinroth has given them the name *intention movements*.

In its original form, the intention movement as such quite definitely represents a by-product of action-specific stimulus production with no species-preserving function whatsoever. With very many social animals, however, innate releasing mechanisms have been developed which 'understand' and respond to regularly occurring intention movements of conspecifics. In primitive cases, the arousal effect which is elicited is frequently the same in the 'reactor' as that which produced the intention movement in the 'actor'. In this way, response-specific arousal acts 'infectiously'. With social animals, it is almost always advantageous for preservation of the species that all members of a society should as far as possible simultaneously exhibit the same 'motivation' (e.g. for eating, sleeping, locomotion, escape, etc.). Any case of so-called *motivational induction* is based on just this function of innate releasing mechanisms which respond to intention movements of conspecifics. This also applies to man. Assumption of 'psychic resonance' as a primary phenomenon not requiring further physiological explanation is nonsense. Further, many phenomena which are repeatedly erroneously interpreted as imitation are based upon similar processes.

As soon as a previously non-functional intention movement is 'understood' by conspecifics on the basis of receptor correlates, it not only acquires considerable survival value: from that moment on, it is subjected to all the factors which otherwise determine the further differentiation of all structures and motor patterns operating to preserve the species. The manner in which this process of further differentiation of releasing intention movements progresses is particularly characteristic with *optically* effective movements. They undergo 'gestural exaggeration' – i.e. their optically effective components are underlined and overemphasized even to a grotesque degree. Certain form and colour characters which further the optical effect are developed, whilst the original mechanically operative components of the motor pattern are reduced or lost. Gestural exaggeration can go so far that the original root of the motor pattern – the intention movement of a mechanically operative behaviour pattern – is scarcely or not at all recognizable. Only by examining related animal species, where formalization of the motor pattern is less advanced can the root be identified through comparison. In view of the enormous accumulation of examples of this phenomenon in the last few years, the reader is referred to the literature cited. Releasing motor patterns, which have originated in the manner described from intention movements and have been further differentiated in a direction different from that of the original motor pattern in arriving at their releaser function, have previously been termed *symbolic motor patterns*. Since the analogy to genuine symbols is not very extensive, I suggest the new term *formalized intention movements.*[32]

The autonomy of the new releasing function of the formalized intention movement has the automatic consequence that a motor pattern functioning purely as a signal can outlive the originally programmed, mechanically effective pattern. For example, as Darwin quite rightly observed, baring of the teeth in human beings by raising of the upper lip has been retained as an angry display pattern whilst the motor pattern of actual biting, which gave rise to the original intention movement of the display pattern, has completely disappeared from our species. Nowadays, we can add a whole collection of examples for this phylogenetic process. To take just one: The males of some original, antlerless Cervids (e.g. the musk-deer) possess elongated upper canine teeth which are used during rut fighting. The animal raises its head and strikes downwards with the teeth. The intention movement of this striking movement has been retained as a threat gesture by many species of the family in which both the canines and the original fighting movement have completely degenerated. We shall encounter still more human display patterns (in connection with the innate releasing mechanisms which respond to them) which quite definitely represent genuine formalized intention movements and are thus releasers in the narrowest sense of the word.

6. BEHAVIOURAL SYSTEMS OF SOCIAL ANIMALS INVOLVING ETHICAL ANALOGIES

Detailed analysis of 'social' action and response patterns of animals (taking 'social' in the widest sense) has shown that these are based upon more-or-less highly differentiated systems of releasers, innate schemata and innate species-specific motor patterns, which interlock like the teeth of a delicately constructed clockwork mechanism. This applies in a similar manner from Annelid worms and Cephalopods to the highest mammals. The conditioned response plays a surprisingly minor rôle in the co-ordination of adaptive (i.e. species-preserving) interaction of conspecifics for joint functions. For example, the stickleback (*Gasterosteus aculeatus*), which exhibits considerable learning ability in its behaviour towards the extraspecific environment, exhibits *not one conditioned response evoked by conspecifics*. In other words, the entirety of intraspecific behaviour is based upon the above-mentioned system of interlocking innate behaviour patterns. Nevertheless, even within the Sub-Class Teleostei, we know of definitely established conditioned responses to conspecifics. All the same, the essence of such responses is completely restricted to a process of increasing the *selectivity* of a response elicited through innate releasing mechanisms and directed towards conspecifics, by additional acquisition of complex conditioned Gestalts. (Seitz has demonstrated this with the Cichlid fish *Astatotilapia strigigena*.)[32a] Even in birds, as I demonstrated at some length in 1935, fixation of response patterns relevant to conspecifics on the biologically appropriate object is virtually the most important function which is performed by the conditioned reflex in the social interaction of the individual animals. The only other learning function which plays a considerable part in the sociology of birds and mammals is the development of personal recognition of specific individuals, which is characteristic in the structure of closed societies, e.g. in Corvids, greylag geese and pack-dogs. Personal recognition of individual animals, which is naturally an acquired phenomenon, is a prerequisite for the two fundamental characters of such closed animal society, i.e. 'exclusive' distinction from non-members and the internal rank-order prevailing between group members.

With that, however, the function of acquired elements in the structure of animal societies is more-or-less exhausted. Even with the highest and – with respect to the structure of their societies – furthest differentiated vertebrates (e.g. the jackdaw, the greylag goose and social Canids), we have not yet encountered a major structural character of such societies which could be modified by conditioned responses. However much the behaviour of such organisms towards their extraspecific environment may be modifiable through experience and acquisition, all behaviour patterns directed towards conspecifics remain relatively unaffected. Apart from fixation on a particular generic or individually determined object, I am literally unable to quote one single case – even with dogs or monkeys – where a behaviour pattern relevant to conspecifics is influenced by conditioned responses. What a jackdaw eats, where it seeks its food, the enemies which evoke alarm and flight, and even the nest-sites which are preferred – all are extensively dependent upon the individual's personal experience and in fact upon the 'tradition' of the society. With respect to these behaviour patterns, we can identify relatively great variability and adaptability. In Northern Russia and Siberia, the jackdaw exhibits no fear whatsoever towards man, nests in any low-built peasant house, constructs the nest mainly with straw and lives on insects trapped on the open ground. In our large towns, the jackdaw is extremely timid, nests only on high and inaccessible parts of buildings, constructs its nest with a great variety of materials (particularly employing a lot of paper) and specializes according to its locality on plundering pigeon nests, feeding on refuse, etc. However, the behaviour of the birds *with respect to one another* exhibits not the slightest variability. The motor display patterns and vocalizations – together with the corresponding innate responses which ensure the social co-ordination of the colony members – are 'photographically' identical. However evident this may be to an experienced animal observer, it is still astounding whenever one hears a well-known species 'speaking the same language' in far-flung places as they do at home.

Even when deprived of any contact with conspecifics from a very early age, a young animal of such a social animal species exhibits virtually all of the characteristics and behaviour patterns which it would exhibit within the framework of a normal conspecific society. However, as is understandable from what has already been said, these behaviour patterns are performed towards a 'wrong' object, usually towards a human being, as long as the latter transmits a sufficient proportion of the stimuli appropriate to the releasing mechanisms concerned.

In higher vertebrates, these systems of intraspecific behaviour, which are almost exclusively based upon innate action and response norms, frequently exhibit extensive functional analogies to the social behaviour patterns of human beings. For this reason, naïve observers are frequently misled into making extremely anthropomorphic value judgements. Of course, a comparative ethologist is particularly wary about simply regarding analogous processes occurring on entirely different psychophysiological levels as 'the same'. Without doubt, the ethologist can see more clearly than anyone else the fundamental difference between these functional analogues of ethical behaviour in social animals and the unique, phylogenetically unprecedented phenomenon of rational responsibility exhibited by mankind.[33] Nevertheless, comparative behavioural research – on the basis of an undoubtedly adequately broad foundation of observational fact – leads to the inevitable conclusion that the structure of human social behaviour incorporates a whole series of functions which are generally regarded as rational/responsible/ethical phenomena, but which in reality should quite definitely be classed together with the innate social behaviour patterns of higher animals exhibiting only functional analogies to ethical processes. In this respect, it is very instructive to delve further into the functional mechanism – and particularly the oft-occurring disruptions – of such behavioural systems in social animals exhibiting ethical analogies.

Characteristic of these systems is the finely balanced equilibrium between the individual components concerned, between the various endogenous-automatic motor patterns and the factors which inhibit them, between releasers and the innate schemata which respond to them, etc. As an illustrative example of such an equilibrium and the disruptions which can occur, we can take the relationship between species-specific aggressive drives and certain inhibitory mechanisms, which normally prevent operation of these drives in a manner detrimental to the species. There is no single organism capable of self-defence, in particular no large carnivore capable of killing large prey, which does not possess a quite particular system of inhibitions, innate schemata and releasers extensively preventing the killing of conspecifics to such an extent that such killing can never reach a frequency sufficient to adversely influence survival of the species. Without further ado, a wolf could with one bite suddenly rip out the jugular veins of a conspecific standing beside him; a raven could hack out the eye of a conspecific with a single jab of the beak. In addition, apart from being equipped with these killing motor patterns, these animals incorporate a considerable level of endogenous stimulus production. For this reason, these very patterns are particularly prone to exhibit threshold-lowering and performance with inadequate substitute objects. Any lively dog playfully 'shaking to death' his master's slippers can convince us of this fact. Thus, mild damming of such responses could particularly easily endanger conspecifics. Solitary carnivores (e.g. the polar bear and the jaguar), which only encounter conspecifics for mating – when the preponderance of sexual responses naturally excludes predatory responses to a large extent – are most able to dispense with mechanisms preventing damage to conspecifics. Accordingly, these are the animals which most frequently kill one another in captivity. With social carnivores and predatory birds, and with species exhibiting a lasting pair-bond, certain specific inhibitory mechanisms *must* be present. A raven would otherwise hack at the eye of his consort just as he pecks at all glistening objects with a quite unspecific response pattern, and a wolf would otherwise fly at the throat of another pack member just as he would at any other organism of the same size.

Anybody who has not had personal experience of these inhibitory mechanisms would find it difficult to imagine their dependability and efficacity. A raven not only refrains from pecking at the eye of a conspecific or an acquainted human being, but actually diligently avoids holding its beak near this vulnerable organ. If one should move one's eye towards the beak-tip of a tame raven perched nearby, the raven will turn its beak away with an almost anxious movement, rather like a parent moving an open razor out of reach of a young child. The raven only brings its beak close to the eye of an acquaintance in one situation – in the responses of 'social preening' (W. Köhler). Just like many other social birds, ravens preen one another's head feathers. In particular, they preen the eye area, which the recipient can clean only in a much cruder fashion by scratching with the inner claw of the foot. The releaser of this behaviour pattern consists of a specific motor pattern whereby one bird *presents* its head to a companion with the feathers fluffed and the eye half-closed on the presented side. A corresponding movement performed by an acquainted human being (despite the lack of fluffed feathers) is regularly 'understood' by a tame raven, and it provokes the bird to draw the eyelashes through his beak with the typical movement for preening tiny feathers. The use of the massive predatory beak so close to an open human eye quite understandably has an almost menacing appearance, and unaccustomed observers who are shown this response regularly warn that the raven 'might take a peck sooner or later'. But the raven really cannot do that! Just as compulsive and reliable are the inhibitions which a dog has against biting a bitch or a puppy of its own species. The increase in range of variability brought about by domestication does have the result, however, that deficiency mutations affect these inhibitions with appreciable frequency in some breeds subjected to intensive breeding (e.g. Doberman, Deutsche Dogge, Barsoi). One has to watch out with dogs which inflict serious bites on bitches or pups. They are psychopaths whose social inhibitions are in some way abnormal, and sooner or later they will bite their own master. Such dogs are extremely dangerous with children.

Releasers which activate social inhibitions against use of 'weapons' by conspecifics are particularly important and interesting. Heinroth refers to them as 'submissive postures'. All of these share the common feature of a revealing relationship both to the characteristic killing pattern of the species and to the most vulnerable areas, which are attacked with the intention to kill. All of us have seen the characteristic submissive posture of the domestic dog. A dog which is attacked and feels itself to be subordinate remains motionless – often abruptly in the middle of the affray – and turns its head away from the opponent with a peculiar, stiff posture. In this way, the most vulnerable part of the dog's body – the protruding side of the neck – *is presented defencelessly to the opponent* (i.e. exactly the area where dogs try to bite one another in fighting!). But, strangely, the dominant dog 'cannot' bite. The fact that the latter undergoes a genuine conflict between drive and inhibition is evident from the fact that clear-cut intention movements of biting are made at the neck of the submissive, immobile opponent. In fact, one of my Chow-Alsatian crossbreds (which were very close to the wild form) performed in such cases the shaking-to-death movement *in vacuo*, with his mouth closed right alongside the opponent's throat.[34] The second submissive posture of the dog – which is mainly observed with juveniles – shows the same correlation to the specific pattern of attack. Fighting dogs attempt to throw one another down by ramming with the shoulder, and more-or-less the worst thing which can happen to a dog whilst fighting is to fall on its back. Correspondingly, young dogs which are afraid of an adult conspecific will from the outset lay on their backs and stay still with the ears laid back and the tail wagging with intensive side-to-side jerks. The adult then sniffs at the sexual organs of the young dog, and the latter – at this point at the climax of the response – will generally expel a small quantity of urine. As soon as the dominant dog responds amicably, as usually occurs (i.e. by beginning to tail-wag), the juvenile leaps up and attempts in a specific manner to induce the former to join in chasing play.

The same correlation between a submissive posture eliciting inhibition and a species-characteristic attack pattern is very evident with many social birds. The killing method of these animals is represented by pecking at the back of the opponent's head; Heinroth regularly identified haemorrhage in the cerebral membranes as the cause of death in birds killed by conspecifics. When exhibiting the submissive posture, jackdaws and other Corvids display the back of the head in attempting to appease a conspecific. Gulls similarly present the back of the skull, but they do this with a different movement – by lowering and extending the head. Herons behave in the same way. In the water-rail (*Rallus aquaticus*), the young bird possesses a morphological releaser in the form of a naked area at the back of the head which is abundantly supplied with blood vessels. When this is presented to an attacker, a specific orientation of the feathers exposes the area even more and there is a simultaneous reddening. The area seems to protrude as if it were underlain by an expandable structure like that histologically demonstrated with the red head-cap of the crane. It is doubtless no chance effect that it is the water-rail – the only predatory species among our endemic Rallidae, and capable of killing prey of some size – which exhibits differentiation of this highly specialized inhibition-releaser in the young.

It need scarcely be mentioned that only the conspecific, in which the corresponding receptor correlates are inherently incorporated, 'understands' all of these inhibition-releasers. I was unable to keep my young water-rails together with ducklings, which are actually much more harmless, because the latter naturally pecked at the proffered red head-caps of the rails. A peacock does not 'understand' the submissive posture of the closely-related turkey-cock, which lies stretched out on the ground in front of its opponent, etc. The fixed, automatic nature of the submissive postures is extremely obvious from the fact that a sub-mitting animal, when confronted with 'failure' of its releaser, becomes even more set in its submissive posture and permits itself to be beaten to death without resisting. In the case of the turkey-cock involved in a fight with a peacock, this regularly leads to the downfall of the former.

The relationship existing between an attack pattern directed at a specific vulnerable part of the body and an inhibition-eliciting sub-missive posture involving 'presentation' of just this body area, which is common to so many social animals, must have a common explanation. It is doubtless one of the greatest puzzles in ethology that a vulnerable body area, which at one moment still represents the goal of a directed attack, can undergo a remarkable inversion of valency so that a moment later – when presented in a clumsy manner – it will elicit exactly opposite behaviour from the attacker.[35] This phenomenon is all the more significant since it obviously plays a part in human behaviour. A whole range of submissive gestures of human beings exhibit such an extensive analogy to the described 'inhibition-releasers facilitating fatal attack' of social animals, that chance correspondence can be reliably excluded. Dropping to the knees, bowing of the head, the many ceremonies of handing over ('presenting') a weapon, the removal of a helmet (which has been preserved to the present day as the mild submissive gesture of taking off a hat), and many other human gestures belong in this category. Even if the actual motor patterns themselves are definitely not innate, they are all certainly underlain by the same valency-switch of vulnerable body areas as with the innate inhibition-releasers of animals.

A further important correlation exists between the social inhibitions against the use of weapons and the *thickness of the skin* in the species concerned. In their relationships with acquainted conspecifics, both in play and in occasional non-serious tussles, carnivores only bite with strongly inhibited pressure. Playing cats, dogs and other carnivores with thin skins always bite very gently in play, even though this may not be quite gentle enough for human skin. Nevertheless, one can also play with a tame lion without being seriously injured. By contrast, the badger (which has an extremely thick pelt) will bite so roughly even in good-natured play that a human being who plays with him without gloves finds himself in a situation similar to that of someone taking part without armour in a mediaeval tournament, where armoured knights amiably jabbed at one another with lances.

'Peaceable' herbivores, which on the one hand do not possess weapons suitable for killing large organisms and on the other are protected against attacks by their highly differentiated ability to flee, do not normally need special inhibitions preventing damage to conspecifics. An indivi-dual dominated by a conspecific in a fight can get away from the victor by means of flight responses which would be effective even against a much more dangerous pursuer. However, if pigeons, hares, deer and other symbols of gentleness and harmlessness are kept in groups in captivity, so that the subordinate cannot escape his persecutor by flight, there is frequently violence and killing of a kind which is quite unusual with crows, wolves or lions kept under the same conditions. One really has to see for oneself how one turtle-dove can attack another cowering terrorized in the corner of a cage and peck hour after hour with its gentle little beak until the whole surface of the subordinate exposed to the beak-jabs of the victor, from the back of the head to the rump, is transformed into a single, bloody wound.

Unfortunately, it would take too much space to discuss in detail the analysis of complex social behavioural systems in higher animals. Suffice it to say that even extremely complex behaviour patterns which exhibit amazing functional resemblances to the responsible-moral behaviour of human beings are entirely based on systems of releasers, innate releasing mechanisms, endogenous motor patterns, etc. This applies to the courageous, altruistic defence of companions by jackdaws, ravens, dogs and monkeys; to the extremely interesting 'police response' of the jackdaw, whereby the entire society protects the nest of a low-ranking bird against attack by a higher-ranking individual; to the peace-making of penguins, in which fights on the densely populated brooding site are 'prohibited because of the danger to the eggs', with outsiders rushing up to separate sparring males, etc. Learning and insight play a part in these behavioural systems only to the extent of *restricting* an innately releasing stimulus situation (p. 147). Nevertheless, the 'exclusivity' of the behaviour which is so determined can be very important. Thus, jackdaws and even most monkeys will 'anonymously' defend an attacked conspecific (in the case of the jackdaw as a result of a demonstrably very simple releasing mechanism), whilst with ravens, dogs and wolves defence of a companion is bound to the conditions of individual recognition.

The above, compressed description of functional analogies of ethical behaviour in animals is intended to demonstrate the rôle played by fixed, innate behavioural components in highly differentiated social structures, and the manner in which they *determine* these structures. We shall now examine the extent to which the presence of innate releasing mechanisms, genuine releasers and endogenous stimulus-production processes can be similarly identified in human behaviour. We shall attempt to see whether it is possible, even with human beings, to demonstrate, in addition to responsible, ethical features, motivational aspects of social behaviour with deeper roots and greater phylogenetic age.

7. INNATE RELEASING MECHANISMS AS FIXED STRUCTURAL
COMPONENTS OF HUMAN SOCIETY

The fact that human beings also possess endogenous-automatic behaviour patterns, innate releasing mechanisms and (in particular) releasers, together with the responding receptor correlates, would not have struck the majority of human psychologists, since they were not aware of the same processes in animal behaviour, where they are far more obvious and striking. Quite naturally, the rôle played by these innate elements in human behaviour is incomparably slighter than that in animal species, and in human beings they are interwoven with, and extensively hidden by, the higher functions of the brain – learning and insight. To start with, we shall briefly consider what is known about innate releasing mechanisms of human beings and about their social function.

Since it is not possible to carry out with human beings the experimental process of rearing in isolation, which is otherwise usual for the analysis of innate releasing mechanisms, we are compelled to make use of other criteria distinguishing the innate schema from the acquired conditioned Gestalt. In the first instance, these criteria are: limited number of characters, Seitz's stimulus summation phenomenon (Tinbergen: *law of heterogeneous summation*) and the identity of response of all normal human beings to specific, biologically relevant stimulus situations.

A good subject for analysis is presented by the innate releasing mechanisms with which we respond to small children. A relatively large head, predominance of the brain capsule, large and low-lying eyes, bulging cheek region, short and thick extremities, a springy elastic consistency, and clumsy movements represent the major characters following the law of summation and combining to give a child (or a dummy such as a doll or an animal) a loveable or 'cuddly' appearance. The products of the doll industry, which are literally the results of dummy experiments carried out on a very wide basis, and also the various types of animals (e.g. pug-dogs and Pekinese) which are taken over by childless women as substitute objects for their parental care drive, permit clear-cut abstraction of these characters. Interestingly, certain German names for animals exhibit a close correlation with the releasing mechanism concerned: species which have a 'loveable' appearance due to the possession of several of the characters mentioned – in particular the very 'strong' characters of the protruding forehead and cheek regions – very frequently bear names ending with the diminutive syllable '-chen', e.g. *Rotkehlhcen* (robin), *Eichhörnchen* (squirrel), *Kaninchen* (rabbit). In all of these cases, the final syllable does not express the smallness but definitely the 'loveable' nature of the animals

Fig. 4. *The releasing schema for human parental care responses.* left: *head proportions perceived as 'loveable' (child, jerboa, Pekinese dog, robin).* right: *related heads which do not elicit the parental drive (man, hare, hound, golden oriole)*

concerned. Closely related forms of the same size – or even smaller – which have small eyes and flat foreheads never bear names ending in '-chen'.

Another process which proves on closer analysis to be a function of genuine releasers and innate releasing mechanisms responding to them is that of human motor display patterns and the response to these. The so-called process of 'physiognomic experience', even where inanimate environmental objects are concerned, is (contrary to the opinion of some developmental psychologists) by no means based on a general, diffuse form of experience which does not sufficiently separate the ego and the environment, and which is also distributed in the animal kingdom. Instead, it is based upon a sharply-defined process of biologically 'erroneous' response to releasing mechanisms, whose actual species-preserving function is the understanding of specific human motor display patterns. The simplicity or character-limitation of the releasing mechanism and the qualitatively identical releasing effect which is produced even by individually presented characters, have the result that the receptor correlate adapted for human display characters will respond extremely easily even to very simple stimulus combinations in our animate and inanimate environment. In this way, the most amazing objects can acquire remarkable, highly specific emotional values by 'experiential attachment' of *human* properties. The countryside can 'smile'. 'The lake laugh sand invites us to bathe.' ('Es lächelt der See, er ladet zum Bade' (Schiller)). Steeply rising, somewhat overhanging cliff faces or dark storm-clouds piling up have the same, immediate display value as a human being who is standing at full height and leaning slightly forwards, etc., etc. The same phenomenon can be even more pronounced in our response to the far greater character combination found in the 'dummies' which we encounter in the form of various animal faces. Our innate releasing mechanisms adapted for *motor display patterns* evoke specific, conspicuously emotional responses when animal heads are sighted, even when the releasing relationship characters are represented by completely fixed morphological structures of the organism concerned. For example, in the camel and the llama the fact that the nostril is located higher than the eye, that the angle of the mouth is drawn somewhat downwards, and that the head is normally carried just above the horizontal, is based upon morphological characters which tell us nothing about the emotional state of the animal concerned. The species-specific carriage of the head is determined by the orientation of the horizontal semicircular canal in the labyrinth.

Anybody who wants to know whether the animal is amicably or negatively disposed, whether it is inclined to eat out of the observer's hand or spit at him, must look at the ears. However, the anthropo-morphic physiognomic response transmits – with the incorrigibility of the typical innate schema – the false impression that the animal is always looking haughtily at the observer. In human beings the gesture of haughty rejection (i.e. the receptor correlate of the releasing mechanism concerned) is a formalized and gesturally exaggerated intention movement of withdrawal, in which the head is lifted backwards, the nostrils are retracted and the eyelids are half-closed. All of this 'symbolizes' resistance against all sensory modalities emanating from the disdained counterpart. In people from Southern Italy and very many oriental

Fig. 5. *The haughty or disdainful impression given by the facial expression of the camel is based on the fact that an innate schema adapted to the motor display patterns of human beings 'misunderstands' the relative level of the eye and nose, which signifies disdainful rejection in a human counterpart*

regions, the same gesture in a less exaggerated form simply means 'no'. Darwin, who recognized and exactly described all of these processes, observed that there is an accompanying brief expiration through the nostrils as if a draught of air were intended to drive away an unpleasant odour. Children from East Prussia accompany this by saying 'pe' with a strongly explosive consonant and the 'e' muffled. In English, the verb *sniffing* is generally used as a term for haughty rejection, and the same phenomenon is summarized in yiddish with the extremely expressive 'Er blost vün sach' (he blows arrogantly).

In an analogous fashion, we experience as an *expression* of courageous determination the *morphological* structure of the head of many predatory birds, which possess prominent bony arches over the eyes and mouth angles which are narrow, closed and drawn backwards. Thus, the eagle has become a symbol of courage and its name gave rise to the root of the German adjective 'edel' (noble). Many further examples of 'erroneous' physiognomic experience of animal forms could be cited.

The great part played by the *eye* as the most important relationship feature in the relative characters of innate mechanisms has the remarkable accompanying effect that we always exhibit pronounced physiognomic experience of almost all human constructions which have *windows*, to the extent that these openings are definitely evaluated as eyes. The structures located above and below the window are 'pressed' into the physiognomic rôle of forehead, eyebrow and cheek regions by the innate releasing mechanism, and their spatial relationships to one another determine (just as we have seen with animal heads) the display

Fig. 6. *The Golden Eagle. Bony arches over the eyes are interpreted as a frown. Together with the pronounced backward sweep of the corners of the mouth, this gives the bird the expression of 'proud determination'*

value of the entirety. I remember quite plainly to the present day that when I was a child a specific carriage of the Viennese City Railway, because of the ventilation flaps located some way above the windows (which gave the impression of raised eyebrows) had an unpleasant – partially disdainful, partially dumbfounded – expression. In children, physiognomic experience is quite generally more pronounced than in adults, presumably because the original character-limitation, and there-fore 'broadness', of the releasing mechanism always undergoes a process of 'entrenchment' (i.e. increasing selectivity) through additional opera-tion of acquisition during the life of the individual, in agreement with what was said on p. 147 and p. 153.

The innate character of the mechanisms concerned expresses itself in the fact that the evoked experience is completely *incorrigible*. Even when one is quite aware of the fact that one's own sensation is just the same as what we refer to as a *misplaced response* in animals, one is unable to stop regarding the camel and the llama as 'disagreeable', in fact almost unaesthetic, whilst feeling the eagle to be 'noble' and 'splendid'. Αισθανομαι means 'I experience', and the original meaning of aesthetic is 'that through which one experiences something', although restriction of the significance of this word has now given rise to a positive experi-ential value.

We thus come to the peculiar releasing mechanisms, usually con-structed around a very small number of *simple* relationship characters, which evoke aesthetic and ethical *evaluation feelings* in human beings. The conceptual separation of these two adjectives is entirely artificial;

nevertheless, we shall adhere to this customary division and turn first to the aesthetic relationship schemata which are 'tailored' for specific proportional characters of the human body. The fact that innate response patterns are actually involved can be deduced through the same criteria as those already established above. An analytical evaluation very similar to that possible with the doll industry proves to be applicable with representational art. Indeed, this best applies not to really high-ranking art but to phony creations generally described as 'corny', which are not dictated by the taste of an artist but by the requirements of the receptive public, as is the case with fashion designs, cheap novels and cheaply made films. Just as in the case of the doll industry, the industries concerned carry out thoroughgoing dummy experiments on a very broad basis with their public, since quite obviously the greatest financial success accrues to the producer whose product exhibits the greatest elicitatory effect. For this reason, such products permit clear-cut abstraction of the form and relationship characters to which the innate releasing mechanism responds. Aesthetic evaluation feelings are evoked, with the same quality as by the sight of a beautiful human being, by extreme simplifications and following extensive interchange of the proffered relationship characters. Just as with the erroneous response of a schema to the characters of human motor display patterns, the innately answered relationship character effects the registration of simplified 'abstract' proportional characters down to arithmetical detail. There is good reason for the suspicion that the aesthetic effect of the so-called *golden section* is underlain by an innate releasing mechanism adapted to the proportions of a beautiful human body and not (as would be the only possible alternative) by 'selective sight' of a mathematical harmony based on acquired Gestalt perception.

The strongly sexual aesthetic responses to specific 'beautiful features' of the male and female body demand particular attention. When one discounts characters which correspond in the ideal pictures of beauty in both sexes, almost *all* of the aesthetic feelings evoked by the male and the female body prove to be elicited by characters *which are immediate indicators of hormonal sex functions*. The contrasting relationship between hip and shoulder width in men and women, the hair boundaries, the distribution of fat in women (which, by the way, doubtless represents a true releaser in the sense established on p. 140 et seq.), the form of the female breast and a small number of other characters present such indicators of sexual fitness. These are 'realized by instinct and not by the head', as was stated by Schopenhauer, who quite correctly recognized almost all of the phenomena discussed, in writing his book *Metaphysik der Geschlechtsliebe* (*The Metaphysics of Sexual Love*). All of the releasing characters of these schemata are represented in exaggerated form in 'corny art' and in fashion in order to produce 'superoptimal dummies' (to use an inelegant but fitting expression from our colloquial scientific terminology). Anybody can produce an enormous number of examples of this.

Very similar statements, based on the aesthetic analogous observations just discussed, can be made about certain equally anthropomorphic ethical evaluation feelings. What applied to morphological relationship characters above, applies here to behavioural characters. In this case too, representational art and, still better, 'representational industry' can be taken as a suitable object for investigation. The number of motifs which elicit an emotional attitude from us is quite small. They evoke 'fear and sympathy' and therefore reappear repeatedly in poetry. Certain immortal forms, such as the maiden threatened by the enemy and freed by the hero, the friend sacrificing himself for a friend, etc., etc. occur repeatedly, from the *Eddas* and the *Iliad* to the wild-west film. In this case too, we encounter the already described characteristic phenomenon which is associated with the function of innate releasing mechanisms – the operative relationship characters, even when presented singly and in very simplified form, elicit the same quality of emotional response as the real situation for which the schema is adapted. Can one find a more marked schematic form of a specific, ethically evaluated behaviour pattern than the rendering given by Schiller: 'Hier bin ich, für den er gebürget?' ('Here am I, for whom he stood pledge?') And yet this has, for anyone of normal sensibilities, the complete emotional value of a real occurrence! One can observe very well in oneself the utter incorrigibility of one's own, unconditional reflex response. Knowing better about the dummy nature of proffered objects changes nothing in the emotions which are released, even when the dummy concerned is so crude as that represented in the modern film. The maltreated child or the virgin raped by the 'villain' (and of course saved just in the nick of time) elicit defence responses even if one is able to laugh at oneself at the time.

As with schemata responding to human display patterns, it is possible to identify typical 'misplaced responses' in the ethical sphere in cases where *animal* behaviour exhibits a purely external, formal similarity to ethically relevant human behaviour patterns 'envisaged' by human innate schemata. Defence of offspring, maternal care responses, social defence responses and so on unfailingly elicit sympathy and a positive ethical evaluation feeling – and this does not only apply to the naïve observer. The compulsiveness of the releasing mechanism is particularly evident where *our own* defence responses are elicited. For example, when a fox kills a hare – particularly when the latter is young and appealing and evokes a response from our 'Kindchenschema' – our own impulse to help the underdog is virtually irrepressible. On one occasion when I violated my own innate responses on a quite rational basis, by feeding, much against my inclination, young and still very appealing capuchin rats to a python, I subsequently suffered from mild neurotic damage to the extent that I repeatedly *dreamed* in an exaggerated emotional manner about the events! One only needs to imagine a powerful quantitative intensification of the same experience to arrive at the furies which follow the criminal! All animals whose social behaviour departs to some extent from that of human beings and yet exhibits parallels, such that comparison is provoked, are subjected to stubborn response of moralizing value judgements. The cuckoo, which does not take care of its own offspring; the billy goat, which exhibits a strong copulatory drive and has no monogamic ties; the ant, which works with 'altruistic' diligence for the good of the community; etc. – all are ethically evaluated as if human conspecifics were concerned. For a zoo attendant, it can gradually become very trying to hear every naïve visitor respond straight off to an animal seen for the first time with completely false and biologically nonsensical value judgements, although the initiate should actually be pleased by these beautiful examples of 'misplaced responses'.

Demonstration, and adequate emphasis, of the enormous part which is doubtless played by innate releasing mechanisms – in particular by those of an aesthetic nature – as relatively entity-independent components and skeletal elements of human social behaviour, by no means signifies that the importance of other, and less immediately anthropomorphic, aesthetic and moralistic action and response patterns is underrated or denied! I have discussed in detail the nature and function of the existence of non-anthropomorphic (in a certain sense genuinely *a priori*) value judgements in a previous publication, and the reader is referred to what was stated in that oft-quoted article. We shall return to the question of functional *limitations* of rational responsibility later on in this paper, in the section on the special dangers to mankind. What immediately concerns us here, however, is the following fact: What we feel to be the ethical value of a fellow human being is not the achievement of his responsible moral code but that of his innate, species-specific 'inclinations'. The objective conduct of a human being may correspond very closely to the ideal of social requirements of the individual, but we still do not regard this as 'good' if the motives do not stem from the deep, emotional layers of innate, hereditarily determined behaviour. 'You will never work heart-to-heart if it does not come from the heart' (Goethe). It was no less than Friedrich Schiller who first clearly recognized and criticized the weak point in Kant's theory of moral behaviour – blindness to the values of natural inclination – in particular in the fine epigram: 'I am always glad to help my friends, but unfortunately I enjoy doing it,/and so I am often troubled by the fact that I am not virtuous./ The only advice one can give is to try to dislike them, and then obey with distaste the demands of duty'. Nevertheless, high estimation of innate ethical responses is thoroughly compatible with that of rational, responsible moral behaviour. When *a human being* is judged as a whole according to his ethical values, we are doubtless correct in valuing most a man whose social behaviour is most 'heart-felt'. On the other hand, when we are concerned with judging the *actions* of a single given human being / for example ourselves / we would be equally justified in valuing highest those which are least provoked by natural inclination and most by rational responsibility.

8. THE ENDOGENOUS AUTOMISM IN HUMAN SOCIAL BEHAVIOUR

Without a trace of doubt, human beings exhibit the *smallest* range of endogenous-automatic motor patterns found in any higher organism.[36] Apart from certain motor norms of food-uptake (seizing, placing-in-the mouth, chewing and swallowing), mating (frictional movements) and possibly certain automatic elements in walking and running, an adult human being appears to have virtually no centrally co-ordinated motor patterns based on endogenous automatisms. However, this paucity of genuine instinctive motor patterns is not a primary feature but the result of a *process of reduction*. In the case of most instinctive motor patterns of man, only *motor display patterns* have remained. Where these owe their origin to intention movements, they permit recognition of the original form of the motor pattern – as was seen with the display of anger (p. 145 et seq.), which was correctly interpreted by Darwin as a for-malized intention movement.

We are, in principle, in agreement with McDougall's view that the qualitatively separate emotions of human beings each correspond to an 'instinct' in the sense of an action-specific arousal modality and behavioural motivation. With very many of these specific behavioural motivations, assumption of an endogenous-automatic basis is supported by the fact that the stimulus threshold sinks during periods without response and rises following abreaction of the drive concerned. This applies to coarse sexual responses and also to the completely independent behaviour patterns of falling-in-love, to demonstrative behaviour and to other patterns. Endogenous accumulation of response-specific behavioural motivation is most clearly evident, however, with the behaviour patterns which were interpreted by Freud as products of the *aggressive drive*. Anyone who has ever worked under a mildly excitable and not quite self-controlled supervisor knows that the emergence of a 'threatening atmosphere' is a quite periodic phenomenon and that, after eruption and abreaction of the dammed-up arousal in a 'purifying thunderstorm', the good will of the despot is not reduced but definitely augmented. After a 'normal office row', a peculiar atmosphere of increased human affection prevails! One of my aunts regularly became involved in arguments with her house-maid, each time giving notice to leave. The typical shift in the perceptual field which, as is well known, accompanies the changes in the existing cumulative value of response-specific energy, expressed itself wonderfully in my aunt's behaviour in that she was inordinately pleased with each replacement encountered immediately after the discharge of her aggressive condition. She never realized that these 'pearls' were compulsively and repeatedly converted to more-or-less hateful creatures in the course of a few months. The accumulation of aggressive responses can become very disruptive, even dangerous, when a very small community is completely isolated from conspecific surroundings on which the dammed-up drives can be abreacted. The 'polar malady' which emerges among members of expeditions, the crew of small boats, and so on, is nothing less than massive threshold-lowering of the behaviour patterns of angry outbreaks. Anybody who has become acquainted with this knows how minor irritations can eventually have a ridiculously angering effect. Even when one has full insight into one's own response, one is unable to prevent oneself from boiling with rage at certain small characteristics of a companion, for example, a cough or a peculiar way of speaking. In so responding to a friend, one behaves fundamentally just like the male of an isolated Cichlid fish pair which will finally attack and kill the female following the absence of threatening conspecifics to chase away from the family. This response pattern is particularly typical of *Geophagus*, and one can prevent this by placing a mirror in the aquarium for the male to abreact his aggression.[37]

Another response pattern, which will be given special treatment here because of its particular importance, is that of *social defence*. Its subjective experiential correlate is the emotion of *enthusiasm*. An especially interesting feature of the response is its association with motor patterns *which are homologous with those of the chimpanzee*. Any man with strong emotions knows from his own experience the overpowering feelings of the onlooker in moments when combative involvement for the society is elicited in us. This emotion is evoked by erection of the hairs on the neck, the upper part of the back and – interestingly – on the outside surface of the upper arm. The gestural motor display patterns consist of pronounced erectness of the body posture, raising of the head, furrowing of the brows, downward retraction of the corners of the mouth, forward projection of the lower jaw, forward extension of the shoulders, and rotation of the arms on the shoulder joints such that the hairy dorsal surface is pointed outwards. The facial expression is the same as that which evokes in us the described emotional responses to the 'dummy' of the eagle's head. Inward rotation of the arms and the contraction of the *musculi arrectores pilorum* does not contribute much to the visual impression of the overall behaviour in human beings, and it would presumably not have been noticed if anthropoid apes did not possess exactly the same motor patterns. A chimpanzee advancing to carry out social defence similarly pushes out his chin, rotates his arms inwards and erects the hair on the upper back and the outside of the upper arm. (On these areas of the body, the hairs have undergone elongation to enhance the releaser concerned, just as is the case with very many pelage and plumage areas of mammals and birds adapted for an analogous function.) As a result of the forward-inclined body posture and the relatively great length of the arms in the ape, these motor patterns produce a considerable enlargement of the body outline, which has a demonstrative, intimidatory function and quite definitely has an 'infectious' effect on fellow members of the society. It is a neat example of a *rudimentary* behaviour pattern, in the true phylogenetic sense, that human beings in analogous cases 'spread out the hair which they no longer have'! The response is elicited by a very simple relationship schema; one which one can justifiably describe as 'unfortunate', since – however valuable it may be for internal cohesion of societies – the innate incorrigibility of its response and particularly the nature of the releasing situation carry great inherent dangers to humanity. The vital relationship character of the releasing mechanism concerned is an external *threat* to the society, and demagogues through the ages have misused this (in itself ethically valuable) response to set nations at one another's throats with the simple dummy of a fabricated enemy and a fabricated threat to the society.

9. THE DOMESTICATION OF MAN

It was no less a man than Schopenhauer who first recognized that human beings exhibit a whole range of characters distinguishing them from free-living animals and shared with domesticated animals. In his already cited work *Metaphysik der Geschlechtsliebe*, he made the very noteworthy statement that certain racial characteristics of the white man are not 'natural' at all but have only emerged in the course of civilization. He states: 'The reason for this is that blond hair and blue eyes themselves represent a variety, almost an abnormality, analogous to the white mouse or at least (!) the white horse.' Anybody who has just a mild ability to recognize such things and compares our species in an unprejudiced fashion first with free-living organisms and then with our domestic animals cannot doubt for a moment that man is a 'domesticated' animal. On the basis of a wide range of factual evidence, E. Fischer has demonstrated that very many characters of modern man – above all his racial characteristics – are based upon alterations of the hereditary complement in a manner quite analogous to those characteristic of 'effects of domestication' in animals. This is not the place to discuss the nature and the probable biological causes of domestication effects. What concerns us are just two typical alterations of innate, species-specific behaviour, which without a shadow of doubt play a considerable part in human social life.

We understand by *expansion of the innate releasing schema* the phenomenon whereby these responsive mechanisms regularly *lose their selectivity* to a marked degree in the course of domestication. It is extremely characteristic of the physiological functioning of the releasing mechanism as a stimulus *filter* that deficiency mutations, which afflict individual characters of the innate schema, do not hinder elicitation of the response concerned, but on the contrary facilitate such elicitation by lowering selectivity. To take one example: according to Heinroth a mother hen of the Burmese jungle fowl (the ancestral form of our domestic chicken) when leading her chicks will only respond with brood-care responses to chicks exhibiting plumage with the typical marking patterns of the top of the head and back, which are characteristic of the wild form and perform a releasing function. Chicks with any other coloration pattern are killed. This selective behaviour is only found here and there with some domestic chickens close to the wild form, with gamecocks, with phoenix chickens and with some dwarf races. Our farmyard chickens do not generally exhibit discriminatory responses towards different colour patterns of chicks, though many still respond in a quite selective manner to the display vocalizations of the chicks and will not accept goslings or ducklings. With the heavy, furthest domesticated races of chicken, such as Orpington, Plymouth Rock and Brahma, one usually finds that even the acoustic characters of the releasing mechanism have disappeared, and such hens will even take care of young mammals which are placed beneath them. The expansion of sexual releasing mechanisms greatly facilitates breeding of many domestic animals in comparison with the corresponding wild forms. Whereas in wild animals, for example greylag geese, a large number of conditions must be fulfilled for development of their highly differentiated sexual and family life to take place, in a domestic animal enclosure together of two individuals of different sexes suffices to obtain breeding success.

The second considerable alteration regularly brought about in the species-specific behaviour of domestic animals by domestication concerns the quantity of endogenous stimulus-production with certain behaviour patterns based on automatisms. Without alteration of the co-ordination of the motor pattern as such, in domestic animals the frequency and intensity of performance of the response undergoes all imaginable degrees of variation. The increase in production of certain motor sequences can in some cases reach such a degree that this becomes the most prominent feature of the domestic races concerned and may achieve a virtually pathological character. In pigeons hypertrophy of the specific motor pattern of escaping from raptors striking from above (which is a pattern common to almost all birds capable of flight) reaches such proportions in the so-called *tumblers* that the birds are literally unable to fly a few yards in a straight line without being thrown off course by 'eruption' of this response. In this case, the originally extremely adaptive motor response has a quite pathological appearance, rather like an attack of cramp. Analogous examples of hypertrophied motor patterns can be found in great numbers in different domestic animals. Just as frequent are quantitative reductions in endogenous motor patterns. In particular, parental care responses of a wide variety of domestic animals often exhibit quite sharply defined deficiencies. The motor patterns of fighting are, in comparison to the wild form, almost always reduced. The endogenous drive to fly is reduced in all domesticated birds with the exception of pigeons and doves, and may even be completely absent. And so on.

Quite generally, one gains the impression that the phylogenetically oldest, most primitive stimulus-production processes – above all those of feeding and mating – incline to hypertrophy; whilst the younger, more finely differentiated behaviour patterns – above all those of family cohesion, parental care and defence of offspring (in short, all social responses) – incline to disappearance. We shall return shortly to the 'beastly' coarsening of social behaviour which results from this process, and to the remarkable correlation which is exhibited between this and the ethical relationship schemata of man.

Unfortunately, there is no room here to demonstrate with a wide range of details the incredibly extensive parallelism between the two briefly sketched domestication-induced alterations in innate action and response norms of domestic animals and certain deficiency symptoms in human behaviour. One would have to be equipped with the inductive basis of Oskar Heinroth and the literary descriptive skills of Thomas Mann in order to transmit to the reader the conviction compellingly forced upon the observer of these parallels: In animals and man, we are concerned with fundamentally similar phenomena based upon the same physiological, i.e. *genetical*, causes. I am completely aware of the fact that this largely intuitive conviction is, from the inductive-scientific point of view, little more than a working hypothesis and requires very exact examination on a factual and experimental basis. However, the justification – in fact the obligation – for publishing this working hypothesis with full emphasis is its practical value, which would be extremely great granted the very probable outcome that it is fundamentally correct. It can in any case be maintained with certainty that complete neglect of the genetic approach in the study of deficiency symptoms of social behaviour in civilized human beings represents a momentous methodological error.

Finally, it is necessary to mention a fact which is extremely remarkable and, in a certain sense, may be brought as an argument for the assumption that certain deficiency symptoms of human social behaviour, which exhibit such extensive parallels to domestication-induced behavioural changes in many domestic animals, actually do have a *genetic* basis. There is an extremely peculiar *correlation* between the innate releasing mechanisms which evoke aesthetic-ethical value feelings and hereditary changes wrought by domestication.

In the aesthetic sphere, our emotional value judgement categorizes as repulsive characters which have arisen through typical domestication effects, whilst characters which are threatened by the same effects of domestication are classed as desirable. There is scarcely one typical domestication effect in the morphological realm which does not evoke our pronounced aesthetic revulsion. Almost more important than this statement is the fact that the converse also applies: virtually all characters which we perceive as specifically ugly are genuine domestication effects.

Muscular flabbiness, a hanging stomach, weak connective tissue and their side-effects such as flabby skin, bow-leggedness and so on, relatively small looking eyes, expressionless facial features lacking in 'striking' qualities, pug-head and many other 'ugly characters' are typical results of domestication. If a large series of pictures of wild forms and their domesticated derivatives is assembled, one is again and again amazed by the 'beauty' and 'nobility' of the wild animals in comparison to the domesticated forms.

The configurational characters which elicit positive or negative response of our anthropomorphic sensations of beauty in such cases can also be abstracted from 'dummies' which evoke a 'misplaced response' of these value judgements. Just as we have done with respect to other releasing mechanisms, the responses of human beings to the products of 'representational industry' and to animal forms can be evaluated as such dummy experiments. If fashion designs are regarded as an example of the former, we once again find the typical tendency towards production of 'superoptimal' stimulus combinations, and we can easily pinpoint the characters which are *exaggerated* for this very purpose. With male figures, these are predominantly the proportional character of broad

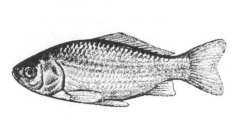

(7a)

(7b)

(7c)

(7d)

Fig. 7. *Wild animals and corresponding domesticated derivatives. a. crucian carp and veil-tailed goldfish. b. wild and domestic goose. c. wild and domestic chicken. d. wolf and domestic dog. Note the shortening of all skeletal structures and the retarded nature of locomotor organs in the domesticated forms*

shoulders and narrow hips, the 'striking' angularity of facial features, the upright body posture, and other characters. With females, they are the narrowness of the waist, the flexibility of the body, the general 'boneless' contours with more-or-less sinus-like curves, and certain proportional characters of shoulder, waist and hip width, which can in fact be transformed following changes in fashion to fit fatter or slimmer body forms, but nevertheless remain approximately constant both in vertical arrangement (probable relationship to the 'golden section'!) and in horizontal projection. Common to the representation of both sexes is an almost limitless exaggeration of the length of extremities. Analogous relationship characters can of course also be abstracted from the products of true art, and here it would seem to be significant that in the decay periods following the full flowering of different art epochs there is frequently the occurrence of an exaggeration of the described relationship characters analogous to that in fashion design.

Wherever an artist attempts deliberately to give a representation of ugliness, he by no means chooses random distortions of the ideal Gestalt, but regularly seizes upon typical domestication characters: The sculptors of classical antiquity represented Silenus as having short, bowed legs and as a fat chondrodystrophic type with a hanging stomach and a pug-head. With Socrates, too, who is historically recorded as an ugly man, the pug-head was used in representation.

Fig. 8. *Socrates is always represented in Greek sculpture as a chondrodystrophic pug-head. For comparison, a bust of Pericles which is to some extent fashionably flattering*

In the same way, the caricature – in cases where ugliness is deliberately represented – in the majority of cases hits out at the domestication characters already mentioned. Take, for example, Wilhelm Busch's Knopp or the dwarfs of the Swede Högfeldt, with their almost demonic ugliness.

It is also possible to abstract many of the discussed configurational characters from the animal forms which are perceived as beautiful or ugly. When a hippopotamus or a toad is interpreted as ugly and a gazelle or a heron is interpreted as beautiful, the analogy to Silenus and fashion ideals is immediately clear. The blind anthropomorphism of our response is particularly clear, since the hippopotamus is actually just as finely equilibriated and harmonic a systemic entity as the gazelle. Self-examination straight away shows the very close relationship of the aesthetic feelings concerned to the 'physiognomic' sensations of animal forms discussed above, which are certainly nothing else than misplaced response of innate releasing mechanisms adapted for true human releasers.

The postulated correlation between our aesthetic sensations and typical domestication characters briefly sketched here can be demonstrated with a vast number of further examples. The exceptions which do not fit the hypotheses are so few in number that they statistically scarcely effect the clarity of the correlation. In addition, many of them can be accounted for by supplementary hypotheses (domestication-induced disruption of the appropriate releasing mechanism) such that they confirm rather than question the rule.

I regard it as extremely significant for the relationship with which we are concerned here that exactly the same correlation exists between our ethical evaluation feelings and domestication-induced alterations of behaviour as between aesthetic feelings and morphological domestication characters. In this case too, the ethically highly valued behaviour patterns are just exactly those which are adversely affected by typical domestication-induced deficiency, whilst those judged to be 'bad' and inferior are those which tend to hypertrophy through domestication.

Among the endogenous-automatic behaviour patterns of human beings, each was originally equally valuable and necessary for the preservation of the species – food-uptake and mating just as much as parental care responses or more highly differentiated social impulses. The fact that we perceive one to be ethically valueless, indeed sinful, and the other as a highly estimable moral attribute, is no doubt closely related to the fact that the former are overdeveloped in civilized human beings just as in domestic animals, whilst the latter tend to disappear. It is a peculiar inverted irony on the part of mankind that we should describe as 'animal' the excess of certain drives which occurs in just this fashion only in man and some of his domestic animals! All of the prophets and religious founders who campaigned against 'sensual lust' as such, intuitively recognized the destructive part played by such drive-hypertrophy. Apart from drive-hypertrophy, it is mainly certain effects of the expansion and loss of selectivity of some innate releasing mechanisms which provoke our negative ethical evaluation feelings. The most common results of a relatively restricted expansion of innate schemata and the consequent lack of discrimination of certain responses are just exactly what we perceive as 'vulgar'.

It is characteristic of all of these purely emotional value judgements that they do not respond to random, monstrous distortions of human social behaviour. Rare and irregular deficiency symptoms in social behaviour elicit our emotional indignation far less than the day-to-day 'sordidness' of typical domestication effects. A **sexual** or mass murderer does indeed elicit horror and amazement, just like any impersonal natural catastrophe, but our emotions do not respond with anything like the intensity which might rationally be expected. Ethical indignation stemming from the deep, emotional levels of our soul responds only to more 'understandable' crimes. This very 'understanding', in my opinion, is based on genuine innate correlates to certain behavioural relationship characters.

Even if these relationship characters were not to correspond down to the last detail with the typical dedifferentiation symptoms in the innate behaviour of domestic animals, as is actually the case, the relationships just discussed would themselves support the assumption that there is also a genetic basis for disruption of human social behaviour. Our *response* to these disruptions is, with a probability close to certainty, inherited, and I find it difficult to imagine that human beings should incorporate inherited innate releasing mechanisms for non-hereditary characters of human behaviour. Apart from this, the evident relationship between our aesthetic and our ethical value judgements speaks in favour of this assumption. The object to which the above-discussed aesthetic relationship schemata are adapted is doubtless the morphological domestication character, and this is just as certainly genetically determined. It is thus an obvious step to assume the same for certain, equally narrowly anthropomorphic ethical value judgements, which introspectively cannot be separated at all from aesthetic judgements and are objectively linked to the latter by several intermediates, i.e. to regard the behavioural disruptions to which they respond as similarly genetically determined.

I emphasize once again that by no means *all* aesthetic and ethical value judgements are based on such a narrow, anthropomorphic innate releasing mechanism.[38] What I maintain here is simply that *such mechanisms do exist* and that they represent important elements as relatively entity-independent components of human social behaviour. They cannot be neglected by sociological research-workers without giving rise to grave misinterpretations.

IV   The constitutive dangers to mankind

1. DOMESTICATION-INDUCED DEFICIENCIES AS A PRECONDITION OF HUMANIZATION

Arnold Gehlen's comment that man is a *'cultural being by nature'* proves to be a bold conception which is convincingly correct in more than one aspect, from the standpoint of comparative behavioural research. It has already been stated that the human being represents the 'instinct-reduction organism'. The 'openness to the environment' exhibited by human beings, which is regarded as a constitutive character by Gehlen – the extensive freedom from specific, hereditarily-determined adaptations to the environment – is a feature largely resulting from domestication-induced deficiencies in fixed, innate action and response norms. It was already recognized by Charles Otis Whitman, one of the first pioneers of comparative behavioural research, that loss of 'instincts' in domestic animals by no means signifies a retrogressive step in the development of intelligence – as would be expected from the theory of Spencer and Lloyd Morgan, who held 'the instinct' to be the phylogenetic predecessor of intelligent behaviour. Whitman demonstrated with a series of excellent observational examples that domesticated animals are frequently capable of solving by insight problems which the wild-form cannot master, and that the exclusive reason for this is that they have attained novel degrees of freedom in plastically purposive behaviour by loss of certain fixed, instinctive action and response norms to which the non-domesticated form of the same animal species remains firmly bound. In reference to the relationship between domestication-induced instinct deficiencies and the insight function which these render possible, Whitman made the notable statement: 'These "faults of instincts" are not intelligence, but they are the open door, through which the great educator experience comes in and performs every miracle of intellect.'

Whitman himself established an initial link between the specific 'openness to the environment' and behavioural liberty of human beings on the one hand, and such domestication-induced deficiencies on the other. It is quite definite that the disappearance or expansion of certain innate releasing mechanisms is an indispensable prerequisite for the versatility and cosmopolitan nature of man. Our closest phylogenetic relatives, the anthropoids, are all specialized for narrowly defined ecological niches and the (in geological terms) abrupt transition from the very 'stenecic' ancestral form to the extreme 'euryecic' mode of life of human beings cannot be explained on the basis of the normal processes of speciation. This can only be understood through the assumption of domestication-induced dedifferentiation processes taking place in fixed innate mechanisms, which would be possible within a few centuries.

2. THE SPECIALIST IN NON-SPECIALIZATION

Domestication is the precondition for the emergence of quite another important and peculiar human characteristic. In agreement with Gehlen, we recognize one of the constitutive characteristics of man – perhaps the most important feature of all – in his persistent, inquisitive and exploratory interaction with the world of concrete objects; in his specifically human activity of building up his own specific world in the environment.[39] However, active modification to produce an individual environment through active, curious investigation certainly occurs in fundamentally the same form with certain animal species. All animal species with which this occurs to a noteworthy extent share one common feature: they are all forms which lack highly developed, differentiated special adaptations to a specific ecological niche and a specific mode of life. In other words, they are to a certain extent average representatives of their respective zoological subdivision, being in this sense 'more primitive' than their specialized relatives. The Norway rat – a typical example of such an animal – lacks the magnificent swimming adaptation of the beaver, climbs less skilfully than the squirrel, burrows less effectively than the vole and runs far less superbly than the jerboa; but in each case the rat excels each of these four fellow members of the Order Rodentia in the three activities which are not the 'speciality' of any given species. Whereas Gehlen refers to man as the 'creature of deficiency', because of the lack of all particular specializations, I should like to lay emphasis on the nucleus of the same phenomenon by highlighting the *versatility* of such unspecialized organisms, especially since one must certainly not neglect consideration of the enormous human *brain* as a somatic organ. Even in the purely morphological aspect, man's versatility is still fairly evident in comparison with other mammals. In establishing a 'threefold test' to examine general physical adaptedness, by prescribing a 20-mile march, a climb up a 12-foot, freely suspended rope and a dive 60 feet in length at a depth of 12 feet to attain the goal of retrieving a sunken object, we set up requirements which can be fulfilled by any average citizen and which no single mammal could accomplish.

Apart from the versatility of bodily characteristics, all 'specialists in non-specialization' share a characteristic structure of innate behavioural disposition: In all cases, the juveniles exhibit peak development of curiosity and learning ability. Such young animals are irresistibly drawn to all phenomena *whose Gestalt perception lies within the realm of their abilities*. Any organism can only acquire conditioning-eliciting characters which can be perceived as Gestalts, and it is therefore understandable when the appetite to learn is particularly evoked in such young animals by objects which are rich in significant Gestalt-applicable characters. In any stimulus situation which is in some way conspicuous because of such significance, the young of unspecialized 'creatures of curiosity' literally try out all of the behaviour patterns represented in their species-specific system of actions. A young raven performs its entire repertoire of innate motor patterns towards any novel object, attempting in a series of actions to peck it to pieces, to break it up by 'prising', or to turn it over with the same motor pattern if it is large and heavy, to hide it by performing certain innate motor patterns, and so on. A young rat will experimentally sniff and gnaw at every conceivable object, will crawl through any available crevices, will climb anything which can be climbed and will 'learn by heart' all possible pathways in its accessible range.

The species-preserving function of this appetite for the unknown and this experimentation of all conceivable behaviour patterns of the species is easily discernible. The specialist in non-specialization actively constructs its environment for itself, whereas an animal with more extensive special adaptations in morphology and innate behaviour is largely born with this knowledge of the environment. In the environment of a 'specialist', such as the great crested grebe, virtually everything which is of biological relevance – the water surface, the prey, the sexual partner, the nest-material, and so on – is determined by highly differentiated innate releasing mechanisms in the species. Learning is predominantly restricted to the localization of stimulus situations which are of significance for the species. There is no capacity in the range of its abilities for self-conditioning to alter any feature in these 'a priori' inherited and species-specific conditions of the environment.

By contrast, the investigative non-specialists are always equipped with very few and extremely broad (i.e. character-*restricted*) releasing mechanisms and a relatively small number of innate motor patterns. It is quite characteristic of the latter that, as a direct result of their minor degree of specialization, they have great versatility of application. Through the fact that such animals at first treat everything novel as if it were of the greatest biological importance, they inevitably become acquainted with every small detail of the most extreme and varied ecological niches which can contribute to the preservation of their existence. *Literally all higher animals which have become 'cosmopolitans' are typical non-specialized 'creatures of curiosity'.*

Without a trace of doubt, the way in which man masters the problems of species survival is fundamentally similar to the described adaptive type of 'specialists in non-specialization'. The strength to which man predominantly owes his biological success and cosmopolitanism is doubtless the dialogue, the active interaction, with the environment, which we can briefly refer to as *investigation*. The intrinsic feature of learning through curiosity in the animals discussed lies in the *objective* interest in all novelties. When a young raven or young rat 'investigates' a novel object – i.e. tries out all conceivable behaviour patterns in its system of actions one after the other – the behaviour patterns exhibited naturally include those whose function is directly or indirectly concerned in food-acquisition; in fact such patterns are frequently more evident than others. Nevertheless, it would represent a fundamental misunderstanding of the drive-goals of the animal to arrive at the interpretation that what is ultimately concerned is appetitive behaviour directed towards feeding. In the large category of purely spatial curiosity behaviour, which leads through 'learning by heart' of all possible pathways to very exact *spatial representation*, this interpretation is excluded from the outset. But even with investigatory 'trying-out' of motor patterns whose species-preserving function is really related to food-acquisition, in a choice experiment one can always demonstrate without difficulty that what is involved is an appetite for novelty, and not feeding, which drives the animal to perform the behaviour: The very best tit-bit known to the animal is not enough to distract it from the investigation of a novel object, even when the behaviour patterns tried out include a number concerned with feeding.[40] To express this in anthropomorphic terms: The animal does not want to eat, but wants to 'know' the whole range of objects in the given surroundings which can 'theoretically' be eaten.

Active investigation by the animal is literally material to the extent that it gives rise to an environmental representation whose centre of gravity is located in *object-related* knowledge and whose treasure of 'known' details greatly excels that of other sub-human organisms. This rich 'theoretical' knowledge of the surroundings is itself the feature which permits such animals to determine, in such extremely different environments, all biologically relevant phenomena which can be exploited for continued survival. Gehlen regards it as a specifically human achievement when the subject becomes 'intimately' acquainted with every novel – and therefore attractive – object through investigatory, active interaction from all accessible aspects and then 'lets it rest there', i.e. places it literally *ad acta* so that in case of need it can at any time be referred to. But it is this very feature which is evident in exactly the same manner in all cases of 'learning by curiosity' exhibited by animal specialists in non-specialization. To give just one example: The innate behaviour pattern of food-concealment in the raven and other Corvids consists of pushing of the object concerned into a dark corner (preferably a crevice) with a predetermined species-specific motor co-ordination pattern, followed by covering with indifferent material. The precondition for smooth performance of this behaviour pattern is that there should be available material with which the bird is already intimately acquainted and which is therefore 'uninteresting'. For example, if a raven should hide a morsel of meat in a crevice in a sofa, and then – on looking around for suitable covering material – find nothing on hand (or rather 'on beak'), one cannot aid the bird by throwing down paper fragments or other novel objects. This regularly disrupts the bird's behavioural intentions, since investigation of the novel object at first fully preoccupies him. The most that can happen is that, after detailed, material investigation of the paper, the bird (more-or-less by chance) will encounter the meat once again and then cover it with the paper. On the other hand, if the bird has previously investigated the paper until it has become utterly uninteresting, it will immediately be referred to when required as concealment material.

Of course, the division into 'specialists' and 'specialists in non-specialization' can only be carried out distinctly between extreme types in the animal kingdom. There are all conceivable intermediates between the two, and genuine appetitive behaviour directed at learning situations occurs with almost all higher animals during certain stages of juvenile development. Most of the behaviour patterns of offspring of higher mammals which appear so 'human' and are commonly assembled under the poorly-defined heading of *play*, prove on closer investigation to be the inquisitive trying-out of species-specific behaviour patterns on novel objects possessing significant Gestalt-applicable features. In every instance where innate releasing mechanisms permit a certain range of variation in the object and simultaneously require restriction through acquisition, it is common to find in the 'construction' of the species-specific system of actions, at the appropriate site, a 'pre-arranged' appetite for novel and Gestalt-applicable features. The young cat, which attempts with its magnificently gracious predatory motor patterns to catch anything which in any way fits into the 'mouse schema', and continually finds novel objects for such play, provides a very well-known example of this process. A young mongoose (*Herpestes mungo* L.), in the extent of its investigative drive, approaches very closely the typical specialists in non-specialization. Anybody who would like to read an appealing and humorous description incorporating acute observations of the curiosity behaviour of such animals should read Rudyard Kipling's wonderful mongoose story *Rikkitikkitavi*.

The importance of the part played by learning through curiosity in the behavioural biology of an animal species is of course closely correlated not only with the absence of specific adaptations, but also with the absolute organizational level of intelligence – in particular learning ability – of the animal. Therefore, curious investigation by young animals is very pronounced in the mammals with the greatest powers of intelligence – the anthropoid apes. It is at least as intensive as in Norway rats or Corvids, although all living anthropoid apes are far greater 'specialists' than the former. For this reason, the 'theoretical', object-directed curiosity of young chimpanzees and orang-utans is particularly impressive, since its interaction with the well-developed spatial representation of these grasping climbers produces extremely complicated 'play behaviour' which is both formally and intrinsically identical with the 'experimental play' (Charlotte Bühler) of young human children. It is amazing how much is exhibited along these lines by the young of lower monkeys (e.g. the capucine monkey, *Cebus*) in playful construction and interlocking of objects, in the employment of lever actions, and so on. One is repeatedly astounded that this intensive investigatory behaviour, which is so similar to human behaviour in its material relation to objects, ultimately gives rise to no more than a skilfully-climbing monkey, who knows which branches are brittle and should therefore be avoided, which fruits can be opened by smashing with a stone, etc. This amazement reaches its peak in the observation of young anthropoid apes. The discrepancy between remarkably human-like curious investigation by the young animal and the behaviour of the adult ape, which is so distinct from its human counterpart, is so great that I am repeatedly led to assume that the ancestors of living anthropoid apes possessed far greater capacities of learning through curiosity and applied manipulation of objects than do the recent forms, in which these higher functions emerge in a vague manner only in the play of young animals. This is, of course, pure speculation, since in this case the question 'rudiment or oriment' will hardly ever be open to definite solution.[41]

3. THE INCOMPLETE CREATURE

This title is once again allied to a concept established by Gehlen. As we have seen, active, dialogue-like investigatory construction of an individual environment is not an achievement peculiar to man. Nevertheless, the openness of man to his surroundings is different from that of animal 'specialists in non-specialization', not only in a quantitatively graded manner but also qualitatively. This considerable difference is based on the fact that in man investigative interaction with the environment *remains preserved until the onset of senility*, whereas with all animals – even the most intelligent and inquisitive – this represents no more than a brief phase in individual development. Even with the most adaptable of all sub-human organisms, what is acquired by learning through curiosity *becomes fixed* in fundamentally exactly the same manner as the individual acquisitions of far less intelligent and more specially adapted animals. In their *completed* condition, behaviour patterns actively established in the wake of learning through curiosity are just as rigid as any other conditioned patterns of behaviour, in fact almost as rigid as innate, species-specific action and response norms. The saying that 'an old dog cannot learn new tricks' applies without restriction to all other unspecialized 'creatures of curiosity'. An old raven or an old rat has no single trace of the openness to the surroundings which strikes us as so 'human' and closely related when observing a young animal. The appetite for novel stimulus situations has completely disappeared, and the animal reacts *adversely* to such by exhibiting intensive flight responses. If such an animal is forcibly placed in novel surroundings in captivity, it exhibits an almost disappointing lack of adaptability. Particularly with old ravens, one can in such cases observe a form of behaviour which exhibits significant parallels to senile dementia in human beings. The latter similarly exhibit complete orientation in their habitual surroundings, and appear to know how to behave properly by insight. However, if they are forcibly subjected to a change in environment, they prove to be mentally unbalanced through their inability to adapt in any way. In new surroundings, old ravens are subject to typical fear neurosis. They prove to be completely disoriented, no longer recognizing acquainted persons, and they completely forget the unpenetrability of cage-wire, flying against the latter just like freshly-captured birds.

But what is the source of this remarkable persistent juvenile characteristic of investigative curiosity in human beings, which is so fundamental to the essence of humanity? The first answer that can be given is that curiosity and openness to surroundings is far from being the only persistent juvenile characteristic of man. As was first observed and convincingly demonstrated by Bolk, a whole range of morphological characters in which man differs from his closest phylogenetic relatives are the result of a peculiar developmental inhibition which, so-to-speak, results in persistent 'juvenescence' of human beings. The relative lack of hair on the body combined with the presence of hair on the head, the predominance of the cerebral part of the skull over the facial region, the pronounced (almost perpendicular) angle of the cranial axis relative to the vertebral column and the accompanying forward position of the *foramen magnum*, the relatively large brain-weight, the curvature of the pelvic axis, a whole collection of structural peculiarities of the female sexual organs, the small degree of skin pigmentation, and a number of further characters, represent features which man has in common with early – in some cases foetal – developmental stages of anthropoid apes. For this reason, Bolk gave the name 'foetalization' to the whole character-complex of human beings.

In essence, this involves the same phylogenetic process as that long recognized in zoology under the term *neoteny*. In Crustacea, Diptera, Urodela and many other animal groups, it can occur that the final stages of ontogenetic development are (in geological terms) abruptly lost. The animal species concerned therefore does not attain the previous final stage of development and instead reaches sexual maturity in a condition which previously represented no more than a transitional juvenile, or larval, stage. The number of persistent juvenile characters in human beings is so large, and they are so decisive for his overall *habitus,* that I can see no cogent reason for regarding the general juvenescence of man as anything other than a special case of true *neoteny.*

For anybody who has correctly grasped the fundamental unity and conceptual inseparability of form and function, it will be immediately obvious that the persistence of juvenile behavioural characteristics in man is intimately correlated with that of morphological characters. *The constitutive character of man – the maintenance of active, creative interaction with the environment – is a neotenous* phenomenon. Whoever, moved by awe of the past, has observed the experimental play of young anthropoid apes and has been accessible to the influence of the absolute intrinsic identity of such play and the corresponding activity of young children; whoever has experienced, with his own children, the general development from the experimental play of the 'chimpanzee age' (Charlotte Bühler) to the manipulations of the growing boy; and, finally, whoever has observed in his own behaviour the smooth transitions from the play of the child to the investigative activities of the grown man, will never doubt the fundamental identity of all of these processes. If Nietzsche's statement 'in the true man, there is a child concealed – who wants to play' did not so exactly fit the phylogenetic facts and the constitutive mental neoteny of human beings, one would be tempted to invert it to read: 'In the true child, there is a man concealed – who wants to investigate.'

The characteristic which is so vital for the human peculiarity of the true man – that of always remaining *in a state of development* – is quite certainly a gift which we owe to the neotenous nature of mankind. On the other hand, however, neoteny is itself most probably *a result of domestication of man,* just like the liberation from the rigid bonds of innate action and response norms discussed in the last chapter. Hilzheimer has shown that a very large number of characters arising in various domestic animals and distinguishing them from the wild type are persistent juvenile characteristics. Drooping ears and short hair in many dog breeds, the generally distributed shortening of the skull base and the consequent bulging of the cranium found in domestic animals, the shortening of the skeletal extremities, and many other features, are characters which are evident in the wild type only during a brief phase of ontogenetic development, but which in domestic animals have become persistent breed characteristics.

The same applies quite distinctly to behavioural characters. To take an example: if a young wolf, jackal or dingo is reared in the family circle from an early age just like a domestic dog, it will at first behave just like a house-dog. In other words, the animal quite simply transfers to certain human beings the juvenile attachment which it would have exhibited towards its mother (and later the leader of the pack) under natural conditions. But whereas a domestic dog retains these essentially 'childish' bonds throughout its life, individuals of the wild forms mentioned – particularly the males – exhibit, as soon as they are full-grown, a conspicuous tendency to become independent, i.e. to aspire to the rank of leading animal. They then become hostile to the former master, attempting to intimidate him and to make him hierarchically subordinate. It is a remarkable fact that a dog, which fits into human society better than any other domestic animal, owes its major behavioural characteristics to neoteny, just like man himself: just like actively investigative openness to surroundings in human beings, fidelity to a master represents a persistent juvenile characteristic in the dog.[42]

It is worth noting in passing that persistent retention of investigatory interaction with the environment, although it is the most important feature, is not the only constitutive behavioural characteristic which man owes to neoteny. The results of psychoanalysis convincingly show the large part played by the continual persistence of certain bonds with the father in the social behaviour of human beings. The idea of an anthropomorphic god, which is common to so many civilized races, is (almost certainly correctly) traced back to these phenomena by Freud.

4. THE 'JEOPARDIZED' CREATURE

Gehlen recognizes a further constitutive aspect of man in that the human being represents the endangered or 'jeopardized' creature – the creature 'with a constitutional chance to encounter mishaps'. From what has been said about domestication phenomena as a prerequisite of humanization, it is sufficiently obvious that this conception presented by Gehlen also incorporates a profound truth. Origin of the specifically human characteristic of behavioural liberty was quite definitely dependent upon the reduction and disruption of rigidly structured action and response norms. Like all other rigid structures, innate behaviour patterns also exhibit the property of supporting and reinforcing. The consequent, adaptable 'rigidity' of behaviour could only be dismantled at the expense of the supporting function and therefore with the loss of safeguards. Each new element of behavioural plasticity had to be bought in exchange for certain degrees of security.

Every process of organic further development – particularly with respect to intelligence – is always a peculiar compromise between these two inseparable and yet so contrasting aspects of all rigid structures. Without rigid structures, no organic system with a high level of integration is possible; but in every case the structures of the existing system must be undone if a system with a still higher level of integration and harmony is to be attained. This unfortunate dilemma is a fundamental attribute of all organic further developments. When a crustacean moults, when a human being undergoes an alteration in personality structure from that of the child to that of a man at puberty, or when an archaic human social order is transformed to a new one, the developmental advance is in every case accompanied by dangers. The reason for this is that the old structure must be dismantled before the new one has achieved full functional capacity. No other organism is or was exposed to these dangers to the same extent as man, since no other in the entire history of life on our planet has experienced, or is experiencing, such headlong development.[43] Phylogenetically and ontogenetically, man is 'the incomplete creature'; ontogenetically and phylogenetically, he is involved in a virtually continuous series of 'moults', and is never in the state of statically equilibriated structural adaptation which can persist for geological epochs of enormous duration with other organisms.

There are very few philosophical dicta which maintain the opposite of the truth so fundamentally as the old saying: *natura non facit saltum!* From the events within the atom to those in the history of mankind, inorganic and organic developments occur in leaps. Even though certain cases of quantitative summation in developmental processes may appear to be continuous when superficially observed, they are basically just as discontinuous as the large qualitative changes occurring in organic development, which were first clearly recognized as such by Hegel. The dangers discussed above as inherent in all of the more significant leaps in organic developmental processes are, understandably, proportional to the magnitude of the individual leaps. We are therefore not at all surprised that one of the greatest qualitative changes that has ever taken place in the history of organic events – that of the evolutionary leap from the anthropoid ape to man, which (in geological terms) took place so extremely rapidly – is accompanied by enormous dangers for the newly evolved creature.

Even somebody who doubts the hypotheses of comparative behavioural research sketched above – in particular the rôle played by domestication – must admit that the structures whose dismantling has led to the endangerment of mankind are those of *innate behaviour*. The price which man had to pay for his constitutive liberty in thinking processes and behavioural acts is that of adaptedness to a specific environment and a specific form of social existence, which in all sub-human organisms is guaranteed by species-specific, inherited action and response norms.

This adaptedness signifies, in the social context, nothing other than complete agreement between inclination and necessity, i.e. the problemless life in paradise which had to be sacrificed in return for the fruits of the tree of knowledge. ·

The functional process which substitutes for the lost 'instincts' in man is that of dialogue-like, *investigatory* interaction with the environment, the process of 'coming to an understanding' with external reality as is etymologically expressed in the word *Vernunft* (*reason*). Man is the creature of reason. But he is not *exclusively* a creature of reason; his behaviour is by no means so thoroughly determined by reason as is assumed by the majority of philosophical anthropologists. There is a far greater degree of influence exerted by innate, species-specific action and response norms than we usually like to believe and accept. This particularly applies to human *social* behaviour. It has been stated above (p. 147) that in animals of advanced intelligence behaviour towards a conspecific is controlled far more by innate components and far less by higher intelligent functions than behaviour towards the extra-specific environment. That this is unfortunately equally true of human beings as well is crudely expressed in the incongruity between man's mastery of his external environment and his stunning inability to solve the intraspecific problems of mankind.

This is by no means due to the fact that these intraspecific (in the broadest sense, *social*) problems are in any way more difficult than those of the external environment. The opposite is true. The fission of the atom, without a trace of doubt, presents the human mind with far more difficult tasks than the question of how one can prevent human beings from wiping one another out with the aid of atom bombs. There are many people of above-average intelligence whose ability for abstract thought is simply not adequate for performing the non-descriptive, mathematical thought processes on which modern atomic physics is based. On the other hand, even somebody of sub-normal intelligence can immediately see what would have to happen, and what must be avoided, in order to prevent the self-destruction of mankind. Despite the enormous difference in conceptual difficulties between these two problems, mankind has solved that of atomic processes within a few decades, whilst man is today even more helpless against the danger of self-destruction – which emerged with the invention of the first weapon, the hand-axe – than at the time of Pekin man!

The fact that even the most modest powers of reason are adequate for recognition of what should not happen, and that this nevertheless occurs, gives much food for thought. Wherever something of this nature occurs in the more transparent behaviour of the human individual, where self-observation is possible (i.e. where, despite full insight into a situation of vital importance, something contrary to reason nevertheless irresistibly takes its course), there is almost always *blockage* of the application of rational thought by dominant innate, species-specific action and response patterns. It is a fairly obvious step to assume the same for analogous, supra-individual, collective failure of rational application. At least, this assumption is promising enough as a working hypothesis for disfunction of innate species-specific behaviour patterns to be seriously taken into account as a probable cause of the otherwise completely unintelligible failure of collective human reason in the face of relatively simple problems. I shall therefore give a compressed account of a series of possible – indeed, probable – disruptive mechanisms of social behaviour patterns:

The first, and probably most important, of these mechanisms is the following: With every organism that is plucked out of its natural environment and placed in novel surroundings, behaviour patterns occur which are neutral or even detrimental for the survival of the species. This phenomenon always arises through the fact that a specific behaviour pattern, based upon endogenous stimulus-production and adapted for a quite specific, species-preserving function, is robbed of its normal releasing situation, such that accumulation of action-specific energy leads to its eruption in a completely inadequate stimulus situation. This is referred to as a *misplaced response.*

Modern man represents such an animal, torn from his natural environmental niche. Within a space of time which – from the geological-phylogenetic standpoint – is immeasurably short, the flowering of human culture has so extensively changed the entire ecology and sociology of our species that a whole range of previously adaptive endogenous behaviour patterns have become not only non-functional but extremely disruptive. We have become acquainted with the most important example of this in the so-called aggressive drive (p. 149 et seq.). For a chimpanzee, and even for early stone-age man, it would be doubtless quite valuable and necessary in the sense of maintenance of individuals, families and the species that internal stimulus-production should be adequate to produce, say, two major outbursts of rage per week. But since such innate action/response norms, in so far as they are not affected by sudden deficiency mutations induced by domestication, can only change at the same phylogenetic tempo as organic structures, it is not particularly surprising that modern man, immersed in his police-protected existence, does not know what to do with these rhythmically-occurring outbursts of rage. In colloquial language, there is a very neat expression of the human quality of 'looking for a good row', summarizing the fact that a relatively harmless discharge of this accumulated response-specific energy has the value of curative catharsis.

The increased motivation for aggression, which is a result of just this accumulation of response-specific energy, is doubtless the cause of the easily *incitable* nature of man. Everybody is pleased to some degree to find a 'permissible' substitute object for his stored aggressive tendencies and happily seizes upon the clumsiest 'dummy' offered by a clever demagogue. I maintain that without this purely physiological basis all of the past cases of demagogically directed mass cruelty, such as witch-craft trials or anti-semitic persecution, would have been fundamentally impossible.

A very similar rôle of 'misplaced response' is played by the more complex behaviour pattern of social defence, which has also been mentioned previously. As already indicated, this response is also only too easily evoked by dummies presented by demagogues. Because of the highly pleasurable character of its subjective experiential correlate, that of social or national fervour, this response is particularly dangerous. It should be unreservedly admitted that it is a magnificent experience to sing the national anthem, overcome by a 'holy' paroxysm, and it is only too easy to forget that the paroxysm represents the hair-erection of the old chimpanzee pelage and that the entire response is fundamentally directed *against* one 'enemy' or another. Above all, nowadays when cave-bears and sabre-toothed tigers no longer exist as dangers to human society, this 'enemy' is always a society of fellow human beings, who feel just as committed to enthusiastic defence of *their* society! The social and (in the profoundest sense of the word) ethical value which doubtless exists in the *unifying* function of the human response concerned will only be accessible to mankind when we have learnt to insert into the 'schema' of the enemy the dangers which really threaten humanity and not a chosen group of fellow human beings set up by a demagogue!

The next mechanism of disruption affecting social behaviour patterns to be discussed finds its cause, just like the preceding case, in the headlong change in social conditions, with which the phylogenetic mutability of species-specific innate action/response norms cannot keep pace. But in this case the disruption is not based on the fact that *lesser* exhaustion of action-specific stimulus-production provides a disruptive excess of impulses; instead, rapid further differentiation of the human social order has led to the necessity for a *greater occurrence* of certain social behaviour patterns which our innate system of social action and response patterns is unable to provide. Among the culturally determined alterations of human social life involved, the predominant effect is probably based on the change from an originally *closed* form of human society to an *anonymous* type. With a very large number of innate social response patterns of human beings, one of the prerequisites for release is that the fellow human being towards whom they are directed should be a personally acquainted member of the society – a 'friend'. Among the ten commandments, those which concern behaviour towards fellow men are followed as a matter of course from natural inclination without any demand upon responsible, moral decision, as long as the 'neighbour' is a personally well-acquainted friend and companion. When one remembers what was said in the section covering animal behaviour patterns exhibiting moral analogies, and calls to mind the close-knit nature of the society represented by a chimpanzee troop – despite jealousy and rank-order squabbles, then one must assume that innate social behaviour patterns played at least the same rôle in primitive human groups. We fundamentally disagree with the biblical thesis defended by some child psychologists and psychoanalysts, that man is utterly 'wicked from childhood on'. Our primitive ancestor, before the actual process of 'humanization', was – at the very least – just as 'good' as a wolf or chimpanzee, in both of which youngsters and females are spared from harm and in which even a jealously fought male society member is protected against an external enemy without hesitation and with all possible vigour. I should like to paraphrase the biblical text to read: Man is not wicked from childhood on, but just good enough for the requirements which were made of him in the primitive human group, in which the small number of individuals were personally acquainted with one another and 'loved' one another after their own fashion. He is not good *enough* for the requirements set by the enormously expanded, anonymous society of later cultural epochs, which demand that he should behave towards any completely unacquainted fellow human being as if he were a personal friend.

Another, extremely special case of this described phenomenon of increasing inaccessibility of innate social action/response norms also entered into the penetrating, abrupt change in human relationships brought about by the *invention of weapons*. One must call to mind what was said in the section on behavioural systems exhibiting ethic analogies, where we discussed the finely-balanced equilibrium which operates between the ability to kill and innate killing inhibitions of an animal species. It then becomes immediately clear how great a danger is presented for the further survival of the species by any disruption of this equilibrium favouring the side of killing ability. Whenever an old male chimpanzee, despite his powerful aggressive drives, refrains from killing or even damaging a weaker conspecific (which would be to the detriment of species survival), it is thanks to species-specific innate inhibitions, which are elicited by highly specific releasing mechanisms. We have become acquainted with 'submissive' postures and calls which represent releasers of such inhibitions. These 'sympathy-releasing' inhibition-evoking factors are, of course, only operative for the species-specific, somewhat slow and gruesome methods of killing with the natural weapons of the species. If one now imagines that such an excitable and vicious creature is quite suddenly presented with a 'more humane' method of killing, whose extremely rapid operation completely excludes functioning of the described inhibition-releasers, then one can understand the terrible consequences which the invention of weapons – from the hand-axe to the atom-bomb – had and has for mankind. The biological situation is fundamentally the same as if a gruesome freak of nature had suddenly equipped the turtle-dove, which (as we have seen) possesses no killing inhibitions whatsoever and no equivalent releasing mechanisms, with the beak of a raven, but without at the same time fitting the dove with the inhibitory mechanisms which are correlated with the presence of this weapon in the raven. However, it must immediately be added, as a corollary to this, that in exact terms the invention of a weapon by a *non-responsible* animal is impossible; the example is purely imaginary and simply intended to demonstrate the mechanism of endangerment. The emergence of a genuine invention, such as that of the hand-axe, is dependent upon an extremely high degree of differentiation of dialogue-like, investigative interaction with the environment, which itself is very close to genuine setting of questions and understanding of the answers. The ability for invention and that for responsibility are dependent upon the same prerequisites.

The failure of killing inhibitions in the situation produced by the invention of weapons is principally based on the fact that the innate mechanisms releasing an inhibition do not respond in the new situation. The deeper, emotional layers of our natures to some extent fail to 'understand' the consequences of the use of weapons, and it is obviously not quite sufficient that reason should grasp something which is emotionally inaccessible. The amazingly small degree of inhibition which thoroughly sympathetic and agreeable civilized human beings exhibit with respect to killing animals, or even other human beings in battle, is entirely understandable on this basis of inability to 'understand'. Like all other emotions, those of sympathy only respond to situations for which we have a predetermined, innate receptor correlate. If an armed man were brought to realize the actual consequences of his actions – the fact that through tensing of his finger on a trigger he can rip out the entrails of a living creature – in a manner not only accessible to his reason, but also immediately accessible to his emotions (i.e. in a manner *similar to that operating in the use of natural weapons*), only very few human beings would hunt for pleasure and the vast majority would be conscientious objectors. The firing of a long-range gun or the dropping of a bomb is so thoroughly 'impersonal' that normal human beings who are absolutely incapable of throttling a mortal enemy with their hands are nevertheless able, without further ado, to apply finger-pressure to deliver up thousands of women and children to a horrible death.

Whereas the three disruptive mechanisms so far discussed are basically derivatives from the same cause, i.e. the conservative nature and incorrigibility of innate species-specific behaviour patterns, the mechanism now to be discussed is based upon domestication-induced *mutability* of some of these patterns. One change is naturally bound up with another, and the mutual relationships between the different mutable and immutable aspects is in reality extremely complex. The fact that the conservatism in *one* type of behaviour pattern is at all able to exhibit a disruptive effect of the kind described is ultimately dependent on the fact that *other* patterns have been lost and thus gave man new degrees of behavioural liberty and therefore the possibility of achieving amazing transitions in his ecology and sociology. The second dichotomous feature of domestication effects – the entire 'audacity' of human behaviour – is of course based on the fact that individual action/response norms *had to be* lost so that 'man could become human', whilst at the same time others *could not* be lost (or even markedly quantitatively augmented or decreased) so that man would remain human. With the blind randomness of all mutational effects, domestication-induced changes affect one just as easily as the other. Domestication on the one hand gave us the constitutive liberty of our behaviour and on the other spreads clear-cut *pathological* hereditary changes and lethal factors. The phenomena referred to as *emotional deficiency* and *value blindness* in psychopathology (P. Schröder) are definitely based on genetic foundations, and very probably on the loss of ethical and aesthetic relationship schemata. Certain pathological increases in aggressive behaviour and so-called over-assertiveness are based on the processes of domestication-induced hypertrophy of the endogenous stimulus-production underlying these behaviour patterns.

It is characteristic of this disruptive mechanism, which is not a generally human feature but a special pathological case, that rational morality is unable to compensate for it. In conclusion, we shall now need to give a closer consideration to the essential restriction in the power of rational thought.

5. THE FUNCTIONAL LIMITATIONS OF RATIONAL MORALITY

The aim of this article is to demonstrate the absolute obligatory requirement for consideration of innate, species-specific action/response norms of human beings in the investigation of inter-human relationships. It is not intended to discuss the nature of rational thought and its specific compensatory and regulatory function in human beings. For this, the reader is referred to the article which has already been extensively cited. Nobody is further from underestimating the difference between man and animals than the comparative behavioural investigator, and nobody can more clearly calculate the absolute *novelty* of the enormous regulative powers over maintenance and further development of existence which are inherent in the rational responsibility of man. The character of a hitherto unknown, novel creation which is exhibited by our moral law affects the comparative behavioural investigator more than any other 'with ever-recurring feelings of bewonderment'.[44] I maintain that one can only recognize the uniqueness of man in its entire, impressive magnitude when this may be *separated* from the background of old, historic characteristics which man still shares today with the higher animals.

But what we are concerned with in this article is just exactly this old aspect of human behaviour, which can only be explained historically and which in fact does *not* obey the laws of rational, responsible morality. The misinterpretation against which this article is directed is the general *overestimation* of the influence exerted by the totality of human society on the structure of the individual and the combined *underestimation* of the influence exerted on the structure and function of the supra-individual society by fixed, phyletically/historically transmitted structures of the individual. As regards theories of morality, this misinterpretation is represented in overestimation of the function of rational morality and underestimation of the rôle played even in human beings by moral-analogous systems of innate behaviour, such as we have encountered on pp. 146–153 in animal behaviour. I continue to hold the opinion expressed in a previous publication, '. . . that in no single case of regularly occurring action by an individual human being bearing upon the welfare and woe of the society is there exclusive operation of the categorical imperative providing impulse and motive for the altruistic act. Instead, in the great majority of cases, the primary active impulse is provided by the response of innate schemata and inherited drives. It is exceedingly difficult to construct situations which are really indifferent as releasers of innate responses, but at the same time demand of us an active and altruistic attitude along the pathway of rational consideration.'

On the other hand, I do not believe that I am guilty of the equivalent misinterpretation of *underestimating* the function of responsible thought in social behaviour of modern man. The culturally determined changes in human ecology and sociology are so profound that hardly one of our natural 'inclinations' is *completely* sufficient to meet the requirements of modern social structure. A supplementary spur in the form of a categorical 'thou shalt' or a supplementary inhibition in the form of a 'thou shalt not' is necessary at every stage. No modern human being can give free rein to his innate inclinations, and presumably this provides the basis for the age-old human longing for the 'lost paradise'. Not only civilized men, but all human beings everywhere are afflicted by 'discomfort in their culture' (S. Freud). No human being is 'happy' in the sense applicable to a wild animal, whose innate inclinations are entirely in accord with what 'should be done' in the interests of species-survival.

Similarly no human being is 'normal' in the same sense. P. Schröder defines the *psychopath* as a human being who either suffers himself from his constitutional psychic predisposition, or makes human society suffer instead. Following what has been said above, it at first seems that we are all – without exception – psychopaths according to this definition, since we all 'suffer' from the necessity either to restrain or to supplement our innate action and response patterns through rational responsibility. However, Schröder's concept at once becomes clear and utilizable when the verb 'suffer' is used in the *medical* sense. With the augmentation in breadth of variation typical of domesticated organisms, human beings also exhibit in their innate social behaviour patterns an extremely wide margin for the average, so that the concept of 'normality' is just as impossible to determine with respect to our inclinations, and the consequent behavioural impulses, as it is with respect to morphological characters. For this reason, the function of regulative compensation afforded by rational morality shows great variation in extent from one human being to another. But even if we completely discard the concept of normality, the division between the *healthy man* and the psychopath intended by Schröder remains completely distinct. This division is based on the fact that the higher personality structure of a human being – together with his rationalistic social morality – breaks down with an *abrupt* transition when the compensatory function is stretched beyond capacity. A human being then exhibits either *asocial behaviour* or *illness*, i.e. developing what is termed a neurosis (or – particularly – a neurotic symptom) by psychopathologists. To take a simile from pathology for this pathological process: A mentally healthy human being does not bear the same relation to a psychopath as a physically healthy person does to a physically sick one, it is more nearly that of a person with a compensated hear-defect compared to someone with decompensated *vitium cordis*. This simile symbolizes very well the distinctness of the boundary between the healthy person and the psychopath and renders immediately understandable the enormous and unpredictable individual differences in tolerance for moral overloading in so-called normal human beings.

V Summary and conclusions

This article is directed against the widely-occurring methodological error found in sociology and ethnological psychology, which consists in utterly neglecting the fixed structural properties of the human individual which are *not* accessible to influence exerted by the totality of the society. This methodological error is derived from two sources, which are considered separately.

The first source – *false generalization of principles of Gestalt psychology* – is discussed in the first section. It is utterly impermissible to generalize properties of the perceptual Gestalt to all organic entities. Examples of absurd overestimation of the principle of primacy of the entity over its components are discussed (pp. 116–119). The nature of organic systems is briefly discussed, and it is demonstrated why they are not 'entities' in the same sense as perceptual Gestalts. There follows a description of the method of analysis on a broad front which is obligatory for study of organic systemic entities (p. 119 et seq.).

No organic system is entirely covered by the definition of an entity as a system of general, reciprocal causal relationships, since each includes fixed *relatively independent components*, which are linked to the totality in a more-or-less one-way (i.e. non-amboceptor) causal relationship (p. 121 et seq.).

The second source of the methodological error laid bare in this article rests in neglect of *innate, species-specific behaviour patterns*. This provides the content of the second section. It is first demonstrated how the theoretical dispute between the mechanist and vitalist schools of behavioural research exerted an inhibitory effect on the discovery and investigation of innate, species-specific behaviour patterns (p. 126 et seq.). It is shown that the predominant principles governing innate behaviour could only be identified from the broad inductive basis of comparative research, and that this is a major reason for the late discovery of such patterns (p. 129 et seq.).

There follows, in compressed form, the research history relating to the nature and peculiarity of the two most important individually invariable components of animal and human behaviour – the *endogenous-automatic motor pattern* (p. 131 et seq.) and the *innate releasing mechanism* (p. 135 et seq.).

A special chapter (p. 140 et seq.) is dedicated to the so-called *releasers* (i.e. differentiations of structure and behaviour whose function lies in the transmission of specifically-answered signal stimuli). The phylogenetic origin of releasing motor patterns through the *formalization of intention movements* (p. 145 et seq.) is extensively discussed. This is of importance, since the majority of human motor display patterns owe their existence to this process.

Subsequently, there is a demonstration of the functional operation in social animals of highly complex systems exclusively based on the function of endogenous-automatic motor patterns, innate releasing mechanisms and stimulus-transmitting releasers. In these, faculties of higher intelligence (e.g. involving acquired components) play an extremely minor rôle, and yet there are nevertheless extensive functional analogies to the rational-moralistic behaviour of human beings (p. 146 et seq.).

The human being also possesses innate releasing mechanisms. The first examples provided are of those which respond to human *motor display patterns* (p. 154 et seq.). These themselves are genuine releasers, in fact of the type which we have already encountered above under the heading of formalized intention movements. In addition, certain aesthetic and ethical value judgements made by human beings are based on the response of innate releasing mechanisms (p. 158 et seq.). It is shown that there is a remarkable correlation existing between these extremely rigid and compulsively responding schemata and certain morphological and behavioural *domestication effects*. Such effects are valued as negative, whilst the characters which they endanger are positively valued (p. 159 et seq.).

One can just as reliably demonstrate in human beings the existence of endogenous-automatic behaviour patterns which play a particularly great part in social behaviour. Even in cases where the endogenous-automatic motor patterns of man have been extensively reduced or only persist in the form of formalized display intention movements (p. 162 et seq.), the effects of endogenous stimulus-production – particularly the phenomenon of threshold-lowering – are quite evident. This especially applies to the so-called *aggressive drive* (p. 163 et seq.).

It is concluded that in human social behaviour, innate species-specific action and response norms play a far greater rôle than is generally assumed in sociology and ethnological psychology (p. 164 et seq.). Exact investigation of such behaviour is therefore an extremely urgent necessity, since certain functional disruptions produce specific dangers which are an integral part of human nature.

The third section of this paper deals with *constitutive dangers to mankind*. In the first place, *domestication* of man is considered; human beings exhibit the same complex of characteristic hereditary modifications as their domestic animals (p. 165 et seq.). The hereditary changes in innate, species-specific behaviour patterns forming part of this complex are briefly considered (p. 167 et seq.). There is a remarkable correlation between morphological and behavioural domestication characteristics and the innate mechanisms releasing value judgements discussed on p. 168 et seq.: specific, typical morphological domestication characteristics compulsively evoke negative aesthetic value judgements, whereas characters contrasting with these effects of domestication (i.e. the characters threatened by domestication) are emotionally evaluated as positive.

At the same time, however, domestication is an unconditional prerequisite for certain constitutive properties of human beings:

1. Man owes his novel, constitutive behavioural liberty to domestication-induced *deficiencies* in innate releasing mechanisms and certain fixed, automatic motor patterns (p. 173 et seq.).

2. Man is a *specialist in non-specialization*. This expression is used to characterize a certain type of organism, also evident in the animal kingdom, whose system of actions is characterized both by a paucity of specially adapted releasing mechanisms and endogenous, automatic motor patterns, and by the large part played by *active, inquisitive learning* (p. 174 et seq.). Perhaps the most predominant constitutive human characteristic is the retention of active, investigatory interaction with the environment (*openness to the surroundings* in the sense intended by A. Gehlen) into old age (p. 178 et seq.). It can be demonstrated that this particular property, just like many morphological characters of man, are component features of general *neoteny* (*foetalization* in Bolk's terminology), which is itself a genuine effect of domestication.

By virtue of its peculiar double action, domestication provides man on the one hand with his constitutive freedom of thought and behaviour, along with his persistent openness to surroundings, whilst on the other hand robbing him of the secure adjustment to the environment which an animal owes to its rigid innate, species-specific behaviour patterns. As a result, certain dangers inherent in the nature of man have emerged.

Man is the *jeopardized* creature, the organism 'with a constitutional chance to encounter mishaps' (A. Gehlen: p. 181 et seq.). The dangers which nowadays threaten the existence of all mankind are obviously derived from disruptions in inter-human relationships. Failure of collective human reason and morality in the face of these disruptions is caused by the fact that they are very largely based on disfunction of species-specific innate behaviour patterns, which are barely accessible to control through rational thought. Several possible mechanisms of specifically human functional disruption in innate social behaviour patterns are discussed. Headlong, culturally determined changes in human ecology and sociology have the result that many previously species-preserving (adaptive) action and response norms, which are no longer employed in modern living, are no longer appropriate. In other words, some of them have a disruptive effect because of their persistence (as, for example, with 'aggressive drives'), whilst others are no longer fitted for the requirements set by the more highly differentiated modern form of society (p. 182 et seq.). A particularly menacing special case of the latter phenomenon is presented by the gradually developing inadequacy of species-specific *killing inhibitions*, which are powerless before the rapidly growing technical possibilities for extermination (p. 186 et seq.). These behavioural disruptions, based on the *conservatism* of innate releasing mechanisms, inhibitions and endogenous drives, contrast with disturbances which are caused by abrupt domestication- (i.e. mutation-) induced *alterations* of these species-specific action and response norms. In the face of these disturbances, the compensatory function of rational responsibility (p. 188 et seq.) is equally inadequate.

This treatise ends with a discussion of the function and functional limitations of responsible morality. The regulative operation of rational responsibility is capable of approximate bridging and compensation of the tensions existing between innate social action/response norms adapted for the primitive ancestral forms of human societies and the requirements of the modern social order. This compensatory function is not achieved without sacrifices and expenditure of energy. 'Discomfort within our culture' in the normal case, and neurosis in the pathological case, represent the price which the individual must pay. The discrepancies between the equipment of each individual with innate social responses and the requirements of the society are extremely variable in man because of domestication-induced augmentation of the range of variation. Nevertheless, the functional capacity of compensatory morality is adjusted for a relatively sharply defined equipment of the individual human being with innate social action and response norms. If the magnitude of the discrepancy between these innate social inclinations and the requirements of the society greatly exceeds the average, as is the case with every 'monstrous' hypertrophy (Schröder) or mutational deficiency of an innate action-response norm, the compensatory function of responsible morality fails at a relatively sharply defined limit, and the human being concerned becomes either asocial or neurotic. The Schröder concept of psychopathy is presented in this light.

The conviction carried by the above, compressed account of our interpretations of human innate, species-specific behaviour patterns necessarily suffers from space limitations. As is the case everywhere else in inductive natural science, the probability of correctness of all results is proportional to the breadth of the inductive basis, and our basis is definitely considerably broader than is indicated in this article. Even if emotionally-coloured resistance is exhibited by many philosophically oriented psychologists and sociologists towards drawing the natural consequences of the unquestionable fact of evolution and giving adequate consideration to the historically-phylogenetically determined characteristics of human beings, the modern level of inductive natural scientific research nevertheless permits us to reliably predict that they will have to pay attention to these theoretical considerations in the near future. That human beings possess innate releasing mechanisms of the same kind as those found in higher animals is a straightforward fact, as is the important part played by endogenous-automatic stimulus-production processes. On the other hand, I am fully conscious of the fact that all of what can be said from comparative behavioural research about the rôle played by functional disruption of innate, species-specific behaviour patterns in the catastrophic social confusion of humanity must provisionally remain purely hypothetical in nature. All the same, I see the most important *practical* task of our branch of research in profound investigation of these hypotheses. One only has to think of the almost overwhelming importance which would accrue in the pedagogical, corrective educational and (above all) ethnological-psychological realms to an initial discovery of *which* disruptions in social behaviour are influenced by rational morality (and therefore by education) and which are not. What we do know is that both phenomena exist. One must remember that the dangers threatening modern man with extinction are derived exclusively from disruptions in social behaviour: it is not the external environment, but man himself who is the threat to humanity. It is only necessary to recall the horrifying simile of the turtle-dove equipped by a gruesome freak of nature with the beak of a raven. Nobody can deny that man finds himself in an analogous position.

One thing, however, is not simply hypothetical but established truth: *The only means of eliminating a functional disruption in a system lies in causal analysis of the system and the disruption.* One might possibly be able to 'understand' an archway through intuitive, holistic appreciation, without possessing knowledge of the form and function of the component building-blocks, but one is unable to *repair* it. Even the queen of applied science – medicine – owes her ability to re-establish a functional entity, which has gone awry, entirely to causal analysis of the component functions. At the moment, humanity represents a functional entity which has gone fundamentally awry. The misunderstanding between the development of the weapon and the inhibitions against using it threatens to extinguish mankind. Will it be possible for us, through collective human striving for knowledge and the collective responsibility of all human beings, to restore the equilibrium between ability to exterminate and social inhibition, which (just like so many other reliable, static conditions of equilibrium) had to be sacrificed in exchange for the dynamic developmental opportunity for human thought and behaviour? The future of mankind will be decided by the answering of this question!

Psychology and phylogeny (1954)

I Introduction

Every living organism is a system produced by a process with a past history, and *every* life phenomenon of an organism is fundamentally only open to understanding after rationalistic and causalistic retrospective tracing of the process of its phylogenetic emergence. Nowadays, this fact is self-evident to any biological thinker. On the other hand, it is a slow and tedious pathway towards recognition of the fact that the same applies to all phenomena of conscious behaviour – that our psychological and intellectual functions are similarly dependent on all other living processes for their emergence. The insight that every single one of our conscious processes is accompanied by a parallel, corresponding nervous physiological process still encounters remarkable resistance from modern philosophers. Just recently, prominent psychologists such as Sombart (1938) and Buytendijk (1940) have questioned with unmistakable emotional fervour the dependence of the human psyche upon biological laws, in particular those of heredity. On the other side, for diametrically opposed reasons, the associationists and behaviourists have denied the existence of inherited psychological structures, since within their mechanistic-atomistic interpretation of all psychological processes the conditioned reflex is the sole element, on the basis of which 'everything' should be explicable. Thus, as a peculiar philosophical irony, the most bitterly opposed schools of psychology were completely united on the one point, that rigidly structured, phylogenetically inherited behaviour patterns do not exist.

Leading schools of psychology are indeed still divergent as to whether the object of psychology is a general natural phenomenon and in particular a living phenomenon, but they are united in the belief that it has nothing to do with theories of heredity and evolution. Medical psychologists have in fact recently begun to take notice of the results of research into heredity, but on the other hand the significance of phylogeny for psychology has remained unrecognized by most qualified psychologists. This is based on the simple fact that they have no knowledge of evolu-
196

tionary research as such: very few such psychologists are equipped with a reasonably thorough knowledge of the approach, methods and results of modern phylogenists.[45] Scarcely one of them can dispose of a basis of personally acquired observational matter justifying an independent judgement about the inductive basis, probability and value of evolutionary theory. Frequently, apparently objective scepticism conceals an unwillingness to carry out the enormous quantity of learning necessary for a justifiable analysis of evolutionary theory. Thus, the synthesis of phylogeny and psychology, envisaged as necessary so long ago by Wundt, today remains very largely a *programme*. I shall here attempt, very briefly, to present a report on the origin, approach, method and present results of a new branch of psychological research, which has only recently been accepted as a true 'field'. This branch deserves the name 'comparative' in the same, phylogenetic sense as the morphologically oriented branches of comparative phylogenetic research. In order to demonstrate the mutual dependence between this branch of science and evolutionary theory, I have to some extent deliberately selected several fields of study in which this relationship is particularly prominent.

II The origin of the comparative psychological approach

It will always remain highly paradoxical that research work in our particular field was initiated not by psychologists seeking clarity about the origin of psychological attributes in animals and man, but by zoologists who – strictly speaking – were at first not intent upon conducting research into animal psychology and were predominantly interested in phylogenetic questions. There are fairly distinct reasons for this: specialized study of phylogeny is more dependent upon a finely developed sense generally referred to as 'intuition' than any other branch of inductive natural science. However, this 'intuition' proves on closer examination to be a special function of *Gestalt perception*.[46] As with any other perceptual process, subconscious mechanisms of the central nervous system which are not open to introspection produce a 'result' based on a wide range of sensory data, and 'accepted as valid' by the human subject. Helmholtz regards these processes as *subconscious conclusions*. Even if they are definitely not of this type, but are based upon the function of much more primitive central nervous organic structures, and even if they occur completely mechanically and with very little regulation – exhibiting the utter incorrigibility of so many inherited response patterns – they nevertheless share with genuine conclusions reached on a higher psychical plane the feature that all of the various perceived details are integrated into a *single* 'conclusion'. The direction of the perceptual pathway for all so-called intuition leads *from the particular to the general* just like that of the inductive process! Since intuition is not a 'wonder' – as is explicitly or implicitly believed by many people – but rather a highly natural physiological function of our perceptual apparatus, which determines from concrete facts their inherent laws in a manner analogous to that of induction, then both induction and intuition *are dependent upon a basis of perceived details.* Following any falsification of the 'premises', intuition (which is supposedly so infallible) produces false information just like any other perceptual process, for instance depth perception in a stereoscopic experiment. The correctness of the intuitively obtained result is just as dependent upon the correctness and range of the underlying provision of individual data as is the result of induction.

This function of Gestalt perception referred to as intuition plays a very large part in the systematic presentiments of all successful phylogenists. For this reason, prominent morphological systematists are always men who possess not only a broad inductive basis of known, consciously accessible individual facts, but also an extremely large hoard of individual facts which are *not* consciously accessible. Instead, when woven into the complex qualities of familiar Gestalts, they form the 'intuitive basis' for the judgements of systematic presentiment. Thus it is that the best and most refined of all systematists are frequently unable to state the reasons for their quite plausible conclusions about certain fine systematic relationships. The 'premises' for such 'subconscious conclusions' in Gestalt perception are in fact not immediately accessible to introspection. In Bronn's *Klassen und Ordnungen des Tierreichs (Classes and Orders of the Animal Kingdom)*, Gadow conducted the intellectual experiment of setting up a '30-character systematic arrangement', by assembling the Orders and Sub-Orders of birds in a table according to thirty recognized taxonomically important characters. The resulting taxonomic schema of the birds exhibited a range of surprising departures from 'obviously correct' details of the habitual systematic arrangement. Gadow implicitly produced the somewhat resigned conclusion that systematic presentiment cannot be replaced by statistical character-evaluation. However, in this article an attempt will be made to subject this discrepancy between 30-character systematics and phylogenetic presentiment to closer psychological scrutiny. This is particularly important, because it emerges that there is a methodologically extremely important reciprocal dependency relationship between comparative behavioural research and phylogenetic systematics.

The failure of the 30-character table is primarily due to the simple fact that every comparative phylogenetic judgement of a true *authority* on the objects concerned is based on evaluation of *a much larger* number of characters. A systematist does not judge a given living organism solely according to the characters given in his list, but instead follows an *overall impression* in which a virtually endless number of characters are interwoven in such a way that they not only *determine* the unalterable peculiarity of the impression, but at the same time *fuse with it*. It therefore requires fairly difficult analytical study in order to separate these characters individually from the overall quality in which they are no longer immediately recognizable as separate features. The *'complex quality'* of perceived Gestalts is a phenomenon with which the psychologist is fully acquainted and which has been relatively thoroughly investigated. The phylogenist must also investigate this phenomenon in order to provide an exact foundation for the best and most important of his activities. Only when it is possible to grasp the characters whose subconscious evaluation provides the basis for 'systematic presentiment' is it possible to evaluate scientifically phylogenetic conclusions.

The limited number of characters employed in any systematic table is not the only reason for their inadequacy. A further, and certainly more important, reason is the following: Every systematic arrangement which incorporates characters determined in an *anticipatory manner* is consequently open to a considerable source of error, to the extent that *no single character* within the various divisions of the related group of organisms subjected to phylogenetic arrangement can be regarded as having *even approximate uniformity of significance*. The rapidity with which a single character can undergo phylogenetic alteration can vary greatly between closely related animal and plant types. The fact that the character behaves in a 'conservative' manner in one division of a group tells us absolutely nothing about the probability that in another division the same character is subject to quite irregular variability. The result is a *continuous variability in the taxonomic reliability of each individual character*. Tabular systematic arrangements cannot in fact take account of this variability, but this is achieved by 'systematic presentiment', which is based on an enormous number of characters simultaneously evaluated on a subconscious level, and which is therefore capable of excluding an unpredictable 'leap' of an otherwise reliable relationship character by following the greater weight of the majority of unaltered characters. To express this in extremely coarse terms: no reasonable person would exclude a completely featherless parrot (something which is far from rare in captivity, as a result of certain pathological processes) from the Class Aves on the basis of this character, though this is quite conceivable with a table based on preconceived characters. On closer analysis of the process under discussion, the special function of 'systematic presentiment' is based on the following: One does not attribute from the outset a specific taxonomic reliability to each of the individual characters considered; instead such reliability is estimated in each individual case from the *relative* variability of the characters. This 'estimation' of the weight of each individual character in each animal type is based on the laws of probability. It is extremely improbable that *many* characters should have simultaneously undergone mutational leaps in the same direction, whilst an individual character – even one regarded as 'conservative' – has remained unaltered. For example, to keep to the same coarse simile, it is unlikely that a featherless group of animals should have produced a type which resembles the parrot in all other characters. Even in less clear-cut cases, we are justified on grounds of probability in assuming that sporadically appearing characters which fall out of the framework of the group are younger, whilst the majority of corresponding group-characters are older, whatever the nature of the characters considered. However, since two directly related species rarely exhibit exactly the same character, and since it is usually the faster or slower flow of characters which provides the basis for varying estimation of the relative reliability of each individual character, the entire – extremely important – process of estimation is *exclusively based upon relativity judgements* and can theoretically only be free of error when the evaluator is aware of *all* characters altered in the evolution of the investigated group of animals. This is, of course, fundamentally impossible. Nevertheless, it emerges that the greatest approximation to genuinely correct character evaluation coincides with the mastery of the largest number of characters inherent to a particular group of animals or plants. The productivity of a phylogenist increases not just in arithmetic, but in geometric proportion to the number of group characters with which he is acquainted. This is because every new additional character corrects and improves the evaluation of *all* previously known characters. As is well known, the diagnosis of monovular twins is based upon the same deductive process: the more numerous the shared inherited characters, the greater is the probability that they are monovular. The probability of chance correspondence of n characters amounts to $1/2n$.

This brief excursion into the field of methodology in phylogenetic systematics was necessary because it unveils an important relationship between behavioural research and phylogenetic study. We can now understand why justifiable pronouncements on phylogenetic relationships are to be expected not from studies of one *organ* in all of its different forms in a wide range of animal groups (a common trend among comparative anatomists), but from those where *a group* of animals has been investigated to determine a maximum number of characters in a maximum number of representatives of the group. This is quite particularly the case when a phylogenetically thinking biologist is acquainted with a group of animals not only through skins and preserved specimens, but also *by study of the living organism*. He is then more or less driven to phylogenetic/comparative consideration of the *characters of innate behaviour*, and this gain in the inductive basis leads his phylogenetic studies on to unexpected successes. At the same time, these facts indicate that a man who is, in a certain sense, 'obsessed' by a group of animals is able to perform an inestimable service not only for the systematic study of the group concerned, but also to phylogenetic methodology in general. In this way, Whitman – who we must now regard as the pioneer of our research approach – investigated in great detail the Order including the Columbidae (pigeons and doves) and in 1898 he produced the remarkable statement (initially completely ignored by professional psychologists): 'Instincts and organs must be studied from the common standpoint of their phylogenetic origin.' Heinroth (1910) similarly studied the anatomy and innate behaviour of the duck group (Anatidae), while Antonius (1937) conducted analogous investigations on the Equidae. One is frequently unable to decide whether to regard these workers as psychologists or as phylogenists. They all share an extraordinarily great love for a certain object, which admittedly originates from a pronounced amateur spirit usually developed very early in life. Nonetheless, their studies have produced to date the methodologically most reliable, in the truest sense 'holistic' (overall) investigations of groups of phylogenetically related animals known. The fact that their successes are solely due to *simultaneous* study of phylogeny and the psychological behaviour of a group of animals shows us quite clearly the heart of the matter: the reciprocal dependency relationship between phylogenetic and psychological knowledge.

The insight which we owe to the two pioneers of comparative behavioural research is, in itself, simple: There exist individually unaltering, species-characteristic motor patterns, which change just as slowly in the course of evolution as morphological organs. But this single fact demonstrated with one sweep the utter falsity of all interpretations of 'instinctive' behaviour which had previously been made, on both the vitalistic and the mechanistic side. According to the view of the vitalists, the 'instinct' was a 'directive factor' intrinsically inaccessible to causal explanation, which set specific *goals* for animal behaviour. It was therefore a logical conclusion for representatives of 'purposive psychology' – in particular McDougall – to regard all instinctive behaviour as fundamentally possessing the typical variability of all *purposive* behaviour, and to simply equate the species-preserving function of such a behaviour pattern with the goal towards which the animal subject strives. On the mechanistic side, by contrast, there were *two* schools of thought. The behaviourists maintained that complex innate motor sequences simply do not exist, no more than innate 'goals' of behaviour. The

Pavlovian reflexologist school, on the other hand, admitted the existence of fairly long innate motor sequences, but explained them simply as chain arrangements of unconditioned reflexes. McDougall in fact produced quite early on the basically correct objection to this theory, in stating that the spontaneity of many 'instinctive' behaviour patterns cannot be explained from the principle of the reflex. 'It is obviously erroneous', he justly wrote, 'to speak of a re-action to a stimulus which the organism has not even received.'

Neither Whitman nor Heinroth ever made a statement about the physiological nature of inherited motor sequences. But whilst they proceeded without preconditions or hypotheses to observe, describe and order the motor patterns concerned, their systematic intuition subconsciously performed a very remarkable function. It has in fact been discovered since then that virtually all of the motor patterns of the wide variety of animals evaluated by Whitman and Heinroth for phylogenetic investigation exhibit a series of very remarkable physiological peculiarities, which more or less cried out for a uniform causal explanation, as indeed eventually emerged. This is a classical example of the automatic emergence of the nomothetic stage from the systematic stage in the organic development of a natural science.

III. The discovery of endogenous stimulus-production and its analytical consequences

The first notable point to come to light was a peculiar *correlation between spontaneity and individual invariability* of inherited motor patterns, which was not at all to be expected following the vitalistic and mechanistic interpretations outlined above. According to the vitalistic-teleological interpretation, a given innate behaviour pattern directed at a specific 'instinct-goal' should *ipso facto* exhibit the typical variability of all purposive activities, which are in fact constant with respect to the ultimate success, but are extensively open to adaptive change in performance. On the other hand, according to the reflex-chain theory, a completely inherited behavioural chain should definitely not exhibit spontaneity. But in reality it is *just* these completely fixed behaviour patterns, with every detail of their motor sequence inherited in a species-specific manner, which exhibit a certain extremely characteristic type of spontaneity. We shall be dealing with this in more detail shortly, since closer investigation of this phenomenon led to discovery of a previously utterly neglected *elementary function of the central nervous system* which is quite independent of the reflex process – the discovery of endogenous automatic rhythmic stimulus production. This discovery of the part played by this autonomous primordial function of the nervous system in the overall behaviour of animals, and doubtless of man as well, represents the most important result to date of comparative behavioural research. On the one hand, this provides a satisfactory explanation for the spontaneity of so many animal and human behaviour patterns, which has repeatedly been used by vitalists as an argument not only against the reflex-chain theory of the mechanists, but against *any* assumption of possible physiological causal explanations of behaviour. Thus, vitalism is forced out of a position which had previously been stubbornly and successfully defended. On the other hand, by contrast, the discovery of automatic-rhythmic stimulus-production disposes once and for all of the explanatory monism of the behaviourists and reflexologists, who believed that they had found in the reflex and conditioned response the sole explanatory principles for all animal and human behaviour. Let us turn to a brief outline of the history of this discovery:

The fact – initially emphasized by Whitman – that certain behaviour patterns act like organs in phylogeny leads on to the assumption that they are organ functions, and a search for the underlying structures in the central nervous system seems advisable. At the prevailing level of nervous physiology, it was almost self-evident to regard these structures initially as *reflex pathways* and to explain innate behaviour patterns lock, stock and barrel as chain-reflexes, as H. E. Ziegler (1910) did with a quite explicit formulation. He defined the 'instincts', whose manifestations were at that time regarded without further analysis as innately adaptive behaviour patterns, as reflex-chains operating through inherited 'klcronomic' pathways. However, he did not in fact provide histological or physiological support for this theory. It soon emerged that *the very nucleus of those behaviour patterns* drawn in to phylogenetic comparisons by the pioneers of comparative behavioural research differed in extremely important features from reflexes. Reflexes, both with respect to their elicitation and to the particular form of the movement involved, are dependent upon external stimuli. It is one of the constitutive characters of the reflex, in fact underlying the formation of the term itself, that – rather like an unused machine – it can remain unnoticed and in readiness for a limitless period, such that appearance of the elicitatory stimulus situation the centrally conducted excitation is projected back into the external environment as a species-preserving motor or secretory response. This does in fact apply very largely to a specific group of inherited motor patterns: to the *orienting responses* which we refer to as *taxes*, following A. Kühn. *But, remarkably, the motor patterns employed by* Whitman *and* Heinroth *in their phylogenetic considerations had relatively little in common with taxes.* On the contrary, a very large section of these patterns represented courtship motor patterns and *motor display patterns* in the broadest sense, and these formally pre-determined motor co-ordination patterns, which are so characteristic of species and groups, exhibited an unbelievable *independence of directive stimuli*. Apart from this, they remarkably did not follow the rule, valid for all pure reflex processes, of passive attendance for the eliciting stimuli: Lorenz (1937) demonstrated experimentally that the elicitation of genuine 'instinctive motor patterns' becomes easier with the length of time since the last elicitation. This *lowering of the threshold* for releasing stimuli can proceed to such an extent, with certain instinctive motor patterns which are normally employed frequently, that after a long period of 'damming' they will be performed *in the absence of* any demonstrable external stimulus. In this 'vacuum activity', the entire motor sequence is a truly photographic replica of the normally performed pattern, though of course the species-preserving function is not fulfilled. The phenomenon of continuously increasing motivation in the interval between two elicitations of the instinctive motor pattern was itself suggestive of internal *accumulation processes*. This supposition was considerably reinforced as it emerged that 'damming' of the instinctive motor pattern not only leads to passive lowering of the threshold value for releasing stimuli, but actually induces the entire resting organism to become restless and *actively search* for the releasing stimulus situation. As early as 1910, Craig referred to this searching activity as *appetitive behaviour*, conceptually separating it from the instinctive performance which the organism seeks to attain. Such behaviour extends from the simplest motor restlessness to the complex, purposive behaviour patterns of human beings, involving an enormous variety of functions. *None of these phenomena can be explained on the basis of the stimulus-response schema of the reflex*. Nervous physiology and consequently general physiological theory had long been constructed on the working hypothesis that the reflex is the sole element from which all nervous functions are constructed. Their practical studies were therefore restricted to the experiment of inducing a change in conditions and then recording the resulting response. This technique *necessarily* led to the opinion that the functioning of the central nervous system is restricted to *response* to external stimuli. It was therefore a fundamentally new phenomenon which had been discovered: the remarkable motor co-ordination of instinctive patterns does not passively await the elicitation of their function, like reflexes or unused machines, but instead comes actively to the fore, renders the entire organism restless and *drives* it towards behavioural performance. In short, they act like *hormones* in that they *produce* stimuli. Physiological investigation of non-reflex processes, which explained in one sweep all of the previously described phenomena departing from the reflex theory, was first carried out by von Holst

(1936, 1938). His results have thoroughly disposed of the theory that the reflex forms 'the element' of all central nervous processes. According to his findings, *automatic stimulus-production processes* in the central nervous system of worms, fishes and higher vertebrates transmit impulses which are already centrally co-ordinated and bring about well-ordered, species-preserving motor processes *without the participation of any sensitive conduction of excitation*. Von Holst pictured these stimulus-production processes as *material* in form, and thus arrived independently of Lorenz at the hypothesis of *accumulation processes*.

The discovery that the nervous system *spontaneously* produces energy parcels which are allotted to certain highly specific motor patterns, on the one hand developing a general *drive* (appetite) for their elicitation and on the other hand lowering the stimulus threshold for such elicitation, is extremely important in fields other than physiology. In the sensualistic associational psychology of the turn of the century, which attempted with an erroneous imitation of scientific methods to develop any understanding of human psychology on the basis of the element of a 'sensation', the attempt was made to find a regular quantitative relationship between cause and effect in the psychological realm. Since only the sensory stimulus was admitted as 'cause', and since evaluation and response to such external stimuli was regarded as the only function of the central nervous system, success was understandably only possible in areas where this very specialized working hypothesis was valid. This was predominantly the case in the field of sensory physiology, where associational psychology produced results of lasting value – for example the Weber-Fechner Law. However, when the quantitative value of the external stimulus was related to the overall response of the organism (i.e. in the actual field of psychology), every attempt to determine regular relationships initially failed. The impossibility of finding this relationship between cause and effect in the field of psychological function – a relationship which was at that time regarded as the only conceivable one – unfortunately produced a general digression from the natural scientific approach among psychologists. Through the discovery of the *internal* causes of the varying motivation of any given organism to perform certain response patterns, the investigation of the quantitative relationship between the releasing external stimulus and the response which is produced by the organism as a whole has now reached a new level of scientific analysis.

Anybody ignorant of endogenous stimulus-production and its 'damming' during long rest periods of the instinctive motor pattern concerned, and unaware of the steep rise in the threshold level for releasing stimuli following repeated stimulation, must initially regard as utterly 'irregular' the behaviour of an experimental animal which at first responds intensively to a specific stimulus situation and on the subsequent trial remains utterly indifferent. However, if one takes into account the prevailing internal motivation of the experimental animal in investigations of the quantitative efficacy of releasing stimulus – as Seitz (1940) did for the first time in precisely programmed experiments – one arrives at an astoundingly constant efficacy of individual stimuli. Seitz used the fighting and courtship responses of teleost fish, which present extremely good objects for quantitative experiments on account of a very exact sequence of intensity levels, to test the quantitative efficacy of individual characters of dummies, in which he could omit selected characters of the normal response-releasing fighting and mating partner. After each individual experiment, the momentarily prevailing readiness to respond (the 'actual level of response-specific excitability') was investigated by presentation of the adequate object. In this way, it proved possible (so-to-speak) to reduce the recorded response intensities to a common prevailing level. The same response intensity could be elicited either by a very efficient dummy with a low level of response motivation, or by a dummy lacking many decisive characters employed after a long period of 'damming' of the instinctive motor pattern concerned. It emerged that there is an *invariable releasing efficacy for each individual character*. The efficacy of each dummy corresponded precisely with the *sum* of the efficacities of each included individual character. Seitz referred to this as the *Law of Stimulus Summation*.[47]

A further, perhaps even more important, analytical extension of the recognition of the physiological peculiarity of instinctive motor patterns was the analysis of the processes (endogenous-automatic and stimulus-directed, reflexive) underlying all motor sequences previously referred to briefly as 'taxes' or 'instinctive behaviour patterns'. Even the simplest 'positive taxis' of any given organism steering towards a stimulus is far from being a pure reflex. Instead, it consists of the disinhibition of a locomotor movement, which is almost always endogenous-automatic in nature; and only the restricted left/right and up/down orienting movements steered by the stimulus are genuine reflexes. In many cases, the stimuli disinhibiting the automatism can be quite sharply demarcated from those according to which the tropic steering of the overall movement is directed. Tinbergen (1938), Lorenz (1938) and Kuenen (1939) have carried out relevant investigations on birds.

The Craig-Lorenz schema of the instinctive behaviour pattern outlined here (endogenous stimulus production – appetitive behaviour – appearance of the specific stimulus situation, which sets the innate releasing mechanism in motion – disinhibition of the consummatory action) has since proved to be over simplified. However, as with many such simplifications, this has itself proved fruitful for analytical research. Particularly Tinbergen and Baerends, together with their pupils, have shown that it is only in relatively rare, special cases that primary appetitive behaviour directly leads to attainment of the stimulus situation in which the consummatory action is elicited. Instead, primary appetitive behaviour of a general kind brings the animal to a stimulus situation in which a specific releasing mechanism activates a *more specific* appetite. For example, a stickleback which has entered 'reproductive motivation' at first seeks a biotope with abundant vegetation: quite specific environmental conditions must be present for the fish to choose a territory, to develop a nuptial coloration and to attain the hormonal condition of full reproductive motivation. A fish which has already acquired this costume is at the same time subject to a special state of behavioural motivation – it is in the 'motivational state for demonstrative behaviour'[48] and exhibits conspicuous appetites for the seeking out of conspecifics. Whether the fish will then fight or court depends upon a further releasing stimulus situation, namely upon the behavioural response exhibited by the conspecific when approached. The activation of the individual behavioural motivations ('Stimmungen', or 'moods', in Heinroth's terminology) takes place in a sequence of integrational levels, passing from higher to lower levels of integration. This begins with the augmentation of a highly integrated, very general behavioural motivation which incorporates *several* special motivations and acts as a precondition for their appearance. The ultimate effect is the release of the most specific goal-behaviour, which incorporates no other elements and represents the *consummatory action* (Craig). This assembly of subsequent, more limited behavioural motivations is aptly referred to by Tinbergen and Baerends as the 'hierarchy of motivations'. There exists usually – though not always – between the governing components at the *same* level a relationship of reciprocal inhibition, eventually reaching complete exclusion. For example, fighting and courtship in labyrinth fish and Cichlid fish are at the same level of integration, and both are governed by the prerequisite of 'demonstrative motivation' with adoption of the display costume. Mixed responses involving the two do indeed occasionally occur, but 'switching' between them (from one behavioural motivation to the other) usually requires a measurable time-interval (response latency), which tends to be longer, the higher the integrational level of the behavioural motivations concerned. Motivations for the individual endogenous-automatic motor patterns do not therefore exist side-by-side in an amorphous mosaic, but represent the terminal components of hierarchically ordered general and more specific chains of appetites, arranged in a branching system. Only in individual, extremely simple cases does the action system of an animal species correspond to a mosaic of action/reaction norms really complying with the Craig–Lorenz behavioural schema outlined above. In higher animals, there is almost always a highly complex hierarchical system of reciprocal inclusion and exclusion of sequences of more restricted behavioural motivations. These various cycles and epi-cycles exhibit great variations in the structure between different animal species, and in particular this applies to the *number* of links involved. Any generalization from one species to another leads to errors. So far, the number, type and integrational characteristics of the hierarchically organized and interacting components, or 'centres', have only been exactly investigated in two animal species – the stickleback (*Gasterosteus aculeatus* L.) by Tinbergen and the digger-wasp (*Ammophila campestris* Jur.) by Baerends.

Our concept of a hierarchy of graduated governing and subordinate components of the central nervous system was originally exclusively based on observation of intact organisms. The concept which has been formed about these components, or 'centres', is therefore primarily a purely functional one. Nevertheless, it is quite justifiable to speak of centres in the true sense of the word, since all of these concepts of comparative behavioural research are confirmed in a very instructive manner by the findings of experimental, vivisectional neurophysiology, with which they entirely conform. Through the investigations of both Hess and von Holst, much important information has emerged regarding the *localization* of the 'governing components', which activate both general and more specific behavioural motivations. The predominant, significant correspondence between these findings and the results of comparative behavioural research lies in the following: The centres discovered by Hess, which are located in a *higher* area of the central nervous system (the hypothalamus) in fact govern more general behavioural motivations at a high level of integration – e.g. those of sleeping, eating or fighting – together with the entire system of subordinate component appetites and motor patterns belonging to these governing cycles in the animal investigated (the cat). On the other hand, the components investigated by von Holst in the *lowest* area, namely directly above the anterior horn motor cells of the spinal cord, each activate only one single motor sequence at the lowest level of integration, which thus has the character of a *consummatory action*. The observational evidence obtained from the intact organism is, as has been said, in full accord with these results. However, this indicates that *between* the very high and very low centres located in vivisectional experiments there is an entire series of intermediate levels of integrating components awaiting discovery. In this respect, exact analysis of the behaviour of intact organisms can provide neurophysiologists with extremely valuable indications as to the *number* of intermediate centres to be expected. With *Gasterosteus* and

Ammophila, this has been very exactly determined. Barcroft and von Holst have already undertaken the attempt to approach the hierarchical series of sequentially governed centres, using a new method of graduated narcosis (or suffocation).

The successes of experimental analysis briefly outlined above, which in fact introduce a new stage of scientific investigation into psychology because of the inherent possibilities for relatively exact quantification, *only became possible through prior comparative phylogenetic description and classification of animal behaviour*. Evaluation of innate behaviour patterns as taxonomic characters not only represented a sharp break from all previously accepted theoretical views, thus providing the impulse for novel analytical research; in fact it introduced a preliminary *order* into the described factual evidence, which already incorporated the distinction between tactically-steered movements and endogenous automatisms, and consequently raised the question of the physiological peculiarity of the latter. Understandably, all motor patterns in which there are significant reflex movements steered by stimuli (i.e. *taxes* in the modern restricted sense) are far less suitable for taxonomic application, because of their dependence upon (often very specific) external stimuli. With taxes, the specific form of the movement in any individual case is dependent upon the nature and direction of the stimulus, whilst the automatism produces thoroughly constant motor patterns performed in a species-characteristic manner even in the complete absence of adequate stimuli. With the orienting response, the *response norm* is innate, as for example with the response of directing the back in the direction of incident light. According to the conditions in each individual case, the animal performs a turning movement of anything from a few seconds of a degree to 180 degrees. The response rule can be abstracted from a large assembly of individual observed cases. On the other hand, with the endogenous automatism the form of the movement itself can be directly described and compared as an innate character of the species. The response norm of the orienting movement is indeed, in the modern restricted sense, just as 'conservative' as any given instinctive motor pattern; but taxes in the earlier, broader sense – which prove on the basis of our analysis to be complex intercalations of reflex-steered and endogenous-automatic motor patterns – are extremely plastic, simply because of the number of their components. For this reason, both Whitman and Heinroth, with the fine intuition of vocational systematists, avoided employing such compound motor chains as phylogenetic characters. In this way, there had already emerged a coarse division on which further causal analysis could be based.

IV   Special phylogeny of motor display patterns

Whitman and Heinroth themselves directed particular attention to a
specific group of instinctive motor patterns, which are now known to be
virtually 'purely' automatic. In other words, they are not overlain by
orienting responses; or where the latter do occur, they are extremely
simple and easily discernible. This group contains automatisms whose
adaptive value lies in the *transmission of stimuli*, to which the conspecific
responds in a regular manner. These instinctive motor patterns have the
further advantage of being simple and yet characteristic, easily described
characters, as is immediately obvious from their function as 'signals' or
'communicatory agents'. Thirdly, they possess an inestimable advantage
for phylogenetic research in that one can extremely reliably exclude a
disturbing factor which is otherwise a major headache for phylogenists –
the *phenomenon of convergence*. For example, if one finds with two otherwise unrelated Anatid species a so-called 'goose bill', with cornified
lamellae reinforced to produce biting teeth, this similarity might quite
easily have arisen because of the fact that both species have undergone
the same adaptive process for external reasons – perhaps the transition
to grass-eating – and thus independently developed the same alteration
of the lamellar bill which was doubtless originally present in all Anatids.
Although the crass examples of convergent adaptation in different
animal classes are easily recognizable as such (take, for example, the
structural similarities between fishes, Ichthyosaurians and Cetaceans),
the possibility of convergence presents a major problem in fine systematic considerations. Confronted with this source of error, phylogenetic
researchers of signal motor patterns ('releasers') find themselves in the
same pleasurable situation as philologists (students of language): when
the latter find words of extremely similar construction in two languages,
they immediately assume that they have the same evolutionary origin.
This is, in fact, justified, since it is actually extremely improbable that
(for example) the indo-germanic words *Vater, pater, padre, père*, etc.
would have such similar construction purely as a chance effect. As far
as their *significance*, in other words their *signal function*, is concerned,
they could just as well have entirely different sounds, as is the case in
other, unrelated languages. By analogy, the same applies to instinctive
motor patterns which develop a releaser function. When drakes of two
duck species rear up in the water during courtship – dipping the extended, inclined head into the water, spraying a small fountain of water
with a lateral movement of the bill and simultaneously uttering a shrill
whistle – it is very improbable that the resemblance between these complex motor sequences and the response of the innately reacting female

would have arisen through convergent evolution in the two species.[50] There is a further advantage for comparative phylogenetic research in that elicitatory instinctive motor patterns are evidently recent evolutionary developments and that in closely related species they are often present at different levels of differentiation, which are open to productive investigation. All of these 'technical' advantages of the releaser as an object of phylogenetic research combine together such that the comparative behavioural researcher is often able to make phylogenetic statements of an exactitude rarely permissible in comparative morphology. For this very reason, we know far more about the phylogenetic history of signal motor patterns than of other instinctive motor patterns. In this case too, phylogenetic investigation of homology has led to elucidation of physiological causal relationships. Comparative description of motor display patterns in closely related animal species had some time previously led Heinroth (1910), Huxley (1914) and Lorenz (1935) to the conception that some signal motor patterns have evolved in a quite specific manner from other instinctive motor patterns, whose species-preserving value was originally purely mechanical and not at all 'communicatory'. All instinctive motor patterns possess the property of appearing at low response intensities as incomplete acts not fulfilling the species-preserving function of the motor pattern concerned. These intrinsically non-functional initiations of specific behaviour patterns, referred to as *intention movements*, can indicate to an observer the direction in which the behaviour of the animal may be expected to proceed with further increase in the same type of arousal. Obviously, the regular, predictable appearance of such movements introduced the possibility that in the course of phylogenetic development a quite innate, functional response to these expressions of specific types of arousal could also be developed in the conspecific. In many cases, this response consists in a resonance of the same type of arousal. Such receptor correlates of highly specialized combinations of external stimuli are known from other sources, and they are referred to as 'innate releasing mechanisms'. However, as soon as a functional signal-apparatus is presented by the presence of an elicitatory instinctive motor pattern and a specifically responding receptor apparatus, the 'intention movement' has passed from being a non-functional neurophysiological side-product to representing a 'means of communication', with a definite species-preserving value in social animals. Evidently, there is subsequently widespread *higher differentiation* of the stimulus-transmitting motor pattern, accompanied by an equivalent development of the receiving innate 'schema'. There is an extremely large quantity of reliable evidence for this particular process. In all cases, the novel function of the motor pattern has led to further differentiation in a quite specific direction: The signal function of the motor pattern is rendered *more effective* through certain *exaggerations* of visually effective components and *simplified* by omission of certain details which were actually vital in the original, mechanical function. In very many cases, morphological differentiations of form and colour are added, thus increasing the visual effect still further. This gestural exaggeration of visually effective individual characters, combined with simplification, is functionally quite similar to formation of genuine *symbols*. Therefore, releasing instinctive motor patterns derived from intention movements as described are termed *symbolic motor patterns*. Without research into homology conducted according to the methods of classical comparative anatomy, such symbolic behaviour patterns could not be understood. In many cases, they have in fact become so different from the original form of the motor pattern that nobody would be able to surmise their origin without comparison with related species. On the other hand, for the reasons given on p. 210 et seq., their phylogenetic derivation can be conducted with a great measure of reliability.

Comparative phylogenetic investigation of motor display patterns has led to the discovery of a second type of derivation of signal motor patterns completely independent of that of the symbolic motor pattern and causally quite distinct. Tinbergen (1940) and Kortlandt (1938) recognized independently of one another that with high general arousal quite unexpected motor patterns often emerge. These do actually have a sharply defined species-preserving function, but they are not appropriate to the prevailing biological situation. There is a '*sparking over*' of unspecific – or exactly speaking *extra* specific – arousal into the pathways of an instinctive motor pattern which is normally associated with a quite particular response-specific type of arousal, through which it is exclusively and 'autochthonously' activated. The phenomenon of sparking over of 'allochthonous' arousal is extremely widely distributed. A male snow bunting, which is involved in a territorial dispute with its neighbour and does not quite dare to make an active attack, abruptly pecks at the ground as if searching for food. In a similar situation, a greylag gander will exhibit body-shaking, and a threat-displaying stickleback performs feeding movements.[51] Doves, shelduck and other birds preen themselves when sexually aroused. If a chimpanzee is not given the accustomed reward after solution of a conditioning test, it will begin to scratch its entire body. And an avocet subject to fighting motivation exhibits – even immediately before mating – an apparently quite aberrant motor pattern; it inserts its bill under its shoulder feathers, as it does when sleeping! In all of these cases, the allochthonous arousal sparks over into *quite specific*, foreign pathways. Tinbergen has attempted to analyse the conditions under which sparking over effects (*displacement activities*) occur.[52] In many, though not all, cases there is a *conflict* between two more-or-less antagonistic drives. For example, in the snow bunting, goose and stickleback, fighting and escape drives are in conflict. Even displacement head-scratching in human beings occurs regularly in conflict situations. However, displacement activities can equally easily occur in cases where the releasing stimulus situation for a particular, specific instinctive motor pattern is present, but where the pattern itself is for some reason out of action. For instance, if the instinctive motor patterns of rolling eggs into the nest are exhausted in a greylag goose to the point of extreme lowering of the prevailing level of response-specific energy, instead of performing egg-rolling in the adequate stimulus situation the goose will exhibit instinctive nest-building movements. In addition, when an animal attains a drive-goal with unexpected rapidity, so that energy is still free after 'satisfaction' of the response-specific behaviour pattern, arousal sparks over into foreign pathways. For example, birds and many teleost fish 'unintentionally' drift into mating responses when an opponent suddenly flees (or is removed by an experimenter) in the middle of a fight. The common feature of all these cases is that excess arousal energy remains and must evidently find some outlet or other.[53] A further common factor is present in many displacement activities of a wide variety of animals in that the allochthonous energy almost always flows into the pathways of endogenous-automatic motor patterns – usually those which are extremely *commonplace* (e.g. preening, scratching and feeding movements). Purely reflex motor patterns are apparently *never* evoked by sparking over of extraneous specific arousal. Even with motor patterns in which endogenous automatisms and reflex orienting responses normally form a functional whole, *the latter are absent* when the motor pattern is set in motion by allochthonous energy. For instance, a normally eating stickleback fixates with both eyes the goal on the substrate at which it snaps; but when the fish exhibits 'displacement eating' in threat behaviour, it fixates the opponent with one eye. A threat-pecking domestic cock behaves in exactly the same fashion, and in this case one can directly observe the non-directional nature of the displacement pecking movements. Sparking-over therefore does not elicit the entire, species-preserving system of directed and automatic movements, but only the endogenous-automatic component.

In a manner analogous to that described for the intention movement on p. 211, the displacement activity – which is also primarily a completely non-functional 'atelic' side-product of special functions of the nervous system – can provide the basis for the evolution of visually operative releasers. As with the 'autochthonously' activated symbolic motor patterns, there is often extensive 'ritualizing' exaggeration and simplification of the motor pattern, and as with the former its derivation from an instinctive behaviour pattern originally set off as a displacement activity can only be determined by comparative studies of homology. In this historical investigation, there automatically emerge remarkable material and methodological parallels with comparative linguistic research. The special form of the releasing instinctive motor pattern is frequently maintained far more constantly than the innate schemata which respond to it, such that comparative historical investigation can reliably demonstrate *a change in significance* of a signal motor pattern.[54] For instance, the so-called tail-beating movement of many teleost fish represents a distinctly formalized symbolic motor pattern with an immediately evident threat significance. Through comparison of many related forms, the movement can be clearly recognized as a gestural exaggeration of the peculiar lateral body movement with which fish push themselves forward before heading for a goal (prey or opponent). In Cichlid fish where both sexes exhibit brood-care, this threat movement has evolved via reciprocal demonstrative display between the partners to become a courtship pattern and in particular a ceremony for nest-relief. In this process, especially in *Hemichromis bimaculatus*, small differences in the motor pattern – which are also evident to the human observer – have emerged to give a motor display pattern with a significance fundamentally different from, and opposed to, that of the original, threatening tail-beat. At the same time, the original tail-beat with its threat significance has been maintained unchanged. Philologists are thoroughly acquainted with similar dichotomies of significance in the evolutionary history of words. The functional analogy between the historical development of these entirely hereditary, releasing motor patterns and the traditionally inherited language of human beings is a continual source of surprise, in view of the fundamental difference in origin and causal development of these two means of social communication. In particular, the minute differences in significance of homologous motor display patterns between very closely related species is compulsively reminiscent of the slight differences between the concepts attached to the same – but hardly ever completely synonymous – words in closely related languages. In *Nannacara*, *Geophagus* and some other Cichlids, for example, a brief lateral head-movement (which originated as the symbol of gesturally exaggerated departure swimming) signifies an almost continuously performed mild *summons* for the young fish swarming around the parent. In analogy with the summoning call of the domestic hen, this is referred to as 'clucking'. *Cichlasoma biocellatum* now performs this motor pattern (which in its original form is also noticeably augmented in response to danger – just like the clucking of the hen) only as a response to mild disturbance. With *Cichlasoma nigro-*

fasciatum (the Honduras Zebra Cichlid) the same pattern exhibits a well-defined warning function at higher intensities and induces the swarm of young fish to collect beneath the mother, like goslings seeking cover. In *Neetroplus carpintis*, the Texas Cichlid, the head movement is very exaggerated and possesses only this described warning function. This function is greatly enhanced, whilst the original summoning function has disappeared.

The examples provided, to which countless others could be added, should suffice to demonstrate the indispensable significance which the phylogenetic approach bears for the understanding of innate behaviour patterns, and also the value which the study of motor display patterns – conducted in a methodologically correct manner – can develop for an investigator of phylogenetic relationships. Comparative investigation of signals derived from symbolic motor patterns and allochthonous displacement activities has a further theoretical and practical value, since for the time being this presents the only possibility for relatively exact elucidation of the phylogenetic development of innate behaviour *and thus of psychological phenomena in general.* Such investigation demands just as much patience and modest examination of apparently unimportant details as comparative morphological systematics, which one nowadays takes rather too much for granted. Only in this way can one acquire the necessary evidence for the inductive basis of all further analysis. This work has been initiated with two groups of animals which – for purely technical reasons such as ease of maintenance and breeding, easy availability of closely-related, comparable species, abundance of comparable motor patterns, etc. – represent particularly favourable objects for comparative behavioural research, namely the Anatidae among the birds and the Cichlidae among the teleost fish. Following what was said in the introduction about the reciprocal dependency relationship between behavioural research and phylogenetic systematics, it is self-evident that these investigations, which are purely psychological *in intent,* must automatically provide an abundance of detailed systematic data on the animal group studied, so-to-speak as a side-product! In my paper 'Vergleichende Bewegungsstudien an Anatinen', 1941 (*Comparative studies of motor patterns in the Anatinae* – see pp. 13–112), which presents our preliminary results, I devoted a large amount of space to this systematic analysis. The Cichlid investigation has only just commenced.

V The genetics of innate behaviour patterns

The question regarding the evolution of species has already been posed so successfully in the field of morphology that extension to the field of behavioural research is an obvious step. Particularly nowadays, where psychological studies dominated by conceptions of heredity are gradually increasing in extent, it has become necessary to acquire exact knowledge about the manner and causes of hereditary alterations of psychological structures. Whitman himself conducted interbreeding experiments with his pigeons and doves. Heinroth made the important observation with Anatid hybrids that they frequently exhibit behaviour which is not *intermediate* between that of the parental species, but instead corresponds to a more ancient type present in other (in this respect more primitive) members of the Anatidae. This effect was already well known for morphological characters, and it permits certain conclusions about the manner of inheritance of the phenomena concerned.

Unfortunately, genetic investigation of species-specific innate behaviour is as yet so little advanced that we are unable to make statements about the hereditary factors of one single describable behavioural character. Our supposition that the inheritance of behaviour patterns proceeds in exactly the same way as that of morphological characters is provisionally based on observations which are so few in number that interpretations cannot be statistically supported. Therefore, a research programme covering genetic aspects of behaviour initially involves quite primitive tasks. In the first place, one must breed hybrids of animal species or races which are closely enough related to provide unlimited fertility of the hybrids, and yet distinct enough from one another in their species-specific repertoires of innate behaviour patterns to permit tracing of the hereditary history of individual characters. The ideal would, of course, be 'instinct races' which differ only in one or a very small number of characters. However, we have as yet failed to find such an object, which is at the same time easy to maintain and to breed. For this reason, the best possibility for genetic behavioural research to my knowledge appeared to be long-term breeding of hybrids between mallard and pintails. The parental species differ only slightly – but nevertheless characteristically – in the repertoire of instinctive courtship patterns. Two pintail species – the Bahama pintail, *Anas* (*Poecilonetta*) *bahamensis*, and the South American pintail, *Anas* (*Dafila*) *spinicauda* – have been discovered which are zoologically very closely related, produce fertile hybrids and nevertheless exhibit marked qualitative differences in courtship behaviour. We intend to trace the hereditary relationships of individual instinctive motor patterns with this material.[55]

VI   The preconditions for human evolution[56]

The huge gulf separating man from the highest Primates (the Pongidae), which must have been bridged at some time or other during human phylogeny, and which Heberer (1952) refers to as the 'animal-man-transitional field', represents one of the central problems of evolutionary research. Various thinkers have concerned themselves with this problem; some of them believed that they had discovered the nature of the unique qualitative transition from animal to man. Wilhelm Wundt regarded the important step from animal to man as the transition from purely associative behaviour – which he regarded as the sole attribute of animals – to insight-controlled, intelligent behaviour. Arnold Gehlen (1950), on the other hand, regards as man's most important peculiarity the lack of adaptation to a specific environment, which permits man to be 'open to the world' and to actively construct his surroundings. Finally, Bolk (1926) gave 'foetalization' (i.e. the presence of certain peculiar neotenous features and the retardation of ontogenesis) as the most constitutive character of man.

All of these characters are indeed specifying properties of man, but none of them alone defines the nature of human beings – in fact, even the combination is insufficient. I shall not attempt here to provide an 'explanation' for the evolution of man, nor to provide a 'definition'. Instead, setting out from animal behaviour, I shall repeat the question posed by Johann Gottfried Herder: 'What was lacking in the animal most similar to man (the ape) which prevented it from becoming a man?' In other words, I simply intend to discuss a series of *preconditions* which must *all have been fulfilled together* in order to make the huge leap at all possible. These preconditions are:

I. CENTRAL REPRESENTATION OF SPACE AND THE GRASPING HAND

Before attempting to answer Herder's question quoted above, it is necessary to ask another: 'What is it that the animal most similar to man – the Pongid – possesses that provides the particular basis from which man could arise?' The answer agrees entirely with that given by Wundt: a specific form of *insight* behaviour which does not occur, and has never occurred, in any other animal. However, we can draw certain conclusions about the phylogenetic *evolution* of this behaviour, and this provides the task for this section.

The current definition of 'intelligence' is restricted to *negative* pronouncements. A behaviour pattern is 'intelligent' or 'insight-controlled' when it is: (1) not governed by special instinctive motor patterns and innate releasing mechanisms fitting the situation concerned, and (2) immediately copes with the situation without trial-and-error or any other learning processes. One might be tempted to add a further clause to this exclusive definition, which would also exclude from the concept of intelligent behaviour any solution of the problem on the basis of innate *orienting responses* or taxes. But one is initially extremely surprised, and then (on closer examination) struck with the significance of the fact, when this proves to be impossible.

Let us take, as an extremely simple example, the behaviour of a higher teleost fish which perceives a prey behind a transparent, but impassable, aquatic plant, and then swims around the obstacle to take the morsel. This can doubtless be understood on the basis of interaction of *two* orienting responses, which are innate attributes of the fish. It responds with a 'negative thigmotactic response' to the plant and with a 'positive telotactic response' to the prey. Thus, the fish's behaviour is the resultant of these two components in just the same way as a projected missile's path is the resultant of inertia and gravity. However – and this is the vital point – such simple resultants of two taxes can be used as a basis for derivation of all conceivable intermediate stages up to behaviour patterns which are universally and evidently regarded as insight-controlled. There is no clear-cut boundary between the detour of the fish and the insight-controlled 'methodical behaviour' (Greek: $\mu\varepsilon\theta o\delta o\varsigma$ = detour) of the highest living organisms; instead there is a quite smooth transition from one to the other. If, on the other hand, one attempts to employ in the definition of insight an introspective estimation of the *experience* (referred to so fittingly by Karl Bühler as the 'Aha-experience'), there is – significantly – still no clear-cut delimitation from quite simple orienting responses. It can easily be demonstrated that this experience occurs qualitatively in exactly the same manner whenever a state of non-orientation is *replaced by* orientedness. This is true of the simplest postural responses, which are definitely governed directly by the labyrinth, just as much as for the most complex scientific insights.

If one compares various animals – initially in a completely naïve way – as regards their 'intelligence', there is once again evidence of a remarkably close relationship between this and the development of orienting responses. Organisms from environments with little structural differentiation require a less exact and less differentiated orienting behaviour than those which must continually come to terms with complicated spatial conditions. The most homogeneous of all environments is provided by the open sea, and this in fact contains certain living free-swimming organisms which *completely* lack genuine orienting responses. For example, the jelly-fish *Rhizostoma pulmo* does not possess a single spatially oriented response to external stimuli, either for its prey (which is obtained by filtration of the sea-water – virtually homogeneous with respect to its content of small food animals) or for gravity, since the weight-distribution between the umbrella and the oral peduncle automatically balances the jelly-fish. The only stimulus reaction exhibited by this jelly-fish is involved in the fact that one beat of the umbrella elicits the next via certain receptors (the so-called 'marginal corpuscles'). 'It perceives nothing more than the beat of its own umbrella,' as Jacob von Uexküll remarked, combining apt description with poetic expression. This jelly-fish is thus the most 'stupid' free-living, many-celled animal that we know.

But even far more highly organized animals of the open sea frequently exhibit an amazing paucity of orienting responses. Once, on the Adriatic coast, I saw thousands of young fish of a needle-fish type (*Belone*, a genus adapted to life in the open sea) quite simply swimming at the shore-line. They swam up individually, but aligned exactly in parallel to one another, and were evidently driven by a common response to some orienting stimulus – light, heat, salinity or the like. The fish, which were still a few yards from the shore-line, were completely healthy; those which were in the intertidal zone were already fighting against death, and on the shore-line there was a small wall of corpses. This unforgettable experience made me realize that it is not only the *sense-organs* which determine the range of environmental conditions that the animal is able to 'represent' in its internal life processes! In fact, the sense-organs of *Belone* are no less highly differentiated than in any given fresh-water fish, which is not only able to 'understand' a vertical obstacle as such, but can even solve simple detour problems as and when required. And, of course *Belone* – just like all optically hunting fish – is able to localize its *prey* very exactly with binocular 'telotactic' orientation. However, as we have seen, it cannot apply this to a rock barrier stretching transversely across its path.

Similar narrowly specialized abilities for central representation are found in *steppe animals*. To a certain extent, the steppe exhibits in two dimensions what the open sea does in three. Even among the steppe-living birds and mammals there are some which are unable to comprehend a *vertical* obstacle and are unable to master it even through a learning process. For example, partridges in a confined space will for hours on end run to-and-fro along the best illuminated wall (i.e. against the wall opposite the window in a normal room). In doing this, they press against the wall to such an extent that they soon wear off the feathers on the neck and breast, and frequently the horny layer of the upper bill as well. If a part of the room is separated off as an exercise area with a knee-high board, as I did with my hand-reared birds, they never learn to overcome this obstacle by flying, even when they have repeatedly flown over the board after a mild surge of flying impulse. When I showed my very tame birds a mealworm from above, on a window-sill fitting flush with the wall, they immediately flew up to it. But they are unable to master the same problem when a table is used instead of the window-sill, since they always end up *under* the table and then no longer know what to do. Thus, they were quite able to aim *upwards*; but they were unable to take account of a solid obstacle standing at a right angle in the intended direction. However, the same birds behaved quite differently as soon as they *flew* instead of running. Despite the rapidity and impetuosity of their flights, they never collided against the walls. A *running* partridge is unable to take account of vertical obstacles, but a *flying* partridge can – and must – do so, since in flight it must be able to cope with the edges of woods, vertical earth faces and the like. But the remarkable thing is that the necessary central representation of space is evidently not accessible to the animal when it finds itself on the ground. In fact, we know of many examples of such restricted attachment of insight behaviour to quite specific situations.

If this behaviour of the partridge is compared with that of a closely-related form which lives in forests – such as the Californian grouse – one is amazed to find that it is able to master extremely complex spatial structures without further ado. This, despite the fact that there is no noticeable anatomical difference from the steppe-living form, either in the sense-organs or in the central nervous system. An analogous result is obtained from a comparison of steppe antelopes and the closely-related chamois.

Now if one asks which animals are forced to cope with the most complex structures in the course of their daily movements, the answer is quite decisive: the *tree-living forms*. Foremost among these are neither those which use claws nor those which employ adhesive pads, but those which climb by means of *grasping extremities* which enclose branches with a piner-action. For animals which climb by means of claws or adhesive pads, it is sufficient if the object at which a leap is directed is correctly localized in terms of *direction* alone. On impact, at least one of the grasping organs will find a hold. For example, one can observe tree-living frogs, and – with longer leaps – even squirrels and dormice, project themselves roughly in the direction of the tree they aim to reach and yet never come amiss. With the grasping extremity, the situation is entirely different. Here, there must be quite exact central representation in the animal's central nervous system not only of the direction, but also of the distance and the exact localization of the goal of the leap. Such representation must include the diameter of the goal and yet other features, and all this must be determined *before* the leap. This is because the grasping extremity must close in a definite spatial position at exactly the right moment; if open or closed into a fist, no hold will be obtained.

In fact, it was consideration of tree-climbing mammals which first demonstrated to me the very close association between the physiological type of optical space-perception and the central representation of spatial features. Among both marsupials and placental mammals, all those forms which are grasp-climbers (and particularly those which leap over long distances and then grasp the goal-object with the grasping extremity), *possess forward-directed eyes*. This fact is well-known for Primates (lemurs, monkeys, etc.). By contrast, claw-climbers have lateral, bulging eyes located some way back on the head. Thus (e.g. with a squirrel), there is no difference from closely-related ground-living forms. This is doubtless correlated with the fact that grasp-leapers fixate their goal with *binocular vision*, since only stereoscopic depth-perception is sufficient for exact perception of the spatial localization of the goal of the leap.

However, this correlation between greater exactitude in spatial discrimination and fixation of environmental objects goes much further back down the phylogenetic tree than binocular spatial vision. Even among fish, we can find a sharp demarcation between those which orient exclusively by peripheral vision and the parallactic illusion of movement of environmental objects, and those which (so-to-speak) scan their surroundings in all directions by persistent fixation. Among fishes, too, it is the former which (other things being equal) live in open water, and the latter which must cope with complex spatial structures. For example, orfs and other free-water forms of the cargo family – which orient only with the first method – only respond appreciably to obstacles when they themselves are moving. If such a fish happens to stop moving just in front of an aquatic plant, when it moves off again it will at first swim directly towards the obstacle and only begins to steer away from it when on the move, when the plant's position is indicated by parallactic movement. It is quite different with a stickleback, a Cichlid or a wrasse. Such fish dart with lightning speed from between rocks or plants, stop abruptly in the water, actively survey on all sides by fixation, and then dart off just as abruptly. This is done with exceptional accuracy of localization; the fish steer around complex obstacles and disappear into narrow crevices. This behaviour – in fact just the scanning fixation movements of the eyes – gives a naïve observer the impression of far greater intelligence than that given by the rigid 'fishy eye' of fish which are spatially oriented by parallactic means.

In the fish Class (Pisces), one can also find relationships between eye-position and spatial orientation analogous to those demonstrated above for mammals. Substrate-living fish with a reduced swim-bladder, which find their way amongst a maze of rocks and must virtually 'climb', always have inclined foreheads which allow for convergent forward vision (e.g. Bleniidae, some Gobiidae, etc.). Particularly with the Family Gobiidae, which includes free-swimming forms with a functional swim-bladder, it is possible to demonstrate quite convincingly the correlation between eye-position and climbing. The 'record' for both spatial orientation and for eye-position, fixation and spatial intelligence is held by the 'terrestrial fish' the mud-skipper, *Periophthalmus*, which is a member of the Gobiidae found climbing among mangrove roots. This fish literally does fixate like a monkey any branch to which it intends to leap. However, the best example for the correlation under discussion is provided by the sea-horse, whose head-shape and eye-position is quite well-known. It is the only fish which possesses a genuine grasping organ, in the form of a rolled-up tail, and it is a magnificent sight to see how the sea-horse binocularly fixates a coral outgrowth with intent to 'make fast' to it.

Even with the stickleback and other fish, there is an impression of intelligence when orientation occurs as a kind of planning operation prior to movement, so that the latter emerges as a *prepared* solution of a given spatial problem. At a much higher level, we find even with the most intelligent mammals an (at least functionally) analogous process, though this precedes not just a single, simple locomotor act, but an entire series of complex purposive activities. Advanced development of central representation of environmental objects, with all of their spatial structures and relationships, permits a few mammals to solve spatial problems not only through locomotion of their own bodies, but also through movements of environmental objects. It is no surprise to learn that the animals which are able to do this are all tree-living animals, the most talented among them being monkeys. The only carnivore so far shown to have such a capacity is the racoon, an animal which has almost monkey-like versatility in the use of its grasping hands. The ability to employ sticks as tools and to stack boxes and such like in order to reach an elevated tit-bit under the operation of insight – first demonstrated by Wolfgang Köhler with the chimpanzee – has since been demonstrated in capuchine monkeys of the New World and, to a limited extent, in the racoon as well. However, whereas the latter two, extremely agile, animals always 'think in the course of acting', so that it is impossible to exclude a certain degree of trial-and-error from their problem-solving, the large anthropoid apes behave in a way which has surely left an ineradicable impression on anybody who has seen them. This can be illustrated with an example: A banana is suspended with a cord from the ceiling of a room so high that an orang-utan is unable to reach it from the floor. (I have only been able to observe this myself with an orang-utan so far, and this only in a film.)[57] In one corner of the room, there is a crate which is tall enough to serve as a ladder for the ape. The orang-utan has already been subjected to a number of experiments on insight-controlled behaviour, but is not acquainted with this new problem. It looks first at the banana, then at the crate, then glances once or twice from one to the other. Whilst doing this – just like a man engaged in deep thought – the orang-utan scratches its head (and other areas of its body). Then it is seized by a fit of rage, stamping and screaming, and finally turns its back on the banana and the crate, as if insulted. But the problem refuses to disappear, and the orang-utan turns back to it, once more glancing between the bait and the crate. Suddenly, the previously sullen expression of the face 'lights up' (this is the only way to describe it), and the ape's eyes now wander from the banana to the empty area *beneath* it on the floor, from this to the crate, then back to the same area and then back on up to the banana. A moment later, the orang-utan utters a cry of joy and rushes towards the crate, performing a somersault from sheer exuberance. It then pushes the crate, with complete certainty of success, beneath the banana in order to reach the bait. Nobody who has seen such an event can doubt the existence of a genuine 'Aha-experience' in the ape.

A stickleback engaged in its 'pseudo-planning' type of scanning fixation of the surrounding space only provides the conditions towards which the subsequent locomotor acts will orient the response. An anthropoid ape, by contrast, is really in the process of *acting* whilst surveying the surroundings – but this activity is restricted to central representation of the environmental objects. Within its 'imagination-space' (a term which is certainly justified), it moves around the central representations of the crate and the banana. The 'central spatial model' is employed with great economy of energy in order to perform the entire operation, more-or-less as a 'rehearsal', without employing motor activity. And this is the beginning of all thinking processes!

It is more than likely that the entirety of man's thought processes originated from these operations emancipated from actual motor activity in 'imagined' space. In fact, this original function probably provides the indispensable foundation for our highest and most complex processes of thought. I am unable to think of any kind of thought process which would be independent from the central spatial model. The opinion that all thought is spatial in origin is supported by *language*. Porzig (1950), in his extremely informative book *Das Wunder der Sprache* (*The marvel of speech*), states: 'Speech translates all non-pictorial relationships into spatial phenomena. Indeed, this is not a property of just one language or a single group of languages; it applies without exception to them all. This peculiarity is one of the unchanging characteristics ("invariants") of human speech. All temporal relationships are expressed spatially: "before or after Christmas", "within a time-span of two years". Psychological processes are referred to not only in terms of "external" and "internal", but also with respect to "above and below the threshold" of consciousness; the "sub-conscious"; "the foreground" and "the background'; "depths" and "levels" of the soul. Quite generally, space serves as a model for all non-pictorial relationships: "Besides working, he also teaches", "love was greater than pride", "This intention lay behind the measure taken". It would be superfluous to add more examples, innumerable quantities of which can be collected from any passage of written or spoken language. This phenomenon is significant because of its quite general occurrence and the rôle which it plays in the history of language. It can be demonstrated not only in the use of prepositions, which are all originally indicators of spatial relationships, but also in verbs and adjectives.' I should only like to add to these philologist's comments that the phenomenon concerned is of fundamental significance not only for the history of language, but even more so for the phylogenetic development of all thought (i.e. including pre-articulate and non-articulate thought). It is evident how little this significance has been lost even in the highest activities of human thought (supposedly linked uniquely to speech) from the terms which we still employ today for the highest and most abstract realms of thought. It is in fact *particularly* these areas where the attachment to central representation of space is most direct. We achieve 'insight' into an 'intricate' 'relationship' – like an ape in a maze of branches – and we only really 'grasp' an 'object' when we have completely 'caught on'. In fact, the last three expressions neatly illustrate the ancient primacy of manual factors over visual factors. This should serve as a caution for modesty to many philosophers who deny the evolution of man from Primates explicitly because of his psychological prowess; in the presentation of even their most elevated philosophical operations, they are compelled to employ expressions which exhibit their origin with extreme clarity.

2. SPECIALIZATION IN NON-SPECIALIZATION AND CURIOSITY

Arnold Gehlen (1950) refers to man as the 'deficient organism', expressing the opinion that human beings – owing to the lack of special morphological adaptations – have been driven to the production of tools, weapons, clothes and the like. This is not considered in biological terms – there is no such thing as a non-adapted organism, or at least where such occur they are individuals bearing lethal factors and doomed to succumb. Gehlen also overlooks the fact that the *brain*, with its enormous size, represents a very tangible special morphological adaptation. Nevertheless, his tenet contains something fundamentally correct and important: an organism *with* pronounced, specialized morphological adaptations would never have been able to evolve into man. Perhaps we might have a clearer view of the significance of the *lack* of special adaptations if we change our standpoint and consider the *versatility* of and organism lacking special adaptations. Take, for example, a comparison of some fairly closely related rodents with extensive specializations in different directions (the jerboa (running adaptation), the flying squirrel (climbing and flying adaptation), the mole rat (adaptation for subterranean life) and the beaver (swimming adaptation)) with a non-specialized rodent (the Norway rat). The latter greatly exceeds any of the four specialists in the three activities for which the given specialist is *not* specialized, and exceeds it even more in ultimate biological success – number of individuals and distribution of the species. If we now compare purely physical (i.e. completely non-intellectual) activities of *man*, with respect to versatility, against those of mammals of roughly the same size, we find that human beings are by no means as fragile and deficient as one might think. For example, if one sets the following three tasks – walking 22 miles in one day; climbing 15 feet up on a rope; and swimming 15 yards under water at a depth of 12 feet, accurately picking up a number of objects from the substrate (all activities which a quite unsportive armchair human being – such as myself – can perform without difficulty) – *there is no single mammal which can make the same performance.*

In addition, the lack of special adaptations in body structure is always accompanied by extremely characteristic *behavioural* versatility. Highly-specialized organs always require a central nervous system differentiated in the same direction, incorporating *instinctive motor patterns* and usually even more highly specialized *innate releasing mechanisms* which direct each instinctive motor pattern towards its specially defined object. Non-specialists, on the other hand, only possess a few instinctive motor patterns with a small degree of differentiation and thus with a *far more general range of applicability* than the wonderfully differentiated patterns of a specially adapted organism. Even less specialized and selective are the innate releasing mechanisms, which set the unspecialized instinctive motor patterns in operation. With an inexperienced young animal, these mechanisms respond repeatedly in a great variety of environmental situations. It is *exploratory, latent learning* which directs the performance of the pattern towards *specific, appropriate* objects. In order to illustrate this, I shall take from the Class of the birds two extreme types – one specialist and one non-specialist. It is no chance effect that the former is the most stupid and the latter one of the cleverest of birds.

In the environment of the great crested grebe (*Podiceps cristatus* Pontopp), almost everything to which the bird responds (the water-surface, the prey, the nest-site, etc.) is already predetermined down to the smallest detail in the inexperienced young bird by highly specialized innate releasing mechanisms, which elicit equally special instinctive motor patterns with a wonderful degree of adaptation. The bird does not need to learn much additional information – in fact it *cannot*. For example, the innate releasing mechanisms for prey-catching and eating require the movement of the fish, and the bird never learns to eat a sufficient quantity of dead fish, even when these are utterly fresh and would be physiologically quite adequate for the metabolic requirements. Adaptability in the bird's behaviour is largely restricted to path-conditioning, which serves in the location of places and situations in which the innate action and response patterns 'fit'. By contrast, there is virtually nothing predetermined in the behaviour of a young raven (*Corvus corax* L.), with the exception of a few instinctive behaviour patterns with great versatility of application. These patterns are em-ployed with *all unknown objects*. The raven first approaches such an object with an extremely high level of *flight motivation*. The raven literally spends several days carefully eyeing the object before approach-ing it. The first active interaction is very commonly represented by a powerful blow with the beak; the raven instantly flees and observes the effect of this action from an elevated perch. Only when these security measures have carefully been applied does the bird begin to try out the instinctive motor patterns of *predation*. The object is turned in every direction with prising movements of the beak, it is grasped in the claws, pecked with the beak, plucked, torn to pieces if possible, and – finally and without fail – concealed. Living animals are always approached from behind by the young raven, and with even greater care than for inanimate objects. It may take weeks before the approach is close enough to permit a vigorous jab with the beak. If the animal then flees, the raven immediately follows with increased courage and kills it, if it can. How-ever, if the animal actively attacks, the raven withdraws and soon loses interest. The innate releasing mechanisms which elicit all this trial-and-error behaviour have an extraordinarily low degree of selectivity. It is only with the handling of living animals that there are evidently mechan-isms available to tell the inexperienced raven 'which is the back and which the front'. The oriented attack on the back of the head and the eyes of other animals also seems to be directed by innate orienting mechanisms. But this more-or-less completely exhausts the innate instinctive equipment which the raven possesses for interaction with the extraspecific environment. The rest is achieved by exploratory learning and the overpowering *greed* for new objects (curiosity). The strength of this curiosity is demonstrated by the following fact: When all the strongest attractants – raw eggs and living grasshoppers – failed, I could always lure my ravens into their cage by placing my *camera* inside . . . an object which they were never allowed to investigate for obvious reasons. With our mongoose, my brother's doctorate diploma played the same rôle for similar reasons.

The undoubtedly great survival value of this curiosity behaviour is doubtless based on the fact that the animal quite generally treats *everything* as being of potential biological significance. As we have seen, there is a series of treatment ranging from that appropriate to predators, to that suitable for prey and food, and this exists until thorough self-conditioning has taught the animal whether a given object is significant as predator, prey or food . . . or of no significance at all. Objects which the raven has 'rendered intimate' through the application of all motor patterns concerned with predators, prey and food and which have been 'set aside' as of no significance (to use Gehlen's fitting expression) can be *returned to* at any later date. For example, objects which have acquired an indifferent status in this way can be employed to cover a food-morsel for concealment, or may simply be used as perches.

The method of inquisitive experimentation with all possibilities has the automatic consequence that such specialists in non-specialization can maintain an existence in a *wide range* of environments, since they find sooner or later everything which they need to survive. On bird-inhabited islands, the raven leads a life very similar to that of skuas and other such parasites upon the great colonies of sea-birds, feeding upon eggs, off-spring and transported food. In the desert, on the other hand, a raven lives just like a vulture, sailing along in thermal up-currents and searching for afflicted animals. Finally, in Central Europe the raven exists as a predator of small animals and insects.

Among the mammals, the Norway rat (*Epimys norvegicus* L.) is the prototype of a non-specialized creature of curiosity. One of its most prominent characteristics is the tendency towards inquisitive 'learning-by-heart' of all possible *pathways* in a given area – in particular escape pathways leading back to its retreat. In this case too, 'return' to pathways which had originally been set aside as insignificant can be very neatly demonstrated. The expression *latent learning* is particularly appropriate here. Within the canal system of a maze, the rat at first crawls along *all* of the pathways, but later ceases to use those 'which lead to nothing'. However, if one later slightly alters the conditions (e.g. by changing the site of the food-area), it becomes evident that the animal has by no means forgotten what it has 'filed'. The most efficient revised pathways are not learned afresh; the rat can, when so required, make use of its latent knowledge. With the rat, the biological success of an unspecialized creature of curiosity is particularly evident. This animal literally occurs everywhere where civilized man has travelled. It lives in the holds of ships just as in the canals of big towns; it thrives in farmers' barns, and it can even live independently of man, occurring on islands as the only terrestrial mammal. Everywhere it is found, the rat behaves as if it were a specialist in its element.

All higher vertebrates which are *cosmopolitan* are typical unspecialized creatures of curiosity, and man is undoubtedly one of their number. Human beings also construct their 'significant environment' through active, dialectic interaction with the extraspecific environment, and thus we are also able to adapt to such a wide variety of environmental conditions that many authors are of the opinion that one can no longer refer to a human 'environment' in the sense understood by von Uexküll. However, I merely wish to demonstrate the close fundamental *relationship* between this active, dialectic construction and dismemberment of the environment and the curiosity behaviour of the animals mentioned.

The most outstanding and essential character of curiosity behaviour is its *objectivity*. On observing a raven with a novel object, first conducting exploratory 'security measures' and then trying out one after the other all the instinctive motor patterns concerned in predation, one is at first inclined to think that the bird's entire activity is ultimately to be interpreted as *appetitive behaviour* for food-uptake. However, it can easily be shown that this is not the case. In the first place, the inquisitive investigation is at once abandoned when the raven is genuinely hungry: it immediately turns to an already familiar food-source. Young ravens exhibit their most intensive phase of curiosity behaviour immediately after fledging, i.e. at a time when the youngsters are still fed by their parents. If they become hungry, they follow the parental bird (or human foster-parent) in an insistent manner, and they *only* exhibit interest for unknown objects when they are satiated. Secondly, when the raven is moderately, though still demonstrably, hungry, the appetite for unknown objects prevails over that for the best available food. If one offers a tit-bit to a young raven actively engaged in investigating an unknown object, the tit-bit is almost always ignored. In human terms, this means: The bird does not *want* to eat, it wants to *know* whether the particular object is 'theoretically' edible. The young raven conducting its 'investigations' is not motivated to eat, and in the same way a young Norway rat repeatedly dashing back to the entrance of its retreat from various points within its range is not motivated to flee. This very *independence* of the exploratory learning process from momentary *requirements*, in other words from the *motive of the appetite*, is extremely important. Bally (1945) regards it as the major characteristic of *play* that behaviour patterns really belonging in the area of appetitive behaviour are performed 'in a field released from tension'. As we have seen, the field released from tension – a *sine qua non* for all curiosity behaviour just as for play – is an extremely important common feature of the two kinds of behaviour![58]

Independence of a momentary drive goal governing the animal's actions has the effect that *different* properties of the object relevant to different drive goals are simultaneously 'rendered intimate' and 'filed'. These 'files' remain as engrams in the animal's central nervous system, evidently arranged according to objects. It is only objectivating recognition of the objects – requiring the entire arsenal of perceptual constancy phenomena – which permits the animal to 'return' to objects and exploit their latently learned properties. This demonstrably occurs when an appetite occurs in a serious functional context. Through this process of learning the properties attached to *things*, independently of the momentary physiological condition and requirements of the organism, curiosity behaviour has an *objectivating* function in the most literal and important sense of the word. *It is only through curiosity behaviour that objects come to exist in the environment of an animal as in that of man.* In this sense, Gehlen is quite right in stating that man constructs his environment himself, since his environment is an objective one! However, this is also true of all unspecialized creatures of curiosity, though to a lesser extent.

A second constitutive property of curiosity behaviour lies in the fact that the organism *does* something in order to *experience*. In fact, this behaviour incorporates no more and no less than the principle of the *question*. An organism which 'constructs objects' through its curiosity behaviour, determining the properties inherent in an object by means of its own, active efforts, to some extent maintains a *dialectic* relationship to extra-subjective reality. And this – as Baumgarten (1950) correctly emphasized – is one of the most important characteristics of mankind.

From this dialectic interaction with objects, man has developed a function which, like language, is scarcely indicated even in the highest animals. When a human being works on an object, this function is based on the fact that *in the course of* this activity, the 'response' of the object is continuously registered and that further activity is steered accordingly. For example, when a nail is being hammered into something, each blow of the hammer must compensate for the unnoticeable lateral deviation imparted to the nail by the previous blow. Anybody not familiar with animals, who – despite exaggerated ideas of the peculiarity of man – habitually imagines higher animals to be far more similar to man than they are, does not generally realize that the ability for such activity regulated through continuous observation of the success is almost completely lacking even among anthropoid apes.

This is particularly evident in the chimpanzee's crate-piling activity. The animal places one crate on top of the other, but never straightens them up; the most that happens is that when one crate overlaps considerably on one side, the next may possibly be placed somewhat further to the opposite side in compensation. That is all. The foremost achievement in this direction so far known was exhibited by Köhler's chimpanzee Sultan, which gnawed at a detached wooden wall-strip until it could be inserted into the hollow of a bamboo-tube in order to extend its sectional 'fishing-rod'. The chimp repeatedly tested to see whether the strip of wood was thin enough, and continued to gnaw until this was actually the case. However, in order to manufacture a genuine tool, such as a hand-axe, incomparably greater differentiation of continuous success-control of behaviour is necessary. In fact, it seems that this intimate connection between action and recognition, between *praxis* and *gnosis*, requires a *special central organ* which only man possesses – in the *Gyrus supramarginalis* of the temporal lobe of the brain. If this area of the brain, which (significantly) also incorporates the 'speech centre', is damaged, the human being exhibits – in addition to speech disruption – certain omissions in activity and recognition (*'apraxia'* and *'agnosia'*). It has not yet been possible (Klüver 1933) to demonstrate the existence of similar centres in monkeys, nor to provoke similar omissions.

Although I have, in the foregoing, contrasted the raven and the rat (as typical unspecialized creatures of curiosity) with the great crested grebe (as an instinct and organ specialist), this does not mean that curiosity behaviour is completely lacking in other, somewhat more highly specialized organisms. The rôle played by *curiosity learning* is dependent not only on the lack of specialization, but also upon the general level of differentiation of the central nervous system. A young orang-utan greatly exceeds the raven and the rat in the achievements of its exploratory learning, although this species is extremely highly special-ized in certain directions. Assume that one is observing a young anthropoid ape – preferably a chimpanzee – performing its magni-ficently logical object-directed curiosity behaviour, which exhibits the character of *play* even more than that of the raven or rat. One would be repeatedly amazed by the fact that, for all this remarkably intelligent – almost creative – experimentation, nothing *more* emerges than the know-ledge as to which nuts can be cracked, which branches can be climbed and (at the most) which stick is best suited for fishing for objects. When I observe how such a young animal plays with building blocks or places boxes inside one another, I am repeatedly struck with the suspicion that these creatures were, in the distant past, once of *much higher intelligence* than they are today, and that in the course of their specialization they have *lost* abilities which now only appear as a silhouette in the young animal's play![59]

One thing in fact fundamentally distinguishes the curiosity behaviour of *all* animals from that of man: it is restricted to a brief developmental phase in young animals. What the raven acquires in early life with its so human-like experimentation soon rigidifies into conditioned patterns, which are later so invariable and adaptable that they are scarcely distinguishable from instinctive behaviour. The need for novelty gives way to a pronounced aversion to all unknown things. An adult raven, and not just a really old one, which is forced to make a basic change in its environment is quite incapable of finding its way in the new situation and falls into a neurotic fear state in which it is even unable to recognize a well-acquainted keeper. A raven which has just reached maturity behaves in such a situation very much like a man suffering from senile dementia. A senile man, whose loss of adaptability is inconspicuous as long as he is in familiar surroundings, immediately exhibits extensive dementia when forced to change his surroundings. In order to avoid misunderstandings, it must be explicitly emphasized that it is not learning ability itself which has been eradicated, but the positive orientation to the unknown. For example, an old raven is perfectly able to learn that a given novel situation is dangerous from a single, unpleasant experience. But this learning process only occurs subject to the immediate compulsion of a quite specific, biologically relevant situation. Old rats or old anthropoid apes do actually behave in a more plastic manner than old ravens, but in principle the gulf between the young and the old animal is the same.

In reply to Herder's question, 'What does the animal most similar to man – the ape – lack that prevented it from becoming man?', we can now provide two quite specific answers. Although spatial representation and insight are already present to an almost human degree of development, although the obligate bond between spatial intention and action existing in other animals is broken, and although there is a true dialectic, inquisitive, objectivating interaction with the environment (at least in the young animal) . . . the anthropoid ape *lacks: firstly* the intimate reciprocal relationship between action and recognition (praxis and gnosis), which permits activity continuously controlled by success and which can apparently only be ensured by the appropriate human centre in the *gyrus supramarginalis,* so that the ape also lacks a basic precondition for speech; *secondly*, in the fully-grown, mature Pongid, there is almost complete absence of curiosity behaviour which in human beings remains active up to the onset of senility. Only the human being continues to *develop* up to old age.

3. DOMESTICATION AND OPENNESS TO SURROUNDINGS

The domestication of certain animal species is the oldest biological experiment conducted by mankind. For this reason alone, this experiment is better suited than any for aiding the synthesis between evolutionary and genetic theory. One commonly uses the term 'domesticated' for a race of animals when it is distinguished from the free-living ancestral type in a number of typical, hereditary characters which have been developed in the course of domestication. Almost all domestic animals exhibit mottling, shortening of the extremities and the skull-base; reduction in tautness of the connective tissue (leading to formation of flabby lobes, drooping ears, reduction in muscular tonus, and the like), a tendency to fattening, and – above all – a quite general and considerable increase in the range of variation of species characteristics. In the expression of these, and many other, characters of domestication, even widely different domestic animals show remarkably extensive parallels. For example, hybridization experiments show that even with species belonging to separate Families (e.g. the Muscovy duck, *Cairina moschata* L., and the mallard, *Anas platyrhynchos*), mottling, drooping belly and other characters are based on homologous hereditary loci. One might possibly be inclined to think that similar environmental conditions (e.g. limitation of freedom of movement; scarcity of air and light; imbalanced, vitamin-impoverished and yet copious food; etc.) have favoured homologous mutations. However, this would definitely seem to be a false assumption; instead the blame for appearance of these characters seems to be exclusively due to the removal of natural selection. According to Herre's observations, the Northern European reindeer (*Rangifer tarandus*) seems to exhibit virtually all the typical domestication characteristics, although admittedly in less extreme form. This, despite the fact that this animal lives in its original environment and in complete freedom. Its environmental conditions differ from those of the wild form in (not even thorough) protection from wolves and a certain selection of breeding stags; the Laps in fact castrate the strongest stags in order to reduce their animosity.

Other organisms which are, so-to-speak, 'self-domesticated' (the cave-bear and man) demonstrate that close confinement and deficiency phenomena are not responsible for the production of the described changes in the hereditary complement. The cave-bear would appear to have been the 'Lord of the Earth' at the time of its greatest distribution, as man is now. It is, in any case, difficult to imagine that any other carnivore was at that time dominant over the powerful cave-bear. And this species in fact exhibited, in the apparent heyday immediately prior to its disappearance, typical domestication characteristics. In the 'Drachenhöhle' (dragon's cave) near Mixnitz in Steiermark, there were many cave-bear skeletons heaped together which exhibited virtually all of the changes which the domestic dog has undergone in the process of domestication. There are giant bears alongside dwarf ones, long-legged animals with a markedly greyhound-like head alongside some whose shortened skulls are strikingly reminiscent of bulldogs, and whose abbreviated legs are similar to those of a dachshund. One needs little palaeobiological imagination to picture the possessors of these skulls as having dangling ears and spotty coat when they were alive.

The fact that man also exhibits genuine domestication characteristics was, interestingly enough, first noticed by Schopenhauer. He clearly states that the blue eyes and the light skin of the European are 'far from natural' and that they are 'analogous to white mice, or at least to white horses'. It is especially noteworthy that there is a fine biological sense expressed in the words 'at least'! Eugen Fischer pointed out a long, long time ago that the kind of pigment-distribution found in the blue or grey human eye does not occur in one single free-living animal species, and yet is found in exactly the same form in almost *all* domestic animals. It is, no doubt, unnecessary to expound further on the predominant occurrence of typical domestication characteristics in modern man. Anybody who has eyes to see such things sees them as a self-evident fact of life, and nobody would doubt their inherent identity with those exhibited by animals.

It is quite certain that a number of domestication-induced changes belong among the preconditions for human evolution, which are lacking in modern anthropoid apes. The most important among them is the developmental inhibition referred to by Bolk as *retardation* or *foetalization*, which fixates juvenile characteristics of the wild form as persistent adult characters. I can see no reason why one should not employ the term *neoteny*, which is otherwise usually used in biology, for the described phenomena – at least for some of these. The reduction of the facial skeleton relative to the brain capsule; the relative shortness of the extremities; flabby ears; short hair and curling of the tail together provide sufficient examples for persistence of juvenile bodily characteristics of the wild form in the domesticated dog, and for domestic ruminants if the last feature is replaced by 'lack of horns'. Bolk (1926), Schindewolf (1928) and other authors have indicated a really convincing number of adult human characteristics which exhibit extensive parallels to those of young, and even foetal, anthropoid apes. The head proportions; the curvature of the vertebral column and – above all – the pelvic organs; the distribution of hair; and the relative paucity of pigment can be given as examples of neotenous characters.

But far more important for the problem of human evolution are neotenous features in *behaviour*. In many extensively domesticated animals, the fighting drive of the adult male is greatly reduced, as is the full manifestation of sexual dimorphism seen in the wild form. If a boar, a bull or a stallion were tame and yet just as aggressive as the wild-living equivalent he would be extremely dangerous and quite useless as a farm animal. However, the domestic animal whose usefulness is most dependent upon neoteny of its behaviour patterns is the *dog*. Its literal fidelity and attachment to a given person doubtless stem from the drives which – in the free-living form – are related *to the mother*, and perhaps later to the leader of the pack. A hand-reared jackal, dingo or wolf behaves towards a human being just like a domestic dog during the first years of life. However, the keeper is later disappointed to see how his charge becomes independent in a quite un-doglike fashion, even though the adult animal still exhibits a certain degree of collegial friendship towards his master. I find it utterly stunning that the dog owes his most important characteristic (fidelity to his master), just as man owes his constitutive *openness to surroundings*, to domestication-induced behavioural neoteny.

In fact, this continuous, inquisitive communication with extra-subjective reality – recognized as one of the constitutive characters of human beings by Gehlen, and accepted as such in this essay – is quite definitely a persistent juvenile characteristic! Inquisitive play also persists in extremely neotenous domestic animals such as the dog! The fact that Gehlen, who extensively discusses morphological neoteny in his book, did not notice the close relationship between neoteny and persistent inquisitive behaviour is a result of his lack of knowledge of the inquisitive behaviour of young 'specialists in non-specialization'. He believed that an animal learns only under the pressure of immediate biological necessity, as was maintained by many contemporary investigators of the conditioned reflex. All purely material research conducted by a human scientist is pure inquisitive behaviour – appetitive behaviour *in free operation*. In this sense, it is *play behaviour*. All scientific knowledge – to which man owes his rôle as master of the world – arose from playful activities conducted in a free field entirely for their own sake. When Benjamin Franklin drew sparks from the leash of his kite, he thought no more about the possibility a lightning conductor than Hertz thought about the possibilities of radio when investigating electric waves. Anybody who has seen in his own activities the smooth transition from inquisitive childhood play to the life-work of a scientist could never doubt the fundamental identity of play and research. Nietzsche states that the inquisitive child (completely departed from the nature of a full-grown, completely animal chimpanzee) is *hidden* within the 'true human being'; but in fact it completely *dominates* him!

The undeniable fact of partial neoteny of man must be given far more consideration in the construction of his probable evolution than is generally the case. *Dollo's 'Law' of irreversibility in specialization meets with important exceptions as soon as neoteny occurs.* The neotenous, gill-breathing axolotl quite definitely evolved from lung-breathing terrestrial animals, and not – as one would necessarily conclude from Dollo's Law, in ignorance of the nature of neoteny – from aquatic primitive Stegocephalians. (Terrestrial axolotls are, of course, more specialized than the larval form.) And exactly the same applies to all hypotheses regarding human evolution, which attempt to exclude Pongids as the possible ancestral form because they are more specialized than man, who, with his primitive organ characteristics, 'cannot' therefore be a derivative from them. The earliest common ancestor of man and chimpanzee was doubtless less specialized than the modern chimpanzee (I have already stated that it was, in fact, possibly more 'human'). But this ancestor was equally certainly *more* specialized than man, and must have been so, since the grasping hand and the correlated phenomenon of central spatial representation could only have developed in an arboreal environment.

Thus, man owes to partial neoteny (and thus indirectly to self-domestication) *two* constitutive features: the almost life-long retention of his environmentally open inquisitiveness, and reduction in specialization, which itself has given him the purely structural stamp of a 'creature of curiosity'.

In addition, man's 'self-specialization' has given him yet other qualities, some indispensable for his intellectual development and the structuring of his cultural life, and some which persistently threaten the survival of his species. We shall first briefly consider analogous qualities in the behaviour of domestic animals and then examine their detailed significance. The innate, species-specific behaviour of many different domesticated animals is typically exposed to certain *disruptions*, which can be summarized into three groups:

In the first place, *endogenous stimulus-production* of some instinctive motor patterns is open to considerable *quantitative* changes, leading either to tremendous hypertrophy or to utter disappearance. The production of locomotor movements decreases in almost all domestic animals, usually in correlation with the disappearance of muscular tonus and an inclination towards obesity. Similarly, in most domestic animals all of the more finely specialized instincts of brood-care and social life tend to disappear, whilst those of eating and mating are usually enormously exaggerated.

Secondly, the specific selectivity of innate releasing mechanisms is lost to a great extent in the majority of domestic animals. Responses which, in the wild-form, would be evoked at their full intensity only by stimulus situations characterized by a whole range of identifying features can be elicited in the domestic form by much simpler substitute stimuli.

Thirdly, functionally correlated behaviour patterns, which only exhibit survival value in combination, can become completely independent of one another. For example, in the domestic goose the instinctive behaviour patterns of 'falling-in-love' (i.e. those of formation and monogamic maintenance of pairs) become dissociated from those of copulation.

Even this very brief outline of disintegration processes in instinctive behaviour strongly highlights points of comparison with human disintegration phenomena. However, we shall first consider the *positive* side. Whitman (1898) had already clearly seen that these domestication-induced losses in innate behaviour by no means imply a backward trend with respect to the higher functions of learning and intelligence. In his work *Animal Behaviour*, he says of certain instinct deficiencies observed in domestic pigeons: 'These faults of instinct, so far from indicating psychological retrogression, are, I believe, the first signs of greater plasticity in congenital co-ordinations, and, consequently a greater facility in forming these new combinations, implied by the choice of action.' Elsewhere, he states: 'These faults of instinct are not intelligence, but they are the open door through which the great educator experience gains entrance to work all the wonders of intelligence.'

There is very little to add to these words of the great pioneer of comparative behavioural research. The Pongid ancestors of man were doubtless just as stenoic (i.e. bound to specific, narrowly defined environmental conditions) as all modern anthropoid apes. It is just as certain that reduction of many innate releasing mechanisms was necessary in order for man to become the most *euryoic* of all living organisms in such a short time-span (geologically speaking), so that he is now equally at home on the Arctic ice and in tropical jungle. Inherent variability between individuals – which is a result of instinct deficiencies and does not occur in any wild-living animal – is also very important. This provides the immediate precondition for the highly developed *division of labour* which is a fundamental requirement for all human cultural developments. But above all, as Whitman so clearly indicated, the constitutive *freedom* of human behaviour is the direct result of domestication-induced reduction of rigid instinctive behaviour.

Freedom often entails danger, and there is a particular danger in the manner in which man acquired his inherent behavioural freedom – by undergoing in an irregular fashion loss or alteration of the proven, species-preserving action and response norms. Domestication-induced alterations of instinctive behaviour are, by nature, processes bordering closely on pathological events, and the deficiencies to which man owes his specific freedom are closely allied to those which drive him to destruction. Gehlen's statement that man is 'the jeopardized creature', the organism 'with a constitutional predisposition towards mishap' seems to be only too apt, in view of the following considerations:

Hypertrophy of drives for food-intake and mating (which we wrongly refer to as 'animal' – it is really only 'domesticatedly animal'), definitely occurs in civilized human beings as a degeneration phenomenon just as much as the disappearance of the more finely differentiated social instincts and inhibitions. The dissociation of love and copulation in human beings, particularly in the male, occurs almost more frequently than their association in a species-conserving, adaptive context. In order to reach a correct appraisal of the disastrous consequences of this single instinct dissociation, one must clearly realize that *falling-in-love* (the selection of the best and most beautiful available partner) is more or less the only factor which today still directs natural selection in a positive manner. In the midst of spatial competition among civilized human beings, almost all of the described domestication-induced instinct disruptions unfortunately have a *positive selective value*. A reduction in the social drives and inhibitions is extremely useful in modern competition, and thus it is that sparingly social or asocial human beings are much more successful than their behaviourally intact counterparts, who in fact enable the former to exist. Individuals with behavioural deficiencies penetrate peoples, states and cultural circles in just the same way (and for quite similar reasons) as malignant cancer-cells penetrating the human body. As with cancer-cells, such individuals can eventually destroy the host organization, and thus themselves. I am convinced that regular collapse of human cultures, as recognized by Spengler, is brought about to a considerable extent by these very processes. It is not an inevitable 'logic of time' which results in 'senescence' of cultures, as Spengler believed; the effect is due to quite tangible processes which are open to experimental investigation.

Having fully recognized these dangers threatening mankind, it requires almost an act of will to retain any optimism about our future evolution, especially since there are other, equally large, dangers in addition to those mentioned. The great developmental leaps in human intellect which have fundamentally altered man's entire ecology in quite short, historic time-spans, naturally resulted in an *insufficiency* of human equipment with drives and inhibitions. Many social behaviour patterns, which automatically appear in response to a personally acquainted society member, naturally failed as the increase of numbers of individuals in human societies required that the same behaviour should be exhibited towards anonymous, unknown human beings. The inhibitions against killing conspecifics proved to be insufficient when the first weapon facilitated and accelerated the deed to such an extent that the factors which previously evoked the inhibition became ineffective.

Each *invention* with which man – in the process of actively constructing his environment – altered his previous ecology and sociology, could have sufficed to destroy him if *the same* ability which had made it possible for him to invent had not been adequate for the *regulation* necessary for bridging the gap between inclination and obligation. This ability involves man's prediction of the results of his actions. The further development of success-controlled activity found in human beings, which was doubtless necessary for the manufacture of even the simplest weapon, the hand-axe, presumably also provided the basis for simple self-questioning: 'What have I done?' And this question contains the foundation of all human moral responsibility. When we clearly picture what it really means for a creature, with the explosive aggressivity doubtless typical of our prehominid ancestors, to suddenly acquire with the hand-axe the possibility of wiping out his equals with a single blow, it almost seems surprising that this invention did not lead to self-destruction of the species. Can we derive from this the hope that human moral responsibility will successfully master the innumerable dangers now threatening mankind? The pervading degeneration of his social instincts, the continually mounting horror of his weapons, the increasing overpopulation of the Earth; all seem to forbode the destruction of mankind. Or are all these evils, in the final analysis, nothing more than symptoms of 'the force that always seeks evil and always brings good'?

The three preconditions of humanization discussed above – central spatial representation derived from climbing with the grasping hand; the versatility and explorative curiosity of the unspecialized organism; and neoteny plus liberation of rigid instincts – are certainly not the only ones. And they by no means provide an *explanation*. How and why did the centre for *praxis, gnosis* and speech arise in the *Gyrus supramarginalis*? How and why did the human brain undergo its enormous enlargement and further differentiation, providing the basis for conceptualized thought and the entire intellectual development of mankind? We are just as unable to provide answers to these questions as we are to give a reliable causal explanation for many far-reaching epigenetic processes involved in evolution.[60] Nonetheless, there seems to be a significant close correlation between these further developments and the three preconditions we have discussed.

VII Summary

In this account of the development of comparative psychology, I have reported on a number of subsidiary fields within this discipline, which bear relatively little relationship to one another. I did this, because these particular fields of knowledge indicate with especial clarity the indispensability of the comparative phylogenetic approach.

Even in the very first pioneer studies of our discipline, one finds the foundation for a far more exact causal analysis of animal and human behaviour than was ever achieved in the (only apparently scientific) field

of experimental psychology. The order introduced among the phenomena concerned (p. 201 et seq.) by the phylogenetic approach led
directly on to the analysis of the endogenous-automatic instinctive motor
pattern and thus to the overthrow of the reflex as the sole possible
'element' of all neurological processes. This itself led to a more exact
formulation of the reflex concept. The elicitatory effect of external
stimuli was investigated from another angle and, because of the understanding of the endogenous processes involved, entered into a new stage
of quantified causal analysis. The result was extensive rationalization of
the apparently completely chaotic relationship between stimulus strength
and response strength (p. 206 et seq.). Apart from this, clear conceptual
distinction between the automatism and the reflex provided a further
possibility for analysis of spatially oriented movements (p. 206). The
introduction of the comparative phylogenetic approach led to the
establishment of a research programme which will provide the foundations for behavioural research genuinely incorporating the concept of
hereditary control (p. 215 et seq.). Finally, the comparative phylogenetic
approach has led us to the problematic transition field between animal
and man. Without attempting any 'explanation', or even just a definition, of the human condition, three *preconditions* for humanization were
discussed: The first is central representation of space based on orienting
responses, which achieves its highest degree of differentiation in animals
which climb with grasping hands. This doubtless provides the basis for
human *spatial* form of visualization, which itself provides the basis for
all thought (p. 217 et seq.). The second precondition is active, exploratory inquisitive behaviour, which only occurs in organisms which are
not bound by highly-specialized differentiation of organs and innate
behaviour patterns. The 'material' and object-related nature of inquisitive behaviour leads to active construction of an objectivated environment. Because of its relationships to play behaviour and human research
activity, inquisitive behaviour emerges as the basis for all dialectic interaction with the environment, and thus as a precondition for speech.
However, no other animal exhibits attainment of an additional, indispensable precondition – close coupling of *praxis* and *gnosis* in the centre
for activity control and cognition. The third main precondition is represented by human self-domestication. This leads to partial *neoteny* in
human beings (p. 233 et seq.), as a result of which human exploratory
inquisitive behaviour – restricted in animals to a brief developmental
phase – is extended to persist until the onset of senility. Domestication,
through the dismantling of rigid instincts, also leads to a new degree of
behavioural freedom (p. 236 et seq.), though at the same time it introduces great danger. A brief outline is given of the rôle of moral responsibility in compensation for the insufficiency of human instincts.

VIII. Review and forecast

It is presumably unnecessary to emphasize any further the fact that the
phylogenetic approach, as applied to the field of comparative psychology, has already led to investigations which go far beyond pure description and systematizing. They have penetrated deep into the third
developmental phase of all natural science – causal analysis aimed at
identification of inherent laws. Nevertheless, it would be rash and pre-
mature to believe that the work of descriptive phylogenetic systematics
has already been completed in behavioural research, and that this aspect
is now dispensable.[61] We shall certainly not permit imposition of restrictions on our inclination to experimental, exact inductive research by any
pedagogical research taboos relating to methodology. Still less will we
permit ourselves to be prevented from an immediate assault upon the
analytically important research tasks. But, at the same time, we should
not forget that the establishment of an inductive basis has not carried us
any further than the very first step along our branch of investigation. The
simplest description of the characters of animal and human behaviour,
conducted without presupposition with the naïve motive of 'finding out
all there is to see', still has a terribly long way to go. To date, we possess
only a very few studies providing adequate descriptions of behaviour in
groups of phylogenetically closely related animals. By 'adequate', I mean
that the exactitude of detail and the number of species covered provide
the basic minimum of reference points for the purpose of comparative
phylogenetic investigation, as has been taken for granted in any morphological study for a number of decades. The studies concerned are:
Whitman's investigations of pigeons and doves, Heinroth's work on the
Anatidae, Antonius' studies of the Equidae and Faber's studies on
Orthoptera (1929; 1932). In addition, there are several fragments such
as Verwey's studies of herons (1936) or Goethe's study on Mustelids
(1940). Among more recent studies, one can mention the following
(without any attempt to provide a complete survey): Orthoptera (Jakobs
1950), Diptera (preening activities: Heinz 1949; *Drosophila*: Milani
1951; Spieht 1951; Weidmann 1951), Salticids (Crane 1949), stickle-
backs (Tinbergen and van Iersel), Cichlids (Baerends 1950; Seitz 1950;
Lorenz), Anura (Eibl-Eibesfeldt 1953), birds (intention movements:
Daanje 1950; gulls: Tinbergen and Moynihan 1952; passerines: Nice
1943; Prechtl 1950; herons: Koenig 1952; Anatids: Lorenz 1941),
mammals (Canids: Seitz 1950; rodents: Eibl-Eibesfeldt 1950, 1951).[62] All
the same, our knowledge of 'all there is to see' is so restricted that we
must continue to operate modestly and patiently to describe natural
behaviour in an exact and unbiased manner. This will *eventually* provide

the necessary inductive basis for later extension of our exact, analytical research framework.

Comparative behavioural research involves a particularly strong obligation to adhere strictly to the methodological principles of inductive scientific research. Without a trace of doubt, this field will shortly take over the rôle of linking inductive natural sciences and disciplines concerned with man himself, which are as yet largely unrelated to inductive research – such as human sociology, ethnology and a large part of general human psychology. It is not difficult to understand why these fields, which have all originated from philosophy, have not (or not *yet*) found a link with the firmly organized system of inductive research fields.

In inductive natural science, as in everyday speech, *explanation* of a particular process means no more than tracing of an observed special principle back to an already established, more general principle. Therefore, a researcher into special natural principles always requires access to a natural science at a more general level, whose basal laws will serve as a reference framework for the special principles he is investigating. A metabolic physiologist requires access to organic chemistry and a chemist requires access to atomic physics in order to provide more profound explanations for the processes they observe. As a general rule in the history of natural sciences, general principles have in fact been identified *earlier* than the more special ones for which they provide the necessary explanatory basis. In most cases, more specialized fields of research pursued to a penetrating analytical level already had access to the well-prepared basis of a more general field of knowledge, whose broad principles provided a foundation for the investigated special processes. For example, the advance which carried physical chemistry into the atomic sphere was met by a broad basis of known facts and principles in the field of atomic physics. And when metabolic physiology began to penetrate into the arena of chemical processes, there was already a long-established foundation of known fact in the field of organic chemistry, which provided the explanatory material for the physiologists. The same relationships existed in all other specialized natural sciences.

Yet with psychology, as with all other disciplines concerned with man himself, the historical situation is completely different. The concept of psychology as an academic discipline is an age-old one, dating back to antiquarian times. It existed as a purely introspective philosophical field long before genuine inductive natural science existed in the sense that we understand. As a *natural science*, psychology is indeed an extremely young field, but it is still much older than neighbouring fields at a more general level. As Darwinian evolutionary theory gradually extended its influence to include psychology as well, man came to be regarded as a living organism which had emerged through natural processes. Psychologists began to investigate human behaviour, as well as the internal workings of man's mind, as life processes. But at that time one knew virtually nothing about the more general principles governing the behaviour and 'mental processes' *of living organisms in general*. When Wilhelm Wundt, at the turn of the century, made the first call for comparative psychology in the phylogenetic sense, there was a complete and utter lack of unbiased data necessary for the inductive foundation for such a field of knowledge.[63]

In the decades which followed, the obstructive dispute between vitalists and mechanists barred the way to such unbiased data-collection in behavioural research. The few behavioural investigators not drawn into this dispute (H. S. Jennings, C. O. Whitman and O. Heinroth) were zoologists and they were therefore so distant from the circles of 'professional' students of behaviour and psychologists that the latter never learned anything about their work. In other words, human psychology as a natural science remained until quite recently as an island in space. There was an un-bridged chasm between this field and the more general natural sciences. In cases where human psychologists attempted at all to proceed in a scientific manner, they understandably tried in vain to forge links with fields of knowledge which were much too basal. That is, they made use of far too broad and simple principles for the explanation of very specialized learning processes. The only soil from which a natural science can draw healthy nourishment is provided first by its own inductive basis and secondly by the inductive basis of the *immediately* adjacent, broader field of knowledge. Both criteria were completely lacking in so-called scientific psychology at the beginning of this century, and so desperate roots were pushed into thin air in a vain attempt to draw nourishment from the barren soil of mechanistic behaviour studies.

The lack of success of this procedure, which is only too understandable on methodological grounds, was so obvious that there was an antagonistic movement through human psychology. Unfortunately, this led not only to rejection of (methodologically unsound) atomistic-mechanistic attempts at explanation, but also to rejection of the natural scientific approach as a whole. The American school of purposive psychology moved to an utterly one-sided, vitalistic-teleological approach. And German Gestalt psychology – which in fact should have been led to introduce a genuinely holistic, yet at the same time inductive-analytical, approach – unfortunately assumed a pronounced vitalistic character in most of its operations. The concepts of Gestalt and entity more and more assumed the character of vitalistic 'factors' which were regarded as being neither in need of, nor accessible to, natural explanation.[64]

Anyone who regards human psychology as a natural science, and intends to investigate on this basis, must regard it as a binding duty to get rid of this philosophically engineered state of affairs, which is so extremely obstructive to advances in research. Research fields involving investigation of the intellectual and emotional attributes of man must also be developed into natural sciences in the true sense of the word.

Nobody who wishes to study human psychology as an inductive natural science can possibly ignore the fact that man is a *living organism*, and that he – like all other living organisms – has developed from other, more simple organisms through natural processes. If we, as natural scientists, wish to provide a natural explanation for the special, immeasurably complex principles governing human behaviour and the human mind (i.e. by tracing them back to the adjacent, more general level of natural principles), then we are faced with the question: 'What *are* these more basic principles?' There can be no other answer: 'The principles concerned are *those which govern the behaviour of living organisms in general.*'

This general methodological point of view is joined by the special phylogenetic aspect. The unquestionable and unquestioned fact of evolution automatically leads to recognition of the corollary fact that an enormous number of structural properties of human behaviour and the human mind owe their particular nature to the unique historical pathway of phylogeny. Without knowledge of phylogenetic relationships, these features must remain incomprehensible. This is particularly true of the *social* behaviour norms of human beings, since these norms – more than any others – are bound to inherited, species-specific action and response patterns.

It is therefore quite definitely *not* a patriotic assertion, but a statement which is completely unquestionable from the standpoint of inductive research, when I maintain that all fields of knowledge concerned with man (in so far as they would claim to be natural sciences) are in need of comparative behavioural research for exactly the same reasons that metabolic physiology needs chemistry and physical chemistry is dependent upon atomic physics.

Looked at the other way round, however, the comparative behavioural investigator, as representative of a *more general* field of knowledge, is not bound to concern himself with adjacent, more specialized fields. The atomic physicist does not need to master chemistry, and an organic chemist does not have to encompass metabolic physiology. Comparative behavioural research includes its own, immeasurably large, area of research activity. Not only is there no obligation, there is no *room* for consideration of (specialized) human psychology or sociology. Following the laws of inductive science, it would be an *illegitimate* extension for comparative behavioural investigators to attempt to explain any complex special principles governing human intellectual or social life which are not covered by general behavioural data[65] . . . something which the mechanistic schools have done repeatedly.

However, it is *not* an illegitimate extension of this kind if we draw attention to certain principles governing human behaviour which can be identified from our own, comparative phylogenetic, inductive basis *and only from this framework*. For example, let us assume that comparative behavioural research provides proof that endogenous-automatic stimulus-production processes and innate releasing mechanisms, together with functional disruptions in these induced by domestication, also play a part in human behaviour. The obligation for consideration of these results lies exclusively in the *more special* field of knowledge. Comparative behavioural investigators can themselves only make the statement *that* such things are certain to influence human behaviour as well. But they cannot state *the manner* in which the influence is exerted, for the simple reason that they do not know the many other, more specialized principles operating within human psychology and sociology. The more specialized field of knowledge, however, exhibits a most serious breach of the laws of inductive research if these factors are ignored. This amounts to a *refusal of knowledge*!

Recognition of this fact is beginning – slowly, but definitely with geometrically increasing speed – to spread into the circles of all psychologists with a natural scientific train of thought. It can be regarded as virtually certain that in the very near future the entire field of scientific psychology (in the real sense of the word) will soon find a link with phylogenetically comparative behavioural research, and thus with the collective organization of *all* natural sciences. Characteristically, child psychologists, who – as unbiased observers – have been true natural scientists from the outset, were the first to begin to evaluate our results for their own use and to speak our language. It is extremely rewarding to see that depth psychologists and psychoanalysts gifted in unbiased observation are beginning to follow their lead. Many of the undoubted errors of both schools can be corrected through synthesis with comparative behavioural research. Even if this synthesis will require the entire life's-work of more than one research-worker, the result will be access to an unimaginably large and fertile – as yet completely untilled – field of exact, inductive research.

As soon as human psychology and depth psychology have been established on a *common* scientific basis, their synthesis *with one another* (so painfully lacking at present) will automatically be achieved. But at the same time, this would give rise to a basic field of knowledge which itself could provide a foundation for a link between human *sociology* and inductive natural science. Sociology is also a daughter of philosophy, and at present it is still quite resistant towards inductive, scientific research. This attitude was unfortunately strengthened by justifiable rejection of the above-mentioned, illegitimate extensions made by mechanistic biologists and psychologists. The term 'psychologism' has generally assumed among modern sociologists a derogatory meaning equivalent to that attaching to the term 'biologism'. But when the entire field of human psychology (including depth psychology and psychoanalysis) has found its solid, scientific anchor in an adjacent field (which must indubitably be taken as the next *broader*) and when psychology itself consequently *offers* human sociology an equally solid basis of known principles, then sociologists will not only be *able* to employ this foundation in their attempts at explanation, but will *have to* if they are to deserve the title 'scientific'.

At this very time, we need an inductive, scientific discipline of human sociology more than any other discipline, for the most pressing problems of mankind are *social* problems of such a kind *that they cannot be solved by philosophical speculation, but only by patient, inductive research work.*

Methods of approach to the problems of behaviour (1958)

It is my belief that the central importance of a Harvey lecture imposes upon me the duty to speak about problems of central importance, and the most important task I can set to myself on a trip to the United States is paving the way to a mutual understanding of American psychology and the branch of behaviour research generally termed 'ethology'. The first stone which I hope to contribute to that pavement consists in correcting the widely spread error that ethology is characterized by a new and original method of approaching the problems of behaviour. The whole aim of my present lecture will be to show that these methods are as old as natural science and that, if there is any merit in ethology at all, it is due to its strict observance of an epistemological discipline, long ago developed by natural science in general, and to the application of comparative phylogenetic methods developed by Charles Darwin (1859), in particular. To achieve this aim, I must begin at the beginning, that is to say with:

I Epistemological considerations

We are living in a time in which it has become fashionable to assess the 'exactitude', and with it, the value, of any scientific result exclusively by the degree to which quantifying methods took part in obtaining it. This opinion is one of the dangerous half-truths which fashion is all too prone to accept. While it is entirely true that quantification invariably has the last word on *verifying* the correctness of any scientific statement, it is a fundamental error to assume that knowledge can progress on the basis of quantification alone. The current overrating of quantification as a source of knowledge has very serious epistemological consequences. The first and worst is that it leads to contempt of observation pure and simple which, as I am going to show, undeniably is the basis of all inductive science. The depreciation of observation has gone so far that the term 'naturalistic', as applied to scientific work, has assumed, with some

246

behaviouristic psychologists, a definitely derogatory connotation. Another highly dangerous consequence of overrating the importance of quantification lies in forcing the several branches of inductive science into an entirely unnatural and unjust scale of values, in which physics, particularly atomic physics, not only range first, but are regarded as the paragon and only genuine representative of a 'science' while, on the other hand, those branches of inductive research which are chiefly occupied with the description of structures, are entirely beneath contempt.

It is easy to demonstrate the fallacy of this attitude, which, incidentally, is by no means that of atomic physicists. What concerns us first is that the derogation of structure as such leads to despising all cognitive functions which convey to our knowledge the existence and the special configuration of structure. This again leads to *atomism*, which can be defined as the erroneous belief that natural laws prevailing in matter can be explained on the basis of more general laws of nature without taking into consideration the way in which the matter in question is structured.[66] Not even the simple lawfulness of the functioning of a clock, for instance the 'law' that the big hand moves twelve times faster than the little one, can ever be understood without a preceding morphological, in other words *descriptive*, study of the clock's structure in general and the relative numbers of cogs on certain cogwheels in particular.

The 'atomistic' procedure of trying to explain the 'one-to-twelve law' of the clock *without* previous investigation of its structure, on the basis of knowing the properties of the materials of which the clock is built and of general laws of physics, like those of the lever, the pendulum, etc., is not, on principle, entirely hopeless: only it equals the attempt to *invent* that clock. Anybody could do it, and much more complicated systems have been invented. There is even one extremely interesting case on record in the history of biological science in which a certain type of self-regulating system had not yet been fully analysed by biologists when it was invented by technicians, by cyberneticists. So, I repeat, atomism is not wrong *on principle*, it only is *bad strategy* in most cases in which an investigator is confronted with a complicated system to analyse. No cyberneticist, on being given the task of repairing an electronic computer of unknown structure built by somebody else, would ever start 'from scratch' by trying to reinvent that computer on the basis of the known elements of electronic tubes, switches, and so on. He indubitably would start with a morphological investigation of its structure. Anybody ever having constructed a system which really works will have sufficient respect for structure. Also, he would be aware of the fact that the same or analogous functions can be achieved by using different structures and that, therefore, the reinvention of a system performing a function identical with the one we want to explain, offers us a model of, rather than insight into, the system which we are trying to understand. But as all physiology has the all-important task of serving medicine, in other words the faculty of *repairing* systems that have got out of order, exact insight into those systems is imperative.

Another fallacy, infinitely more dangerous than atomism, also arises from contempt of structure. Let me again use a parable to explain my meaning. Assuming that scientists from Mars have just landed on our planet and are now trying to understand some sort of system found on earth, for the sake of simplicity let us suppose that the system they happen to find first is an automobile and let us, for the time being, pass by the question whether they could ever attain any real understanding of the machine before realizing what it is made *for*, in other words before ascertaining that it is a locomotor organ of *Homo sapiens* L. This, of course, they could find out only by observing the system in the frame of reference of an enveloping system, watching the car in its 'natural habitat', driven along a road by a man sitting in it. Supposing all this to be already known to them, what would be the best way for them to proceed in order to 'understand' that automobile? Obviously they would take it to pieces and put it together again. And just as obviously they would have to use *all* the pieces in order to achieve this resynthesis.

The same difficulty which our Martians would encounter in trying to understand the interaction of parts within a system, also confronts us, however completely we understand it ourselves, whenever we try to explain its working to somebody else who does not. We are forced to begin at *some* point, for instance by describing the crankshaft turning and pushing up and down the connecting rods and pistons, conveying at first a rough survey knowledge of anatomy and mechanical functions. Then we go on to say that, in going down, the piston sucks 'mixture' out of the 'carburettor', though, in using this term, we are fully aware that the recipient of our explanation cannot have, as yet, any idea of what a mixture or a carburettor is. What we hope is that our pupil will form a vague idea of what those things might be, and reserve, in the diagram of the engine we are trying to convey to his or her mind, some empty spaces corresponding to these conceptions, to be filled in later by detailed knowledge. At whatever end we begin, *no* single part can be understood, in the full significance of its form and function, before *all* others are. In other words, the parts interacting in a system can be understood only simultaneously and together, or not at all.

Thus the very nature of systems, built up of differently structured parts interacting with each other, imposes upon analysis a very definite strategy of procedure, beginning with making an inventory of all parts, investigating their several forms and structures *to the point of knowing these by heart*, though one does not, at that point, grasp their significance, pushing forward the knowledge of all parts and their interactions *simultaneously*, or at least never forgetting, while investigating one part, that there are innumerable others, nor where the object of the present concentration of interest is situated within the whole. R. Matthaei (1929), in his book on the Gestalt problem, has likened this procedure to that of a painter who begins his representation of reality by a very generalized provisional sketch and then advances by furthering all parts of the picture in equal proportion, until the whole presents itself, often more simple and easily intelligible than was expected. This method is best termed that of the *analysis on a broad front*. It is imperatively imposed on research by the purely physicalistic recognition of a system consisting of different and mutually interacting parts.

To attempt the resynthesis of any such system on the basis of insufficient investigation of the question how many and what sort of different parts enter into its construction, is very dangerous, but what, for the reasons just given, must be regarded as entirely unpermissible, is to assert dogmatically, at the very beginning of analysis, that only a certain number of parts are sufficient, as explanatory principles, to explain the whole system. This fallacy is what I propose to call *explanatory monism*, though maybe the word 'monopolism' would be better, as the concept under discussion has, of course, nothing to do with metaphysical monism, as opposed to dualism. If our Martians, after detaching a few nuts and bolts, should turn their backs on that automobile, retire to their laboratory, and there try to resynthesize the whole system on the basis of these two sorts of elements, their procedure would not be less logical than that of scientists who sincerely believe that all behaviour can be explained on the basis of reflexes and conditioned responses. Not that nuts and bolts are not among the most important elements that must be understood in order to understand the function of the whole they take part in. Not that the same is not true of conditioned responses. Not that both do not have the all-important function of holding the other, mosaiclike, oddly shaped parts of the system together. They indubitably do. But to assert that *there are no other parts* or *explanatory principles*, is obviously nonsense.

Atomism and explanatory monism, though usually associated, must be conceptually distinguished. Also, the second is a much more serious obstacle to progress of knowledge than the first. The most confirmed atomist can, as we have seen, still invent a system, but explanatory monism blinkers the outlook because it channels investigation into a narrowed range of experimentation which precludes the discovery of other explanatory principles. What, in my parable of the Martians and the car, has been described as turning away from the object and taking the few detached parts back to the lab, is something which most deplorably happens in real life: further unbiased observation, which alone might lead to the discovery of further explanatory principles, is not only deemed unnecessary, but outright unscientific. A good example for this sort of deadlock is furnished by the rôle the reflex concept plays in the development of neurophysiology. The hypothesis that responding to stimulation was the one and only function of the central nervous system led to a manner of experimentation which could not but confirm the preconceived theory – and that is absolutely the worst thing a working hypothesis can do. With few exceptions, the experiments of that time and school confined themselves to keeping the animal or the preparation under constant conditions, then letting a change of conditions, a 'stimulus', impinge upon it, and then recording the response thus elicited. In that sort of set-up, the central nervous system, poor thing, never even got the opportunity to show that it could do much more than just react to stimulation!

Explanatory monism is pardonable only in the genius who has discovered a new explanatory principle. Nearly every genius and discoverer of such a principle has availed himself of that prerogative. I. P. Pavlow sincerely believed that all problems of behaviour could be solved by the theory of conditioned reflexes. Jaques Loeb (1913) thought the same of tropisms, and so on. Perhaps it does little damage if the discoverer of a really new and important explanatory principle thus overrates the extent of its applicability, but when disciples tend to do the same, the discovery which originally was a great step forward towards our understanding of nature, may develop into a very serious obstacle to the next steps.

Atomism and explanatory monism are the more detrimental to research and the method of analysis on a broad front becomes the more imperative, the more the object investigated bears the character of a whole or system and the more complicated its structure is. In all the world there is no object exceeding, in these respects, the neurophysiological organization of the central nervous system which determines behaviour. For this reason, atomistic approach and explanatory monism have less prospect of ultimate success in behaviour study than in any other branch of natural science.

It is my conviction that the ardent endeavour to concentrate on quantification alone and to neglect all other cognitive functions, particularly those which convey knowledge of structure, is due to a misapprehension of the methods employed by physics. Physicists, more than most other scientists, are disciplined to think in terms of systems. I still remember, with gratitude, Dr Vinzenz Blaha, my teacher of physics at the Schottengymnasium in Vienna, who unceasingly tried to impress on our juvenile minds the fundamental fact, that there is, in all the world, no action which is not interaction. *Actio* equals *Reactio* was the equation which he had printed in golden letters on a large board and hung in our classroom, and, in our first lesson of physics, he sat each of us in turn on a revolving table set on a roller bearing and told us to try to turn round. Obviously, he regarded the strategy of thinking in terms of systems as the first and most fundamental thing which the novice in physics ought to be taught, and this was his unforgettable way of doing it.

As physicists indubitably do think in terms of systems, they are also aware of the importance of studying structure and of the cognitive functions purveying knowledge of structure. No physicist ever believed that quantification was the only legitimate source of knowledge. If, in observing a physicist at work, we do see him, for most of the time, occupied with calculations, it is not because he neglects structures, but because he already *knows enough* about the structures which concern him. The basis of induction, on which the imposing building of modern physics is erected, consists just as much of observation and description as that of any other natural science. That the physicist is not ashamed of being 'naturalistic' is beautifully borne out by a paper which Max Planck published in 1942. In this he demonstrates that the sequence of cognitive acts through which the physicist attains a partial understanding of the surrounding universe, does not differ, in principle, from the procedure by which an absolutely naïve person or even a child achieves essentially the same understanding, if on a simpler level. All knowledge begins with perception aided by exploratory behaviour; this results in what is termed latent learning in animals. In the chaos of stimulus data, we, animals, children, and scientists alike, learn to discern syndromes, that is recurring combinations of data. I use the word syndrome in a very wide and literal sense, meaning stimuli 'running together', occurring together in space and time, just as the etymology both of the Greek and the Latin word implies. Young Adam masters the immense multiplicity of these syndromes with the help of giving names. Some of these names are generic: All dogs are called 'bowwow' by our little Adam, and this all-important feat implies, in itself, that he has succeeded in arranging many syndromes in an order of similarities and dissimilarities. The next step is the discovery of a certain lawfulness underlying that order. This sequence of three cognitive functions, by which the child attains a tolerably adequate picture of the surrounding world, are absolutely identical with the three phases discerned by Windelband (1894) in the development of inductive natural science: the idiographic, the systematic, and the nomothetic phase.

Our ability to discern and recognize sets of regularly concurring stimuli as natural units is based on the function of a very wonderful, but by no means miraculous organization within our central nervous system, that of perception. Our conceptions of objects in space, as well as those of processes in time are based on its function. A set of extremely complicated nervous mechanisms performs the highly important task of keeping our perception of objects and processes constant, in spite of the varying accidental circumstances in which we perceive them. I perceive the paper before me as white, whether I am seeing it in yellow electric light, in the more bluish daylight of early morning, or in the reddish light of the setting sun. I perceive the head of an approaching person as having a constant size although the area on my retina covered by its picture increases tremendously with the decrease of distance. I perceive the form of my pipe as constant while turning it to and fro before my eyes, in spite of the fact that its retinal image assumes astonishingly different contours. All these 'constancy phenomena' perform a function which is *objectivating* in the same sense in which this word is applied to rational scientific procedures: accidental sensory data, dependent on fortuitous circumstances are suppressed while lawfulnesses constantly inherent to the objects and/or processes are 'abstracted'.

True Gestalt perception indubitably is nothing else than one of the constancy functions, though, of course, it is by far the most complicated one and includes, or has for prerequisites, most other constancy mechanisms, such as those mentioned above. The constancy of form, as illustrated by the central interpretation of the retinal image of the pipe turned before my eyes, involves functions of stereometric computations attaining an immense complication – indeed, the phenomenon of form constancy with all the classic criteria of a Gestalt, such as transposability, independence of elements, etc. English-speaking psychologists are not usually aware that the German word *Gestalt*, in common parlance, means just external form. It is indubitably in the service of form constancy that the mechanisms of Gestalt perception have originally been evolved in higher organisms. But a central nervous organization, as well as a man-made computer, occasionally has an interesting way of being able to perform other functions besides the one for which it has been built. It is on record that an electronic device built to compute compound interest unexpectedly proved to be able to perform differential calculus. In an essentially similar way, just by performing their typical functions of detaching relevant configurations from a background of 'white noise', that is to say, of inessential stimulus data, the mechanisms of Gestalt perception achieve the amazing feat of *abstracting generic conceptions*. It amounts to an erroneous rationalization to believe that this is done by abstract thinking. When little Adam invents his first noun, calling all dogs 'bowwow', this is not owing to his having abstracted the diagnosis of *Canis familiaris* as given by Linnaeus, but to the functioning of his Gestalt perception, which enables him to disentangle the essential configuration common to all dogs from the background of inessential differences and which permits him to perceive, in the aunt's peke, the neighbour's dachshund, and the butcher's mastiff, *one* common Gestalt, that of *the* dog!

All these functions of the constancy mechanisms, including that of Gestalt perception, are performed entirely without any participation of reasoned thought; most of them are quite inaccessible to rational self-observation. Yet their procedure is so strictly analogous to that of ratiocination that the two have actually been confounded even by most profound thinkers. Helmholtz declared the processes of distance perception and size constancy to be the results of 'unconscious conclusions'. Egon Brunswik (1957), in order to stress the analogy, as well as the physiological differences, existing between the two kinds of computing processes, coined the term 'ratiomorph' for those here under discussion.[67]

Useful though this distinction doubtless is, I doubt whether it does not imply the danger of suggesting too strict a dichotomy between two types of functions which, in reality, merge into each other by all possible gradations. The functions of perception are cognitive functions, notwithstanding the fact that their mechanism is inaccessible to self-observation and incorrigible by ratiocination. They are *aprioristic* in the strictest sense of Kantian theory of knowledge, being in existence previous to all personal experience and being indispensable in order to make experience possible at all. It is my epistemologically heretical, but firm, conviction that the Kantian 'forms of ideation', space and time, are by no means two independent entities, but mere abstractions of two aspects of *one* functional system, that of the mechanisms which enable us to move and to perceive movement in space *and* time.

The philosophy of inductive science does not concede absolute validity to *any* of the 'aprioristic' forms of ideation or of the 'aprioristic' categories of thought. The scientist must necessarily attribute, at least as a working hypothesis, the character of reality to the world he is endeavouring to explore. For the physiologist or psychologist who claims to be a scientist at all, it would mean the highest degree of inconsistency, not to attribute the same character of reality and, on principle, the same degree of relative cognizability both to outer reality and to the physiological mechanisms to whose function we owe its cognizance. The biologist thinking in terms of evolution necessarily must regard all cognitive functions as having evolved in interaction with, and in adaptation to, the things and the laws of outer reality. He does not expect them to convey, to us, absolute truths about outer reality, but just that kind of working knowledge which is necessary for the survival of the species.

The biologist, therefore, is not in the least surprised when the physicist tells him that the picture of the world conveyed by our 'aprioristic' forms of ideation and categories of thought, though adequate for the practical purposes of survival, do not, on close investigation, fit reality in a very exact way. Space, as we are wont to visualize it, stirringly infinite, beautifully homogeneous, and intelligibly three dimensional, is shown by the physicist – and we must believe him unless we want to cast overboard all the laws of mathematics – to be not only finite, but to possess a fourth dimension in which it is surprisingly crooked in the most unexpected manner. Time gets off no better than space; the statement that two things took place simultaneously does not have any precise meaning for the physicist and even the category of causality itself, logical and inescapable as it would appear to be, is shown to correspond to facts only in rather haphazard, roughly statistical manner.

What the physicists have done in order to achieve this pitiless critique of the world picture conveyed by the cognitive functions we are naturally endowed with, was a most revolutionary and, from the viewpoint of idealistic theory of knowledge, a strictly illegitimate procedure. Physicists have had the temerity to doubt the absolute necessity and validity of all the rational forms of ideation[68] and of thought and to treat them exactly as if they were nothing else than working hypotheses. And that, of course, is exactly what they really are!

The old contention waged by idealists and empirists, whether some forms of ideation or thought are given to us a priori or a posteriori, loses most of its epistemological importance the very moment one regards Man as a product of evolution. The empiristic assertion that there is nothing in the human intellect of which Man had not previously been informed by his senses, would, of course, be the merest nonsense if we should interpret it to mean that the central nervous system is, in the young organism as yet devoid of experience, a completely unstructured mass and attains structures only through experience as conveyed by the sense organs. But if, on the other hand, we consider the mechanisms by which evolution achieves the creation of adapted structure, then their functioning appears analogous to experience in so many points that we cease to be astonished by the similarity of the results attained by evolution on one, and by learning on the other, side. The genome, the set of chromosomes, contains an unbelievable store of information which would fill innumerable textbooks of anatomy, physiology, ecology, behavioural sciences, and what not, were we able at all to express its contents in written words. All this treasure has been collected by a procedure closely akin to trial-and-error learning. The arrangement of the genes within the chromosomes, the limited dosage of their mutability, the possibility of their recombination through the processes of sexual reproduction, all taken together represent an apparatus which performs an altogether successful series of experiments, progressively gathering information concerning the powers that be, forever daringly staking part of the progeny and yet prudently never jeopardizing the survival of the species – in other words, the amount of information already collected. The overwhelming success of this method is demonstrated by the fact that all higher organisms, plants as well as animals, are descended from the creatures that have 'invented' it, from the flagellates. Campbell (1958) has shown very convincingly that the evolutionary procedure under discussion is essentially identical with that of pure, e.g. deductionless induction. The same, of course, is true of the process composed of pure trial-and-error plus conditioning.

As far as is known at present, these two mechanisms are the only ones by which an organism can attain information concerning the universe surrounding it. All structures and/or functions, including those of behaviour, which possess a definite survival value, owe it either to one or to the other. The question, to which of the two? is of obvious importance from the viewpoint of causal analysis of behaviour, but from that of theory of knowledge, its answer is irrelevant.

Thus, all cognitive functions with which we are endowed, indubitably are, like all other adaptive life processes, the function of organic systems evolved in age-long interaction between the organism and its environment. The recognition of this fact has repercussions in many directions. One of them, directly important to the subject of my lecture, concerns the assessment of the relative values attributed, in the day's work of inductive research, to the several cognitive functions ranging from the highest, rational ones implying the categories of causality and quantity, down to those of perception and the functions of receptor organs. The most important conclusion to be drawn from all the above-mentioned evolutional and epistemological considerations is that *all* these cognitive functions go to form a functional unit in which no single part can be dispensed with without doing damage to the whole. Therefore, no single function can be regarded as being 'more important' than any other.

As a rule, overrating the highest thought processes and underrating sensory and perceptual functions is a failing characteristic of philosophers rather than of scientists, and it was at the former that Wolfgang Metzger (1936) directed his witty satire when he said that there were some people who, by epistemological considerations, were incurably prevented from using their senses as a source of scientific cognizance. Yet much the same is true of many behavioural scientists who, under the misapprehension that quantification is the only truly objectivating cognitive function, endeavour to use it exclusively to the extent of despising all others. Of course, the epistemological inconsistency of this attitude is much easier to show up than that of the idealistic philosophers at whom Metzger is poking fun. It simply consists in denying to perception the character of cognitive function when it is used in direct observation, devoid of hypothesis, yet endowing it with that self-same character whenever it is used to read a measuring instrument.

Yet a worse inconsistency lies in forgetting that, whereas the objectivating function of perception is independent of that of quantification, the basic function of the latter, simple counting, is absolutely dependent on perception in general and on Gestalt perception in particular: The latter irrefutably is the indispensable purveyor of the equal, or at least comparable, entities which are to be counted. I never can help a shrewd suspicion that the worshipper of quantification and despiser of perception may occasionally be misled into thinking that two goats plus four oxen are equal to six horses. Counting pecks of pigeons in Skinner boxes without observing what the birds inside really do, might occasionally add up to just this. It is not at all a rare experience that, in studying central nervous processes, one finds this sort of one-sided dependence of the higher, more derived and complicated function on the phylogenetically older and more primitive one. I confess that I absolutely fail to understand why this universal and unconditional, one-sided dependence of counting on perception is not in itself sufficient to authenticate, in the eyes of every scientist alive, perception as a legitimate and independent source of scientific knowledge.

As it is, however, I have recently written a whole paper on this subject (Lorenz, 1959), addressed exclusively to a comparatively small yet important group of scientists who are underrating the importance of structure and that of the cognitive functions which convey to us knowledge about structure. These scientists are American psychologists strictly adhering to behaviouristic concepts and methods. They are the only atomists I know of. Atomic physicists are not atomists by any means; quite the contrary, they are all thinking in terms of structured systems and they would not have succeeded in splitting the atom if they had not.

Also, atomic physicists are in the most complete agreement with the evolutionist's theory of knowledge. This I endeavoured to formulate in a little paper (Lorenz, 1941b) which appeared just prior to Max Planck's aforementioned paper (1942) 'Die exakten Naturwissenschaften,' in which he stated very much the same opinions. The temporal sequence was lucky, not because the priority of my paper is of any importance, but because the obvious independence of the conclusions is. Nobody will ever think that Planck was influenced by me, whereas the opposite suspicion would indeed be pardonable. I feel free to state that it was the proudest moment in my life when I read, in a letter from Max Planck:

'Es erfüllt mich mit grösster Befriedigung dass man, von so völlig verschiedenen Induktionsbasen ausgehend zu so völlig übereinstimmenden Ansichten über das Verhältnis zwischen realer und phänomenaler Welt kommen kann' [It gives me great satisfaction that, starting from such entirely different bases of induction, one can reach so entirely consonant views concerning the relationship between the real and the phenomenal world].

There are other interesting consequences of our fundamental conviction that all our 'aprioristic' forms of ideation as well as all our categories of thought must be regarded as being nothing but working hypotheses developed in phylogenetic interaction with reality, sufficient for our survival, but by no means conveying absolute truth. The most important of these consequences is the recognition of the interdependence of all branches of science, as well as of science and theory of knowledge. It is, to any scientist, a matter of course that every branch of science is, for the success of its analysis, dependent on the existence of another, more general, more basic neighbouring branch. What we call *explaining* a process or a lawfulness found in nature means making it intelligible on the basis of *more general* laws of nature *and* the *special structure* the function of which they govern. Describing in detail the special structure of the object investigated is the very own task of the investigator, the task from which he cannot be excused. But as regards the more general laws, he *has* to rely on the findings of the 'man downstairs', that is to say, of the scientist investigating the adjoining level of more simple and more basic natural laws. Otherwise he would have to undertake the impossible task of pushing analysis down to the level of atomic processes all by himself. Thus, it is a necessary arrangement that each story of the collective building of inductive science is erected on the supporting structure of the next-lower one. The accent here is on the word 'next', as obviously it is impossible to skip a level. When, for example, Sutton and Boveri sought an explanation of the Mendelian laws it would not have helped them, if they had had even the profoundest insight into the biochemistry of chromosomes, or any such more basic laws and processes. What they needed to know was the general gross structure of chromosomes and the processes of their division and reunion during reduction and fertilization. The detailed knowledge of biochemistry may, as a further step, prove necessary to explain the lawfulness of the latter processes, in their turn. Jumping levels means neglecting structure and is, therefore, again equivalent to the methodological fault of atomism.

One prerequisite for the successful collaboration of all the innumerable particulate levels on which investigation is being carried forward is, of course, that of a certain temporal sequence proceeding from the lower levels upward. The upper storey remains, for the time being, literally hanging in the air, unless the next one downstairs is far enough advanced to offer, ready-made, those natural laws which the man upstairs needs for his explanatory endeavour. This type of deadlock does not seem to have occurred very often in the history of science. In most cases, the man downstairs was just ready with the necessary support in the form of more general laws where the man boring downward from the next higher storey had got deep enough to need them. This certainly was the case with atomic physics when chemistry had advanced far enough to need its support. The fusion of physics and chemistry is indeed the classic example of analysis achieving ultimate success. The word analysis actually means dis-solution and what it dissolves is not, as many think, the independent existence of a natural law: The latter remains a law as much as ever, even when we attain full understanding of why things work that way. What analysis really disintegrates, if only in the case of ideal success, is the seemingly strict boundary line separating natural processes which take place in different structures and on different levels of complication and/or integration.

The procedure of 'giving an explanation' as I have just defined it, determines, by its very nature, the direction in which inductive analysis invariably has to progress, that is the direction *from* the more complicated more highly integrated process *towards* the simpler and more basic one. As an important consequence of this universal directional trend of all inductive research we find a queerly asymmetrical one-sided relationship of dependence between the several branches of science. On whatever level of complication an investigator is working, he must know practically all about the results which the men on the next-lower level have brought to light, but he need not, on principle, know anything about what is going on in the investigation of processes more highly complicated and integrated than those which he is himself trying to analyse. The organic chemist must know all about inorganic chemistry, but need not know anything about the physiology of metabolism; but the physiologist investigating metabolism certainly won't get far unless he is thoroughly conversant with organic chemistry. Thus, all the branches of science form a functional unit, fitting into each other like a system of Chinese boxes. The beauty of this imposing structure lies not only in the fact that *it is humanity's one and only really* collective endeavour, but also in another fact: It is not man-made, but is imposed on all our striving for knowledge by the real structure of the real universe.

This grandiose frame which holds all Man's cognitive efforts has for a basis, two assumptions: the aforementioned assumption that the outer world is real, and the second one, that it is governed by *one* set of ubiquitous and uncontradictory laws which never suffer the least exception, however complicated and integrated the structural systems whose function they govern. This assumption is absolutely compatible with our conviction that, far from containing absolute truth, all our formulations of these laws are but rough approximations, and this applies equally to empirically gained, scientific laws and to the 'aprioristic' axioms imposed on our ideation and our thinking by the organization which our brain has acquired in phylogenetic interaction with reality. The most fundamental among these laws are, on the empirical side, those of physics and, on the aprioristic side, those of mathematics of logic. The ultimate goal of our explanatory endeavour must be to trace back, to the basis of these laws, all the structures and functions we encounter in the universe, proceeding from one level of complication to the next lower one by the ancient means of examining structure and reducing its function to more general laws derived from the next-lower level. Hence all natural science necessarily is 'mechanistic', or, since physicists themselves have lost their absolute trust in the laws of classic mechanics, *physicalistic*.

Yet atomic physics is not the ultimate, absolute fundament, on which the pyramid of all other sciences is built and which represents rock bottom to all human cognitive endeavour. Some scientists who still are naïve realists, and some philosophers who are transcendental idealists, tend to think so.[69] Atomic physicists do not. They are fully aware that our a priori forms of ideation and of thought, inevitable and logical though they seem, are nothing more than working hypotheses which fit the facts of reality no better than man-made ones do and which are accessible to constructive criticism in exactly the same way. The great physicists have abundantly shown that forms of ideation and of thought can be confronted with experimental results and the limits of their explanatory validity can be thereby determined, using the same procedure which is applied in examining man-made working hypotheses. Doing just this has been the revolutionizing deed of men like Planck and Einstein. Though their views deviate fundamentally from those held by Kant, it is nevertheless doubtful whether the great physicists, without the basis of Kantian philosophy would ever have been able to formulate their own criticism of human cognitive functions as clearly as they have done. In any case, it was no coincidence that Max Planck was a great admirer of Kant and a highly learned expert in Kantian theory of knowledge.

At this point we discover an unexpected interdependence of science and philosophy – if we concede that theory of knowledge belongs to the realm of the latter. We find that, on the one hand, it is impossible to push our knowledge of outer reality any further without critically examining the cognitive functions through which this knowledge is conveyed to us, and also that, on the other hand, it is quite impossible to effectuate this constructive criticism without pushing forward, in its turn, our knowledge of outer reality. Any attempt at a theory of knowledge which does not take these facts into account is comparable to the procedure of thoroughly examining a photographic camera, say a Leica, without taking into consideration that it is an apparatus made to take pictures of the outer world and that its makers have developed it, from simpler models, by a procedure in which the relative quality of the pictures taken has had an influence on the development. This kind of 'pure Leicology' would afford a very poor idea of the camera's essential nature. For analogous reasons, theory of knowledge is dependent on science.

The reasons for which science is dependent on theory of knowledge are just as obvious, but are different ones. They are the same for which a man using a microscope must have a thorough knowledge of all the optical properties of the instrument he is using, in order to escape the danger of mistaking, for real properties of the things perceived, those peculiar characters which are imposed on all pictures by the limitations and shortcomings of even the best optical instrument (Lorenz, 1941b).

The views stated in the preceding paragraph were published, as conclusions drawn from purely biological, evolutionistic considerations, in my little paper of 1941 when I was living in Koenigsberg, in the shadow of Immanuel Kant himself. So it was not surprising when they were most emphatically rejected by philosophers. But it was a surprise, and a most pleasant one, when great physicists emphatically agreed. I could not summarize my own views more succinctly than P. W. Bridgman did in his remarks (1958) on a talk given on the subject under discussion by Niels Bohr (1958): '*The object of knowledge and the instrument of knowledge cannot legitimately be separated.*'

The epistemological attitude of which I have attempted to give an outline is identical with the one that Donald T. Campbell (1958), in his brilliant paper on the subject, has termed *hypothetical realism*. It is the attitude which, consciously or unconsciously, *all* scientists take in respect to theory of knowledge, provided they have outgrown naïve realism at all. I may add that it does not do much damage to most branches of natural science if they have not. It is no coincidence that, among all scientists, atomic physicists and physiologists of behaviour are the ones who are most intrigued by the problems of theory of knowledge: Quite obviously these problems are the responsibility of the science concerned with the ultimate, basic objects of knowledge and the one concerned with the physical instrument of knowledge. If the goal of understanding the inner mechanisms of our brain to the extent of explaining the limitations of our cognition is a Utopian one, it is nevertheless one that is inescapably set to us by the structure of the universe which dictates the strategy of our possible advance.

All scientists working on the levels of complications and/or integration which lie *between* the levels of physiology of cognition and atomic physics are, on principle, free to act, in their day's work, as if they were naïve realists. No damage can be done by this attitude as long as they remain really naïve, and trust their sense organs, their perception, and their power of reasoning to an equal degree. Man's cognitive organs and functions are *made* so that they work tolerably well within the 'middle ranges' of their application and naïve realism does not interfere with the rules which, in the game of research, command certain things and forbid others. To collect one's basis of induction without as yet having formed a theory biasing the act of collecting, to investigate structure conscientously, to think in terms of systems consisting of universally interacting parts, never to believe that any one single explanatory principle can achieve, by itself, the understanding of such a system, never to skip a level of integration, on the long journey analysis has to go through on its way downward to atomic physics, these are some of the commandments which are practically never broken by natural scientists.

With psychologists, this is an entirely different matter. I have already said that, in the historical development of natural science, either by design or by sheer luck, the research on the more basic levels had, in the majority of cases, advanced far enough when the analysis in progress on the adjoining higher level began to reach downward far enough to need the 'man downstairs' for further support. Physics had progressed just that far when chemistry began to need it, organic chemistry when physiology of metabolism did so, and so on; in short, the more basic processes were, on the whole, investigated earlier than the more complicated ones. With psychology, this was not so. Psychology is the daughter of philosophy and is, for this reason, much, much older than any natural science. It was very old indeed when, at the dawn of this century, it discovered that Man was, after all, part of nature and that even the highest functions of his mind ought, on principle, to be treated and investigated as natural phenomena. It was admirable and consistent when psychologists of that time, with Wilhelm Wundt for a leader, took the first steps to make psychology an empirical natural science. The fact that these first steps led in the direction of a deplorable atomism is easily explained – and excused. Psychology started its research on the level of the very highest, most complicated process in the universe. Very little was known about the structure and the functional organization of the central nervous system; the 'man downstairs' of my parable simply did not exist. In the overwhelming chaos of inexplicable facts two tangible processes offered a foothold to research: the reflex and the

conditioned responses. As a matter of course, psychologists and behavioural scientists grasped at what, after all, were by no means straws,
but very real explanatory principles, and it is easily understood that
they modelled their 'stratagem of research' on that of classic physics
rather than on that of biology, though the latter would have been their
legitimate neighbouring and more basic branch of science. All this
conspired to lead the most serious and scientifically respectable among
psychologists to adopt the most absolutely atomistic attitude ever encountered in the history of natural science. They became confirmed in it
by two factors. The first was the tremendous initial success which reflex
and conditioned response had to show as explanatory principles. Indeed,
in a rat's behaviour, so much really is explicable on the basis of these
two things that it is nearly – if not quite – pardonable to believe that *all*
its behaviour is! The second factor was the spirit of contradiction
aroused by the criticism – justified in that one point – which was uttered
by the more or less vitalistic opponents of behaviourism. This historical
development explains why behaviourists so consistently forget the
immensely complicated structure of the central nervous system and why
they despise all cognitive functions which, like Gestalt perception,
pure observation, description, comparison, and systematization, convey,
to the human mind, the knowledge of structure, and which by *all* natural
sciences are regarded as the indispensable steps that must have been
gone through *before* the first attempt at the abstraction of natural laws,
of nomothesis in Windelband's classic terms, is undertaken.

I have had to go into epistemological details rather extensively in the
attempt to convince you of what I said in the first paragraphs of my
lecture, namely, that the methods of approach which many American
psychologists believe to be characteristic of ethology, are, in reality,
fundamentally common to all natural science *except* behaviouristic
psychology, a fact of which some of the more outspoken critics of
ethology quite obviously are not conscious. I can summarize what I have
tried to explain hitherto in one sentence: *The method of approach of all
inductive natural sciences is 'naturalistic'!*

I now come to the discussion of a more special set of problems concerning not the theory of knowledge, but the practical strategy of
research imposed on all biological sciences by the fact of evolution. The
ethological approach has been criticized as being 'finalistic' by Kennedy
(1954) and Lehrmann (1953) and as 'preformationistic' by the latter.

II Treatment of phyletic adaptation

It devolves upon me to show that the treatment of phyletic adaptation
by which ethology has incurred these reproaches, is absolutely the same

in *all* branches of evolutionistic biology. Finalism, in the correct connotation of this word, may be defined as the belief that a metaphysically
determined end or goal enters, as another causal factor, into certain
causally connected chains of events directing them to that particular
end, which is invariably one that has a definite survival value for the
animal or its species. Of course this opinion is entirely untenable from
the physicalistic viewpoint common to all science, as even the slightest
'directing' factor implies a force: Every change of direction has the
dimension of an acceleration and is, therefore, unthinkable without a
force. Thus, the finalistic view implies a breach of the second law of
thermodynamics.[70]

No scientist is farther from assuming the kind of directing factor
assumed by finalism than is the biologist thinking in terms of evolution.
The indubitable fact that the organic world, as we know it today, owes
its existence to a historical process which, at least on principle, is
explicable on the basis and without any infraction of the ubiquitous
laws of physics has, for a consequence, a very specific conception of
structures and functions which 'serve the end' of survival. This conception of what one might call, in English, 'expediency' has nothing in
common with the finalistic conception of an end or goal, still less with
the vitalistic idea of a prestabilized harmony existing between organism
and environment, as implied by J. von Uexküll's conception of a
pre-existing *Bauplan*. If the German word *Zweckmässigkeit* contains,
etymologically, the implication that the structure or function in question
is constructed in such a way as to attain a certain result, why, so it is,
not by a miracle and still less on a pre-existing plan, but by mutation
and selection performing something that is very close to trial-and-error
experimentation.

To an observer whose eye is not sharpened by phylogenetic comparison, any higher organism gives the impression of such a supreme
and absolute harmony that it would appear outright sinful to search for
imperfections and that the assumption of a plan, preconceived and pre-
ordained by a supernatural agency, seems inevitable. But a closer,
comparative look at *many* organisms discloses an entirely unmiraculous,
if still more wonderful fact: Organisms are *never* built on the principle
which must be postulated on the basis of preformationistic concepts,
that is to say, like buildings whose functions a far-seeing architect fore-
saw, whose smallest details were agreed upon before the first stone was
laid, and whose actual erection then took place all in one sitting. Organisms are always constructed on the principle on which a house is built
by a settler, who first erects a simple provisional shack in which to live,
and who later on, as his affluence and his family increase, adds one piece
after the other to the building. In such a house, many parts will, in the

course of time, change their functions completely: What first was the living room, may become the stable or even the lumber room; compromises and temporary shifts will become necessary, many among them of a very doubtful expediency. The efficiency of the building as a whole will necessarily remain inferior to that which could be achieved by the construction of a planning architect, but the latter is unattainable just *because* the house has to be lived in all the time and can never be torn down altogether and wholly reconstructed.

All structures of all organisms came into being in a strictly analogous manner. Had they not done so, we should know still less about the history of their phyletic development than we do. The essentials of this development are, as Goethe formulated it, differentiation and subordination of the parts. This means that, with higher development, all parts become more and more different from each other and, at the same time, more dependent on each other and on the whole of the organic system. This is clearly the consequence of a progressive division of labour, each part becoming more and more specialized for its own function. Here, for the first time, the word 'for' is encountered in connection with function, so here is the point at which we must discuss what it means.

For the biologist conscious of evolution the question 'what for?' makes sense only when applied to the structures and/or functions which have undergone a development, in the above-defined sense of differentiation and subordination and which thereby have become specially adapted to the service of one particular survival value. In other words, the biologist asking: 'What has the cat sharp, crooked, retractile claws *for?*' and answering correctly: 'To catch mice with,' does by no means profess finalism. His question and answer are just 'shorthand', meaning: Which is the function whose survival value exerted the selection pressure which caused, in the herpestoid ancestors of cats, the evolution of this particular form of claws? So this question is definitely directed not at a metaphysical goal, but at a natural cause. The biologist investigating phylogeny is the last man to forget that so-called finality is a direction arrow which we attached to events *post festum*. Every single living organism is a product of the factors causing evolution and is a construction which is 'expedient' enough for survival; were it not, it would not exist. Because we have, before our eyes, only the successful ones among the innumerable experiments which evolution is constantly performing by its patient trial-and-error method, it is all too easy to forget the extinct results of the unsuccessful ones, which are certain to outnumber the survivors by billions.

Knowing where to put and where not to put the question 'what for?' in the above-defined sense, is one of the most important assets to the biologist's strategy of research. Not to put the question where it legitimately can be asked, means neglecting a most important line of causal research. Applying it to a process devoid of survival value means hard work leading to nothing. In medical science, the decision whether to put or not to put the question is equivalent to deciding whether a process or structure is to be regarded as 'normal' or as 'pathological', which is exactly why medical men are particularly good at deciding it. Also, medical men usually possess a commendable awareness of the fact that the conception of the 'normal' cannot be strictly defined and has only the very loose meaning of 'just good enough for survival'.

For the biologist investigating the structure and behaviour of healthy wild animals, it is easier to decide when to ask the question 'what for?'. Whenever an organic system attains a degree of complication and regularity which makes it impossible to assume that it arose accidentally, the question is not only legitimate, but obligatory. If some cows are spotted brown and some black, no biologist will trouble to investigate the survival value of one or the other. But supposing we were the first biologist to come to South America and to shoot a giant anteater. Investigating the bizarre structure of its jaws, its hyoid bone, and its tongue we should know, with what amounts to absolute certainty, that these characters which diverge so strongly from the corresponding ones of other mammals, could have attained their present properties only under the urgent selection pressure of a most definite function. So the question 'what for' is indispensable to the endeavour to attain causal understanding. I may add in parentheses that all these considerations not only hold true, but are of quite particular importance in those cases in which a structure or an innate behaviour pattern has lost, as a secondary step in phyletic history, the survival value whose selection pressure had caused it to originate. The 'adaptation of yesterday', the so-called *vestigial* character, is one of the chief sources of phylogenetic knowledge and of particular importance to the student of innate behaviour. It is an empirical fact that fixed motor patterns are apt to be even more 'conservative' than morphological characters. Probably a small vestigial hump on the body surface or a blind appendix to an intestine is more liable to impede some function, and thus set off selecting processes leading to its disappearance, than is the performance of some senseless motor pattern which therefore, to the joy of the phylogeneticist, often is carried over almost indefinitely.

Having now said what I considered it absolutely necessary to say about fundamentals, in respect to which ethological approach is identical with that of science in general and that of the vast unit of biological sciences in particular, there still remains to me the task of comparison between the ethological approach and that of other schools of behaviour study.

III Comparing the ethological approach to that of other schools of behaviour study

A. BEHAVIOURISM

In my endeavour to set forth, as clearly as possible, the methods of approach characteristic of ethological behaviour study, I have been forced to begin with epistemological fundamentals and then to go, in some detail, into the consideration of the part which the problems of survival value take in determining our method of approach. I hope you will pardon it if, in addressing an American audience, I have felt it necessary to *defend* the ethological strategy of research against some misunderstandings contained in the criticism which ethology has aroused on the behaviouristic side. I have tried to do this by showing that the epistemological attitudes and the ways of treating the question of survival value, in which ethology differs from behaviourism, are the very same ones in which most or all inductive natural sciences, particularly the biological ones, differ from it in exactly the same respects.

This attempt has inevitably entailed some serious criticism of the behaviouristic approach, and if this seemed too aggressive I hasten to redeem this impression by emphasizing the tremendous debt owed to behaviourists by science in general and quite particularly by ethology. I am, at the moment, not speaking of the vast success which behaviouristic thought and experimentation have had in unravelling the problems of learning, and which is absolutely undisputed.

The values which the world owes to behaviourism are by no means restricted to the field of practical research only. Its importance is even greater concerning the theoretical approach to the body-mind problem. By its radical self-restriction on what can be objectively observed in the behaviour of an organism, it has put an end, once for all, to the general confusion of psychological and physiological causes and effects.

The student of animal behaviour is in a highly conflicting situation regarding the problem of the relationship between objective, physiological, and subjective, psychological processes. While fully aware that it is only the former that are accessible to the methods of inductive research, he cannot help believing in the reality of the latter. No normal man is able to avoid that type of 'empathy', and it is simply not honest not to confess to it. After all, we profess it by refraining from inflicting torment on animals. But, at the same time one must keep strictly aware that empathy does not convey to us even the slightest degree of knowledge. Though I 'know' that the tame greylag goose accompanying me is 'frightened' when it stretches its neck upwards, flattens its feathers against its body, and utters a certain note, it is not any empathic flow of communication flowing from the bird's soul to mine which gives me information about its behaviour. It is the exact opposite of this process that has taken place. From experience, repeated literally thousands of times, I have learned that in a goose performing just those expression movements all thresholds of escape responses are extremely low and that, in all probability the goose will fly off the next moment. If I admit, as I don't hesitate to do, my own belief that the goose *does* experience, at that moment and in correlation with that behaviour, something like fright, this belief has nothing to do with scientific knowledge. But it is based on scientific knowledge if I predict that the goose will fly off, for science is, in F. Fremont-Smith's aphoristic definition, 'Everything that makes things predictable.'

In human beings of course, psychology proper, that is to say the investigation of Man's subjective phenomena, can be pursued by the method of true induction. But it is a fundamental epistemological error to believe, that these subjective phenomena can ever, even in case of a Utopian final success of research, be 'explained' on the basis of 'underlying' physiological processes. These physiological processes do not 'underly' their psychological correlates, but they go parallel to them in a most mysterious way which, on principle, is not accessible to the operations of our rational thought. The relation between the correlated processes is, as Max Hartmann has termed it, a-logical; even the most cautious parable expressing it by speaking of a certain 'parallelism' is somewhat misleading, because the 'parallel' is very one-sided: All subjective experiences are indubitably correlated with physiological processes, but, on the other hand, by no means all physiological, not even all neurophysiological, processes are experienced as subjective phenomena.

For this basic epistemological reason, psychology proper, as the science dealing with subjective phenomena, does *not* have a branch of natural science for a neighbour, in the way in which any more special branch of research has a more general one to support it. Though psychology proper applies the same methods of observational induction, deduction, and experimentation, it is not 'founded on' neurophysiology, but runs parallel to it in the same fundamentally inexplicable manner in which subjective phenomena run parallel to physiological ones. The eternal impenetrable diaphragm partitioning the field of our knowledge into two incommensurable realms is something we indubitably have to accept – as philosophers. As men, we find it difficult to do so, and most investigators of behaviour would have to confess, if they were quite candid, that they really are gnawing away at the hard bone of the body-mind problem, hoping against hope to crack it, while they are patiently investigating the physiological as well as the subjective side of life processes. At least, even the strictest psychophysiological 'parallelists' ought to confess to their belief, that subjective and physiological phenomena are only two sides of the same reality. I do not hold with any philosophy to which I cannot remain consistently faithful in the realm of commonplace commonsense, and when I say that my friend Frank is sitting there in the second row, I mean neither the objectively observable physiological phenomena of his body, nor the vaguely correlated soul, the existence of which I do *not* infer by certain analogies between his behaviour and my own, but the reality of which is inescapably forced on my conviction by what Karl Bühler (1922) has termed *'Du-Evidenz'*. What I mean is precisely the unity of his body *and* his soul, a unity which the cognitive functions I am endowed with make it quite impossible for me to doubt. And this is exactly why, of the three attitudes it is, in theory, possible to take towards the body-soul problem, one assuming identity, the second interaction, and the third parallelism between both, I find myself compelled to profess the one first mentioned.

For the practical purposes of psychophysiological research it is irrelevant which of these three positions one assumes, as long as one keeps conscious that none of them release us from the obligation to keep constantly in mind the existence and the nature of the impenetrable partition between our two fields of knowledge.

One of the most frequent mistakes is to regard this partition as being correlated to levels of integration or complication of different life processes. This error is already essentially contained in the current use of the terms 'physiological level' and 'mental level', as if the great partition were, in a manner of speaking, a *horizontal* one. In Hempelmann's otherwise admirable *'Lehrbuch der Tierpsychologie'* (1926) one finds this entirely misleading assumption practically on every page. The evolution of life processes, and particularly neural ones, is treated as if, up to a certain level of complication, they were 'still' physiological and as if, above that level, they neither were standing in need of, nor accessible to, a physiological explanation. In reality, of course, the great partition runs *longitudinally* through all levels of complication of all life processes. There are quite simple ones, even on the 'vegetative level', which percolate through the great diaphragm and appear, subjectively, as the most dramatic experiences of pleasure or displeasure, ranging from the ecstasies of voluptuousness to the throes of seasickness. There are, on the other hand, neurophysiological processes which, with respect to the complication of their function, equal the highest mathematical operations of our rational thought, and which are nevertheless entirely devoid of any subjective phenomena running parallel to them, as is the case with the amazing 'computations' performed by many mechanisms of our perception, such as those of the constancy phenomena and those of Gestalt perception.

Another mistake, and probably the one most frequently found in literature dealing with psychophysiological problems, lies in connecting subjective phenomena as causes with physiological processes as effects and vice versa. Let me illustrate the fallacy of this procedure. Supposing a man has been punched on the jaw by another, we can describe what happens to him from the subjective as well as from the objective, physiological side. He experiences shock and pain, both of which frighten him, his fright causes a deep if momentary depression of his self-assurance which subsequently elicits anger and an urgent need for self-assertion which, in turn, finds its satisfaction in retaliating by another punch and enjoying the sweetness of revenge as well as the feeling of self-esteem restored. The objective, physiological account of the identical chain of events would be something like this: A slight concussion of the central nervous system and a strong stimulation of pain receptors causes a quickly passing paralysis of central functions; the man not only remains motionless for a moment 'as if paralysed', he really is, for the time being. His jaw sags, his head droops, his knees give, his skin becomes pale, all in consequence of a severe drop in the tonus of his sympathicus. In the next second the well-known process of rebound sets in, his adrenals spout, his sympathicotonus shoots upward, his eyes pop, his skin turns deep red, his striated muscles get taut, the temporary paralysis in his central nervous system gives way to excitation, and complicated, partly instinctive, fighting responses are released.

Obviously, it would be incorrect to regard any one of these events either on the subjective or on the objective side of the chain as being the *cause* of the phenomenon correlated to it on the other. One cannot be the cause of the other because it is, in fact, identical with it and only viewed from another, incommensurable side. Also, it would be incorrect to regard event number one, on one side, as the cause of number two on the other. The temptation to commit this breach of epistemological discipline is particularly great if the first event is familiar on the subjective, and completely unanalysed on the physiological, side, while the opposite holds true of the second. Thus it is quite usual, in common parlance as in psychosomatic medicine, to say that, for instance, a severe disappointment causes a heart neurosis, etc., etc., connecting cause and effect right across the great partition, ignoring it completely.

These infractions of epistemological discipline would not be very dangerous, were it not for the fact that conceding the possibility of a psychological cause for a physiological effect offers a most welcome loophole for vitalistic 'factors' to creep in. If we have today achieved a more or less general acceptance, in all behavioural sciences, of a dis-

ciplined epistemological treatment of the problems of psychophysiological correlation, this commendable state of affairs indubitably is, to
a great extent, a merit of the behaviouristic school which, by its rigorous
self-restriction to the objective side, once for all severed the Gordian
knot of the body-mind problem which seriously threatened to enmesh
all behaviour study. Perhaps the fact that the schools of behaviourism
and ethology see eye to eye regarding these questions is an affinity that
ought to do more than just compensate the discrepancies concerning
other methodological points.[71]

B. PURPOSIVE PSYCHOLOGY

This school, represented by William McDougall, E. C. Tolman,
E. S. Russel (1934, 1945), Bierens de Haan, and others, makes a point
of studying the purposiveness of animal and human behaviour. E. C.
Tolman (1932) has given a perfectly good definition of a purpose in
exclusively objective terms: A purpose is given whenever an organism
keeps on changing between varying types of behaviour until a *constant*
effect is achieved. If, for instance, a dog first attempts to jump over a
fence, then, finding himself unable to do so, tries to tear a board away
with his teeth, then, this also being of no avail, digs a hole under the
obstacle, and, having got in, eats the rabbit enclosed by that fence, it
makes perfectly good sense for the objective student of behaviour to say
that the eating of the rabbit is a purpose to the accomplishment of which
the other behaviour patterns serve as means.

It is superfluous to emphasize the ubiquity and the importance of this
organization of behaviour and, therewith, the theoretical merit of
pointing out that it *is* an organization of most definite survival value –
which is just what the behaviouristic opponents of McDougall (1933)
and his school have failed to do. It is not a vitalistic assumption, but
plain fact, that life processes very often keep running in one definite
direction and are able to resume it again when put off course by extrinsic
agencies. Any regulative process of this kind, compensating the effects
of outer disturbances, must, of course, unconditionally be regarded as
the function of a 'built-in' regulating system, developed by the species
under the selection pressure of just this function. It is of tremendous
survival value of any species of higher animal if it has at its disposal a
number of mutually exchangeable types of behaviour accomplishing
the same end, and, additionally, the faculty to learn which is the most
suitable under a given set of circumstances. From the viewpoint of the
biologist aiming at a causal analysis of behaviour, showing up the existence of a purpose only means having established the fact that some kind
of regulating system is at work; in other words, establishing the existence

of a purpose means the discovery only, and not the solution, of a problem.

Some among the purposive psychologists cannot be spared the reproach that they did regard it as an answer to the question *why* behaviour was running along certain lines when they succeeded in discovering *to what purpose* it did so. Contrary to behaviourists who tended to disregard adaptedness and survival value of behaviour, purposivists were keenly aware of their importance, but did not consider them as problems to be approached by natural science. 'Wir betrachten den Instinkt, aber wir erklären ihn nicht' [We meditate on instinct, but we do not explain it] Bierens de Haan wrote in 1940.

But in criticizing William McDougall himself, even the most pedantically physicalistic student of behaviour must concede that his insight into the nature of self-regulating systems was surprisingly little impaired by his professed belief that regulation as such neither stood in need of, nor was accessible to a natural explanation. Indeed, his representation of 'instinctive' behaviour and particularly the regulative interaction of 'instincts' contains innumerable factual insights the scientific truth and value of which is in no way diminished by their discoverer's not believing that they were, on principle, explicable on the basis of physical laws. Although this disbelief prevents McDougall from seriously attempting physiological explanations of complicated and regulative processes in animal behaviour, it does not hamper him in *describing* them in a detailed and absolutely correct way, emphasizing just those points which are, amazingly, the ones on which later physiological analysis found a foothold.

And absolutely the same holds true of William McDougall's treatment of the *spontaneity* of animal behaviour. His slogan 'The healthy animal is up and doing' which he continued to throw into the teeth of reflex theory, contains a core of indubitable truth. Exactly as in the case of purposive regulation of behaviour, he did not search for a physical explanation of this truth. It is even somewhat doubtful whether he believed such an explanation possible on principle, but it is *not* open to any doubt that he *did* see the existence as well as the theoretical importance of facts which remained completely inexplicable by the theory of reflex and conditioned response and which, therefore, were simply negated by behaviourists. It is less damaging to the progress of scientific knowledge to refrain from explaining certain indubitable facts than to refrain from noticing *and describing* them – only because they fail to fit in with a preconceived theory. In other words, the impediment of causal analysis inherent to purposive psychology did not prevent it from giving a detailed and correct description of those fundamental phenomena in animal and human behaviour which *stand in need* of causal analysis. In any case, purposivists know what some behaviourists obviously still refuse to believe, that observation and description have to precede analysis in any study of natural processes.

A comparison of observational and descriptive behaviour studies performed by purposive psychologists on the one hand, and by ethologists on the other hand, shows a striking affinity of both: Both would be termed 'naturalistic' in the parlance of behaviourism. In reading McDougall the ethologist cannot help feeling that facts are being brought to his notice which are highly relevant to the understanding of animal behaviour – shortly and naïvely expressed, that McDougall 'knows more about animals' than anybody believing their behaviour to be explicable in terms of reflexes and conditioned responses alone. His descriptions display a most acute vision for natural units in the structure of behaviour, in other words for *organization*. He is quite explicit about the fact that 'appetite', or what ethologists would objectively describe as appetitive behaviour, owes its existence to an entirely different 'organization' than instinctive behaviour patterns. He has formed, in all precision, the concept of patterned organization on the receptor side of behaviour, which he called the innate 'perceptual pattern'. He knows all about the interaction of independently variable instinctive motivations and about the phenomena arising in case of their conflict, down to a quite correct description of what ethologists, much later, were to call displacement activities. Also his basic assumption concerning the different organization of unlearned behaviour and perceptual patterns on one side, and of learning and insight on the other, and quite particularly his views on the manner in which the two last-named functions serve to integrate, into a functional whole, the several particulate elementary unlearned patterns, are nearly identical with the views held by ethologists on the same subjects.

On the other hand, even the greatest admirer of McDougall has to concede that he very often assumes an attitude that is not only indifferent but positively hostile to causal explanation in general and to explanation on the basis of conditioned response in particular. It is characteristic of a great genius with an almost visionary insight into the great coherent contexts of wholes that he tends to despise details and also people insisting that the whole is explicable on the basis of details. If I say that McDougall behaves, in this respect, exactly like Goethe, this surely expresses the rank I am ready to accord to him. What he refuses to see, is that causal explanation is altogether compatible with the existence of wholes or systems, that the possibility of a physiological explanation of behaviour does not preclude subjective consciousness nor the existence of purpose, and that the conditioned response is a particulate element of behaviour which, so far from being incompatible with the conception of wholes or systems, plays the most important part in integrating other behaviour elements into a whole or a system.

Wherever, in his writing, he describes examples of animal behaviour which quite indubitably consist in conditioned responses, he hastens to repudiate this assumption by describing, most correctly, the subjective phenomena, particularly those of perception and of pursuing a purpose, which, certainly in men and possibly in animals, are the subjective correlates of this type of behaviour. It never seems to occur to him that *both* ways of describing the facts are *equally* correct.

Similarly, he treats instinctive behaviour as if the fact that it indubitably serves survival were incompatible with its being naturally caused. As instinct, to him, is an infallible directive factor, he is prevented from taking into consideration what, to ethology, has been one of the most important sources of information: the illuminating cases in which the organization of instinctive behaviour miscarries and fails to achieve its normal survival value. To him, miscarriage is proof that, by definition, the behaviour in question is not caused or directed by instinct. Thus, the only case known to me, in which McDougall actually proposes a causal explanation of behaviour, concerns the case of insects killing themselves by flying into a light. Discussing this in his book *Outline of Psychology* (1933, p. 64), he suggests that a phototropism in the sense of Jaques Loeb (1913) might be the cause.

C. JAKOB VON UEXKÜLL

If there is, in the history of science, one really convincing illustration of Hegel's doctrine that any thesis is true only when taken in conjunction with its antithesis, it is furnished by antagonistic attitudes assumed, by purposive psychologists on one side and by behaviourists on the other, in relation to the epistomological problems already discussed. I have tried to show, in another paper (1950) that both parties tended to extreme positions which neither of them ever would have taken, had it not been in contradiction to the opposite opinion. This was particularly deplorable in respect to the methodological treatment of self-regulating systems: Because directed regulation, as I tried to define it (page 270) was regarded as the effect of an entelechial 'factor' by purposivists, self-regulating systems were strictly ignored by behaviourists who, on principle, should have been ready and able to undertake a physiological, causal explanation of these processes.

I have attempted to make clear, at the very outset of this presentation, that thinking in terms of complicated, structured systems is not only compatible with, but fundamental to, the endeavour to 'understand' life processes in general, and behaviour in particular, in a 'natural', that is to say in a physicalistic, manner. I have tried, in my parable of the motorcar found by the Martian explorers, to sketch the method forced on inductive research by the nature of systems.

Curiously enough, it was a self-professed, dyed-in-the-wool vitalist, who first consciously and consistently applied that method of 'analysis on a broad front': Jakob von Uexküll, whom, in spite of fundamental philosophical dissension, I regard as one of my most important teachers. The point of departure, in all his investigations, is a complexes of observational, empirical facts representing a *system* in which the organism and its environment are found to stand in a relationship of multiple, mutual interactions. Analysis invariably has to begin with the question: Which, among the many data of environment, are the ones that, on one hand, have a releasing effect on certain behaviour patterns of the animal and are, on the other hand, influenced and changed, by the activity thus released, in such a manner that their change has, in its turn, a repercussion on the organism's responses? All data, or complex of data which, in this way, are sending releasing stimuli to the animal's receptors and, at the same time, are offering points of attack to the animal's effectors, represent the 'things' constituting the animal's 'world'. The system which von Uexküll (1921), regards as the elementary unit of behaviour, is the *functional cycle* (*Funktionskreis*). It consists in the circular chain of causes and effects which – running through the organism and its environment, from the stimuli impinging on the animal's receptor organs, on through its nervous system to its effector organs, then back into environment – by the functions of its receptors and its effectors, divide its world into two sectors, the perceptual field (*Merkwelt*) comprising all the receptor cues (*Merkmale*) to which the animal responds, and the effector field (*Wirkwelt*) consisting of all the points of attack which environment offers to the animal's effectors (Fig. 1).

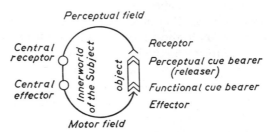

Fig. 1. *See text for explanation. From von Uexküll (1921)*

In this simple diagram, a vast programme of research is implied. The investigation of a species of animals and of its behaviour must necessarily begin with the endeavour to ascertain the number and the properties of its functional cycles, to draw up an inventory of the receptor and effector cues taking part in the cycle, and to analyse their causal interaction with the structure of the organism, on one side, and that of environment on the other. The organism's 'inner world' (*Innenwelt*), comprising the whole of its bodily structures and/or functions, is causally influenced from the side of the 'perceptual field' (*Merkwelt*), that is to say, those parts of environment which affect its receptor organs, in other words those which are selected, out of innumerable others, by the specific organization of the receptors. The conception of the latter does not by any means include the sense organs only, but also the whole organization which, within the central nervous system conveys specifically releasing stimulation in the direction towards effector organizations. The function of receptors is not only to receive releasing stimuli, but also to exclude all others from becoming effective. All the stimulus data originating from receptor cues converge centreward into a network of interactions (*Merknetz*) which constitute the central representation and the unity of the receptor cue. On the effector side, a corresponding network (*Wirknetz*) serves to integrate and co-ordinate the single muscle contractions into an activity which represents an adaptive response to the cues received. The task of investigating the biology of any species of animals can be regarded as fulfilled only when all functional cycles are fully analysed and when we have gained full knowledge of what 'strings' keep the organism suspended, in a steady state, within its environment. These strings of course, are, as we all know, causal chains interlocking by hook and eye. It is mechanical problems that are confronting us on every side.

These statements quoted, for the greatest part literally, from von Uexküll's book *Umwelt und Innenwelt der Tiere* (1921), hardly sound vitalistic! The research programme mapped out in them is pretty nearly identical with that of ethology, very many of the provisional, more or less operational concepts of part functions are the same, even if semantics are different. Von Uexküll has by no means confined himself to stating a programme but has, with very many species of invertebrates, driven causal analysis of behaviour to a point where he 'knew the strings by which an animal is suspended in its environment' to a degree hardly ever surpassed by an ethologist.

Although the starting point and frame of reference for all his considerations always was the animal *as subject*, the method of his research always was objectivistic to the extreme. Together with Beer and Bethe he devised a nomenclature avoiding all subjective terms to describe internal states and processes within an animal's central nervous system. Even his conception of the animal's subjective world is determined by what he found objectively, represented in its responses. Even a purist of objectivism could find no fault with von Uexküll's method in that respect.

In some respects, however, ethologists and, for that matter, all non-vitalistic natural scientists must file a protest against von Uexküll's views. One of these is that he altogether rejects the fact of evolution. As a consequence, he is prevented from regarding adaptation, or, to be more precise, adaptedness of structure and/or behaviour as the result of a natural process of historical, causally determined development, of phylogeny. The *Bauplan*, a pre-existing, pre-established harmony of organic and environmental structure accounts, in his opinion, for the amazing fact that all organisms are equally well adapted to their respective environments, and, more particularly for the adaptedness of behaviour which hinges on the other surprising fact that, in the animal's world, it is always the same thing in which the receptor cues, releasing certain activities coincide with the properties offering points of attack to these activities, in such a way that behaviour achieves survival value.

If it is only the biologist conscious of evolution who takes exception at these decidedly preformationistic views, I doubt whether any natural scientist can follow von Uexküll's philosophy of knowledge which is somewhat reminiscent of Leibnitz's doctrine of 'monads'. Von Uexküll repudiates the belief in the existence of any sort of extrasubjective real universe, common to all organisms living in it. What, in his opinion, is real, are only the innumerable particulate worlds of all the innumerable animal and human subjects.

It was lucky for the progress of behaviour study that von Uexküll, in his day's work, did not remain consistently faithful to his own philosophical doctrines. Even his classic diagram of the functional cycle which proved so fruitful in his research, is fundamentally incompatible with the doctrine of the nonexistence of extrasubjective reality. What is marked 'object' (*Gegengefüge*) in Fig. 1 obviously represents the structure of outer reality which is influenced by the animal's activities and, by being changed, exerts an influence on the organism in return, indubitably is assumed to be real, though it does *not* appear in the animal's 'world'!

Another example of how von Uexküll accomplished grand work by not adhering too strictly to his professed philosophy concerns his experimental treatment of receptor cues, of what ethologists would call key stimuli. According to his doctrine of the *Bauplan*, it is due to pre-established harmony that any 'thing' in the animal's world unites, in itself, those properties which, by sending out receptor cues release the animal's response, with those others that offer the right points of attack to the activities released. The tick, *Ixodes rhitinus* L., whose normal hosts are mammals, responds to two main receptor cues: The releasing object must have a temperature of approximately 37° C. and must smell of butyric acid. In nature, admirably, such an object practically always will offer, to the tick, the 'effector cues' of being soft, stingable, and possessing blood vessels for the tick to suck. Receptor cues and effector cues always coincide, or at least they *did* until von Uexküll himself made them discontinue doing so, at least in the laboratory, by presenting the tick with suitable dummy objects and showing that the tick will blindly sting anything offering the two key stimuli mentioned. This experiment opened the path to the investigation of what physiologists of behaviour today call the innate releasing mechanism, that is to say the organization of sense organs and the afferent structures within the central nervous system which cause the organism to mechanism.

Though von Uexküll repudiates just those problems and just those phylogenetic methods which are most characteristic of ethology, this young science certainly owes more to his teaching than to any other school of behaviour study. He was the first to show clearly that (1) causation and survival function of behaviour are two points of view which not only can be, but have to be, considered simultaneously; (2) subjective interpretation and physiological analysis of behaviour are compatible, though the two aspects must never be confounded or mixed; (3) the realization that organisms and their behaviour are forming, together with their environment, a 'whole' or *system* is not an obstacle at all to the attempt to explain that system on the basis of natural laws.

D.   HERBERT S. JENNINGS

I have attempted to give a very short sketch of the different, independent schools of behaviour study, just sufficient to show their agreement and disagreement with the ethological approach. Even this necessarily crude abstract would be incomplete without paying tribute to the man who, independently of and synchronously with Jakob von Uexküll, took the all-important step of applying to animal behaviour, those methods which are imperatively dictated to research by the nature of its object, namely a structured regulating system. It was H. S. Jennings who, in his classic work *The Behaviour of Lower Organisms* (1904), clearly defined the conception of the *system of actions* characteristic of a species.

Although by virtue of his background and his schooling he probably ought to be regarded as a behaviourist, his methods as well as his results agree and converge with those of von Uexküll in a surprising number of details. It is highly gratifying and, indeed, reassuring that absolutely identical results can be attained even on the basis of entirely incompatible philosophies, if only the good old method of inductive approach is applied, the method that begins with a thorough and unprejudiced observation and description of facts and proceeds to analytical and abstract nomothesis only after having accumulated and systematized a sufficient basis of fact to build upon. This method is not only dictated by the epistemological considerations on which I enlarged in the first part of this presentation, but by the simplest common sense as well. Moreover, this method comes automatically to those whose eyes are held to the object of their observation by that spell which the beauty of organic nature casts on some of us. Because this aesthetic appreciation is closely allied with the faculty of perceiving wholes or systems, in other words of Gestalt perception, no single investigator of nature who is gifted that way will ever be an atomist. On the other hand, this very gift may turn into a curse for the progress of our knowledge for a very simple reason. Remnants of idealistic philosophy, with which our whole Western culture is imbued more than most of us realize, make it impossible to some otherwise astute thinkers to *attribute value to anything explicable in a natural way*. In such cases, the very reverence engendered in the student of organic nature by its beauty and harmony, makes it impossible to him to *want* to analyse and understand it in a natural way. He cannot help feeling that any explication is a devaluation, or even a desecration. This attitude is so characteristic that it could be used as a personality test for students of behaviour, it indubitably has caused innumerable excellent men to join the ranks of the vitalists, and it also explains why so many among the antagonists of natural explanations are, surprisingly, such very nice people.

The uniqueness of H. S. Jennings simply lies in the fact that his gift to perceive harmonious systems and his obvious appreciation of their beauty did *not* in any way conflict with his quest for their causal explanation. It is with a strong sense of indebtedness that I remember how, on Karl Bühler's advice, I read the *Behaviour of Lower Animals* and how it suddenly flashed upon me that acknowledging the existence of wholes or systems did not imply a confession to vitalism. To a young student this truism bore the character of a revelation.

The importance of H. S. Jennings can be expressed in one sentence. He was the first student of behaviour who was not a vitalist, and yet approached its problems by a method adequate to its character of a whole or system.

IV   Methods peculiar to ethology proper

There are no methods that can justly be said to be exclusively characteristic of ethology, unless one regards it only as a school of behaviour study, and not as the branch of biology which it really is. As a branch of biology, ethology originated, as a new branch of science legitimately should, with a discovery that opened a new line of investigation. Charles Otis Whitman (1899), and Oskar Heinroth (1911) discovered independently of each other that there are certain motor co-ordinations which are just as reliable and widely spread taxonomic characters, as any morphologic properties one can think of. In other words, these movements are just as constant characters of a species, a genus, an order, or even larger taxonomic category as any of the bodily structures used in their definition and identification. This discovery had important consequences, mainly because it upset most of the then accepted theories of 'instinct'. In that sense it was something new.

But of the method that had led to it, the very opposite is true: It was the orthodox method of comparative morphology, the method of arranging the properties of species systematically in order of similarity and dissimilarity, the method that had already taken an important part in leading Charles Darwin (1859) to *his* discoveries, that now, when applied to the new field of behaviour study once again achieved unexpected results.

Of course, the very peculiar physiological nature of the fixed motor patterns thus discovered necessitated special methods of investigation. In spite of their great constancy of form, these motor patterns are definitely not chains of reflexlike processes, as was formerly assumed. Rather, their physiological nature is the same as that of certain movements based on endogenous, automatic production of motor stimuli within the central nervous system, a type discovered and investigated by Adrian (1950), von Holst (1935, 1936), Paul Weiss (1941 a, b), K. D. Roeder (1955), and others. They are co-ordinated in a highly peculiar way by processes in which afferent processes in general and proprioceptors in particular take no part and which have been investigated and analysed by E. von Holst. The physiology of these movements, the way in which they are organized to form an integrated regulative system, the physiological mechanisms, inhibiting them during quiescence and setting them off at the biologically adequate moment, and so on, all necessitate methods of research specially adapted to the process investigated.

But again it would be entirely misleading to call these methods exclusively characteristic of ethology. They are also characteristic of the branch of physiology represented by the investigators mentioned above and of others. As a matter of fact we are applying, in my department, such methods, for instance that of electric stimulation in the hypothalamic region, which was first used by W. R. Hess (1943) on cats and later modified and adapted to use on birds by E. von Holst. Our opinion of the importance of these physiological methods is borne out by the fact that I have moved into the same institute as E. von Holst.

V Summary

I hope that I have succeeded in convincingly supporting my anticipatory assertion that ethology does not, in its fundamental philosophy, its epistemological attitudes, its methods of approach, and its 'strategy of research', differ from any other natural sciences, least of all from biology. Where it does differ from certain schools of psychology, orthodox evolutionistic biology does the same. Ethology can be briefly defined as the application of orthodox biological methods to the problems of behaviour. If, in the course of my presentation, I have criticized other schools of behaviour study, accusing behaviourism of atomism, of explanatory monism, and of a neglect of structure, accusing purposive psychologists of finalism and vitalism, and von Uexküll of preformationism, if I have even slightly reproached H. S. Jennings for not introducing, into his considerations, the phylogenetic viewpoint, I must very sincerely beg you to believe that I offer these criticisms without the slightest feeling of superiority. Ethology certainly has no right to claim any merit for adhering to the old methods of biology, which is its mother. All other schools of psychology and behaviour study are descended from philosophy sired by great philosophers – behaviourism by René Descartes, purposive psychology by Aristotle and Plato, and von Uexküll's *Umweltforschung*, by Leibnitz – whereas ethology has, for a father, a very plain zoologist: Charles Darwin.

Gestalt perception as a source of scientific knowledge (1959)

DEDICATED TO KARL BÜHLER ON THE OCCASION OF HIS 80th BIRTHDAY

Ist die Natur nur gross, weil sie zu zählen euch gibt? (Schiller)*

I Introduction and theoretical approach

The general task of this paper has, in fact, already been indicated by Friedrich Schiller's question quoted above: In our day and age, it has become only too common to estimate the 'exactness' (and thus the value) of any scientific result exclusively according to the rôle played by quantifying methods in its attainment. In the first place, this leads to denial of any value or scientific legitimacy for the process which provides the fundamental basis and roots for all inductive research – straightforward, unprejudiced *observation*. This has gone so far that, coming from the mouths of some behaviouristic psychologists, the term 'naturalistic' has assumed a definitely derogatory meaning. Secondly, the various disciplines within the natural sciences are arranged on a quite unjustifiable scale of evaluation. In this, descriptive disciplines concerned with the investigation of structures are ranged at the lowest level, whilst physics (particularly atomic physics) is admired as the highest – in fact, almost as the *only* – form of genuine 'scientific' research. The unfortunate result of all this is that some fields of research concerned with systemic entities of complex structure adhere to the erroneous belief that one can understand function without insight into structure.[72] But one cannot even relate the functional principles of a clock (e.g. the principle that the large hand moves twelve times faster than the smaller) directly to the laws of classical mechanics, without previously investigating the morphological structure of the clock mechanism and, in particular, the numerical relationships between the teeth of the various cogs.

Lack of insight into the theoretical necessity for investigation of structure is coupled with underestimation of the cognitive processes which inform us of the presence of structures. Wolfgang Metzger very

* Is Nature great only because she has given us things to count?

281

wittily said of some philosophers: 'There are some people who are incurably prevented, by theoretical considerations of cognition, from using their senses for the purpose of scientific understanding.' Paradoxically, this applies just as aptly to many otherwise extremely perceptive research workers, who believe that they are operating in a particularly 'objective' and scientific manner by banishing, as far as possible, their own perception from their methodology. The illogicality of this procedure, in terms of perceptual theory, is quite easily demonstrated – more easily than the illogicality of the philosophers ridiculed by Metzger. The core of the problem is that perception is accredited with scientific legitimacy where it is used for reading a measuring instrument, but not where it is used for direct observation of a natural process. Physicists, because of the nature of their research objects, are not merely continuously forced to make recourse to measuring instruments, they are justified in doing so by current insight into the structure of the investigated objects. However, the attempt to investigate a natural process exclusively by measurement, before one has obtained insight (through perception) into the underlying structure, is probably largely based on a misunderstanding of physics, combined with attempted mimicry of its superficial features.

In fact, the physicist himself has quite a different view of the function of perception. Max Planck, in a short publication issued in 1942, showed quite lucidly that the *Weltbild der Physik* (*A World View of Physics*) arises through the perceptual functions of the naïve, pre-scientific human being . . . in fact even through those of the child. All our knowledge about the laws operating in the reality surrounding us is based on the information provided by the wonderful (but nevertheless quite easily analysable) neural apparatus which establishes perception from sensory data. Without this apparatus, and above all without the truly objectivating function of so-called constancy mechanisms (to be discussed in more detail later), we would know nothing about the short- or long-lasting existence of those natural unities which we call *objects*.

This information provided by perception, which is actually unwittingly accepted as genuine even by those who despise it most, is itself based upon processes which – although quite inaccessible to introspection of rational control – nevertheless exhibit close analogies to rational operations (e.g. reaching conclusions). As is well known, this led Helmholtz to equate the two types of process.

These analogies go even further with other, still higher differentiated functions of perception, which are extremely closely related to constancy functions, and to some extent incorporate them. Such are the highest functions of Gestalt perception, which permit us to directly grasp laws operating with the complex arena of natural processes. These laws are dissected from the background of chance, irrelevant items of information which are simultaneously passed on by our sense-organs and by the lower perceptor functions. As I shall attempt to demonstrate later on, the mechanism of Gestalt perception thereby accomplishes feats which are really amazingly analogous not only to 'subconscious conclusions', but also to the classical three steps of inductive natural science – the accumulation of an inductive basis, systematic ordering of this material, and abstraction of a governing principle.[73]

However evidently this process may possess the character of a physiological activity, even resembling some computer functions, it is nevertheless included, along with other functions of the central nervous system which are not open to introspection and are not easily performed at the rational level, within the mystical concept of 'intuition'. This is presumably the reason why many, who otherwise are by no means fools, are inclined to view with mistrust anyone who openly admits that he allows himself to be guided by Gestalt perception in his scientific work.

However, the more the object of research has the character of a complex systemic entity, the greater the reliance one has to place on the aid of Gestalt perception. In the whole world, there is no system that exceeds in structural complexity and regulative integrity the mechanisms determining the behavioural principles operative in higher animals and man. Thus, for the behavioural physiologist it is more important than for any other scientist to know whether, and to what extent, the information provided by his own senses may be accepted as valid. (N.B. The German term *Wahrnehmung* for perception literally means 'taking as true'.) For this reason, the necessity for critically evaluating Gestalt perception as a source of scientific knowledge is derived from the requirements of my daily work. Thence comes the justification for making this particular evaluation the special task of this paper, although I am aware that I am little qualified for mastering it.

II Theoretical considerations of perception

First and foremost, I should like to avoid any misinterpretation to the effect that the following considerations are set down in order to provide backing for hypothetical realism. This may perhaps emerge as a side-product, but the main aim is directly concerned with the task outlined in the previous section. If one accepts the existence of a real external environment, then one must accept that even the simplest forms of spatial orientation and perception provide us with knowledge about extra-subjective reality (by analogy) in fundamentally the same manner as the highest forms of human reason; the difference lies only in the *degree* of analogy achieved. This would mean that they are equally legitimate sources of knowledge. A naïve realist gazes outward, and does not recognize himself as a kind of mirror. An idealist looks only into the mirror, and because of the angle of view he cannot see that this has a non-reflecting rear side. When one investigates animal and human behaviour as a physiologist, it is impossible to avoid the assumption that there is some kind of isomorphy between physiological events and experience; it is heuristically immaterial whether one adheres to a theory of identity or parallelism between the two phenomena. In both cases, one must inevitably conclude that as a scientist – and thus as a hypothetical realist – one must attribute to the mechanisms and functions running parallel to our experience on the physiological side the same kind of reality and recognizability as is attributed to the objects in external reality about which they provide information. And this leads on to the further inevitable conclusion that we cannot advance our knowledge about the 'rear side of the mirror' (i.e. the apparatus which provides our image of the surroundings and projects this into experience) without simultaneously extending our knowledge about the 'reflected' properties of extra-subjective reality, with which it has a real reciprocal relationship. Of course the converse applies just as much. Thus, for a hypothetical realist, investigation into the theory of knowledge implies functional study of the human *Weltbild-Apparat* (*environmental image apparatus*) as an organic system. I am well aware that the term 'theory of knowledge' commonly has a quite different meaning in the realm of philosophy, and that philosophers may object to my regarding simple component functions of the environmental image apparatus (e.g. spatial orientation and perception), or even their analogues in animals, as cognitive processes. However, I do this out of conviction.[74] This paper has been written exclusively to demonstrate that Gestalt perception is a fundamental, indispensable component function in the overall system of human cognitive processes, and that it is thus one of these processes. The following theoretical considerations of cognition are aimed entirely at this goal; indeed they might more fittingly be called *practical* considerations of cognition.

As Max Planck states, any scientist would commit an unforgivable logical error if he were to set out from the assumption that what he was trying to investigate was unreal. The assumption made by all scientists that there exists an external environment independent of the object experiencing it is regarded by D. T. Campbell as a working hypothesis, and he therefore refers to the epistemological viewpoint involved as *hypothetical realism*. This interpretation involves somewhat more than what is expressed in Planck's statement. The concept of the hypothesis incorporates as a constitutive feature the property of testability through confrontation with factual evidence. And this is just what the Kant-disciple would energetically oppose. He would say that all scientific knowledge is exclusively related to the phenomenal world and that the belief that the cognitive functions of human beings can be tested at work and screened for errors is in itself an indication of adherence to naïve realism. I do not consider that this immediate objection is valid.

In fact, I would maintain that modern physics has already achieved what was supposedly impossible. Men such as Planck and Einstein see an image of extra-subjective reality which no longer really fits in with the term 'phenomenal world'. In this image of the world, provided by modern physics, one notices with despair that there is very little of the forms which – according to transcendental idealism – are forced upon all human experience by the 'spectacles' of space, time, causality, substantiality and other categories 'necessary for thought'. If we do not prefer to throw overboard all the laws of logic and mathematics, we must reluctantly accept the fact that the fine – and apparently so clear – phenomenal form forced onto objects by our graphic three-dimensional and infinite Euclidean space is only very approximate and merely adequate for our practical purposes. It fits, so-to-speak, the reality underlying the phenomenon of 'space' only in an 'intermediate range of measurement'; and, to our further disappointment, this reality extends in a hitherto unexpected further dimension in an irregular and confusingly contorted manner. We have to accept the statement that any pronouncement about two events occurring simultaneously is, similarly, only meaningful within the narrow, practical confines of life and that it does not have an exact physical meaning. We have to believe that the thought form of causality, which appears to be so compelling and logically invincible, in the same way only fits the events in a rough, statistical manner, and that in the final analysis matter and energy are the same thing.

Each of the mentioned advances in physical knowledge represents the removal of a 'pair of spectacles', though this does not mean that man can come to terms with all of the spectacles he wears. The new facts unearthed by physicists with respect to extra-subjective reality must, of course, also be attributed to a priori conceptual patterns. But these particular patterns were applicable to factual areas where pre-existing concepts had failed. The 'abandoning' of these concepts occurred in exactly the same manner, and for the same reasons, as abandonment of a working hypothesis which human beings have established and then discarded because of the emergence of phenomena which no longer fit the hypothesis. The fact that one can subsequently advance somewhat with another working hypothesis does not at all mean that the latter is regarded as absolutely valid. In the same way, modern physicists do not need to believe in the absolute validity of cognitive patterns utilized in criticizing the range of applicability of other concepts.

Biologists are not at all surprised that physicists have lost their belief in the absolute validity of a priori patterns of conceptualization and visualization. From the physiology of sensory functions and perception, the biologist knows that the organization of peripheral and central receptor mechanisms is extremely 'narrow-minded' in its concentration on the practical requirements of survival of the species, and that it arbitrarily selects from reality only a restricted segment, which is just sufficient to meet these requirements and thus produces a 'twisted' picture of reality. A prime example for this process is provided by the function of colour-perception, which quite arbitrarily divides the continuum of wavelengths into a discontinuous series of 'spectral colours' for the sole purpose of arranging the extracted information such that pairs of colours exhibit mutual cancelling. In association with this, an 'invented' colour 'white' is specially established. This is a qualitatively uniform perceptual form which has no simple correlate in reality. Since the middle of the spectrum has no correlate, in the form of genuinely existing wavelengths, which could be employed for complementary cancelling, the complementary colour 'purple' has been invented – just like the original 'white' – and this closes the colour series in the form of a ring. The species-preserving function of this entire apparatus is exclusively based on the fact that chance variations in the colour of illumination are compensated such as to extract as constants the inherent reflective properties of objects. This 'objectivating' function, which will be dealt with more fully on p. 304, is thus exclusively related to the perceived object and not to the light as such. To take a rough-and-ready illustration: It is quite immaterial to a bee what reality lies behind the phenomenon 'light'; what the bee must be able to do is to recognize a flower by its constant, inherent reflective properties, independent of whether the incident light is bluish or red-tinted. The great species-preserving value of the described mechanism is indicated by its wide distribution. If, as has been reliably demonstrated, such different organisms as man and the bee possess a colour-constancy mechanism operating according to the same principles, it can safely be assumed that it has been developed independently in the phylogeny of the two under selective pressure dictated by the same functional requirements.

At this point, a counter must be made to the accusation of μετάβασις εἰς ἄλλο γένος[75] which is often levelled at the perceptual physiologist because he unhesitatingly uses perception (i.e. a form of subjective experience) as an indicator of physiological events. He can – and must – do this, because (as has already been said) the assumption of some kind of isomorphy[76] between physical and psychological events is a basic hypothesis of all research into the physiology of perception. It is quite immaterial whether one adheres to a theory of identity, regarding physiological and experiential processes as simply two incommensurable aspects of the same extra-subjective reality, or to a theory of psycho-physiological parallelism. In both cases, the accusation of μετάβασις would apply to the common term 'physiology of perception' itself. Although the manner in which physiologists apply experiential termino-logy to objective events may appear to be somewhat improper to the terminological purist (e.g. when von Frisch and his colleagues talk of 'bee purple' as a colour), this is really no more than illustrative short-hand for the statement of factual evidence which could quite definitely be set out in objectivating language and elucidated by purely objective investigation. Finally, reliance upon the hypotheses of identity or parallelism is further justified by the fact that (for example in the case of the colour-constancy mechanism) one obtains exactly the same answer whether one selects one's own subjective experience or the objective conditioning behaviour of bees as an indicator of physiological function. Anybody who is seriously engaged in perceptual physiology is quite well aware that he is riding two horses at once. But this very fact provides the main stimulus and value of this branch of science; one can analyse the same process both from an objective and from a subjective point of view. One is secretly gnawing away at the tough fare of the 'body-mind problem', and one is unable to disgorge it although one knows full well that 'nobody can digest this old sour-dough between the cradle and the tomb' (Goethe).

Perceptual physiologists provide extremely important results (which should not be ignored by epistemologists) with respect to the remarkable transformation process which occurs between the input of physical in-fluences at the peripheral sense-organ and experience of the perceptual phenomenon. The critique of perception as a cognitive process which emerges from this is significantly similar to that made by modern physicists regarding more central functions of cognition. The relation-ship between 'outside' and 'inside' is remarkably similar in its appearance to the physiologist and the physicist. A great thinker such as Goethe was still able to seriously believe that colours represent objectively un-questionable properties as an object of physical investigation, though not in terms of physiology. Nowadays, hypothetical realists are beginning to accept the fact that forms and categories of conceptualization are also functions of central nervous organization, which bear an analogy-relationship to the inherent reality of objects which is just as incomplete as the relationship between the colour 'red' and the electromagnetic waves of a given range of wavelengths.

The people who are least able to believe in the absolute validity of a

priori forms of thought and conceptualization, however, are those concerned with comparative research relating to the phylogeny of animal
and human behaviour patterns and the operative physiological mechanisms. For such workers, the organization of the sense-organs and the
nervous system – whose functioning provides us with information about
extra-subjective realities – is quite evidently something which arose in
the process of speciation through interaction with and adaptation to
these immutable properties, just like that of all other morphological
structures. They are open to the same methods of comparative phylogenetic research, which show quite unmistakably how smooth a transition there is between the mechanisms of spatial orientation and
perception on the one hand and a priori forms of thought and conceptualization on the other. Despite the enormous differences between
these lower and higher cognitive processes in terms of complexity and
level of integration, they all quite characteristically fit Kant's definition
of the a priori: they are all determined prior to any individual experience,
and must be so for experience to be at all possible.

This evolutionary approach to human 'a priori' forms of thought and
conceptualization produces an opinion about the recognizability of extra-
subjective reality which differs fundamentally from that produced by
that of transcendental idealism. As long as one identifies in the a priori
forms and categories of conceptualization properties which are absolutely necessary for thought and bear no relationship whatsoever to
the world of objects, yet represent the exclusive 'spectacles' through
which we are able to see objects, it is quite logical to refer to an object
itself only in the singular and to refer to it as fundamentally excluded
from cognition. Given a complete lack of relationship between a priori
schematism and the extra-subjective world, the phenomenal world
would of course in no way represent an image of the real one. The
relationship between the two, to use a parallel, would be the same as
that which exists (for example) between experience and the background
of reality when a human being lacking any information about toxicology
is mildly poisoned by some exotic poison. The human being experiences
something, but what he experiences bears no image relationship – i.e.
exhibits no kind of analogy – to the reality of the chemical combination.
This relationship between experience and the reality underlying it is,
however, fundamentally altered as soon as the receiver of the experience
possesses information about the corresponding reality. For example, to
keep to our parallel, this would apply if the poisoned person were a
pharmacologist who was able to 'picture' from personal observation of
his symptoms which substance had produced them.

The organization of our perception, of our forms and categories of
our conceptualization (in short, of our entire 'world-image apparatus')

in fact incorporates quite a lot of information[77] about the real properties about which it notifies us in the form of phenomena. It is not the a priori schematism of our conceptual processes and thought which arbitrarily and independently prescribes for extra-subjective reality the form it assumes in our phenomenal world. In terms of phylogeny, it was the other way around: extra-subjective reality, in the course of aeons of persistent struggle for survival, has forced our developing 'world-image apparatus' to give due reckoning to its properties. Just as the fish fin does not prescribe the physical properties of water and the eye does not determine the properties of light, our forms of thought and conceptualization have not 'invented' space, time and causality. Of course, the fin does determine to a marked extent the manner in which a fish experiences the water, and the eye determines the way in which light paints a picture in our phenomenal world; and of course water and light possess properties which are not transmitted to the experience of the bearer by the relevant organs. But it is just as obvious that the fundamentally coarse and incomplete information provided by our 'world-image apparatus' about the external world has a real correlate in the properties inherent in the external objects themselves.

The fact that our 'world-image apparatus' itself has arisen in the course of evolution by interaction with the unsympathetic properties of the real external world – something which can scarcely be doubted by any scientific thinker – has interesting consequences for the contradiction which exists between idealism and empiricism with respect to the a priori nature of our forms of thought and conceptualization. The contradiction is not actually exposed as a pseudo-problem, but its resolution is shown to be a question of extremely tenuous epistemological value. Of course, the thesis *Nihil est in intellectu quod non ante fuerat in sensu* would be straightforward nonsense if taken literally to mean that the entire central nervous system in a young, inexperienced organism is a completely structureless mass which requires sensory experience in order to become at all structured. However, on the other hand the phylogenetic process leading to the formation of structures favouring survival of the species is analogous to individual learning in so many features that we have no cause for amazement when the end results of the two are often similar to the point of confusion. The genome (the chromosome system) incorporates a virtually unimaginable store of 'information' which would fill many, many textbooks of anatomy, physiology and behaviour if we were actually able to translate it into human language. This entire store has been accumulated by a process which is very closely related to that of learning through trial-and-error. The arrangement of the genes in the chromosomes, their restricted (to some extent prescribed) variability, and the possibility of

novel combination through the processes of sexual reproduction, together provide an apparatus which enters into cautious experimentation
with the properties of the environment. In this, the existence of the
species and all the previously achieved adaptations are never set at risk;
instead, only a probabilistically determined percentage of the progeny
are involved. We know that these methods have been overwhelmingly
successful in biological terms; after all, all animals and plants are
descendants of the organisms which first 'employed' such methods –
flagellate Protozoa.[78] Campbell has demonstrated that the process by
means of which phylogenetic alteration of the genome explores the
properties of the surrounding environment for novel possibilities of
existence is exactly equivalent in all respects to pure *induction* (i.e.
induction free of all deductive processes).

We know of only two ways in which an organism can obtain information about the surrounding environment. Firstly, there is the above-
described genetic-phylogenetic interaction of the stock with its environment. Secondly, there is individual learning through trial-and-error.
But learning is, of course, always a function of an extremely complex
apparatus which has been 'designed' down to the minutest detail in the
passage of evolution, accompanying interaction between the species and
its environment.

The third possible assumption which could explain the evident agreement between the organism and the surrounding environment is that of
pre-established harmony. If one rejects any mystical assumptions and
insists upon a causal explanation, this can only be understood to mean
that structurally-based functional properties of matter within the organism operate in the same way as in the inorganic environment. In view
of the differences in structural complexity, this is so improbable that I
regard further discussion of this idea as unnecessary.

All animal and human behaviour which interacts in a species-
preserving manner with specific features of the surrounding environment
owes its adaptation to one of the two information sources specified above
– usually to both at once. For the behavioural physiologist it is inevitably
of prime importance to trace the adaptation of individual behavioural
elements back to one or other of these sources. For an epistemologist,
however, it is almost immaterial which of the two adapting processes
underlies the existence and specific form of a given structure or function
of our perception, thought or cognition. In the supra-individual, phylogenetic sense, the forms of our conceptualization and thought have
arisen in a manner which is just as much *a posteriori* as the process of
organ-formation. This involves an empirical evaluation carried out not
by the individual, but by the sequence of generations.

Certain forms of conceptualization and thought are 'necessary' only to the extent that certain natural laws are so all-pervading that any higher organism must enter the world with the ability to take account of them. Almost every higher animal incorporates in the organization of its body and behaviour structures which are adapted for such inescapable facts, e.g. that two solid bodies cannot occupy the same area in space, that light passes in approximately straight lines, and that the effect always appears after the cause in time.

There is an almost uninterrupted transition from such central nervous organization, which has arisen in adaptation to quite general and all-pervading natural laws, and that which has arisen in relationship with special requirements of the human environment – particularly the human *social* environment. On observing a specific facial expression of a fellow human being, we can 'intuitively' and directly share his experience. At night, on looking out of the window of a train, we can correctly interpret the relative displacement of a few light-points as parallactic; in consequence, we can not only form a direct image of the distribution of the lights, but also deduce the movement of the train itself. These two achievements are doubtless based on quite different physiological processes. The first (e.g. the response of Spitz's smiling infants) is based on an innate releasing mechanism; the second on one of those extremely complex computing processes which are so characteristic of our spatial Gestalt perception and so similar to conscious calculation that Helmholtz was able to regard them as subconscious conclusions. However, both processes are functions of neural organic structures, which have arisen in the course of evolution of our species in interaction with, and in adaptation to, properties of our environment. The difference between the two, with respect to function, lies in the fact that the first is concerned with a very special and specific human environmental situation, whilst the second is concerned with a quite general situation which is biologically relevant not only for the species *Homo sapiens*, but for the vast majority of optically-orienting organisms.

Thus, the functional difference between the two mechanisms selected as examples in human cognition is not due to the fact that one provides information which is more true and more correct than that provided by the other. The difference lies in the *differing range of application* within which each mechanism can meaningfully operate. A neural computing apparatus which is capable of evaluating all conceivable parallactic displacements with all kinds of perceived objects to provide correct information not only about their position in space, but also about the movement of the viewing eye itself, must necessarily exhibit genuine analogies in a large number of individual features to the properties of the extra-subjective reality which it reflects within our phenomenal world. The experienced phenomenon is, in a more 'abstract' sense, an image of the extra-subjective reality than is the experience of a single emotional parameter produced, for example, by an innate releasing mechanism on seeing the expressive movement of a fellow human being.

It is, perhaps, not quite correct to say of such different cognitive processes that one is more anthropomorphic than the other, as I did in 1942. Of course, in the final analysis, they are all equally anthropomorphic. But the more general formulations of possible experience, determined for ubiquitously operating natural laws, can also be demonstrated in other organisms, whilst the more specialized releasing mechanisms are – of course – quite specifically human. Even the most general forms of experience open to us (space, time, causality, etc.) have – as is known from modern physics – only limited, though individually distinct, ranges of application. Where they all fail, the 'least anthropomorphic' of all categories, that of *quantity*, takes us just a little further. It was a revolutionary act, quite illegitimate according to the transcendental-idealistic laws of human reason, when Max Planck, confronted with a situation where the category of causality was of no further use, simply abandoned it and replaced it with probability calculations.

It is possible that the characteristic feature of extremely wide applicability is what makes so many scientists regard the category of quantity as the sole 'non-anthropomorphic' one. Many oft-quoted statements express the primacy of quantity, e.g. 'any branch of scientific research is scientific in proportion to its mathematical content', or 'natural science consists in quantifying what is quantifiable and to render quantifiable anything that is not so already'. The authors of these aphorisms, which are both highly intellectual and highly erroneous, have completely forgotten the structure of matter, quite apart from the fact that they deny to psychological research the character of a scientific study and to the variegated world of qualities the property of reality. In any case, it is epistemologically invalid to regard the category of quantity as absolute. This, too, is no more than a box which more-or-less fits the properties of extra-subjective reality to a degree adequate for the requirements of natural selection. Wilhelm Busch says 'two times two makes four is a truth: what a pity that it is so easy and so empty'. The counting machine involved in our extensive quantification operates like a mechanical excavator, which adds a shovel-full of something or other to each previous one. The operation is only genuinely precise and free of contradiction as long as it is conducted in a vacuum and only involves counting of the re-cycling shovel ($=$ unity). As soon as this machine is allowed to bite into the non-homogeneous matter of extra-subjective reality, the absolute truth of its pronouncements is immediately lost. To say that two sheep or atoms plus two further sheep or atoms[79] is equal to four others is a statement of only very approximate value, for the simple reason that there are never two really equivalent atoms or sheep, let alone the eight which would be necessary in order to lend the above statement absolute truth. The equation: two million plus two million makes four million, when applied to reality, is far more correct than the statement 'two times two is four'. This is because the individual differences between the counted units are statistically ironed out with large numbers, with a probability verging upon certainty (always assuming that one is not adding sheep to cattle). Thus, our thought form of extensive quantification resembles that of causality in the decisive respect that both involve statements which correspond to extra-subjective reality only with statistical probability and that neither incorporates absolute truths.

An approximate truth, 'information' about extra-subjective properties,[80] is – as has already been shown - incorporated in any behavioural adaptation which results in successful interaction with a given environmental factor. In cases where both simple and complex mechanisms are concerned with the same environmental property, this analogy between behavioural adaptation and genuine cognition is often clearly exhibited. The blind, fixed avoidance response of a *Paramaecium* incorporates only a single element of information about the object blocking its path; namely, that there is at that point an insurmountable obstacle to loco-motor progression. The three-dimensional spatial insight which is provided by our optical depth perception tells the human observer in far more detail about the object blocking the way. However, in the single point which is vital to the *Paramaecium*, its modest information can only be confirmed: it cannot swim on in its previous direction at that point.

The mechanism which enables so many animals to develop conditioned responses is an adaptation to the physical fact of energy-transformation. Preparatory or avoidance response to the conditioned stimulus preceding the biologically relevant one is only adaptive (in terms of species-survival) when the two stimuli occur in sequence with reliable regularity. This is only the case when both are links in the same causal chain. The mechanism of the conditioned response takes in only one piece of information about this relationship – that the effect follows the cause in time. And this 'cognitive feat' is of tremendous survival value! In addition, it is actually a correct piece of information, since it remains quite true even when viewed from the higher level of human causalistic thought.

The more primitive and the more highly differentiated cognitive processes therefore do not differ in that the former provides information about *different* factors: the latter simply involves *more* features of extra-subjective reality. The simpler 'world-image', when compared to the most highly differentiated, is by no means distorted – it is merely por-trayed on a far coarser template.

If anything is suited to fortifying our belief in the reality of the external world, it is the range of functional analogies existing between the simplest and the most differentiated subconscious and rational cognitive processes. These can only be understood on the basis of the assumption that the analogous mechanisms have originated in adaptation to the same structure in extra-subjective reality. Analogies such as the two illustrated in the above examples are found in just the same way when one compares animal with human functions as when comparing lower and higher cognitive processes in man himself. Whilst Egon Brunswik and I were still working in Vienna – he on perceptual mechanisms and myself on innate releasing mechanisms – we were repeatedly amazed in the course of our discussions by the extent to which such analogies frequently apply. Human perception often responds just like that of an animal, and can be misled by crude dummies; whilst animal perception often performs feats which quite clearly come under the heading 'ratiomorphic', later developed by Brunswik.

These considerations, derived from application of an evolutionary viewpoint to the theory of knowledge, agree just as immediately with the basic assumption of hypothetical realism as do the results of modern physics and of perceptual physiology. They fulfil the requirement attached to any new hypothesis of incorporating facts which cannot be explained from the standpoint of other epistemological theories (above all that of transcendental idealism).

One requirement, which I mentioned at the beginning and whose inescapability I had deduced from the assumptions of hypothetical realism in 1942, is that any theory of cognition is obliged to incorporate into its frame of reference all advances in our knowledge about the objects of cognition. This applies particularly where the object proves to be so recalcitrant to being fitted into the 'a priori' forms of thought and conceptualization as is the object of modern physics. One can of course choose for the object of one's investigation the mechanism of these cognitive processes as they are operating *in vacuo*, and thus indulge in 'pure' epistemology. However, in doing so one would proceed in the same manner as somebody investigating the governing principles of the mechanisms of a camera (e.g. a Leica) without taking into account the fact that the entire apparatus exists for taking photographs and was developed by the Leitz Company in Wetzlar from simpler, earlier models to perform this particular function. And above all, using such a procedure, one will not learn what it is necessary to know about the functions or the functional limitations of the apparatus in order to learn about its performance and how to improve it in order to push back these limitations.

The short paper mentioned above, which included the most important aspects of the epistemological considerations I have outlined, had just appeared when Max Planck's publication (quoted on p. 282) followed, showing that he had reached comparable conclusions in very many respects. Niels Bohr, in his lecture given to the American Academy of Arts and Sciences in 1957, set out exactly the same principles, and P. W. Bridgman – in his summarizing comments on this lecture said: 'The object of knowledge and the instrument of knowledge cannot legitimately be separated; but must be taken together as one whole.' I mention the priority of my short paper with respect to the similarly oriented statements of the three Nobel prize-winning physicists taken as 'witnesses' simply because the *independent* agreement is significant, and because one would be more likely to think that I was influenced by them than *vice versa*. All the same, I must admit that it was one of the proudest moments of my life when I read in a letter written by Max Planck that he was extremely satisfied 'by the fact that, starting from such fundamentally different inductive bases, one can come to such congruous views about the relationship between the real and the phenomenal world'.

In concluding this section, one must ask whether there is confirmation for the initial supposition that arguments for the basic assumptions of hypothetical realism can, in fact, be derived from these considerations of the human cognitive apparatus. However, the reply to this question does not affect proof of the legitimacy of perception as a source of knowledge, which I regard as theoretically established.

On superficial examination of the considerations set out above, one initially suspects that the argumentation for the assumption of a reality which is partially accessible to cognition through analogy is really taken through a logical circle, rather like the actions of Baron von Münchhausen in drawing himself out of a bog by pulling his own pigtail. It may in fact look as if both the cognition of physical facts and the recognition of their reality must represent a precondition for arriving at certain concepts concerning the cognitive apparatus, which is equally presupposed to be real. This apparatus projects into our experience to give rise to *phenomena*, as for example in the representation of the mechanism and functioning of the colour-circle given above. In fact, the simplest and didactically most obvious form of description gives a false idea about the path which was originally followed by cognition. The physicists would never have arrived at their concepts about the wave-nature of light if the mechanism of the colour-circle did not divide the spectrum cast by a prism into bands perceived as qualitatively different. However much the mechanism of colour constancy is tailored for its special function, however arbitrarily it may deal with the continuum of wavelengths underlying the manufactured phenomena in assuring this one function, and however misleading it may indicate that white and purple are 'pure colours', it nevertheless assisted physicists in arriving at the one essential discovery that different wavelengths do in fact exist. It was a *further* epistemological advance when knowledge about the wave-nature of light led to further questions about the physiological nature of the colour-circle.

This procedure seems to me to be less like that of the legendary imposter (von Münchhausen) than that of a normal human being placing one foot in front of the other in walking. It seems to me that all non-realistic philosophers give too little thought to the fact that results coming from quite different areas of study and derived from quite different phenomena never contradict one another, but – on the contrary – aid advances in those areas which are farthest from their own origin. To me, it seems absurd to search for any other explanation for this than the fact that there is a single extra-subjective reality underlying all phenomena. This opinion is, admittedly, based on the naïve (though generally trusty) view that the correctness of any testimony becomes more probable with increase in the number of independent, accordant witnesses. If the five participants in a symposium agree in the view that there are five wine-glasses on the table around which they are sitting, I sincerely admit that, with the best will in the world, I am unable to understand how any rational human being can seek any other explanation than that – whatever may lie behind the phenomenon 'wine-glass' – it is really present five-fold.

III   Constancy-functions in perception

I can think of no better evidence for the legitimacy of perception as a source of scientific knowledge than the proof that Gestalt perception not only performs the same functions as the generally recognized processes of rational thought, but actually achieves this through operations which are extensively analogous, though not open to introspection. In order to demonstrate this proof, I have selected two mechanisms which have long been recognized, but whose pattern of operation and adaptation for survival of the species was only recently elucidated – particularly by Erich von Holst.

1. COLOUR CONSTANCY

I always see the surface of my writing-desk to be the same pale-brown colour, whether I look at it in the bluish morning light, in the heavily red-tinged light of the late afternoon or in the yellow light of an electric bulb. In fact, under these differing circumstances, the desk surface reflects quite different wavelengths in each case; but my perception remarkably tells me nothing – or very little – about this state of affairs. What my perception tells me, in essence, is not what colour the surface is, but rather something about a constant property of the object of reflecting light of certain wavelengths better than that of other wavelengths. I shall first describe the manner in which this constant property is ascertained under changing conditions by referring to the process in anthropomorphic terms. This simplifies understanding of the matter, although the physiological 'ratiomorphic' computing mechanism actually operates in a simpler fashion. The perceptual mechanism at first 'surveys' the entire visual field and determines the average of the wavelengths it reflects. If wavelengths of a particular spectral colour are predominant, the mechanism 'assumes' that the light-source transmits these more than those of another colour. The mechanism thus operates on the basis of the probable – but far from certain – presupposition that the objects occupying the visual field reflect all spectral colours equally on average, without preference for one in particular. If the hypothesis is erroneous – i.e. if objects in the visual field predominantly reflect one colour (e.g. red) – the constancy mechanism promptly 'concludes' that the colour of illumination contains a high proportion of red. For this reason, in a manner which is correct in a formal logical sense but erroneous in that it is based on false premises, the objects which reflect red to a lesser extent are erroneously regarded as reflecting other wavelengths in preference to red. But, apart from such special cases, the constancy mechanism concerned informs us with great reliability about the characteristic reflective properties of a given object, and these are directly perceived as its 'colour'.

What I have just described in a 'ratiomorphizing' manner is in reality performed by a physiological mechanism which arrives at the same information using the same stimulus data, but by means of a far simpler pathway than that outlined above. The function of the mechanism depends upon the well-known principle of complementary colours and the 'trick' which the evolution of this mechanism has 'invented' by a virtual stroke of genius is reduction of spectral colours to an 'arbitrarily' selected zero point – *white*. (Remarkably, it is not a mixture of wavelengths corresponding exactly to that of sunlight which we perceive as 'white', but one displaced slightly towards the shorter wavelength side of the spectrum. We do not know why this is the case; but it is somewhat immaterial with respect to functioning of the colour constancy mechanism.) A second great invention is represented by the fact that certain clusters of wavelengths, isolated from one another in the spectrum, are combined in such a way that they are mutually exclusive. In other words, when together they give zero (i.e. white). However, since the spectrum is arranged in linear fashion, there is a great difficulty for this system of reciprocal compensation in paired clusters of wavelengths: however the complementary clusters may be arranged, one of them must always be opposite its complementary partner. This difficulty was overcome with the 'fiction' of a spectral colour which simply does not exist – *purple*. This closes the spectral band to give a circle, by combining the red end with the violet. The colour-circle and its significance were first recognized by Wilhelm Ostwald.

If a retinal area is struck by light of a given wavelength, the sector of the perceptual apparatus which receives this colour-signal and passes it on towards the centre simultaneously begins to indicate the complementary colour. In contrast to the primary colour-signal, this complementary colour-signal diffuses through other parts of the retina and the coupled afferent components of the nervous system, in so far as these are at all affected by light of any kind. Here, we are faced with a widespread activity of the perceptual apparatus – namely active production of a perceptual component which cannot be distinguished from a similar signal coming in from the peripheral sense-organ. The extremely important adaptive function of this 'phantom' lies in the capability of extinguishing signals from the sense-organs in cases where constancy perception requires it, by superimposing a similar signal with inversed sign. Green actively produced through irradiation with red light adds up with genuine red of the same intensity to give white, just like 'genuine' green indicated by the retina. It is for this reason that, under red illumination, our writing-paper still looks white.

The green-signal, produced in perception both actively and in compensation for red irradiation, does not arise – at least not exclusively – through threshold-lowering to green light augmenting and emphasizing a green which is actually present. For instance, if a red-irradiated semi-circle is contrasted with a white semi-circle contrived by mixture of spectral blue and yellow (i.e. which does not reflect genuine green light), the experimental subject sees this white as green in just the same way. However, there is as yet no quantitative investigation showing whether this green is just as intensive as when seen on a white composed of an all-colour mixture.

Segmentation of the continual gradation of wavelengths to give a number of discontinuous, complementary bands with positive and negative signs, the introduction of the zero-colour white, and in particular the active production of 'phantom'-colours, together provide a perceptual organization which has quite definitely been differentiated in evolution to assist in colour constancy, and thus indirectly to further object constancy. The long-familiar contrast phenomena like so many other so-called sensory illusions, are non-functional (but not species-endangering) miscarriages of a highly differentiated organ-system, whose function is paradoxically that of avoiding sensory illusions and of passing on to the higher centres of our 'world-image apparatus' only information which has a genuine correspondence with extra-subjective reality.

2. DIRECTIONAL CONSTANCY

The second constancy mechanism which I am going to employ as an example of a ratiomorphically operating perceptual apparatus is that which prevents us from erroneously interpreting displacement of the retinal image caused by movement of our eyes themselves as movement in the environment.

Helmholtz was already aware of the significance of the fact that passive movements of the eye-ball, brought about for example by finger-pressure or with a suitable mechanical arrangement moving the anaesthetized eye, produce illusory movements of the environment in the opposite sense. He correctly concluded that proprioceptors cannot therefore be involved in the prevention of illusory movements in active eye-ball movements. A significant extension of Helmholtz's observation is provided by an old-established observation of practising ophthalmologists: people with paralysis of the eye-muscles suffer from the fact that when they attempt to turn the gaze in the direction hindered by paralysis, the environment appears to leap in the direction of the intended – but unaccomplished – movement of the eye-ball.

Both of these effects can be elucidated in a 'ratiomorphizing' manner as follows: When the eye-ball is passively rotated, there is no perceptual 'experience' of the movement; the perceptual mechanism must therefore 'conclude' that the image-displacement noticeable on the retina was caused by environmental movement in a direction opposite to that imposed on the eye-ball. In an attempt at active rotation which is hindered by paralysis, the perceptual mechanism 'expects' a displacement of the retinal image. This mechanism, of course, is 'unaware' of the paralysis and operates on the assumption that the command from the centre has been properly carried out, i.e. that the eye-ball has rotated to the degree prescribed by the command. On the basis of these false premises, the mechanism must logically 'conclude' that the environment has performed the same movement as the eye-ball, since the retinal image is in the same position as before.

In reality, the process described in this ratiomorphic manner is carried out by a mechanism described and analysed by von Holst and Mittelstaedt. A 'copy' of the command issued to the motor components is directly conducted to those sectors of the perceptual mechanism which also receive signals from the sense-organ resulting from the response to the command. Such sensory signals directly produced by inherent movements of the organism are referred to as *reafferent signals*, and the signal relating to the outgoing motor command which is transmitted to the perceptual mechanism is the *efferent signal copy*. The constancy function of the entire mechanism is based on the fact that the efferent signal copy actively produces in higher receptor centres a perceptor effect which is exactly equivalent to that evoked by the reafferent signal, but has an inverse sign so that the two together add up to a zero-signal. For this reason, when we perform active, undisturbed eye-movements the environment is seen as completely immobile, although extensive displacements occur on our retina and are actually centrally transmitted.

Of course, the same constancy function could also theoretically be achieved by informing the central perceptual mechanism of the movement actually carried out, by making use of the proprioceptors, and relating this information to the reafferent signal. This solution has in fact been produced by evolution in many cases, and this has apparently occurred particularly in cases where accuracy of compensation is more important than rapidity. The biological advantage of the efferent signal copy is, of course, based on the fact that it more-or-less anticipates the arrival of the reafferent signal in the perceptual sector, or arrives simultaneously.

A further example may briefly be added to these somewhat more extensive descriptions of constancy mechanisms – that of size-constancy. In this case, von Holst has shown that the motor processes of convergence and accommodation occurring on close approach of a viewed object surprisingly produce a compensatory 'phantom' of size-reduction *directly*, i.e. without association with distance-perception. This very probably involves an efferent signal copy. If the two eyes are subjected to greater convergence without any change in accommodation, the visual image becomes smaller. The same thing happens when one induces the eyes to undergo greater accommodation whilst convergence and size of the retinal image are maintained constant. Both processes operate in an additive manner, which has been quantitatively investigated by von Holst. This mechanism, of course, also provides the perceptual mechanism with information about the momentary distance of a viewed object. However, it is surprising that this does not involve a mechanism closer to that which seems more obvious from our ratio-morphizing standpoint (i.e. that of primarily measuring the distance and then determining constant size from the correlation between the distance and the size of the retinal image), though this is accepted as certain in many textbooks. This is all the more remarkable since other mechanisms of size-constancy do in fact utilize this method. The illusion that objects seen in fog appear larger is doubtless based on the fact that in this case the depth-criterion of the air-haze[81] erroneously indicates a greater distance, from which an exaggerated size of the viewed object is ratiomorphically calculated.

3. GENERAL CONSIDERATIONS OF CONSTANCY MECHANISMS

In the above discussion, I have deliberately selected examples of constancy mechanisms which are quite different from each other in their causal-physiological origins, in order to show more clearly the common properties which have evolved in adaptation for similar functions.

Both mechanisms provide their particular selective value by compensating for accidental changes in perceptual conditions – the first compensating for variations in colour of illumination and the second for variations of the spatial position of the sense organ. Both directly inform the perceptual mechanism itself about properties attached to objects in extra-subjective reality.

Both achieve this by actively producing a perceptual phantom. This 'pseudo'-perception, with its inverse sign, is qualitatively and quanti-tatively identical to that evoked by accidental change in the perceptual conditions – to be more exact, identical to that which *would* be evoked if the signal were not fully eradicated by superimposition of the 'phantom'. I have used inverted commas for the words 'phantom' and 'pseudo' because, in fact, genuine perceptual processes are involved. In other words, it is highly probable that the compensatory signals acting to ensure constancy, along the last stages of their afferent pathway, follow the same paths and evoke a response from the same central mechanisms as 'genuine' perceptual processes (i.e. those immediately evoked by signals from the sense-organs). At least, this assumption seems an obvious one for anybody who sees in the complete lack of distinction between two experiential processes an argument for identity of their physiological correlates. A good example for the identity of central phenomena despite differing origin of the signals is provided by vision of movement. When we see a bird flying through a blue sky, it is the retinal elements which – through a temporal sequence of response – initially provide information about the bird's movement. However, a moment later the retinal image is brought to the *Fovea centralis* by 'telotactic' mechanisms. It is maintained stationary at this site by movement of the eye, following the movement of the object. From then onwards, it is exclusively the efferent signal copy of the commands passing to the eye-muscles which transmits information centrally about direction and rapidity of the viewed object. However, our perception of the gliding movement remains the same throughout the entire process. We notice nothing of the transition whereby one peripheral computing apparatus replaces another.

As with those mechanisms discussed in detail in the previous section, all kinds of constancy apparatus are – in principle – 'ratiomorphic' in the most rigorous sense of the term, since all incorporate processes analogous to those of both induction and deduction. All incorporate 'hypotheses', whose validity is not absolute, but simply extremely probable. And, when the inductive basis is erroneous, they can all give rise to false conclusions which they then – often incorrigibly – continue to uphold.

All mechanisms of constancy perception are objectivating in the literal sense of the word. They establish order in the immeasurably vociferous cacophony of the sensory data storming in upon us, by abstracting from many individual cases laws governing them all, using a genuine inductive process. This is all the information with which they provide us; they do not inform us of the sensory data themselves, still less about the process by means of which they arrived at their abstractions.[82]

The vast majority of perceptual illusions, including the best-known examples, are functional miscarriages of constancy mechanisms. Through special, generally improbable stimulus situations, these mechanisms are 'misled' into producing their compensatory 'phantom' where there is nothing to compensate.

4. FORM CONSTANCY

The most complex and awe-inspiring of all genuine constancy mechanisms is that of form constancy. This is really what underlies object-constancy – the recognizability of objects. One only needs to think of Jacob von Uexküll's definition: 'An object is anything which moves in unison.' Whilst I am looking at my pipe as I turn it backwards and forwards in front of my eyes, my perceptual mechanism correctly interprets the many variations in the retinal image as alterations of spatial position of the pipe, and not as shape-changes. This achievement, which is so self-evident to us that it scarcely gives us food for thought, incorporates as integrating components virtually all of the constancy functions already mentioned, together with an enormous number of stereometric computations, which are so complex that one would doubt the possibility of investigating such mechanisms if experience did not tell us that these sometimes function more simply than rational processes with an analogous function. The illustrative-geometrical function of this mechanism remains virtually unimpaired when the contour-alteration of the image is left as the only source of information, with all other sources withheld. This is the case when a silhouette is observed. The only restriction which the information suffers is that the direction of rotation is no longer indicated. As is well known, the rotation of a silhouette can equally well be interpreted as a movement to the left or to the right. However, the perceptual apparatus does not inform us about this ambiguity in information; instead, it 'decides' upon a 'hypothetical' assumption that there is a given direction of rotation. One interpretation can frequently give way to the other – an effect which is extremely familiar and which, with some practice, can even be produced voluntarily. One could ascribe survival value to this abrupt 'decision' of the perceptual apparatus in favour of one of two alternative interpretations. Since the perceptual apparatus, particularly that concerned with processes of movement, is in fact present in order to direct an immediate and appropriate behavioural response, it is not in a position to conduct 'statistical analysis'. It is much more effective to make a wrong 'decision' with 50 per cent probability than to attempt a compromise solution which will be certainly inappropriate. With the drawn-out processes of complex Gestalt perception, as we shall see (p. 305 et seq.), the situation is quite different.

Constant perception of a spatial form involves transpositions which are closely related to those of true Gestalt perception. The image which is projected on to the retina by, for example, the contour-line of a fish's back is a line with multiple irregularities which alters its length, its radii and the sense of its sinuosities according to the angle of view. It can contract to give a short, straight line when the fish is viewed from directly in front or behind and expand to a long line when the fish is seen directly from above. When my perceptual mechanism performs this function under normal observational conditions, depth criteria and other aspects may provide information. But when the same achievement is shown with a silhouette of an object turned backwards and forwards, the only source of information from which the mechanism can deduce constancy of the perceived form is the fixed relationship between the heights, distances and signs of the curve-peaks portrayed upon the retina. Computation of the large number of very 'abstract', constant relationships to give a single perceived quality is a function which realizes all the classical criteria of the Gestalt.

IV   Gestalt perception as a constancy function

I am unable to see any fundamental difference between the above-described mechanisms of optical form constancy and those of Gestalt perception. There is a quite continuous chain of simple and complex mechanisms permitting us to attain an image of surrounding objects which is adequate for our survival, and to recognize these objects as 'the same' despite continual alteration in the perceptual conditions. In fact, it is misleading to talk of a 'chain', since all of the mechanisms together form a system in which there are reciprocal functional relationships between all components. For example, size-transposable form constancy is incorporated in the mechanism of size constancy and *vice versa*.

As has already been said on p. 286 et seq., the characteristic objectivating function of all constancy mechanisms is based on extraction of a principle prevailing in the sensory data. Particularly in the case of form constancy, this principle may be so complex that its distinction from the 'background' of accidental features appears to be analogous to genuine, rational abstraction. The mechanism which carries out this special function actually proves to be capable of more general operation. It is not only able of perceiving as constant those principles (laws) which are evident from the constancy of properties attached to objects, it can also identify constant features inherent in any other stimulus-configurations – particularly with respect to temporal sequence.

In principle, the perception of temporal properties is nothing particular or novel for complex Gestalt perception. This certainly plays a part even in lower perceptual functions, as in the described cases of directional constancy, movement constancy and similar phenomena. The conceptual form of time is remarkably closely related to that of space; it is, of course, only portrayable in terms of analogy with movement in space, as is noticeable from the double use of temporal and spatial prepositions such as 'before', 'after' and from the illustrative etymology of the words 'future' and 'past', etc. The converse, i.e. the description of spatial relationships in analogy with temporal processes, is also quite common, as when we talk of the 'passage' of an 'undulating' line or the 'extension' of an object. These parallels between the conceptual forms of space and time, which extend as far as mutual substitution, are certainly not only characteristic of human linguistic symbolism, but actually derived from the primary property that a movement possesses both spatial and temporal extension. Central representation of space, which is present in many organisms as a precursor of the human conceptual form, of course only evolved in free-moving creatures which were forced to orient their movements in space. Through comparative examination it can be neatly demonstrated that the 'central spatial model' has undergone increasing differentiation hand-in-hand with increasing demands upon the capacity of orientation of movement.

In view of these facts, it is somewhat less amazing – though still extremely remarkable – that, in the perception of spatial and temporal processes and of exclusively spatial Gestalts, the functions of transposition, distinction between accidental and elementary sensory data, and above all distinction of constant laws, are performed in virtually the same manner. For this very reason, it is almost immaterial for the discussion of the most complex functions of Gestalt perception, which are closely related to genuine abstraction, whether one selects examples from the category of exclusively temporal Gestalts (e.g. that of melodies), from that of the spatio-temporal Gestalts of movement, or from exclusively spatial configurations. The latter is the most suitable for illustration, although there is – to be exact – no purely static-spatial Gestalt perception, except in the special case of tachistoscopic presentation. In all other cases, the eye continuously meanders over the observed configuration, which itself introduces mechanisms of directional constancy operating in time.

In exact terms, the perception of any 'time-incorporating' Gestalt incorporates some degree of memory function, since for surveying of its configuration some fixation – however brief – of the initial components is necessary, with the unique exception of the special case mentioned above. I believe that there is a function of learning and memory taking place on another level which plays a decisive rôle in the most complex forms of Gestalt perception now to be considered. The time element involved is far greater, by a matter of several powers of ten. The constant colour and size of a viewed object is literally transmitted in its final form with only a momentary lag; surveying of a short temporal Gestalt lasts scarcely longer than the Gestalt itself. But a really complex Gestalt, for example, a physiognomy or a piece of polyphonic music, must be seen or heard several times before the Gestalt perceived with respect to these configurations has assumed its final quality. In fact, one might perhaps say in somewhat extreme terms that such extremely complex Gestalts never attain a really final quality. Instead, with each slight advance in the degree of acquaintance, the Gestalts might change very slightly; new, minor principles would continually be distinguished from the background of accidental features, permitting and increasing penetration into the structure of the perceived entity.[83]

The participation of learning and memory in the development of complex perception actually permits 'abstraction' of the Gestalt from the background of chaotic stimulus data, even when the 'noise' of the latter is so predominant that a single presentation does not contain sufficient information with respect to Gestalt regularity. In a process of information-collection, which can extend over years or even decades, Gestalt perception – in combination with memory, which is remarkably 'good' in this special context – provides such a broad 'inductive basis' that the principle sought after appears to be 'statistically validated'. The inverted commas in this case indicate that there is a genuine analogy between the ratiomorphic and the rational process. Once, I was engaged in an extensive discussion of these processes at a congress, describing how, in the observation of complex animal behaviour patterns, one can literally see the same process thousands of times without noticing the inherent principle until – quite abruptly – on the following occasion the Gestalt is distinguished from the background of accidental features with such clarity that one asks in vain why it was not noticed a long time ago. Grey Walter summarized my somewhat long discourse with one sentence: 'Redundancy of information compensates noisiness of channel.'

The clarifying contributory effect of exclusion of accidental features, which is only conceivable with participation of learning and memory, is probably the prerequisite for acquisition of an entirely new function by Gestalt perception. This evidently arose very late in phylogeny, and it is only in man that it has reached full flower. The same mechanisms which produce object constancy and which were quite certainly evolved for this function in the course of phylogeny are capable, as we have seen above, of generalizing their function and of encompassing other principles, such as those of short-term temporal Gestalts. Without actual alteration of their physiological structure, the same mechanisms can, in fact, achieve something quite different: From a large number of individual configurations, which can be presented at considerable time-intervals, they 'abstract' a supra-individual principle governing them all.

These same perceptual mechanisms – which permit me to recognize my chow-chow Susi as the same individual from the front and from the back, at a distance and close at hand, in red-tinted and bluish light, and so on – by means of a remarkable functional change also permit me to identify in this chow-chow, in a bulldog, in a terrier and in a dachshund a common, unmistakable Gestalt quality – that of the dog.

This highly specialized function of Gestalt perception undoubtedly underlies the abstraction of generic concepts and most probably represents an indispensable precondition for such abstraction. A young child which is already capable of referring to all dogs as 'bow-wow' and all cats as 'miaow-miaow' has quite definitely not abstracted the zoological identification formula for *Canis familiaris* and *Felis ocreata*. In addition, it is impossible to predict the content of such quasi-abstraction carried out by Gestalt perception. The small son of one of my colleagues obstinately and incorrigibly used the term 'bow-wow' not only for dogs, but also for horses, cats and mice. The parents, both zoologists, only exchanged their disappointment for joy when they found out that 'bow-wow' simply meant 'mammal' and was unerringly applied to members of the Class Mammalia – including his newborn sister.

My elder daughter, at the age of five years, had a restricted knowledge of the variegated bird Family Rallidae (rails); she was only acquainted with the moorhen (*Gallinula chloropus* L.) and the coot (*Fulica atra* L.), but knew these very well. We tested her on the comprehensive bird-collection at the Schönbrunn Zoological Garden, without giving any helpful suggestions. Without any mistake, she identified the rails kept in the various aviaries. She picked out the long-legged Purple gallinule (*Porphyrio*) caged with the waders and spotted the small Rallids such as the corncrake (*Crex crex* L.) kept together with small gallinaceous birds. In the same cage, there were a number of Turnicidae (Button quails), which belong to an extremely ancient group possibly closely related to gallinaceous birds, and whose external appearance is very much like that of corncrakes. When asked about these birds, she replied uncertainly 'They look a bit like chickens,' thus exactly voicing the opinion of the most qualified systematists.

The presence of such highly-developed 'systematic intuition' in a five-year-old provides convincing evidence that this faculty is based on ratiomorphic – and not rational – processes. One becomes extremely conscious of this fact when one attempts, as an experienced comparative zoologist, to study these processes themselves. Through introspection, one may indeed notice that the information provided by Gestalt perception abstracting from the groups involved consists of a single, unmistakable experiential quality. But there is nothing to indicate which characters and character combinations are incorporated as quality-determining components in the overall entity of the quality. I have repeatedly carried out this process of self-examination, taking the multi-Family group Percoidei (perch-like fish). In almost every Family in this group there are adaptations to a wide variety of ecological niches, so that the range of variation within a Family is far larger than the average, externally visible differences between the Families. The characters utilized by taxonomists for the diagnosis and definition of the Families are generally not externally visible. Whilst I was still a schoolboy, I noticed that I was able to correctly place the members of two Families of which I knew many examples (Cichlidae and Centrarchidae) even when I saw a particular species or genus for the first time. My later efforts to find out which characters and character-configurations, woven into unitary Gestalt perception, determine the unmistakable qualities of 'Cichlid membership' and 'Centrarchid membership' produced only the modest outcome of two negative statements.

In the first place, it is not the conspicuous, crude characters such as body-shape, number and kind of fins, and so on which determine the quality. The first time that I saw the tiny dwarf Centrarchid *Elassoma evergladei*, which – because of its rounded body form and the invisibility of the dorsal fin rays – does not at all look 'Centrachid-like', I took it for a number of seconds to be one of the toothed carp Family (Cyprinodontidae). Then I immediately perceived that extremely characteristic uncomfortable feeling which is well known to anyone schooled in Gestalt psychology and is caused by disrupted Gestalt perception. Thereupon, the familiar Gestalt of the Centrarchid sprang out of the background of accidental Cyprinodont-like characters, virtually with an 'audible click' and a truly liberating 'Aha-experience'.

Secondly, it is remarkably *not* a general rule that characters which are present in all the individual Gestalts concerned in an apparently striking form are necessarily incorporated as quality determinants in the quasi-abstraction performed in perception of the super-individual group Gestalt. Both of the Rallids known to my daughter were aquatic birds with an externally duck-like body form. The absence of this character in the first unknown Rallid genus she encountered did not in the least hinder her from recognizing the quality of 'Rallid membership'. All of the Cichlids with which I was acquainted until recently possess marked lateral flattening of the body and a high back. When I saw for the first time the dorso-ventrally compressed forms from the strongly flowing river area of the Congo, which are adapted to substrate-living, I instantly recognized them as Cichlids; the completely altered body form did not in the slightest detract from the unmistakable quality of 'Cichlid membership'.

So which kinds of information indicate in such achievements of Gestalt perception that a crude, conspicuous character present in all known cases is simply an 'accidental feature' of the configuration? A comparison of ratiomorphic and rational accomplishment of the same task permits certain suppositions about the direction in which the solution of this data-processing puzzle should be sought. Any zoological systematist who had tried to reach a 'diagnosis' of the group concerned by applying inductive abstraction to the basis of knowledge which my daughter possessed about the Rallidae and which I possessed about the Cichlidae would undoubtedly have included the aquatic character of the Rallids and the tall body form of the Cichlids in his identification key. In order to avoid this error, the systematist would have had to possess much more information. For example, when the snakes are included in the Tetrapoda in zoological taxonomy, although they lack the four legs determining the naming of this large group, this is done for a very good reason. The conviction given by Gestalt perception to any naïve observer of the animal group concerned, to the effect that the snakes are 'essentially' Tetrapods and that the absence of legs is an 'accidental feature', is in full accord with the phylogenetic consideration that the absence of legs in snakes could only be attributed with the significance of a primary character if it were assumed that all of the other characters agreeing with the Tetrapoda – in particular with the Reptilia – had arisen purely by chance. This assumption is so improbable that its calculable mathematical expression would run into astronomical figures.

Many decades ago, the ornithologist Gadow tried out the extremely interesting experiment of comparing the degree of correctness of 'systematic intuition' with that of rational consideration of phylogenetic relationships based on a known number of evaluated characters. He came to the undoubtedly correct conclusion that Gestalt perception, unbeknown to the perceiver, is capable of taking into account an enormously large number of characters. That this number must obviously be very large is indicated, among other things, by the fact that a comparison of a very small number of species (only two in one of the examples given above) provides enough information to allow Gestalt-based 'diagnosis' of the group.

V   The 'weaknesses' and the 'strengths' of Gestalt perception

If knowledge of modern calculating machines provides more than just a conceptual model anywhere in the physiology of the central nervous system, it is in the physiology of those mechanisms which extract our perceptual information from sensory data. Far from giving an impression of being fundamentally inaccessible to research and leading on to mystical-vitalistic interpretations, their functions – and even more their extremely informative miscarriages – so strongly exhibit the characters of mechanical, or, (better) *physical*, systems that they provide support for research optimism more than all other similar complex living phenomena. Thus, paradoxically, the miscarriages of this apparatus themselves strengthen our conviction that it is something real which interacts with real aspects of extra-subjective reality and provides us with true information about this interaction, even though this is of course no more than approximate. After all, the most general and least 'anthropomorphic' forms of possible experience, the categories of causality and quantity, are unable to achieve more than this.

One must, however, keep a close watch on the specific functional properties of Gestalt perception, in order to avoid their becoming sources of scientific error. Gestalt perception is just one single component of the systemic entity of our cognitive functions, specialized for a quite particular function. The particular species-preserving function whose selective value led to this specialization is that of the *discovery* of inherent principles.[84]

Certain other properties have been sacrificed for the sensitivity of this 'detector', and it is this fact which leads to the possibility of miscarriages. This is very important for critical evaluation of Gestalt perception and will therefore be dealt with first. In a manner analogous to that exhibited by many sensory functions, the sensitivity of response of complex Gestalt perception is magnified almost to the limit beyond which there is the danger that, because of self-excitation within the apparatus, 'information' is produced which does not correspond to any stimulus arriving from the exterior. Exactly the same limitation on the magnification of sensitivity of a receiving apparatus exists in technology. For example, one may not increase the sensitivity of a microphone to the point where molecular noise becomes audible.

In Gestalt perception, the equivalent of this 'built-in-noise' is the phenomenon which has been referred to by various investigators as 'Gestalt pressure', 'significance tendency', 'indiscriminate Gestalt tendency', and so on. Briefly, this phenomenon consists in the perceptual mechanism falsifying sensory data which almost, but not quite, fit an interpretation in the sense of a governing principle, so that they *do* appear to fit. What is evidently the same mechanism can also operate to the effect that sensory data which can be interpreted in terms of two alternative principles are always resolved in favour of the simpler, 'more significant', of the two, even when the more complex, 'less elegant' interpretation is the correct one and retouching of the sensory data is necessary for maintenance of the incorrect conclusion.

When the information contained in the sensory data is equally suited for establishment of two – sometimes opposing – interpretations, our perceptual mechanism does not inform us of this ambiguity; it 'decides' upon one of the interpretations and informs us of this one as 'the truth'. The stubbornness with which this 'arbitrary' choice is maintained varies greatly. Abrupt switching occurs and can be intentionally provoked with practice, as in the well-known case of the direction of rotation of silhouettes. I observed in myself an analogous case on the level of the most complex Gestalt perception based on learning when recognizing exactly intermediate hybrids between two animal species with which I was well acquainted. When I saw for the first time, completely unexpectedly, a hybrid between a domestic goose and a mute swan, I initially 'recognized' it as a swan, but doubted my mental health a second later for having regarded a domestic goose as a mute swan. It was only after a number of to-and-fro switches in Gestalt perception that I realized what I was really observing. Then, with some winking movements of the eyes, I was able to voluntarily switch the bird's Gestalt and see it alternately as a goose or a swan, exactly as one can switch the perceived direction of rotation of a silhouette cast by a rotating object.

Under perceptual conditions which lead to reduction in the clarity of the individual elements of sensory information, the 'phantasy' of the process concerned is given more play. As was shown particularly by Sanders in his well-known experiments with tachistoscopic presentation of incomplete geometric figures, Gestalt perception produces considerable falsification in the sense of greater regularity and significance of what is perceived. With sculptors and painters, one can often observe that they step backwards from their just-completed creation and examine it with the eyelids almost closed, only to look at it quite clearly a moment later. This 'technique' makes use of the 'significance tendency' by deliberately rendering the image unsharp and providing an opportunity for it to change in the direction of the required regularity, thus permitting determination of the discrepancy between the Gestalt which is sought and what is actually present. A portrait photographer makes use of the same peculiarity of Gestalt perception by deliberately avoiding sharp focus. The same is true of fashion – a woman's face appears more regular through a veil than it actually is, and so on.

One can use an old-established experiment to illustrate the interaction of all the discussed miscarriages of the 'significance tendency'. Using thin, black wire (so thin that the relief of the cylindrical thread disappears), one constructs an outline model of a cube, which is then rotated around a vertically oriented spatial diagonal. It is then observed in front of a mirror with one eye, such that the mirror image exactly coincides with the image of the wire cube, with the axes of rotation of both images overlapping. The mirror image then appears to leap forwards into the directly observed wire-cube, so that both appear to turn around the same axis. Simultaneously, the perceived direction of rotation of the mirror image is inversed, so that both cubes are observed as packed together and rotating in the same direction around a single axis. This switch in perception of the location and rotational direction of the cube reflection is accompanied by two easily understandable, but quite interesting, effects. In the first place, the reflection appears to become considerably smaller. This is understandable, since it is now perceived as being far closer to the eye than the actual image plane. Secondly, the reflection appears to perform a remarkable belly-dance; like a flexible shaft, the axis of rotation is continuously distorted at the rhythm of rotation, such that the observer is presented with the concave side. The nearer the eye is brought to the cube, the more pronounced becomes the effect. It can easily be explained from the fact that the perceptual mechanism undergoes a change of interpretation of the retinal image of the wire cube outline, which consists only of black, unsubstantial lines and is therefore ambiguous with respect to front and rear. That is, parts of the cube reflection turned away from the eye are interpreted as being towards the eye, and *vice versa*. Those parts of the real image lying at the rear, but indicated by the perceptual mechanism as lying in front, undergo double size-reduction. There is first of all reduction which the retinal image actually undergoes because of increase in distance and secondly reduction invoked by the size-constancy mechanism which reduces any object in proportion to its closeness (pp. 300, 301).

If this particular miscarriage of Gestalt perception is described in ratiomorphic terms, it has almost the effect of a caricature of the process occurring only too frequently on a rational level in precipitate and uncritical hypothesizing. As a rapid conclusion, an extremely simple and 'elegant' hypothesis is formed, which makes do with the 'conceptually economical' assumption that there is one single axis and a single rotational direction. The data which this hypothesis is unable to incorporate are rendered acceptable by an extremely improbable and forceful 'supplementary hypothesis', which consists of the assumption that the inner cube loses its rigidity and becomes flexible and compressible like rubber. The false information, as with all perception, is accepted 'as true' and stubbornly upheld, just like a false assumption made by an uncritical maker of hypotheses.

This leads on to the second functional property of Gestalt perception which follows the 'significance tendency' as a second dangerous source of error; namely, its fundamental incorrigibility. The mechanism which is constructed to discover principles governing the sensory data, evidently obtains its information almost exclusively from the periphery. To my knowledge, the cases in which one can make the perceptual mechanism switch arbitrarily between two equally good 'hypotheses' provide the only examples for demonstrable influence exerted upon the perceptual mechanism by higher centres of the central nervous system. For this reason, erroneous information provided by the most complex and ratiomorphic forms of Gestalt perception is maintained just as incorrigibly as that of the simplest constancy mechanisms. However, whereas the perceiving person can easily become aware of the illusion with the latter mechanisms, with the highest functions of Gestalt perception their ratiomorphic character itself leads him to perform pseudo-rationalization and to believe that he has reached the result concerned not through subconscious perceptual processes but by means of rational consideration.

A. Bavelas, an information theorist and group psychologist, has reported an impressive case of this kind which actually occurred in a situation where Gestalt perception had been deliberately robbed of any regularity in the data, in order to demonstrate its 'built-in-noise'. Bavelas arranged for several experimental subjects to press a number of buttons in any order they liked under conditions where a sound-signal was produced at irregular time-intervals. The instruction given was that the subject should find out the principle in the series of buttons pressed which called forth the signal. The majority of the experimental subjects believed that they could perceive such a principle and went as far as constructing extremely complicated hypotheses. The subsequent disclosure that no principle was in fact operating met with strong resistance. One of the experimental subjects visited Bavelas a long time after conclusion of the experiments and attempted, with the aid of notes made during the experiments, to convince him that the apparatus providing the random distribution of the signals had not functioned properly and that, unbeknown to the experimental controller, the perceived regularity had, in fact, slipped into the experimental set-up.

The third great weakness of Gestalt perception, which does not in fact lead to actual false information as in the previously discussed functional peculiarities of exaggeration of significance and incorrigibility, lies in the great variability of its development in different human beings. People with a particular inclination towards Gestalt perception tend to look down upon those who are unable to see what they themselves perceive to be quite obvious, and who demand, quite justifiably, a rational verification. Those talented for rational and analytical thought, who seldom at the same time possess great powers of perception of complex Gestalts, regard somebody talented in this latter respect both as an irresponsible prattler, because they are unable to follow the path along which he reached his results, and also as uncritical, because he regards verification of what is perceived as unimportant.

Even if this difficulty in the way of mutual understanding can be easily overcome with a little insight into the nature of Gestalt perception, individual variability in the talent to perceive Gestalts still remains as a limitation on its scientific evaluation, if only because it cannot be taught and can scarcely be improved through learning and practice.

A fourth, intrinsically quite interesting, weakness of Gestalt perception is its vulnerability to introspection. Even if one simply directs attention to its functioning, the latter is considerably disrupted. One of my own experiences illustrates this effect. In my home region, in the summer one finds carrion crows but no rooks. The first rook which I saw flying at the beginning of the autumn transmigration always struck me instantly as such. I never mistook the flight silhouettes of the rooks and the carrion crows, although these differ in only minute proportional details. In every case, my diagnosis proved to be correct when the bird came closer and other characters became visible. By contrast, a conscious attempt to distinguish the flight silhouette gave judgements with a quite random distribution. Rationally controlled attention to perceived details evidently disrupts the equilibrium which must exist between them if they are to fall into place to give a unitary Gestalt. Unfortunately, this considerably hinders the scientific applicability of Gestalt perception.

In the respects so far considered (i.e. the tendency to exaggeration of significance, incorrigibility, unpredictable individual variation, and the fact that it can hardly be taught – if at all) Gestalt perception is distinctly inferior to functionally analogous rational processes. But it is superior to them in two important features.

Firstly, Gestalt perception can uncover an unsuspected regularity,[85] whereas the rational abstraction process is absolutely incapable of doing so. With the exception of some very modern computers, which are able to superimpose a large number of curves and to derive a principle operating in them all, we have no means – in particular, no rational process occurring in the central nervous system – which is able to discover inherent principles. It is always necessary to have a theoretical approach, i.e. a supposition about an inherent principle, before it is possible to verify it.

Secondly, as has been shown, Gestalt perception is able to take into account a greater number of individual details and more relationships between these than in any rational calculation. Even a correlation analysis based on an extremely broad statistical foundation is inferior to Gestalt perception in this respect. The machines mentioned above, which evaluate complex curves, only achieve approximately the same result as Gestalt perception within their narrow range of application. Goethe's statement 'One uses words to ill effect in the attempt to create Gestalts' is correct for the simple reason that it is impossible to maintain rational surveillance over all the data which would have to be passed on in the linear, temporal sequence of the spoken language. Above all, this surveillance can never be sufficient to grasp the innumerable, multidirectional relationships between the individual data. The obstacle involved is probably inadequacy of the memory. For example, if one reads in a zoological textbook the description of a bird, one is unable to 'picture' it mainly because one has already quite forgotten where (e.g.) a brown stripe was described when reading the description of a neighbouring body area. The fact that it is in principle possible to construct a Gestalt from the temporal sequence of individual data is evidenced by photo-telegraphy and television. Here, the transmission of information must take place so rapidly that the positive after-image assumes the task which overtakes our memory in a linguistic rendering.

Memory, which is unable to retain individual data and thus does not permit us to determine rational relationships between them, is remarkably capable of exactly retaining the reciprocal relationships, the 'configuration', of a large number of data over long periods of time, provided that it was the perceptual mechanism which had initially recorded these relationships. In this respect, memory performs veritable wonders, as can be illustrated with an example with which any doctor will be familiar. One may have seen on a single occasion, perhaps many years ago, a given complex of symptoms without consciously having perceived a particular Gestalt quality. On seeing the same complex a second time, it can happen that quite abruptly, from the depths of the subconscious, Gestalt perception will produce the unquestionable message: 'You have seen exactly this pattern of disease once before!'

It is, of course, this surprising feat of the memory in the fixation of Gestalts which permits Gestalt perception to accumulate such a rich hoard of factual material in the course of the years. In numbers of retained facts, it far exceeds any rational knowledge that a research worker may ever possess at a conscious, accessible level. At the same time, the scope of this subconscious knowledge affects the probability of correctness of perceptual information in just the same way as the breadth of an inductive basis influences the reliability of any rationally determined conclusion. In both cases, the probability of correctness is directly proportional to the scope of the factual basis.

The enormous treasure of facts accumulated by the perceptual mechanism plays in its ratiomorphic abstraction processes a rôle analogous to that played by the inductive basis in rational research, and its accumulation takes just as much time. This explains why the discoveries which great scientists make with the same object of research are sometimes spaced over many years. For example, Karl von Frisch published his first paper on bees in 1913; in 1920 he first described their ability to transfer information through dances; and in 1940 he discovered the orientational mechanism employing the position of the sun (which presupposes an 'internal chronometer') together with directional signalling in the hive, operating through transposition of the sun's direction to give a 'symbolic' vertical representation in the dances. Still later, in 1949, he discovered the amazing 'computing apparatus' which is capable of determining the sun's position from the polarization plane of light from the blue sky. However much bee-like activity – experimentation and conscientious verification – may underly these great discoveries of a prominent scientist, it is certainly no chance effect that they mainly emerged during his holidays, when he was using his own beehives at his summer residence. For one of the most pleasant properties of Gestalt perception lies in the fact that it is most active in collecting information when the perceiving person, lost in the beauty of the observed object, assumes that he is thoroughly relaxed intellectually.

VI Critical usage of Gestalt perception

In my opinion, every discovery of operating principles of any degree of complexity is fundamentally brought about by the function of Gestalt perception. This applies to all the natural sciences, and it also applies to mathematics – as is willingly admitted by mathematicians. Although, as has already been demonstrated, ratiomorphic and rational cognitive processes often exhibit extensive functional analogies and are often capable of mutual substitution, I regard Gestalt perception as irreplaceable in this particular function. But for this very reason, I regard it as extremely important that every research worker should be sufficiently well acquainted with the previously described functional properties of his own Gestalt perception in order to compensate its weaknesses with rational processes and to fully exploit its strengths.

The miscarriages resulting from the fact that the 'significance tendency' overshoots the target (p. 312) are particularly dangerous for those research workers who are most talented with an ability for perception of complex Gestalts. However, this danger can in fact be excluded to a great extent either by 'feeding' more and more information into one's own perceptual mechanism, or by giving the mechanism an opportunity to collect data from another 'point of view', e.g. in the perceptual illusion with the rotating wire cube discussed on p. 311, which can be destroyed by opening the other eye. In both cases, it is the perceptual mechanism itself which, on the basis of an expanded 'inductive basis', drops its own 'over-eager hypothesis'. Of course, one may not forget the fact that perception of an inherent principle, however convincing it may seem, does not represent a scientific truth until the entire arsenal of higher rational cognitive processes has mastered the difficult task of 'verifying' what the perceptual mechanism has discovered, or the even more difficult feat of identifying and tracing the process whereby the perceptual mechanism achieved its result. Finally, and most importantly, one must always remain aware that Gestalt perception is only an apparatus of discovery, that where its results contradict those of rational processes it is obligatory to believe the latter, and that in all aspects of verification quantification is decisive.

The second weakness of Gestalt perception – its stubborn incorrigibility – often makes it very difficult to comply with this latter requirement. It can subject the research worker to serious internal conflicts.

The third weakness of Gestalt perception, individual variation in its development and the impossibility of teaching in the proper sense of the the word, can be extensively overcome by increase in 'information', i.e. straightforward observation. What an observer is absolutely unable to see in an object the first twenty times is eventually seen on the two-hundredth occasion. In fact, the disadvantage often turns into an advantage in that somebody who is better talented for observing details and for analytical thought doubts the essentially correct perception of a totality-spotter and finally reaches, along a rational pathway, the verification which the latter would never have attained.

The fourth great weakness of Gestalt perception – the fact that it promptly goes on strike (p. 313 et seq.) when there is a rational attempt to influence its operation – necessitates a peculiar technique which one must learn, rather like practising yoga. In order to render this procedure understandable, I shall attempt to give a phenomenological account of the genesis of a Gestalt produced over a long period of years (p. 315 et seq.). The first sign that the Gestalt perception mechanism has 'caught wind of' some principle inherent in the processes just observed consists in the fact that, rather like a good bloodhound, it begins to 'tug at the lead' in a particular direction. This is manifested by means of its built-in ability to attach to certain stimulus combinations the quality of attraction and interest. This initially completely diffuse overall quality can, as stated, persist for many years as a wholly diffuse vague experience; but at the same time it has such a strong effect upon the entire emotional sphere that one is simply unable to escape from the observational object concerned. In this way, more and more information is automatically forced into the computing apparatus of complex Gestalt perception; something which one genuinely seems to feel. Step-by-step this leads to perception of individual relevant components of the Gestalt sought. It is, at least for me, incorrect to state that in these most complex cases of perceptual processes the Gestalt is determined before its components. Instead, one is first aware of the component complexes which will provide the structural basis for the overall entity, though one does not know the configuration in which they will combine to give the Gestalt. This is very clear in the description which Max Wertheimer gives of the cognitive steps which led Einstein to formulation of relativity theory.

This is the very phase in which one should *not* attempt to induce synthesis of the Gestalt by conscious experimentation with the components recognized as significant. Anyone inclined to introspection knows, for example, that in solving a word-puzzle one should never attempt to find the requisite sequence by permutation. In doing so, one becomes fixated upon one or more syllable-combinations and it is impossible to escape from these. Instead, one must keep one's eye on all of the syllables (components) in the same way, so-to-speak keeping them all free-floating and then make an effort in a quite specific, but barely describable, manner. The implied 'yoga exercise' simply consists in thus applying pressure to Gestalt perception without drifting into conscious contemplation, which would definitely hinder the search for a solution. Nobody who is convinced that all mental processes have a neurophysiological side to them should really wonder at the fact that Gestalt perception requires an energy-supply in order to perform its highest functions.

The subsequent, decisive step is the abrupt 'popping out' of the solution. It usually occurs quite unexpectedly and almost never whilst one is actually concerned with the problem. It is literally as if a messenger whom one had sent off with a particular request for information had returned with news of his success. C. F. von Weizsäcker, at an informal meeting of cybernetically-interested biologists, once gave a very illustrative description of this process, particularly with regard to the phenomenon whereby at the decisive moment one is absolutely certain of possession of the solution, but not yet aware of what it looks like. The accompanying experience is exactly comparable to that where the messenger hands over the expected notification of success, but in a sealed envelope.

Quite remarkable subjective experiences occur when Gestalt perception has produced two mutually incompatible 'hypotheses'; something which is not at all rare. As I unexpectedly saw the already-mentioned goose/swan hybrid and alternately perceived it as a goose and as a swan, this feeling struck me with an intensity bordering on nausea. However, this particular experiential quality emerges not only when – as in that case – two equally distinct Gestalts blatantly contradict one another, but also when a small minority of stored elements of information do not fit a 'hypothesis' which is able to arrange an overwhelming majority of data with disarming elegance. When this occurs, one is 'not quite at ease' with the prevailing interpretation, and a feeling of doubt arises – the ratiomorphic analogue of the rational process of doubt. In Wertheimer's report on his talk with Einstein, there are extremely convincing examples for this process as well. The 'yoga exercise' of critical application of Gestalt perception necessitates first and foremost (though I mention it last) the following achievement: One must learn to attune one's ear to the utmost for the warning which the perceptual mechanism gives us in the form of the above-described feeling of discomfort. Seductively elegant information which it gives us about the existence of complex principles can, under certain circumstances, be completely false. And when the mechanism makes us distrustful of its own information through this specific feeling, there is always something wrong about the information.

VII The rôle of Gestalt perception within the overall functional system of the human cognitive mechanism

The enormous diversity of opinion about the value, and even about the scientific legitimacy of Gestalt perception is undoubtedly largely based, apart from obvious cultural and philosophical factors, on the typological differences between research workers which lead them to enter different disciplines. The zoological or botanical phylogeneticist, the clinical practitioner and the human psychologist with a European background are probably most conscious of this value and make systematic use of it. At the other extreme are the died-in-the-wool behaviourists who deny that Gestalt perception – and thus observation of organisms in their natural environment – has any value or even any scientific character. An encouraging compromise between the two extremes is provided by research workers who in fact allow themselves to be involuntarily guided by their own Gestalt perception, but 'reject' it in the psychoanalytical sense and indignantly deny that this is the case.

Both extremes lead to erroneous epistemological approaches; the former frequently and the second always. Those who venerate their own intuition tend to underestimate the value of rational, particularly intuitive, cognitive processes. Their opinion is that 'Nature cannot be robbed of its veil in broad daylight; and what she does not reveal to your mind, you cannot prise loose with levers and screwdrivers' (Goethe). Thus, even the greatest of all Gestalt-spotters – J. W. Goethe – regards the fundamentalist researcher seeking after extension of the inductive basis and rational verification as the 'most unfortunate of all the sons of the Earth', who is 'always clinging to insipid facts, digging after treasures with a greedy hand, and glad enough to find earthworms'. The bard completely overlooks the fact that the object of his scorn is remarkably interested in earthworms and not in treasures; when he unearths the latter as a side-product of his digging, he usually leaves them unheeded for others to exploit.

Whereas the exaggerated veneration which Goethe lent to 'intuitive revelation' (his term for the functions of his own Gestalt perception) invites the criticism that it is very one-sided, the opinion at the opposite extreme, that all information provided by Gestalt perception is 'only subjective' and lacking in scientific value, is additionally marred by utterly incomprehensible epistemological illogicality. Quite obviously, it is not only information provided by Gestalt perception which is subjective; all cognitive processes are. The preceding epistemological considerations are enough to demonstrate the boundless naïvety of the opinion that perception only provides 'objective' information when used to read a measuring instrument.

In order to provide a correct illustration of the rôle played by our Gestalt perception in the framework of the systemic entity of all our cognitive processes, one would have to know more than I know about the function of rational processes. Therefore, I can only attempt to describe in very coarse outline the division of labour between ratiomorphic and rational processes. In doing this, I am aware of the fact that even a sharp distinction between these two types of processes is probably an artificial simplification of reality.

It is quite definitely a simplification of this kind to represent the interaction between the various cognitive processes, as I have done above, as if there were always a distinct separation between the prior discovery of an inherent principle through ratiomorphic processes and its subsequent verification through rational processes.

Presumably, any scientific discovery begins with the Gestalt perception mechanism drawing attention, in the diffuse manner described, to the presence of something awaiting discovery. However, this does not at all mean that Gestalt perception operates alone to define a Gestalt. It can occur that the mass of data superimposed on an inherent principle is so complicated and full of irregularities that it is impossible for Gestalt perception to extract the Gestalt from the background of accidental features. For this reason, rational, quantifying, statistical and surveying pre-treatment is necessary to permit Gestalt-formation. How often has it occurred that a scientist has first 'seen' a suspected principle in his graphs and diagrams or even in equations; and how often has it emerged that in these results of rational processes he has found a principle different from that which was first suspected?

It seems to me that there is a peculiarly close and direct functional relationship between the process of extensive quantification and that of Gestalt perception. When the mechanical excavator of our calculating apparatus permits coherent statements about concrete objects in the real external world, there is the obligatory precondition that the counted units should be the same as one another. However, the category of quantity is utterly unable to determine this fact – all quantification is, in this respect, dependent upon the objectivating processes of the constancy mechanisms and of Gestalt perception. This applies just as much when a schoolchild counting apples straightforwardly perceives the equivalence of the counted objects as when a physicist perceives the object constancy of his measuring instrument, which enables him to provide each shovel of his calculating machine with the same quantity of the concrete commodity to be measured. In the course of his phylogenetic and cultural evolution, man has counted objects through tens of thousands of years – natural units whose approximate equivalence was indicated by his perceptual mechanism before he arrived at the brilliant invention of measurement, which permitted him to divide a continuum into a number of equivalent objects.[86] The fact that the lower and phylogenetically older function of the perceptual mechanism provides the precondition for the more recent, higher function of quantification, indeed more-or-less contains the latter, is not at all surprising. This relationship frequently exists between lower, older and higher more recent processes in the central nervous system. Nevertheless, it is surprising that this fact is not generally regarded as evidence for the scientific legitimacy of Gestalt perception.

Within the long series of extremely varied processes leading from the mild suspicion of a principle discovered by Gestalt perception to the clear formulation of scientific knowledge, the mechanisms involved doubtless act in a quite irregular sequence, frequently simultaneously. Gestalt perception may intervene at a wide variety of points, in order to determine a regular relationship between other, rational components of the overall phenomenon; as is well known, one sees genuine Gestalts even in numbers or in equations. At other points, rational categories can be applied to complexes whose natural unity was first identified through Gestalt perception and not by any rational process, as for example in the above-cited case of counting of perceived objects, or when we ask whether a particular complex of symptoms, which has been perceived but not yet analysed, has a causal relationship with another, similar complex. The great variety in the interaction of different perceptual, conceptual and interpretational processes is evident just from the variety of pathways which can lead to the same element of knowledge.

In my view, it is only the beginning and the end of this pathway which are determined by the mechanisms of Gestalt perception. Two arguments support this assumption, though they cannot claim to be compulsive proofs – they are simply indications which one should not overlook. In the first place, at the instant where one finds the solution of a problem, whatever its complexity and however 'purely intellectual' it may be, there is exactly the same qualitatively unmistakable experience, which also occurs when, as a result of functioning of completely subconscious mechanisms of spatial orientation or of perception, the state of disorientation is abolished and 'with an audible click' gives way to an oriented condition. Bühler has fittingly referred to this as the 'Aha-experience'.

Secondly, however, the process of finding solutions is so absolutely inaccessible to introspection, as is so characteristic for the ratiomorphic processes of perception. The solution always comes as a surprise, as an illumination, which appears to enter our rational thought from elsewhere, from outside. It is well known that this is expressed in many formulations of non-scientific language. If one is unable to believe in a supernatural origin for such 'inspiration', then the most likely assumption would seem to be that it is the result of the highest evolved processes of our central nervous system with the closest analogy to rational thought – those of Gestalt perception.

My conclusion is that the perception of complex Gestalts is a completely indispensable component function in the overall system of all processes whose interaction constructs our persistently incomplete picture of extra-subjective reality. Thus, it is just as legitimate a source of scientific knowledge as any other process involved in this system. It is in fact, in any series of steps leading to such knowledge, the beginning and the end, the Alpha and the Omega. Though this is only in the quite literal sense, since between these two letters there is the entire alphabet of the other 'a priori' forms of our thought and visualization which must be used to write down the phenomena if we are to be able to read them as experiences.

VIII. Summary

The task of this paper is to show that among the functions involved in the overall operation of human knowledge, no single one – not even that of quantification – is predominant over any other. In the systemic entity of all cognitive processes, the perception of complex Gestalts plays a part which is not only scientifically legitimate, but utterly indispensable.

Do animals undergo subjective experience? (1963)

It may seem paradoxical that, for a lecture to technologists and the friends of the *Technische Hochschule*, I should select a theme concerning the boundary between behavioural physiology and psychology. The question is, in fact, just as impossible to answer, as the border between these two fields of knowledge is impossible to cross. However, it is a fact that behavioural physiologists are frequently more or less forced to employ concepts derived from technology when faced with the most complex nervous processes taking place at the highest level of integration (i.e. where the closest contact with psychology occurs). One of the four departments of the *Institut für Verhaltensphysiologie* (that led by Dr Horst Mittelstaedt) is concerned with biocybernetics, in other words with the control mechanisms of living organisms. Concepts from communication technology, particularly those relating to *information*, have become indispensable for an understanding of the functional operation of the central nervous system. It is no chance effect that a microscopic image or a schematic representation of nervous pathways and their connections is so strongly reminiscent of corresponding images of communications instrumentation, such as a telephone exchange.

Psychology concerns the study of subjective processes in experience; processes which one can only directly observe in oneself. In my opinion, the German term '*Psychologie*' should be restricted to this field and not – as is usual in America – be extended to include all branches of objective research into behaviour. For this semantic, pedantic reason, our Max-Planck-Institut in Seewiesen is labelled 'for behavioural physiology', and not 'for animal psychology'. But this by no means indicates that we are not interested in subjective processes.

The question representing the title of my lecture, 'Do animals undergo subjective experience?', is one which I am often asked to answer. The answer is: 'If I were able to give an answer, I would have solved the problem of body-and-mind.'

If I am walking along with a tame greylag goose which suddenly stretches, extends its neck and softly utters a harsh warning-call, I may say 'now it is alarmed'. However, this subjective abbreviation only means that the goose has perceived a flight-eliciting stimulus and that – in accordance with the principles of stimulus-summation – its threshold values for other flight-eliciting stimuli have been markedly lowered. If, at this very moment, there is nothing more than a Cockchafer suddenly flying past, the goose will take off and fly back to the lake (usually to my annoyance, since my aim is to conduct observations, filming or the like). In saying that the goose is alarmed, I am expressing the freely-admitted *belief* that subjective processes are taking place within the bird. We all believe that animals experience things; after all, we have animal protection laws and we do not unnecessarily cause pain to animals. However, the scientific content of my observation is restricted to the statement that a goose which behaves in the manner described is much more likely to fly away than usual. To use a neat definition given by Frank Fremont-Smith: scientific knowledge is anything which permits prediction.

My knowledge about the subjective experiences of my fellow men and my conviction that higher animals (such as a dog) also experience things are two quite closely related phenomena. They are *not* based on analogization, as has long been assumed by philosophers. One of the greatest achievements of my respected teacher, the late Karl Bühler, was the uneqivocal demonstration that the assumption of other human subjects with similar experience is an inescapable and compulsive train of thought. It is a genuine a priori necessity of thought and interpretation, which is just as evident as any axiom. Bühler therefore spoke of 'Du-Evidenz', the evidence of 'you'. This forms the basis of a remarkable illogicality in the experiential considerations of some great idealistic philosophers. On the one hand, they spurn the evidence of the senses and of perception as being of no account, and therefore regard the essence of existence as fundamentally unidentifiable; yet on the other they assume (in a manner which is actually quite unjustifiable from their own standpoint) that there are other, fellow subjects experiencing things in a similar fashion. This, despite the fact that they know about the existence of fellow subjects exclusively through their own, discounted sense-organs.

This is not to say that conclusions based on analogy are without any validity. Of course, the physiological-psychological parallelism or 'iso-morphy'[87] of processes which I objectively and subjectively observe in myself permits the conclusion that a fellow human being, whose physiological functions are analogous to my own, also experiences in a manner analogous to myself when subject to the same physiological events. When applied to animals, analogization is much less valid. The greater the difference in structure of sense-organs and nervous systems from that of my own, the greater will be the difference in functions. The nature of the accompanying experience is fundamentally inaccessible to me, and remains so even when an inescapable piece of evidence drives me to assume that my dog undergoes some kind of experience. The lower

we descend in the organic series, the greater the invalidity of analogization, and at low levels of organization, even the evidence of the 'you' is
muted. Even I can kill mussels without a trace of sympathetic feeling.

But there is another kind of analogization which possibly leads to
better established views about the subjective experience of animals. One
can ask oneself what nervous processes accompany subjective experience
in ourselves. It has long been known that this concerns only a few of the
many such processes. Many early psychologists and many philosophers
assumed as a self-evident fact that it is the most complex central nervous
processes, occurring at the highest level of integration, which are illuminated by subjective experience. One often hears and reads, for example
in the otherwise excellent textbook on animal psychology written by
Hempelmann, that certain simpler processes are 'still' explicable on a
purely physiological basis, whilst other, more complex, processes have
a psychological explanation. This corresponds with the idea that the
'soul' (so-called) occupies the summit of the pyramid of central nervous
processes, and that subjective experience accompanies central nervous
events only above a certain level of integration. Narrowly associated with
this idea is another one: that at these highest levels of nervous processes
the laws of causality are no longer completely valid, since psychological
factors exert a controlling or directive influence on physiological processes. As a result, a fundamental barrier is presented to research possibilities for both the mental and physical processes involved. Erich
von Holst, when explaining this fundamental and dangerous error in
experiential studies, always used to express himself by means of a
gesture: he held his hand out, flat and horizontal, in front of his forehead
and just above eye-level. On one occasion, as a famous German philosopher and teacher was giving a lecture at a philosophy congress in
Bremen, and was in the course of expressing this very error (though in
an extremely complex and cloaked manner), I wanted to see what
von Holst – sitting in another part of the lecture hall – thought about it.
He caught my glance and held his hand flat in the manner described . . .
but high above his head.

Another gesture which is common amongst us (the masonic greeting of
behavioural physiologists and good psychophysical parallelists) is that of
holding the hand flat and vertical between the eyes, so that one eye
gazes past the palm and the other past the back of the hand. In the first
place, this symbol indicates that the partition between the two great
incommensurables, physiological and psychological, is impermeable. In
other words, as Max Hartmann has said, the relationship between the
two is *alogical*. Secondly, the gesture indicates that the barrier does not
horizontally separate the lower from the higher, but that it is a vertical
division passing from the base to the apex through all living processes.

There are extremely simple nervous processes, in fact some which take place in the vegetative nervous system, which are accompanied by extremely intense experience. One only needs to think of the phenomena of sea-sickness and the various forms of sensuality. On the other hand, there are quite complex achievements, analogous in their function to the most difficult operations of logical and mathematical thought, (e.g. those of the computing apparatus involved in perception), which are not only performed subconsciously, but are even fundamentally inaccessible even to the greatest efforts of determined self-observation.

Thus, the parable involved in the expression of psychophysical 'parallelism' has its drawbacks like any other parable. It is true that everything involved in our experience has a correlate on the side of nervous physiological processes, but not everything which occurs within our nervous system reflects itself in subjective experience. *What* is reflected in our consciousness from all these internal processes depends upon quite different criteria, which can apply both to the most simple and to the most complex processes. In order to bring out the common characteristics of these criteria, I shall first attempt to portray a few extremely simple processes and a few very complex ones, in association with their accompanying experiential aspects.

As has already been said, there are simple nervous processes at the lowest level of integration which occur far out on the periphery of the human organism and yet which occupy our most central *Ego*, even to the extent of excluding all other contents. Sea-sickness and sensual lust have already been mentioned; *pain* is perhaps an even more impressive example. Wilhelm Busch says of pain: 'Toothache, subjectively considered, is doubtless unwelcome; but it has the good property that the life-force, which is often wasted on exterior things, turns towards an internal point and there becomes energetically concentrated.' And, at a later stage: '. . . it is only in the narrow cavity of the molar tooth that the soul finds its home.' It is impossible to give a more apt description of the matter! Apart from pain, whose most important function is obviously that of informing the higher centres of our nervous system *where* there is something out of order, there are many similar physiological mechanisms which are there for the sole purpose of letting us know *that* something is wrong. We feel ill without knowing the reason. The very fact that we have only one term, 'I feel ill,' for a range of conditions based on different causes is extremely characteristic. It appears that the vegetative nervous system has 'probes' (in the sense used in control technology) in a wide variety of homeostatic control systems, which sends the signal 'ill' to the governing centres whenever there is a departure from the biologically required optimal condition. However, these higher centres, whose functions are accompanied by experiences, take such signals extremely seriously; at least they are intensively concerned with them. When we are ill, we allow the experiences of the previous day to drift through the memory. In many cases, a clear-cut association abruptly falls into place. On thinking of the not quite fresh fish which I ate yesterday, I feel even more ill, and I resolve to be more careful than previously when eating fish in restaurants.

Such very simple nervous processes accompanied by experience almost always have the plus or minus sign of pleasure or displeasure and they have a positive or negative conditioning effect on the behaviour which produced them. 'That was good, do it again soon!' is the encouragement of pleasure; 'Leave that alone in future!' is the warning of displeasure. This is the subjective side of the process which Ivan Petrovitsch Pavlov has termed the 'conditioned reflex'. Such positive or negative conditioning mechanisms, prior to any individual learning, already incorporate phylogenetically acquired information. They 'know' in advance what is good and what is damaging for the continued existence of the organism. Yerkes, and many classical behaviourist psychologists along with him, were of the opinion that fulfilment of the requirements of a tissue has a positive conditioning effect. From a purely theoretical point of view, it is conceivable that the signal received by the higher centres simply reads: 'There is something wrong' and that trial-and-error behaviour of the organism has the task of finding out what must be undertaken in order to allay the unwell condition. But in reality, such incorporated learning mechanisms are always programmed on the basis of copious innate information. Signals indicating water-deficiency, hypoglycaemia or hypothermia in our tissues are not diffuse, unnamed feelings of disorder: they are referred to as thirst, hunger, freezing, and so on. An extremely common conditioning mechanism which Hull discovered rewards any behaviour which leads to relief of a previously existing state of tension. The innate information 'do what leads to relief of tension' in the vast majority of cases leads the organism to biologically correct behaviour, furthering the survival of the individual and of the species. There is only a single environmental situation in which this can be dangerous: poisons, such as alcohol and narcotics, also lead to relief of tension, and this acts as a powerful positive conditioning factor in consumption of these damaging substances.

In contrast to these very simple nervous processes, which are nevertheless accompanied by extremely intensive, central experience, there is at the end of a long series passing through all conceivable transitional stages, a range of highly complex processes which are performed without any emotional participation. In fact, as has already been stated, these processes are inaccessible to our introspection. The organization of our sense-organs and nervous system, which constructs perception on the basis of individual sensory data, frequently performs such complex calculations and logical deduction that the great Helmholtz was misled into regarding these achievements as 'subconscious conclusions'. If calculating machines constructed by human hand represent anything more than a model anywhere in biology, then it is in perceptual physiology.[88]

A good example for the functioning of such a computing apparatus is provided by the so-called constancy effects. I see this piece of paper as 'pure white' under a wide range of different lighting conditions – in the pronounced blue-dominant light of day, in the red-tinged evening light and beneath the yellow light of light-bulbs – although, in objective terms, the paper reflects utterly different wavelengths in each of these cases. This achievement is based upon a measuring and computing apparatus whose task it is to determine reflective properties which are constant attributes of the paper, rather than the prevailing colour lent by illumination. The 'subconscious conclusions' which are involved can be described in anthropomorphic terms in order to make them more easily understandable. The mechanism sets out with the 'hypothesis' that all objects located in the visual field together reflect all wavelengths of the spectrum equally in an overall average manner, without preference for a particular colour. It then measures the wavelengths in the entire visual field, extracts the average and takes this as the value predominating in the colour of the incident light. This colour is subsequently subtracted from the wavelengths which my piece of paper actually reflects and the apparatus then tells me directly which colour the paper *would* reflect if the illuminating light were 'pure white'. However, 'white' is nothing more than a value selected arbitrarily by the organization of this apparatus, and in fact it remarkably tends towards the short-wave end of the spectrum as compared to natural sunlight.

Despite the logicality of its 'conclusions', this computing apparatus sometimes produces erroneous results; namely, when the premise of its general hypothesis is inapplicable. In a case where a large number of objects in the visual field predominantly reflect one colour (e.g. red), the apparatus is taken in by this generally improbable situation, which was not 'foreseen' in the programme, and it 'assumes' that there is red illumination. Now if an object were to reflect a spectrum corresponding to the 'zero-colour' white, despite red illumination, it would necessarily have to reflect the complementary colour of red (i.e. green) more strongly than any other wavelengths. This is just what the computing apparatus erroneously 'believes' in the case quoted above, and it tells us that certain objects are green when they are not. This well-known illusion is referred to as *simultaneous contrast*. Very many so-called 'optical illusions' – in fact the majority – amount to analogous erroneous conclusions which are reached by our mechanisms for perceptual constancy under rare conditions not 'foreseen' in the programme.

The achievement of colour constancy in human beings, which has just been described in an anthropomorphic fashion, is actually reached in a much simpler manner. As is well known, calculating machines frequently operate much more simply than our mathematic operations. The apparatus, quite arbitrarily, divides the continuous spectrum into bands of colour and determines that certain (also arbitrarily selected) mixed proportions of these colours will be equal to zero, or white. White can be produced just as much by the admixture of two specific colour bands as through a homogeneous mixture of them all. Any two bands which combine to give white represent our so-called complementary colours. For the middle of the spectrum (yellow-green), a complementary colour is 'arbitrarily chosen'. This colour, like white, does not correspond to a specific wavelength but to a mixture of wavelengths, giving an 'artificial' complementary colour for yellow-green – our so-called *purple*. The incidence of any of these colours on a segment of the retina has the result that all other retinal areas indicate the complementary colour with an intensity which depends upon that of the genuinely incident light and the size of the affected retinal area. This mechanism, the *Farbenkreis* (*colour circle*) discovered by Wilhelm Ostwald, performs the very calculation which I have just described in anthropomorphic terms.

There are other computing systems involved in our perceptual functions. Many of them are far more complex than that discussed above, and accordingly one knows much less about their mechanisms. Just imagine the complexity of the stereometric operations which must be performed by my visual perception apparatus in achieving the following: When I turn my pipe backwards and forwards before my eyes, move it towards them and take it away again, this familiar object maintains a constant form and size. In other words, my perceptual apparatus is capable of correctly interpreting all form and size changes in the retinal image as *movements* and not as corresponding changes in form and size of the pipe! If the pipe really did suddenly draw in its stem or expand when brought towards my eyes (as the retinal image does through perspective shortening), I would doubtless drop it with an exclamation, for my perceptual apparatus would at once 'notice' that these alterations of the image cannot be explained through the stereometry of movement. We are far too used to these wonders of calculation to ponder upon them. One would have to fall into a really meditative mood in order to summon up the correct philosophical θαμμάζειν.

All of these computing systems function in a manner analogous to our rational thought. Egon Brunswik therefore referred to them as 'ratio-morphic', which expresses the fact that they are formally analogous to reason, but must not be equated with it. All of them, I emphasize once again, operate without conscious participation and in fact cannot be rendered conscious even by the greatest effort of will. This also applies to Gestalt perception and even to the most complex of all constancy phenomena, which incorporates many other effects such as the described functions of colour, size and form constancy – so-called object constancy. This mechanism permits objects in our subjective world to appear as uniform and recognizable entities. All such functions are *objectivating* in the literal sense of the word, since they extract properties adhering to the real object from the background of accidental perceptual conditions. They do not inform us of the enormous number of individual sensory data on which the information is based; nor do they indicate the manner in which the results are achieved. Classical Gestalt psychology gave rise to the maxim: 'The Gestalt is prior to its components,' which means that the overall result is first to penetrate to the conscious *Ego*. The small extent to which the component parts of the overall result can sometimes be consciously appreciated derives from an enquiry which follows the transmitted result in time. However, in the realm of physiological processes it is of course the individual peripheral elements of our sense-organs which respond first, and a period of time elapses (which is necessary for nervous conduction and response of the entire series of centripetal centres) before the integrated message arrives at the *Ego*.

My illustration for this process is a military one; though one can see from the mistakes that I make about rank that I am no militarist: Privates Meier, Müller and Schmidt have enteritis (stomach-ache). They report the fact; the corporal informs the sergeant-major, and the 'mother of the company', already taking notice of causes, informs the lieutenant that the kitchen has been using bad fat. Jumping a few steps, the message that the general receives from the battalion commander simply states that a petty officer has been demoted for buying cheap food and embezzling the difference in price. It would be quite useless to search for the individual, peripheral reports about the digestive upsets of the individual privates in the distilled, essential information transmitted to the general. These elements are no longer contained in the information, despite the fact that they provide the 'inductive basis' from which the transmitted information is derived.

Just as the general knows nothing about the sick soldiers, we know nothing (for example) about the data underlying human distance perception. The contractions of the convergence and accommodation musculature transmitted through so-called 'efference copies'[89] no more pass along the entire series of centres to the conscious level than does the absolute size of the retinal image, which is also involved in the calculation. When

I hold my spectacles before my eyes, the only information that I receive is: 'Here, and just here, are my spectacles.'

Afferent transmission of information from lower to higher centres must necessarily be organized such that a lower centre always receives *more* individual data than it passes on to the next higher centre. The competence of each centre rests in the function of analysing (with its own sector of 'responsibility') the reports which it receives, extracting those which are important for the organism as a whole, and passing on a simplified, but more meaningful, message. The organization of transmission of orders resembles in many ways that of afference. If, standing here on the right side of the speaker's rostrum, I wish to return to my notes, I simply give the impulse to do so. I do not give detailed commands to my left leg to lift the foot from the floor by innervation of the hip-rotating and knee-joint bending muscles, and to the right leg to turn my body to the left by contraction of the external rotating musculature, and so on. I leave the details of the performance to my able peripheral centres. These perform their duty best when one does not interfere with their activity. For this, too, I can provide a parallel – though this time a non-military one. The art of being a good departmental director consists in finding co-workers who are all more capable in their more restricted and more specialized fields than the director. This must in fact be the case even when one has oneself taught an individual to fulfil the tasks concerned. What Mephisto says of the art of sorcery applies very aptly here: 'The devil has indeed taught the art, but the devil alone cannot practise it.' Exactly the same applies to the relationship between our voluntary and commanding *Ego* and the motor centres which transform the commands into action. Not only innate patterns, but also motor patterns learnt consciously and quite intentionally, are performed better and more smoothly when the *Ego* does not interfere in their performance. The Austrian author Gustav Meyrinck has portrayed the disruptive operation of the watchful *Ego* in an extremely amusing, satirical pseudo-Indian fable: a millipede is walking along with wondrous co-ordination of his 500 left and 500 right legs when he is met by a malicious toad. The toad looks at the millipede for a while and says: 'Oh most worthy and many-footed millipede, pray allow a humble four-footed being to pose a question: How do you actually manage to raise the 357th foot, whilst just replacing the 358th, and so on?' Thereupon, the millipede is rooted to the spot and is unable to move one step further. A very similar situation can arise when, for example, a clinical director suddenly feels it is necessary to intervene in the well-co-ordinated and smooth-running functions of his subordinates.

The analogy between the conscious Ego and an organization composed of many human beings is much more remarkable than one at first realizes. Once again, this is one of those far-from-obvious self-evident facts which we only too easily forget to marvel at. It poses a number of questions which are perhaps fundamentally unanswerable, but nevertheless very stimulating. Why on earth are there such narrow limits on our consciousness? Why must our consciousness, just like the brain of a commander, rely upon subordinate components which provide from the afferent side 'premasticated', simplifying reports which have been sieved to leave only the most essential information? And why, on the efferent side, can it only transmit very general, equally simple, commands to the subordinate centres, which independently calculate the practical details and transform them into action? After all, all of this takes place in *one* central nervous system, in the most cohesive organ which we know of, and we know that within this system both the very simplest and the most complex processes can be accompanied by emotional experience. So why not all together? Why is our *Ego* so small?

You have just heard me employing the terms 'afferent' (conducting towards) and 'efferent' (conducting away). Leading towards who or what? Leading away from where? We know quite well where the inward conduction originates from and equally well where the outward conduction leads. But what lies between the two? You may know that early neurophysiologists imagined that the processes in the brain were centralized and localized in centres. The opinion was that all inward-coming messages passed to a specific site, which (somewhat like a good civil servant with a well-defined area of operation) makes a decision about the incoming messages, partly takes its own action and partly sends on a report to a director. This opinion in fact incorporates a grain of the assumption of a horizontal boundary between what is 'still' physiological and what is 'already' psychological. The idea of a 'centre' really includes an embryonic assumption that there is a particle of 'the soul' sitting inside it, which 'knows' what it has to do without there being any need for a causal explanation of this knowledge. However, as true psychophysical parallelists, we must ask what physiological apparatus is sitting there, since – in order to fulfil its function – it should really be an entire human being.

With the march of progress in our knowledge of neurophysiology, not much has survived of the theory of centres. Genuine, localized centres with the type of function originally pictured exist only for relatively simple operations, such as that of breathing or that for certain stimulus-production processes (e.g. those evoking the heart-beat). Nevertheless, the theory of centres incorporates a certain amount of truth which coincides with that which may also be attributed, after critical analysis, to the belief in a 'horizontal' barrier between physiological and psychological processes.

Certainly, the nervous structures underlying holistic and functionally cohesive functions are hardly ever banded together in one locality. Equally certainly, the pathway of components, which begins at the sense-organ and conducts 'centripetally', passes in a smooth transition into the other pathway conducting 'centrifugally' and terminating in a motor or secretory effector organ. It is also certain that, over the whole trajectory of this process of excitation-transfer, one can never say: 'Here is the centre; here all the threads run together.' For this reason, our Institute jargon has gradually incorporated, in the place of the terms 'afferent' and 'efferent', the expressions 'in the stimulus upcurrent' and 'in the stimulus downcurrent'. All the same, this stimulus current is centralized in a certain sense: many threads run together and unite. They therefore decrease in number in the stimulus downcurrent from the sense-organ until, on the other side, they begin to branch, increase in number and finally terminate in an enormous number of effector components. The region of the system in which the messages pass along the smallest number of conducting fibres (i.e. the area where the individual elements of information are most decisive and least numerous) is quite certainly the site where nervous functions are most clearly associated with subjective experience. One cannot talk of centres, but one can refer to a 'most central' sector of nervous processes. The latter is itself not hierarchically organized, and certain forms of the field theory probably bring us far closer to an understanding of its workings than did the old idea of centres. But, as a whole, this sector behaves with respect to the peripherally situated components on both sides (i.e. upstream and downstream) exactly like a centre. In this, the most confined and least ramifying, region of the information-transfer system is the seat of our experience, and its behaviour is remarkably similar to that of a spider in its web. Like the latter, it does not remain still at one point, but moves to any area where there is something out of order or something to fetch. It can be despairingly concentrated in the narrow cavity of a molar tooth or happily given over to the enjoyment of equally peripheral processes. Just as the spider has only eight legs, but a far greater number of threads in its web, our *Ego* can (strangely) only summon up a minute section of the range of central nervous processes at any given time. For this reason, it is *unable* to concern itself with too many details, and it seems a reasonable – if speculative – assumption that the most central components, in order to maintain their versatility and plasticity, must be shielded from a too specialized knowledge of the details. Of course, this does not at all answer the question posed previously ('Why are we unable to experience everything at once?'). Like the overworked director in an old Jewish joke from Vienna, we can only exclaim: 'Do you think I am a bird, able to be in two places at once?'

I, as a soul in my own body and as director in my department of the Institute, 'become involved' in three typical cases: When there is a particularly important decision to make, when something has gone wrong, and – finally – (thank God) when there is something very pleasant to report. The message of displeasure ('that was wrong') and of pleasure ('do it like that again') are probably the most powerful generalized and abbreviated pieces of information contained in our *Ego*. The 'ability to experience pleasure and sorrow', as Wilhelm Busch so aptly says, is doubtless the primaeval form of experience. And this is exactly what I feel can be attributed to higher animals. Such an assumption is not based exclusively on conclusion through analogy utilizing the fact that reward and punishment have the same positive and negative conditioning effects as in man. A more conclusive piece of evidence is the observation that very many higher animals exhibit motor and vocal display patterns which do not express a special kind of pleasurable or unpleasant experience, but indicate pleasure or displeasure in general. One can at once see that a dog is sad, but not why this is the case. With a young greylag goose, the discontentment call (which we usually refer to briefly as 'crying', and which alarms the mother goose) can be heard in exactly the same form when it has lost its parents, when it is hungry, when it is cold, or when it wishes to crawl beneath the parent and go to sleep. In brief, the call is given in all unpleasant situations. It will, for example, be uttered even after fledging by a goose which is not yet independent of its parents, when it has fallen through thin ice on the lake and cannot get out. The goose does not readily hit upon the solution of *flying* out of its predicament. On one occasion, an amusing experience with a very tame young Snow goose provided me with some extremely convincing evidence of the 'you' that such a bird also possesses the generalizing negative experience of displeasure. The goose had been greatly spoilt in order to ensure that it would be as closely attached to me as possible. Every day, as I went down to the lake, I used to take it a handful of wheat. On one occasion, the wheat was exhausted, and I had taken along oats as a substitute. The goose – whose name, characteristically enough, was 'Little Princess' – delightedly flew up to me from some distance away. It was just about to pick greedily at the grain when it noticed that it was not wheat, but oats. 'Little Princess' began to cry loudly and heartbreakingly, just like a small child whose doll has been taken away. In such a situation, one automatically feels that an animal really experiences things. My teacher Heinroth, the grandfather of objectivized behavioural research, was often reproached with the criticism that he treated an animal like a machine with respect to its physiological processes. He often used to reply: 'On the contrary, animals are emotional people with very little ability to reason.'

The important decisions requiring the presence of the director always arise when two relatively high-ranking subordinates differ in opinion. Conflicts between the most subordinate centres are solved, either through compromise or through one of them maintaining his opinion, without any report of such activities penetrating through to our *Ego*. I believe it was Henri Bergson who was the first to point out that instinctive behaviour patterns are sometimes performed without the associated emotion, in fact without any conscious participation at all, as long as there is no other motivational factor in the way. Fleeing (fear behaviour) is not necessarily attached to the emotion of fear for oneself. If, whilst I am crossing a street, a careless car-driver forces me to make a number of rapid escape leaps, I do not at all have a sense of fear. If, on the other hand, a small child has fallen over in the middle of the street, and in trying to save it I must expose myself to the rapid approach of a bus much closer than I would in the absence of this second behavioural impulse opposing escape, *then* I have a sense of fear.

All that I have told you so far about the manner in which my own experience is located in a specific area of nervous activity – at the narrowest point of the converging and subsequently diverging current of excitation – and how it can move around to various places, sometimes far out into the periphery, as far as the cavity of a molar tooth; all that is good, descriptive science, like any communication of unprejudiced observation. Since it is *self*-observation which is involved, I cannot really know whether it is the same for all of you. But your repeated laughter strengthens my conviction, which is in any case automatically dictated by the concept of evidence of 'you'. I am also encouraged by your persistent and benevolent attentiveness, in the belief that these relationships are not simply of great interest to myself. However, in concluding, I do want to ensure that you do not believe me to think that I have solved any problems through these considerations. Unfortunately, quite the opposite is the case: the riddle of the relationship between body and soul is only rendered more paradoxical by the facts I have outlined.

Every one of the nervous functions which can have an emotional aspect, can also occur without any experiential component. The plus and minus values, which are determined by reward and punishment as conditioning mechanisms attached to all learning processes occurring in given stimulus situations, can easily be imitated with an electronic machine, as Grey-Walter has demonstrated with his wonderful models. And in human beings, too, they can function without any experiences, without the correlates of pleasure and displeasure. As the control technologists among you know, one can also arrange for machines to perform another process very frequently associated with experiential factors – the making of decisions. We are also aware of this function of decision-making in subordinate components of the central nervous system which are not accessible to our consciousness. For example, when our apparatus for form-perception is confronted with a range of information permitting two equally probable interpretations, our *Ego* is told nothing about its uncertainty; the mechanism 'decides' upon one of the two possible interpretations and stubbornly reports only the one. When we observe the silhouette of a rotating object, our computing apparatus can only definitely state that the object is turning; it cannot say whether it is to the left or to the right. Nevertheless, the apparatus reports that the image is quite definitely turning in a given direction. However, when we send back a forceful enquiry, the apparatus some-times becomes uncertain and suddenly maintains the opposite of what it had previously reported, like a school child who has guessed the wrong answer to a question. The observed rotation direction of the silhouette is thus abruptly reversed. A perspective drawing of the edges of a cube located somewhat obliquely in space can be so interpreted that one might be looking at the upper or the lower of the almost horizontal surfaces. Some people are unable to rid themselves of the impression which is produced first and to see the second interpretation; other people can voluntarily make the two possible interpretations interchange.

Inclination and disinclination can also arise without subjective experi-ence of reward and punishment. Decisions can be made and conclusions can be drawn without any subjective experience occurring in parallel with the nervous processes responsible for these achievements. Why, then, must my *Ego* suffer so that my organism will avoid that particular control-disrupting situation next time? Why is our subjective experience drawn in each time there is an important decision to be made? Since a part of nervous physiological phenomena can occur without experience, why should this not apply to all nervous processes? Conversely, if a proportion of nervous processes is experienced by our *Ego*, why cannot the whole functional system of well-integrated processes provide the content of our experience? Above all, why is it that only a tiny propor-tion of all the processes fundamentally open to experience can be lit up in the confined chamber of our experience at any one time?

It is possible, in fact probable, that most of these questions are intrinsically unanswerable. But even if a scientific answer could be found for one or the other of them, we would not be a hair's breadth closer to solution of the Body-Mind-Problem. As Max Hartmann (in agreement with Nikolai Hartmann) has stated, the relationship between physiological and psychological processes – despite the undeniable occurrence of parallelism and isomorphism – is fundamentally *alogical*. However, although convinced of this experiential fact, many behavioural physiologists and neurophysiologists who are capable of philosophical introspection, cannot restrain themselves from pondering on this, the greatest problem of all. In fact, the choice of their scientific research object is greatly influenced by this interest. They concern themselves with processes which have these two incommensurable sides – one which can be investigated physiologically, and one open to introspection. It is a fine and noble thing that the thinking man is unable to fold his hands idly in his lap even when confronted with insoluble problems. In Goethe's *Faust*, Mantho says, 'My affection goes to him who demands the impossible,' whilst Mephisto says, 'Oh, believe me, those who chew a thousand years on this tough fare; no man can digest this old sourdough between the cradle and the tomb.' One can justifiably set a statement of a great German biologist alongside these quotations from the greatest masterpiece of our greatest bard. Many years ago, Alfred Kühn made a speech to the Austrian Academy of Science and closed with a quotation from Goethe: 'The greatest happiness in human thought is reached when the investigable has been investigated and the non-investigable is calmly worshipped.' He then started nervously, and drowned the rising applause with the sharply uttered words: 'No, not *calmly* . . . *not* calmly, gentlemen.'

Notes

1   *P. 1.* This paper was addressed, in 1963, to the freshmen of the Medical School at the University of Colorado. Much of what is said in it will reappear in a more extensive form in other papers included in this collection. In fact, the little paper might almost be regarded as an abstract of the rest. As I have said in the introduction, a large number of repetitions will be inflicted on the reader. I only hope that the different connections in which some all-important facts will keep reappearing will provide some consolation. Also, the clearness of exposition does, I hope, increase somewhat with each repetition.

2   *P. 14.* This 'systematic intuition' was the first guise in which I encountered Gestalt perception as a source of knowledge, though not yet realizing its great importance.

3   *P. 19.* The genera *Poecilonetta, Dafila, Nettion, Virago, Chaulelasmus, Mareca, Querquedula* and *Spatula* have all been lumped by Mayr and Delacour into the one genus *Anas*. I object to this lumping because it could only be done without loss of information if quite a number of species were correspondingly demoted to subspecies.

4   *P. 20.* Convergent evolution does, however, occur even in signals, Peter Marler has shown that the warning calls, better 'mobbing calls', of many species of song birds have evolved convergently under the selection pressure of interspecific co-operation.

5   *P. 21.* The word 'schema', meaning sketch or diagram, was later dropped by us, because it implies something like a simplified picture, which again makes it seem too closely related to Gestalt perception.

6   *P. 21.* The adjective 'symbolic' is not quite correct in connection with innate motor patterns, as the word symbol has a very definite connotation in cultural history. The analogy, however, is plain.

7   *P. 23.* General arousal as an independent parameter of behaviour was demonstrated in ethological research only in recent years by Anne Rasa. Connecting it with the phenomenon of displacement activity was at the time of writing this, slightly prophetic.

8   *P. 26.* Curiously enough, the ducks and geese themselves seemed to agree with this hypothesis. Mallards whose social responses Dr Schutz succeeded in imprinting on geese (and vice versa) regularly joined in mutual displays in which the geese gave their triumph ceremonies while the mallard drakes indulged in a frenzy of 'raebraeb' palaver.

338

9   *P. 30.* It must be remembered that C. Waddington's great discovery, that modifiability can be selected for, was unknown to me at the time of writing this.

10   *P. 33.* It is a very difficult question whether a gradual rise of intensity, as shown by a series of movements, is the effect of self-stimulation or not. The conclusion seems justified only when 'inertia' of response, a so-called 'warming up' effect, is clearly demonstrable.

11   *P. 35.* Much later we found that the shaking movement is invariably preceded by a tail-waggle, while the grunt-whistle is *followed* by one. If a drake in the introductory posture begins to tail-waggle, one knows that only a shake and not a grunt-whistle will follow.

12   *P. 35.* It is not true that the grunt-whistle is entirely absent in the Bahama pintail, it is only very rare. As D. Kaltenhäuser has demonstrated, the grunt-whistle is potentially and genetically present in all species of surface-feeding ducks, with the exception of the blue-winged group.

13   *P. 36.* U. Weidmann has demonstrated that the grunt-whistle is activated at a lower threshold of specific excitation than the down-up and the head-up-tail-up movement. The former occurs when aggressive motivation is predominant, head-up-tail-up when sexual motivation is.

14   *P. 40.* It was a complete error to homologise this motor pattern of the Bahama duck with the head-up-tail-up, which it superficially resembles. The motor pattern really can be shown to be an exaggerated down-up movement. In the common teal, the same motor pattern exists together with a real head-up-tail-up and is distinctly different from it. See also page 51.

15   *P. 44. Anas rubripes* drakes also nod-swim without prior performance of the head-up-tail-up movement.

16   *P. 50.* It is an error to homologise the raeb-call and burping. In the gadwall, both occur side-by-side.

17   *P. 55.* See note 12, page 35.

18   *P. 58.* Here again the homologisation is wrong, as in *bahamensis* the movement is actually a down-up.

19   *P. 60.* It would be interesting to know more about this species, because otherwise the blue-winged group and all other surface-feeding ducks are clearly separated, as D. Kaltenhäuser has demonstrated through her investigation of hybrids.

20   *P. 79.* It seems retrospectively incredible that I overlooked the down-up movement of the common teals. It resembles that of the Bahama duck, though it is less exaggerated.

21   *P. 94.* Characteristically, the grunt-whistle of all widgeon mallard hybrids is complete, and as well developed as in mallard itself. Hybrids between the mallard group and blue-winged ducks like spoonbills, garganeys etc. show an underdeveloped, incomplete form of grunt-whistle, just like the hybrids between the mallard group and diving ducks. Hence the conclusions of D. Kaltenhäuser already mentioned in 12.

22   *P. 116.* This assumption is often made with regard to the organic entity
     represented by human cultural society. If, as many ethnological anthro-
     pologists tend to assume, human behaviour contained no genetically
     determined elements, in other words if it were entirely formed by cul-
     tural tradition, this procedure of equating the concepts of Gestalts
     on one side and of human social entities on the other would be legitimate.
     However, I shall come back later to the source of error which lies in the
     neglect of phylogenetically programmed norms of behaviour.

23   *P. 117.* The emphatic denial of the very existence of this kind of structure
     in man himself is, of course, one of the fundamental dogmas of the
     pseudo-democratic doctrine.

24   *P. 119.* See also the paper 'Inductive and Teleological Psychology'
     included as the last paper in the first volume.

25   *P. 126.* See also quotation from D. E. Lehrman in the Introduction.

26   *P. 130.* It must be remembered that the field of molecular genetics was
     as yet unknown at the time when this was written.

27   *P. 131.* Some necessary qualifications of this rather simplistic representa-
     tion of inductive procedure are to be found in the paper 'Gestalt percep-
     tion as a Source of Scientific Knowledge', page 281.

28   *P. 134.* Spontaneity of aggression has been conclusively demonstrated
     by Eibl-Eibesfeldt, Anne Rasa and others in some animals. Whether it is
     a spontaneous drive in man, as I myself and also all psychoanalysts
     assume, is still controversial. In fact it is an interesting question why
     aggression and other activities of avoidance are not purely reactive as, in
     regard to the requirements of their function they could well be. It
     simply is a physiological fact that 'pure reactions' in the sense of classical
     reflex theory seem to become rarer and rarer as our knowledge pro-
     gresses.

29   *P. 135.* In more modern investigations the frequency with which a
     certain response occurs has also been used as a measure with which to
     quantify the efficacy of a stimulus-combination.

30   *P. 138.* Seitz quantified the effect of stimulation exclusively by the
     intensity of the response elicited. His data do not preclude the possibility
     of one sign stimulus exerting a multiplicative effect upon another.
     However, Seitz was perfectly correct in assuming a summation of sign
     stimuli, as recent investigations by D. Leong and W. Heiligenberg have
     conclusively shown.

31   *P. 144.* There are, however, some rare cases in which signals have evolved
     convergently in several species. These cases provide the typical kind of
     exception that proves the rule. One example, pointed out by Peter
     Marler, is that of the mobbing calls of some European song bird species,
     which co-operate in attacking owls and other small predators.

32   *P. 146.* For several reasons, not least of them the priority of Sir Julian
     Huxley's discussion of the phenomenon, we now prefer to speak of
     ritualization rather than of 'formalization'.

32a *P. 147.* The difference between the responses of the stickleback and of
     Astatotilapia strigigena are not quite as fundamental as here described.

W. Schleidt has demonstrated that in practically all higher animals the innate releasing mechanism is rendered more selective to varying degrees by additional conditioning.

33 *P. 148.* Rational responsibility is not the only unique property of man, the cumulation of tradition which leads to culture actually provides man with the faculty of inheriting acquired characters. This unique biological property of man is often forgotten and should have been mentioned here.

34 *P. 151.* The existence of this submissive gesture has been doubted by R. Schenkel and E. Zimen. It is always dangerous to assert that a motor pattern *does not* exist in a certain species. H. and J. van Lawick-Goodall and P. de la Fuente have amply confirmed my observations.

35 *P. 152.* As Tinbergen has pointed out, the primary gesture of appeasement very probably was a turning away of the weapon. That, at the same time, the proffering of a vulnerable spot has acquired a signal function in its own right, is borne out by the fact that in many cases special morphological structures or colour markings have evolved in that place as, for example, in the young of the water rail, *Rallus aquaticus,* and the kittiwake, *Rissa tridactyla.*

36 *P. 162.* This statement is only true regarding long and obligatorily linked chains of motor patterns. As P. Leyhausen has pointed out, the higher development of mental faculties in mammals and man was not correlated with a reduction of instinctive patterns of behaviour, but rather with their fragmentation into many smaller and independently disposable parts.

37 *P. 163.* It was Bernhard Hellman who, at the age of seventeen, resorted to this means in order to 'discharge', in a male of *Geophagus brasiliensis,* the accumulated aggressive drive before offering to it a female which the fish then at once accepted and courted. Hellmann may be regarded as the first man to realize the fact that aggressive behaviour patterns accumulate when not released. Anne Rasa (in press: *Zeitschrift für Tierpsychologie*) has demonstrated the same by quantitative methods in *Microspatodon chrysurus.*

38 *P. 172.* On maturer consideration, twenty years after writing this, I doubt the necessity of this cautious qualification. The close interaction and the far-reaching analogies between instinctive and culturally determined norms of behaviour notwithstanding, I am quite convinced that, at the very root of every emotional value judgement, an innate releasing mechanism lies concealed.

39 *P. 174.* I would add to this statement concerning exploratory behaviour that, on its basis, self-exploration developed as the first step to conceptual thinking. The latter, in its complicated integration with tradition, has given rise to syntactic language and, along with this, to all the wonders of accumulated collective knowledge, in other words to culture.

40 *P. 176.* Monika Holzapfel, in her highly important papers on play, has formulated with extreme lucidity the problems here under discussion. In order to explain the fact that the animal is able to try out, in quick

succession and in the same situation, practically all the motor patterns
at its disposal, a common and independent motivation must be assumed
which is able to activate all of them indiscriminately. Play is physiologically akin to displacement activity in so far as a motor pattern is
'allochthonously' activated by a motivation other than the normal one.

41   *P. 178.* A. Kortlandt has developed the interesting hypothesis that the
chimpanzee had, at a time, progressed to far more human forms of
behaviour than those which it shows today, and that it led a far less
aboreal life. In Kortlandt's opinion a secondary 'dehumanization' process was caused by the competition of early human beings, who drove
the chimpanzee back into the forest.

42   *P. 181.* Erik Zimen has demonstrated this by a very thorough comparative
study of the ontogenetic development of social behaviour in wolves on
one hand and in poodles on the other.

43   *P. 182.* What I had not yet quite realized at the time of writing this, was
that this 'headlong development' is caused by the accumulation of
tradition, which is practically equivalent to the inheritance of acquired
characters.

44   *P. 189.* Translation of Immanuel Kant's famous sentence 'Zwei Dinge
sind es, die das menschliche Gemüt mit immer wiederkehrender neuer
Bewunderung erfüllen, der gestirnte Himmel über mir und das moralische
Gesetz in mir.'

45   *P. 197.* I am happy to say that this statement is definitely outdated now,
sixteen years after it was made.

46   *P. 197.* The reader who is more particularly interested in Gestalt-
perception for its own sake may skip what follows and concentrate on
the paper 'Gestalt perception as a Source of Scientific Knowledge' page
281. See also comment 2 on page 14.

47   *P. 206.* See note 30, page 138. Re-reading these pages, I find that they
might give the erroneous impression that, by the procedure of double
quantification, all intervening variables are taken into account, which, of
course, is not the case. A highly important independent parameter,
general arousal, was recently demonstrated by Anne Rasa in the paper
already mentioned. (Note 37 on p. 163.)

48   *P. 207.* Heinroth's excellent German term 'Imponiergehaben' is difficult
to translate into English, except, perhaps, by 'demonstrative behaviour'.
This does to some extent indicate the dual function of intimidating any
rival of the same sex, and attracting a partner of the opposite sex.

49   *P. 208.* At the time of writing Erich von Holst had not yet performed
his now classic experiments of brain-stem stimulation in chickens. They
agreed with, and confirmed, the assumption of a hierarchical organization of instinct even more convincingly than do those of W. R. Hess.

50   *P. 211.* See note 31, page 144.

51   *P. 212.* Later and more thorough analysis revealed that these motor
patterns are actually derived from nest building and not from eating.

52   *P. 213.* The term *displacement activity* (German: Übersprungsbewegung)
has the one drawback that the term 'displacement' has its own connota-

tion in psychoanalysis, where it is used as the English translation of Sigmund Freud's term 'Verdrängung'. Taken in itself, however, 'displacement activity', meaning a motor pattern performed in a biologically inappropriate situation, is sufficiently different from the term 'displacement response', meaning a reaction to a substitute stimulus situation, in other words response to an inadequate object.

53 *P. 213.* P. Sevenster and A. Bol have since advanced another theory, and quite lately A. Rasa, in her study of general arousal as an independent parameter, has further modified our views on the causation of displacement activity.

54 *P. 214.* This has been thoroughly confirmed by G. P. Baerends in his paper on ritualization.

55 *P. 216.* This programme has since been carried out in our department by W. von de Wall and D. Kaltenhäuser, both working on duck-hybrids, and also by Sybille von Hörmann, working on crickets.

56 *P 216* Repeated misunderstandings have made me realize the necessity of emphasizing, at this point, that I am speaking not of the unique and species-specific properties of man (such as rational responsibility and accumulating tradition), but merely of the prerequisites on the basis of which these achievements have become possible.

57 *P. 222.* This was a Russian film made at the behaviour laboratory in Suchum on the Black Sea.

58 *P. 228.* The absence of an activity-specific tension makes it necessary to postulate a special source of motivation activating all kinds of motor patterns, as pointed out by Monika Holzapfel; see note 40, page 176.

59 *P. 230.* See note 41, page 178 on A. Kortlandt's 'dehumanization' theory.

60 *P. 238.* We can now venture a tentative answer to this question. As Jacques Monod has pointed out, in a paper read at the Nobel Symposium in autumn 1969 in Stockholm, it was indubitably the selection pressure of accumulating tradition which caused the rapid growth of the human telencephalon.

61 *P. 240.* It is sad to realize that it is even more necessary today to emphasize the necessity of simple description than it was at the time of my writing this. See also the paper 'Gestalt perception as a Source of Scientific Knowledge', page 281.

62 *P. 240.* A good number of analogous papers have been added since, outstanding among which is the comparative study of fiddler crab species all over the world by Jocelyn Crane.

63 *P. 242.* A more exact rendering of the relationship of mutual interdependence existing between more basic and more specialized sciences is to be found in my paper 'Innate Bases of Learning'.

64 *P. 243.* These are hard words! As to the positive merits of the schools here criticized see the next paper page 246.

65 *P. 244.* Again I want to emphasize that even at the time of writing I did not forget man's unique faculty of accumulating tradition.

66 *P. 247.* See also Introduction. The error here described is, however, not quite identical with that of atomism, but considerably worse.

67   *P. 253.* It has been suggested, by some critics, that these processes
     might still be identical with reasoning, though performed at a sub-
     conscious level. The answer to this is that I should indeed wish I were
     endowed with the mathematical prowess which would be necessary to
     achieve, rationally, all those feats which is easily performed in the
     achievement of form constancy (for one) in every normal five-year-old.

68   *P. 254.* Paul Weiss, in some of his writings, has used 'forms of visualiza-
     tion' rather than the generally accepted English translation, for Im-
     manuel Kant's word 'Anschauungsformen', the term 'forms of
     ideation'. In my opinion, Paul Weiss's term is not only more intelligible
     but actually the better translation by far. It also permits translation of
     'anschaulich' with 'visualizable'. Even the substantive 'visualizability'
     for 'Anschaulichkeit', though difficult to pronounce, is easy to under-
     stand.

69   *P. 259.* At least some of my critics accuse me, very unjustly, of thinking
     so.

70   *P. 263.* The fact that 'finalism' as here discussed is a particular form of
     vitalism, and a fallacy, does not preclude that 'finality' in the sense of
     purposiveness is an important and objectivily describable phenomenon.
     This was discussed in the last paper included in volume I, 'Teleological
     and deductive psychology'. The discussion of the relationship between
     purposiveness and free will is intentionally left out here.

71   *P. 270.* At the time of writing this, I underestimated the deepness of the
     chasm between the approaches of orthodox Behaviourism and natural
     science. See also Introduction.

72   *P. 281.* See also Introduction.

73   *P. 283.* Karl Popper has rightly denied the all-too simple statement that
     collecting information forms the basis of all science, in the way that
     Windelband's separation of the ideographic, the systematic and the
     nomothetic stage seems to imply. Even before our rational processes
     can begin their work, Gestalt perception has already performed all
     these three steps of cognition. In other words, there is no level at which
     human beings perform 'pure observation' entirely devoid of any hypothe-
     tical bias. Perception itself works on the basis of quite a number of
     phylogenetically evolved hypotheses, and very well-founded ones at
     that! Karl Popper's denial of induction would be entirely correct, if
     human cognition were forced to start on the basis of unprocessed sensory
     data, which it only not only does not but *cannot*.

74   *P. 284.* This was written before I had read Donald Campbell's papers,
     a fact which makes our complete agreement even more satisfactory.

75   *P. 286.* The Greek words denote a logically illegitimate jump from one
     category of concept to another.

76   *P. 286.* Isomorphy means identity of external form.

77   *P. 289.* The word 'information' is here used in the sense of common
     parlance and not in that given to it by information theory. In our sense,
     it roughly signifies knowledge without, however, implying rational
     processes.

78 *P. 290.* The same mechanisms of acquiring adaptive information have since been demonstrated to exist even in bacteria.

79 *P. 293.* I have been told since by physicists that atoms of the same element are indeed identical by definition. So let us substitute for 'atom': 'one shovel-full of whatever our counting "excavator" happens to be digging up at the time'.

80 *P. 293.* For the term 'information about something' the term 'knowledge' can always be substituted.

81 *P. 301.* The Latin word *albedo* literally means whiteness, in this case the milkiness or fogginess, which increases with the thickness of any layer of air.

82 *P. 302.* See also note 67, page 253 and note 73, page 283.

83 *P. 305.* This is the case with me every time I hear again a symphony, even if I thought that I knew it very well indeed.

84 *P. 310.* See again note 73, page 283.

85 *P. 314.* This is also why people gifted with a good faculty of Gestalt perception do not proceed scientifically by forming a hypothesis and trying to disprove it. The hypotheses which present themselves to a good Gestalt perceiver have a way of being at least partly true. It would be a lie if I should profess that I am honestly trying to disprove my hypotheses. All I am trying to do is to improve them, because I always partially distrust them.

86 *P. 321.* These pieces, cut out of a continuum by a process of measurement are indeed the only objects whose identity approximates that of the counting 'shovel', in other words of the unit itself.

87 *P. 324.* See note 76, page 286.

88 *P. 328.* The following is redundant and has been better explained in the previous paper.

89 *P. 330.* Also termed 'efferent signal copies', by some translators.

Bibliography

Alverdes, F. Die Wirksamkeit von Archetypen in den Instinkthandlungen der Tiere, *Zoologischer Anzeiger*, **119,** 1937

Antonius, O. Über Herdenbildung und Paarungseigentümlichkeiten der Einhufer, *Z. Tierpsychol.*, **1,** 1937

Armstrong, E. A. Bird display and behaviour, London 1947

Aschoff, J. Tierische Periodik unter dem Einfluß von Zeitgebern, *Z. Tierpsychol.*, **15,** 1958

— Zeitliche Strukturen biologischer Vorgänge, *Nova Acta Leopoldiana*, N. F. **21,** 1959

Baerends, G. P. *An introduction to the study of the ethology of cichlid fishes*, Leiden 1950

— Fortpflanzungsverhalten und Orientierung der Grabwespe (*Ammophila campestris*), *Tijdschrift voor Entomologie*, **84,** 1941

— On the Life-History of *Ammophila campestris*, *Jur. Proc. Ned. Acad. Wetensch.*, Amsterdam 1944

— Specializations in Organs and Movements with a Releasing Function, in *Physiological mechanisms in animal behaviour*. Symposia of the Society for Experimental Biology, **IV,** 1950

Bally, G. *Vom Ursprung und von den Grenzen der Freiheit. Eine Deutung des Spiels bei Tier und Mensch*, Basel 1945

Baumgarten, E. Versuch über die menschlichen Gesellschaften und das Gewissen, *Studium Generale*, **10,** 1950

Bavelas, A. Group size. Interaction and structural environment. Group processes, *Transactions of the Fourth Conference*, 1957, The Josiah Macy Jr. Foundation New York

Beach, F. Analysis of factors involved in the arousal, maintenance and manifestation of sex. Excitement in male animals, *Psych. Med.* **4,** 1942

Bierens de Haan, J. A. *Die tierischen Instinkte und ihr Umbau durch Erfahrung*, Leiden 1940

Birch, H. G. The relation of previous experience to insightful problem-solving, *J. Comp. Psych.*, **38,** 1945

Bohr, N. On atoms and human knowledge, *Daedalus* (American Academy of Arts and Science), Spring 1958

Bolk, L. Vergleichende Untersuchungen an einem Fetus eines Gorilla und eines Schimpansen, *Z. für Anat.*, **81,** 1926

— *Das Problem der Menschwerdung*, Jena 1926

Braemer, W. *Versuche zu der im Richtungssehen der Fische enthaltenen Zeitchätzung*, Verhandlungen der Deutchen Zoologischen Gesellschaft, Münster 1959

Bridgman, P. W. Remarks on Niels Bohr's talk, *Daedalus* (American Academy of Arts and Sciences), Spring 1958

Brunswik, E. Scope and aspects of the cognitive problem, in J. S. Bruner *Contemporary approaches to cognition*, Cambridge 1957

Bühler, C. *Das Seelenleben des Jugendlichen*, Jena 1922

Bühler, K. Die geistige Entwicklung des Kindes, Jena 1922

— *Handbuch der Psychologie*, I. Teil: *Die Struktur der Wahrnehmungen*, Jena 1922

Buytendijk, F. J. J. *Wege zum Verständnis der Tiere*, Zürich and Leipzig 1940

Campbell, D. T. *Methodological suggestions from a comparative psychology of knowledge processes*, Oslo 1959

— Evolutionary epistomology, in Schilpp, P. A. *The philosophy of Karl R. Popper*. La Salle, Open Court Publishing Co. 1966

— Pattern matching as an essential in distal knowing, in Hammond, K. R. *The psychology of Egon Brunswik*. New York: Holt, Rinehart and Winston, 1966

Craig, W. Appetites and aversions as constituents of instincts, *Biological Bulletin*, **34,** 1918

Crane, J. Comparative biology of salticid spiders at Rancho Grande, Part IV: *An Analysis of Display, Zoologica*, **34,** 1949

— Combat, display and ritualization in Fiddler Crabs, *Philos. Trans. Roy. Soc.* London B. **251,** 459–72, 1966

Daanje, A. On locomotory movements in birds and intention movements derived from them, *Behaviour*, **3,** 1950

Darwin, C. *The Expression of the Emotions in Man and Animals*, London, 1872

Dieterlen, F. Das Verhalten des syrischen Goldhamsters, *Z. Tierpsychol.*, **16,** 1959

Dilger, W. C. The comparative ethology of the African Parrot Genus *Agapornis, Z. Tierpsychol.*, **17,** 1960

Drees, O. Untersuchungen über die angeborenen Verhaltensweisen bei Springspinnen, *Z. Tierpsychol.*, **9,** 1952

Eibl-Eibesfeldt, I. Beiträge zur Biologie der Haus- und der Ährenmaus nebst einigen Beobachtungen an anderen Nagern, *Z. Tierpsychol.*, **7,** 1950

— Beobachtungen zur Fortpflanzungsbiologie und Jugendentwicklung des Eichhörnchens, *Z. Tierpsychol.*, **8,** 1951

— Nahrungserwerb und Beuteschema der Erdkröte (*Bufo bufo L.*) *Behaviour*, **4,** 1951

—Vergleichende Verhaltensstudien an Anuren: Zur Paarungsbiologie des Laubfrosches, *Hyla arborea L., Z. Tierpsychol.*, **9,** 1953

— Angeborenes und Erworbenes in Nestbauverhalten der Wanderratte, *Naturwissen.*, **42,** 1955

— The interactions of unlearned behavior patterns and learning in animals, *CIOMS symposium on brain mechanisms and learning*, Oxford 1961

— *Grundriß der vergleichenden Verhaltensforschung*. Munich, Piper Verlag, 1967

Faber, A. Die Lautäußerungen der Orthopteren I, *Z. für Morphologie und Ökologie der Tiere*, **13,** 1929

— Die Lautäußerungen der Orthopteren II, ibid., **26,** 1932

Fischer, E. *Die Rassenmerkmale des Menschen als Domestikationserscheinungen, Z. für Morphologie und Anthropologie*, **18,** 1914

Freud, S. *Vorlesungen zur Einführung in die Psychoanalyse*, Vienna 1930

Frisch, K. v. *Erinnerungen eines Biologen*, Berlin 1957

Gadow, H. *Vögel. Bronns Klassen und Ordnungen des Tierreiches*, **6,** pt. 4, Leipzig 1891

Gehlen, A. *Der Mensch, seine Natur und seine Stellung in der Welt*, Berlin 1940

Goethe, F. Beiträge zur Biologie des Iltis, *Z. für säugetierkunde*, **15,** 1940

— Beobachtungen und Untersuchungen zur Biologie der Silbermöwe (*Larus a. argentatus* Pontopp.) auf der Insel Memmertsand, *Jahrbuch für Ornithologie*, **85,** 1937

— Beobachtungen und Versuch über angeborene Schreckreaktionen junger Auerhühner (*Tetrao u. urogallus* L.), *Z. für Tierpsychol.*, **4,** 1940

Grey Walter, W. *The living brain*, London 1953

Harlow, H. F., Meyer, D. R., and Harlow, M. K. Learning motivated by a manipulation drive, *J. Exp. Psychol.*, **40,** 1950

— and McClean, F. G. Object discrimination learned by monkeys on the basis of manipulation motives, *J. Comp. Phys. and Psych.*, **47,** 1954

Hasler, A. D. and Schwassmann, H. O. Sun orientation of fish at different latitudes, *Cold Spring Harbor Symposia on Quantitative Biology*, 1960

Hebb, D. O. Heredity and environment in mammalian behaviour, *Brit. J. Anim. Behav.*, **1,** 1953

Heberer, G. Fortschritte in der Erforschung der Phylogenie der Hominoidea, *Ergebnisse der Anatomischen Entwicklungsgeschichte*, **34,** 1952

Heinroth, O. Beiträge zur Biologie, insbesondere Psychologie und Ethologie der Anatiden, *Verhandlungen des internationalen Ornithologenkongresses*, Berlin 1910

— Die Brautente, *J. f. Ornithol.*, **58,** 1910

— and Heinroth, M. *Die Vögel Mitteleuropas*, Berlin 1924–1928

— Über bestimmte Bewegungsweisen der Wirbeltiere, *Sitzungsberichte der Gesellschaft der naturforschenden Freunde*, Berlin 1930

Heinz, H. J. Vergleichende Beobachtungen über die Putzhandlungen bei Dipteren im allgemeinen und bei *Sarcophaga carnaria* L. im besonderen, *Z. Tierpsychol.*, **6,** 1949

Hess, E. H. Space perception in the chick, *The Scientific American*, **195,** 1956

Hess, W. R. and Brügger, M. *Das subkortikale Zentrum der affektiven Abwehrreaktion, Helvetica Physiologica et Pharmacologica Acta*, **1,** 1943

Hilzheimer, H. Historisches und Kritisches zu Bolks Problem der Menschwerdung, *Anatomischer Anzeiger*, **62,** 1926/27

Hinde, R. A. Factors governing the changes in strength of partially inborn response as shown by the mobbing behaviour of the chaffinch, *Proc. Roy. Soc.*, **142,** 1954

— Changes in responsiveness to a constant stimulus, *Brit. J. Anim. Behav.*, **2,** 1954

Hinde, R. A., and Tinbergen, N. The comparative study of species-specific behavior, *Behavior and Evolution*, ed. Roe and Simpson, New Haven 1958

Hirsch, J., Lindley, R. H. and Tolman, E. C. An experimental test of an alleged innate sign stimulus, *J. Comp. Phys. and Psych.*, **48**, 1955

Hoffmann, K. Die Einrechnung der Sonnenwanderung bei der Richtungsweisung des sonnenlos aufgezogenen Stares, *Naturwiss.*, **40**, 1952

— Versuche zu der im Richtungsfinden der Vögel enthaltenen Zeitschätzung, *Z. Tierpsychol.*, **11**, 1954

Holst, E. von. Über den 'Magnet-Effekt' als koordinierendes Prinzip im Rückenmark, *Pflügers Archiv für die gesamte Physiologie*, **237**, 1936

— Versuche zur Theorie der relativen Koordination, **237**, 1936

— Vom Dualismus der motorischen und der automatische-rhythmischen Funktion im Rückenmark und vom Wesen des automatischen Rhythmus, ibid., **237**, 1936

— Neue Versuche zur Deutung der relativen Koordination bei Fischen, ibid., **240**, 1938

— Entwurf eines Systems der lokomotorischen Periodenbildung bei Fischen, Ein kritischer Beitrag zum Gestaltproblem, *Z. für vergleich. Phys.*, **26**, 1939

— Aktive Leistungen menschlicher Gesichtswahrnehmung, *Studium Generales*, **10**, 1957

— and Mittelstaedt, H. Das Reafferenzprinzip, *Die Naturwiss.*, **37**, 1950

Hörmann-Heck, S. V. Untersuchungen über den Erbang einiger Verhaltensweisen bei Grillenbastarden (*Gryllus campestris* x *Gryllus bimaculatus*), *Z. Tierpsychol.*, **14**, 137–83, 1957

Hull, C. L. *Principles of behavior*, Appleton-Century, New York 1943

Huxley, J. S. *Man in the modern world*, New York 1948

Jacobs, W. Vergleichende Verhaltensstudien an Feldheuschrecken, *Z. Tierpsychol.*, **7**, 1950

Jander, R. Die optische Richtungsorientierung der roten Waldameise (*Formica rufa* L.), *Z. für vergleich. Physiol.*, **40**, 1957

Jennings, H. S. *Das Verhalten der niederen Organismen*, Berlin and Leipzig 1910

Kitzler, G. Die Paarungsbiologie einiger Eidechsen, *Z. Tierpsychol.*, **4**, 1942

Klüver, H. *Behavior mechanisms in monkeys*, Chicago 1933

Koehler, O. Vom unbenannten Denken, *Verhandlungen der Deutschen Zoologischen Gesellschaft*, Freiburg/Br. 1952

— Zur Frage nach der Grenze zwischen Mensch und Tier, *Freiburger dies universitatis*, **6**, 1958

Kortlandt, A. De uitdrukkingsbewegingen en geluiden van *Phalacrocorax sinensis*, *Ardea*, **27**, 1938

Kooij, M. Prohominid behavior in primates, *Symp. Zool. Soc. London*, **10**, 61–88, 1963

Krätzig, H. Untersuchungen zur Lebensweise des Moorschneehuhns (*Lagopus l. lagopus* L.) während der Jugendentwicklung, *J. Ornithol.*, **88**, 1940

Kramer, G. Die Sonnenorientierung der Vögel, *Proceedings IX. International Ornithological Congress*, 1955

Kühn, A. *Die Orientierung der Tiere im Raum*, Jena 1919

Kummer, G. Untersuchungen über die Entwicklung der Schädelform des Menschen und einiger Anthropoiden, *Abhandlungen zur exakten Biologie*, **3,** 1953

Kuo, Z. Y. Ontogeny of embryonic behavior in Aves I and II, *J. Exp. Zool.*, **61,** 1932

Lawick-Goodall, van, H. & J. *Innocent Killers*. London, Collins

Lehrman, D. S. A critique of Konrad Lorenz' theory of instinctive behavior, *Quarterly Review of Biology*, **28,** 1953

Leiner, M. Ökologische Studien an *Gasterosteus aculeatus, Z. für Morphologie und Ökologie der Tiere*, **14,** 1929 and **16,** 1930

Leong, C.-Y. The quantitative effect of releasers on the attack readiness of the fish *Haplochromis burtoni* (Cichlidae, Pisces), *Z. vergl. Physiol.*, **65,** 29–50, 1969

Leyhausen, P. Über die Funktion der relativen Stimmungshierarchie (dargestellt am Beispiel der phylogenetischen und ontogenetischen Entwickling des Beutefangs von Raubtieren), *Z. Tierpsychol.*, **22,** 412–94, 1965

Lorenz, K. Über den Begriff der Instinkthandlung, *Folia Biotheoretica II,* 1937

— Durch Domestikation verursachte Störungen arteigenen Verhaltens, *Z. für angewandte Psychologie und Charakterkunde*, **59,** 1940

— Die angeborenen Formen möglicher Erfahrung, *Z. Tierpsychol.*, **5,** 1942

— Über das Töten von Artgenossen, *Jahrbuch der Max-Planck-Gesellschaft*, 1953

Marler, P. Specific distinctness in the communication signals of birds, *Behaviour*, **11,** 13–39, 1957

Matthaei, R. *Das Gestaltproblem*, München 1929

McDougall, W. *An outline of psychology*, 6th ed. London 1933

Messmer, E. and I. Die Entwicklung der Lautäußerungen der Amsel, *Z. Tierpsychol.*, **13,** 1956

Meyer-Holzapfel, M. Triebbedingte Ruhezustände als Ziel von Appetenzhandlungen, *Naturwiss.*, **28,** 1940

— Das Spiel bei Säugetieren. In Kükenthal: *Handb. d. Zool.*, **8,** (10), 1–36, 1956

Milani, R. Osservazioni comparative et sperimenti sulle modalità del corteggiamento nelle cinque specie europee del gruppo 'obscura', *Istituto Lombardo di Science e Lettere*, **84,** 1951

Mittelstadt, H. Prey capture in mantids. *Recent advances in invertebrate physiology*, University of Oregon Publ., 1957

Nice, M. Studies of the life history of the song sparrow, II, The behavior of the song sparrow and other passerines, *Trans. Linnaean Soc. of New York*, 1943

Noble, K. G. and Bradley, H. T. The mating behaviour of the lizards, its bearing on the theory of sexual selection, *Annals of the New York Academy of Sciences*, **25,** 1933

Pawlow, I. P. *Conditioned reflexes: an investigation of the activity of the cerebral cortex*, trans. G. V. Anrep, London 1927

Peiper, A. Die 'Instinkte' des Neugeborenen, *Z. Psychol.*, **136,** 1935

Pelwijk, J. J. and Tinbergen, N. Eine reizbiologische Analyse einiger Verhaltensweisen von *Gasterosteus aculeatus* L., *Z. Tierpsychol.*, **1,** 1937

Peters, H. Experimentelle Untersuchungen über die Brutpflege von *Haplochromis multicolor*, einem maulbrütenden Knochenfisch, *Z. Tierpsychol.*, 1, 1937

Planck, Max. Sinn und Grenzen der exakten Wissenschaft, *Naturwiss.*, **30**, 1942

Poll, M. Über Vogelmischlinge, Verhandlungen des 5. Internationalen Ornithologen-Kongresses, Berlin 1910

Popper, K. R. *The logic of scientific discovery.* New York, Harper & Row, 1962

Porzig, W. *Das Wunder der Sprache*, München-Bern 1950

Prechtl, H. F. R. and Knol, A. R. Die Fußsohlenreflexe beim neugeborenen Kind, *Archiv. für Psychiatrie und Zeitschrift für die gesamte Neurologie*, **196**, 1958

Rasa, A. Appetence for aggression, *Beiheft Z. Tierpsychol.*, in press, 1971

Richter, G. P. Behavioral regulators of carbohydrate homeostasis, *Acta Neurovegetativa*, **9**, 1954

Riess, B. F. The effect of altered environment and age on motheryoung relationship among animals, *Annual New York Acad. Science*, **57**, 1954

Rösch, A. G. Über die Bautätigkeit im Bienenstaat und das Altern der Baubienen, *Z. für vergleich. Phys.*, **6**, 1927

Russell, W. M. S. and Russell, C. Human behaviour in an evolutionary setting, IV. *International Congress of Zoology*, **9**, 1954

Sander, F. Experimentelle Ergebnisse der Gestaltpsychologie, *Berichte des* 10. Kongresses für experimentelle Psychologie, Jena 1928

Sauer, F. Die Entwicklung der Lautäußerungen vom Ei ab schalldicht gehaltener Dorngrasmücken, *Z. Tierpsychol.*, **11**, 1954

Schenkel, R. Ausdrucksstudien an Wölfen, *Behaviour*, 1, 81–129, 1947

Schindewolf, H. Das Problem der Menschwerdung, ein paläontologischer Lösungsversuch, *Jahrbuch der preußischen geologischen Landesanstalt*, **49**, 1928

Schleidt, W. M. Wirkungen äußerer Faktoren auf das Verhalten, *Fortschr. Zool.*, **16**, 469–99, 1964

Schroeder, P. *Kindliche Charaktere und ihre Abartigkeiten*, Breslau 1931

Schwassmann, H. O. Environmental cues in the orientation rhythm of fish, *Cold Spring Harbor Symposia on Quantitative Biology*, 1960

— Basic principles of sun orientation in fishes, *The Anatomical Record*, **134**, 1959

Seitz, A. Die Paarbildung bei einigen Cichliden. I. Die Paarbildung bei *Astatotilapia strigigena* Pfeffer, *Z. Tierpsychol.*, **4**, 1940

— II. Die Paarbildung bei Hemichromis bimaculatus Gill, *Z. Tierpsychol.*, **5**, 1943

— Vergleichende Verhaltensstudien an Buntbarschen, *Z. Tierpsychol.*, **6**, 1950

— Untersuchungen über angeborene Verhaltenweisen bei Caniden *Z. Tierpsychol.*, **7**, 1950

Sevenster, P. A causal analysis of a displacement activity: fanning in *Gasterosteus aculeatus*, *Behaviour Suppl.*, **9**, 1961

Sombart, W. *Vom Menschen, Versuch einer geisteswissenschaftlichen Anthropologie*, Berlin 1938

Spurway, H. The causes of domestication: an attempt to integrate some ideas of Konrad Lorenz with evolution theory, *J. of Genetics*, **53**, 1955

Storch, O. Erbmotorik and Erwerbmotorik, *Akademischer Anzeiger der mathematisch-naturwissenschaftlichen Klasse der Österreichischen Akademie der Wissenschaften*, Vienna 1949

Thielcke-Polt, H. and Thielcke, G. Akustisches Lernen verschieden alter schallisolierter Amseln, *Z. Tierpsychol.*, **17**, 1960

Thorpe, W. H. The modern concept of instinctive behaviour, *Bulletin of Animal Behaviour*, **7**, 1948

— *Learning and instinct in animals*, London 1956

Tinbergen, N. Social releasers and the experimental method required for their study, *The Wilson Bulletin*, **60**, 1948

— An objective study of the innate behaviour of animals, *Bibliotheca Biotheoretica*, **1**, 1942

— Die Übersprungbewegung, *Z. Tierpsychol.*, **4**, 1940

— *The study of instinct*, Oxford 1951

— and van Iersel, J. J. A. Displacement reactions in the three-spined stickleback, *Behaviour*, **1**, 1948

—and Kruyt, W. Über die Orientierung des Bienenwolfes (*Philantus triangulum* Fabr.), III, Die Bevorzugung bestimmter Wegmarken, *Z. vergleich. Physiol.*, **25**, 1938

— and Moynihan, M. Head flagging in the black-headed gull; its function and origin, *British Birds*, **45**, 1952

Tolman, E. C. *Purposive behavior in animals and men*, Appleton-Century, New York 1932

Uexküll, J. von. *Umwelt und Innenleben der Tiere*, Berlin 1909

Verwey, J. Die Paarungsbiologie des Fischreihers, *Zoologisches Jahrbuch, Abteilung für Allgemeine Zoologie*, **48**, 1930

Wall, von de, W. Bewegungsstudien an Anatiden, *J. f. Ornithol.*, **104**, 1–15, 1963

— 'Gesellschaftsspiel' und Balz der Anatini. *J. f. Ornithol.*, **106**, 65–80, 1965

Watson, J. B. Psychology as the behaviorist views it, *Psychological Review*, **20**, 1913

Weidmann, U. Über den systematischen Wert von Balzhandlungen bei *Drosophila*, *Rev. Suisse de Zool.*, **54**, 1951

— Verhaltensstudien an der Stockente, *Z. Tierpsychol.*, **13**, 209–71, 1956

Weiss, P. Autonomous versus reflexogenous activity of the central nervous system, *Proc. Am. Phil. Soc.*, **84**, 1941

— Reductionism stratified, in Koestler, A. *The predicament of modern man*, 1969

Whitman, C. O. *Animal behavior*, Biological Lectures of the Marine Biological Laboratory, Woods Hole (Mass.), 1898

Wormald, H. The courtship of the mallard and other ducks, *British Birds*, **5**, 1910

Ziegler, H. E. *Der Begriff des Instinktes einst und jetzt*, Jena 1920

Zimen, E. Vergleichende Verhaltensbeobachtungen an Wölfen und Königspudeln, in *Ethologische Studien*, Munich, Piper Verlag (in press)

Subject Index

353

Author Index